Till the Heart Sings

Other Books by Samuel Terrien

The Psalms and Their Meaning for Today
Job: Poet of Existence
Lands of the Bible
The Bible and the Church
Job: Commentaire
The Power to Bring Forth
The Elusive Presence

SAMUEL TERRIEN

A Biblical Theology of Manhood & Womanhood

Till the Heart Sings

Fortress Press   Philadelphia

Library of Congress Cataloging in Publication Data

Terrien, Samuel L., 1911–
  Till the heart sings.

  Bibliography: p.
  Includes indexes.
    1. Sex—Biblical teaching. 2. Sex—Religious
  aspects—Christianity. 3. Man—Biblical teaching.
  4. Woman—Biblical teaching. 5. Man (Christian
  theology) 6. Woman (Christian theology) I. Title.
  BS680.S5T46 1985   233   85–47731
  ISBN 0–8006–0752–X

48,709

1737E85   Printed in the United States of America   1–752

For Sara

Contents

Preface

The title "Till the Heart Sings" is borrowed from Helen Waddell's rendering of a line from the *Carmina Burana*.* It points to the radiance and the exhilaration of a maturity that human beings of both sexes may reach whenever they seek to translate in modern terms and to enact in their lives the demands as well as the magnificence of a biblical theology of manhood and womanhood. "Till the heart sings" implies a movement toward an end, the celebration of intelligent love on earth, both human and divine.

This book is offered without a "vast cumbrous array" of scholarly footnotes. Let the reader know, however, that it has been made possible only by the labors of many exegetes and historians of the Bible. Debts of gratitude to them are here acknowledged.

References to books and articles have been appended to the last two chapters, because some of the material discussed therein, such as the Nag Hammadi texts, is not yet readily available to the general reader. Biblical commentaries and articles in biblical dictionaries have not been listed in the selected bibliography that appears at the end of the book.

Scriptural quotations generally represent the author's own translation, which often follows the King James Version, for its language and rhythm happily reflect the Hebrew and sometimes the Greek original. No hesitation, however, has prevented emendations of the time-honored KJV whenever modern scholarship has conclusively shown it to be erroneous or obsolete to the point of obscurity.

Librarians of Union Theological Seminary, Columbia University, General Theological Seminary, and Yale Divinity School have been constantly and graciously helpful. The editors and staff of Fortress Press, especially Dr. John A. Hollar and Dr. Barry L. Blose, deserve particular mention for their warm interest and minute care in the preparation of the manuscript for publication.

The author wishes to remember those courageous women students of

---

*"Surge cantilena de pectore," *Carmina Burana*, MSS. of Benedictbeuern cxl. 6 in *The Wandering Scholars: The Life and Art of the Lyric Poets of the Latin Middle Ages*, ed. and trans. Helen Waddell (Garden City, N.Y.: Doubleday & Co., 1955), 116; cf. *Mediaeval Latin Lyrics*, trans. Helen Waddell (New York: W. W. Norton & Co., 1977), 226–27.

Union Theological Seminary and Barnard College, New York, feminists all, who resisted the pressure of their extremist peers and sometimes of their academic advisors in order to study the biblical dynamics of manhood and womanhood rather than to accept the prejudices of the moment. They saw that those prejudices were born out of an uninformed and fossilized notion of Scripture.

Thanks are also extended to the educational institutions and monastic communities of the Roman Catholic church in the United States and Canada, among which dedicated Christian men and women discussed with the author problems of sexual morality and a new theology of priesthood. To these and others, in ministers' conferences and retreats, in theological seminaries and in university departments of religion, appreciation is expressed for stimulus and insight, for corrective criticism and the grace of friendship.

Introduction*

Far from supporting the male sexism of traditional Judaism and Christianity, biblical theology regards woman as the crown of creation. Modern feminists tend to hold the Bible responsible for the subservient status of womanhood in Western civilization. This assumption is understandable, for the rabbis and the church fathers have appealed to Scripture whenever they have sought to justify their misogyny. If the books of the Old and of the New Testament are viewed in their historical growth, however, and due respect is paid to their canonical tensions, they reveal a theology of manhood and womanhood unique in the ancient world. It remains a challenge for modern theology.

The main thrust of the Hebrew Bible and of the New Testament contradicts the disbalance in favor of the male sex that is traditionally ascribed to Holy Scripture.

Hermeneutics and Theology

A biblical theology of manhood and womanhood will seek to describe the vocation of man and woman in society from the perspective of the faith that animated ancient Hebrews and early Christians. The inheritance of Abraham found its critique in the Hebrew prophets and sages. For modern Christians it has received its fulfillment in the figure of Jesus of Nazareth.

Although this study will refer to great men and women in the Bible and to legal proscriptions in the ancient Near East and in the Old Testament, as well as to the ambiguities of the early church concerning women, it will not be a study of biography, psychology, sociology, or jurisprudence. Rather, it will attempt to view the problem of the sexes under the dimension of the Hebrew God, endorsed and adored by Jesus of Nazareth as the Creator, the Judge, and the merciful Father of all.

Biblical hermeneutics—the science of biblical interpretation—lies at the heart of the crisis that smothers Christian life and thought today, at the end

---

*Part of this introduction is derived from S. Terrien, "Toward a Biblical Theology of Womanhood," *Religion in Life* 42 (1973): 322–33; reprinted in *Male and Female: Christian Approaches to Sexuality*, ed. R. T. Barnhouse and U. T. Holmes (New York: Seabury Press, 1976), 17–27.

of the twentieth century. Protestants and Roman Catholics alike suffer from various forms of confusion concerning the inner source of authority in their religious knowledge.

Why should any Christian, disturbed by the problems of sexual fairness in contemporary life, attempt to formulate a biblical theology of manhood and womanhood? Because the Holy Scripture still constitutes the only source of thinking common to all the families of the universal church of Jesus Christ. It is the main channel through which a divine interpretation of human life may filter down to every generation, the most fertile ground for initiating mutual enlightenment, reciprocal correctiveness, and eventual reunion.

Of course, the Bible has been interpreted in many different ways during the past centuries, and the history of Christian thought shows that biblical theology is not identical with modern theology. The biblical theologian should never pretend to be a systematic theologian. Nevertheless, the Christian thinking of our time will be sterile or chaotic if it is not informed, inspired, and checked by the dynamics of scriptural authority, with their peculiar tensions and thrusts at different times of ancient history.

Sexuality and Canonical Exegesis

Krister Stendahl raised important questions when he wrote *The Bible and the Role of Women* (Philadelphia: Fortress Press, 1966). The subtitle of his essay indicated the direction in which the quest had to be pursued: "A Case History in Hermeneutics." Unfortunately, Stendahl in effect ignored the Hebrew Bible as a whole and concerned himself almost exclusively with the ambivalent attitude of St. Paul.

The question remains as urgent as ever: Are the Pauline views organically predicated upon those of Jesus? In what way do they differ from those reflected in the laws of impurity in Leviticus? Was it indeed Moses who excluded women from the sanctuary? Who decreed that woman was a ritual pollutant?

More to the point, perhaps, the question should be asked: Did Jesus intend to constitute his male disciples as an "apostolic college" with the prerogative of male succession? Were the New Testament writers of the second generation progressing or regressing when they stipulated the subservience of woman to man?

In other words, is there a biblical theology of manhood and womanhood generated by faith in the God of the prophets and of Jesus? Here is a "case history for hermeneutics" that shouts for the attention of contemporary theologians in the universal church.

The time-honored and now disparaged practice of extracting proof-texts from Scripture in order to support male sexism in the church must be rejected for precisely what it is. It represents a fossilized view of the Bible that denies its historical character. It considers the Bible as if the Old Testament and the New constituted, Koran-like, an unchanging textbook of religion and morals, even of cosmology and geology. This is what fundamentalists and popes do when in the name of Scripture they reaffirm the inaccessibility to women of the sacerdotal and governing offices of the church.

To be sure, a large number of Protestant churches today accept the ordination of women on a par with that of men. Nevertheless, pulpit committees and ecclesiastical officials, especially in the Anglican and Lutheran families, as well as in the so-called Free churches issuing from the Reformation, are still displaying a subtle malaise if not an implicit hostility to women in the pastoral ministry.

Canonical hermeneutics will respect the modern methods of investigation that are today applied to the text and meaning of Scripture by anyone eager to maintain intellectual integrity. It is no longer decent for educated Christians of the twentieth century to divorce their faith from modern culture. This does not mean that a Christian interpretation of life in general, or of man and woman in particular, should be informed by exclusively secular sciences rather than by faith in a God who still challenges humankind through the men and women of the Bible.

The dynamics of scriptural authority will urge, stimulate, motivate, inform, and restrain but not shackle a modern interpretation of sexuality in our time.

The Gospel and the Law

The faith of ancient Israel began with gospel rather than law. While traditional Christendom has opposed the law of Moses to the gospel of Jesus, contemporary students of Scripture point out that the word "law," which translated the Hebrew word "Torah," originally meant not "legal code" but "nurture through narrative and lore," "teaching," and still later, "law." The first five books of the Old Testament, or Pentateuch (Torah), tell the story of the beginning of our faith in concrete form ("we were slaves in Egypt"), and the legal codes that are found chiefly in the books of Leviticus and Deuteronomy represent six or seven centuries of opinions and precedents in ritual and civil and criminal jurisprudence. These legal opinions and precedents reflect in their final edition not the thought of Moses but the utopian and restrictive viewpoints of the Jerusalem priests who survived the exile in Babylon (597–539 B.C.) and who were concerned, at a moment of threatened annihilation, with preparing a blueprint for the new Zion in a newly created earth.

To isolate the prohibitions of Leviticus on sexual matters from the cultural environment to which these prohibitions addressed themselves is to commit a grievous error of historical anachronism. In a different manner, St. Paul's strictures on similar issues corresponded to the particular situation of cultural decadence in the Roman Empire. They should not be applied to other moments of history without some fair appraisal of the problems and needs of a given century. The relativity of morality and beliefs, as distinguished from absolute trust in the reliability of God, demands the constant renewal of theological thinking in the light of biblical theology. Proponents of an unchanging dogma, whether these might be popes or sectarian fundamentalist pulpiteers claiming to speak for the only church or a moral majority, relegate Jesus of Nazareth to an immoral minority. They also ignore the elementary fact that Scripture is a library of sixty-six books that were twelve hundred years aborning, from the Late Bronze Age in the thirteenth century B.C. to the waning Iron Age in the first century A.D.

When biblicists of the Roman and sectarian varieties appeal to "the law of Moses" or to the letters of the apostle St. Paul in order to justify obsolete codes of sexual ethics as divinely ordained, their procedure displays a literary fallacy and a historical illusion that imply either ignorance or a misapprehension of the way in which the biblical literature was written, selected, and slowly "canonized." Scripture is an anthology of historical records showing the continuity of a peculiar community of people at once faithful and unfaithful who attempted to follow their vocation toward genuine humanhood in spite of the many disruptions, regressions, and revolutions of history. Jesus himself proclaimed the need for facing historical change when he observed that new wine required new wineskins. On the other side of the spectrum, contemporary ethicists of sexuality appreciate the meaning of change, but they often ignore the continuity of purpose that permeates the biblical picture of man's and woman's destiny. They risk falling into the transitoriness of moral pragmatism, thus reducing religion to morality and morality to self-interest.

The Thrust of Hebraic Faith
Within Christianity

A biblical theology of manhood and womanhood shall not seek to be a substitute for modern theology. By analyzing the fields of force that, in the course of twelve centuries of religious vicissitudes and of literary growth, have opposed ritual moralism to enlightened humaneness in the realm of sexuality, one may perhaps see in a new light the scriptural complexity and yet clarity upon which the changing ethics of Jewry and Christendom in our own time need to be founded and erected.

This complexity readily appears when it is recognized that the religious functions of men and women differed markedly before and after the exile in Babylon (sixth century B.C.). Ancient Israel ascribed to woman a religious status that was displaced and lowered in nascent Judaism. Similarly, the unequivocal respect of Jesus for womanhood did not prevent the first- and second-generation church from adopting an ambivalent attitude of male superiority that led second-century Christianity to a practice of ecclesiastical misogyny. Yet, an unbroken but often hidden thread of sexual fairness may be detected in the motley tapestry that was woven over a

4

thousand years from the traditions of Genesis to the grandiose hopes of the Johannine Apocalypse.

The task of the biblical theologian is to retrace the movements of action and reaction that have molded the Hebraic, Jewish, and Christian anthropologies of the sexes. Perhaps unexpectedly, the pursuit of this task will help the contemporary theologian not only to apply the dynamics of Scripture to the problem of sexual ethics but also to formulate the divine reality with the insights of female as well as of male experience.

Religious inspiration and revelation are always interlocked. While psychology is not the source of theology, there can be no theological language that is not at once informed by the visions of a few prophets and the living of human existence as male and female.

A biblical theology of manhood and womanhood may show that the God in whom the ancient Hebrews and the early Christians trusted had elevated their notion of sexuality above that of their cultural environment. At the same time, it may disclose the extent to which their sexual awareness influenced the way in which they spoke of God.

The thrust of Hebraic faith must be kept alive within Christianity. Its fluctuations of progress and regress show a principle of homogeneity standing above the ebb and flow of human culture. From the Yahwist's myth of creation (Gen. 2:4b–25) to the feminine personification of Wisdom *(Sophia),* the Bible moves across the centuries toward a theology of woman's liberation organically related to a theology of man's liberation. Man and woman, created equal, fall under the same dimension of tragic finitude in their historical existence. Both are in need of a radical renewal and regeneration.

Knowing that he cannot prove his innocence without calling God guilty, Job prefers silence when he is asked, "Wouldst thou condemn me in order to affirm thy righteousness?" (Job 40:8). Like him, the poet of Psalm 51, with his *kyrie eleison,* refers to the universal solidarity of the human condition and not to the curse of womanhood when he confesses that man is brought forth in iniquity (Ps. 51:5; cf. Job 14:1). The same psalmist applies the myth of cosmic creation to the microcosm of the self in need of rebirth when he begs, "Create in me a pure mind and will" (Ps. 51:10). This notion is at the root of the Pauline view of male and female in Christ as "a new creation" (Gal. 6:15).

It is from the perspective of their nature and destiny within an eternal transcendence that man and woman discover not only their equality and their complementariness, but also the paradox of their freedom.

> The woman's cause is man's, they rise or sink
> Together, dwarfed or godlike, bond or free.[1]

The Bible does not contain a ready answer to the question of the role of single women in the church or society for the technological age of civilization, but it clearly proposes a set of principles for contemporary theologians to investigate and delineate.

Biblical faith, from Abraham to Jesus the Christ, lays the basis for a theology of manhood and womanhood that goes counter to the traditional attitudes and practices of Christendom and challenges the church of today to rethink critically not only the respective functions of both sexes but also the suprasexual meaning of the gender of God.

Chapter 1

Woman, Crown of Creation

From the days of the church fathers, Christians have generally assumed that woman is the source of evil in the world, or at least of corruption in human nature. Tertullian, for example, addressed her in these words: "You are the Devil's Gateway. . . . How easily you destroyed man, the image of God! Because of death which you brought us, even the Son of God had to die." If the fiery pamphleteer had looked at Scripture more broadly as well as more minutely, he might have added at once that Jesus was "born of a woman" (Gal. 4:4) and that the so-called image of God was not a quality granted exclusively to the male of the species, for the narrator of the later story of creation, in Genesis 1:1—2:4a, explicitly stated, referring to both sexes:

> And God created human kind in his own image,
> Male and female created he them.
> (Gen. 1:27; cf. 1:26)

The expressions "image" and "likeness" designated not human faculties bestowed by the Creator but the manner in which man *and* woman were brought into being.

To this day, many readers of the Bible continue to interpret the earlier story of the Garden as if it promoted an unrelieved misogyny. Scientific studies of Genesis 2:4b—3:24 show that such a view is totally mistaken.

The Two Stories of Creation

Several features of the narrative will have to be omitted from this study. It will be sufficient at this point to observe that Genesis contains two stories of creation: first, the archaic tale of the Garden (Gen. 2:4b—3:24), and second, the prose poem of cosmic creation (1:1—2:4a). The archaic tale gained public attention in the sanctuaries of the United Kingdom of Israel during the reigns of David and Solomon (tenth century B.C.). At a time of triumphant nationalism, traditions on the ancestors were drafted to support political and economic expansionism, and a fatal alliance was de facto sealed between the monarchy and the religious cults of Canaan. Israel became inebriated with self-satisfaction. The somber voice of those who had

7

remained faithful to the creed of Moses in the desert reminded king and people of a truth they had preferred to forget: "Man, thou art dust" (Gen. 3:19).

The story of the Garden was probably chanted liturgically at the ceremonies of the autumn festival, several hundred years before it was incorporated into the present Pentateuch. It was then prefaced with an entirely different description of humankind.

The prose poem that now begins Genesis and the whole Bible (Gen. 1:1—2:4a) was originally independent of the story of the Garden and became, during the exile in Babylon (sixth century B.C.), a festive lesson for the celebration of the weekly Sabbath. When Jerusalem was destroyed and the temple of Solomon razed in 587 B.C., a handful of Judahites survived and were forcibly deported to the torrid marshes of Lower Mesopotamia. Some of their leaders, inspired to bring pastoral comfort, transformed the yearly feasts and the Sabbath itself into a rhythm of "holy times." The temple on the rock of Zion—center of the sacred space—was gone. Judaism was born when sacred space was lost and time, its substitute, was made holy. Whereas the ancient creed, in an epoch of national success, had to offer the stern voice of penance and humility, the new creed, in time of national disaster, was intent upon lifting the despair of the Judahites. It sang to them, "God created human beings in his own image, according to his own likeness." The deported Judahites and their children became the first Jews. With its contemplation of the cosmic Creator, Judaism was on its way.

Obviously, the two stories of the creation of man and woman obtain an unexpected and extraordinary meaning when they are placed back into the respective situations of history from which they received their final form. Each story answers a peculiar need of existential significance. Both are proclamations of religious truth. They do not aim at reminiscing over a distant past. They are a parable of the human situation, a true *mythos*.

Modern investigation into the origin and meaning of mythology has demonstrated that most myths originated in cultic contexts. They were part of a celebration of a feast in a sanctuary. Their purpose was to describe the phenomena of nature and especially the mysteries of the human heart. In spite of the popular misunderstanding of the word, a "myth" is not necessarily a false account of some historical fact that reasonable persons are bound to disbelieve. Some myths are erroneous and obsolete. Others are "true" myths, particularly the narratives that point to a psychological or sociological aspect of human existence. As the Roman historian Sallust put it in the first century B.C., "A myth has never happened. It happens every day."

The Myth of the Garden

The myth of the Garden was first told as a pungent description of every man and every woman. When, during the exile in Babylon, the Jerusalem priests embedded that story within their history of the world, they placed it at the beginning ("genesis"), in what is now Genesis 1. At the same time, the myth of the man and woman in the Garden was transformed into an account of "the first couple." "The man and the woman" received the proper names of Adam and Eve (Gen. 3:17–21) and became the ancestors of the successive generations (Gen. 4—11). An important distinction needs to be made between the ancient story of "the man and the woman" (Gen. 2:1—3:16) and the editorial link that transformed "the man," literally, in Hebrew, *ha-adam,* a common noun, with the definite article, into Adam, a proper name, without the definite article (Gen. 3:17). Until the moment of human rebellion and the curses, "the woman," *ha-ishshah,* was not named either (3:3, 13, 16). She received the appellation Eve, "the Life-Giver," only when she was presented as "the mother of all living beings" (3:20).

For this reason, as well as for a number of others that emerge from the study of comparative folklore and ancient Near Eastern literature, the story of the Garden, in its original form, should never be viewed as the chronological, historical, factual report of monogeniture.

The priestly editors of the Pentateuch, obsessively concerned with chronology, may have unconsciously attempted to relegate Adam and Eve to the most remote antiquity in order not to see themselves in the mirror of "the man and the woman." Likewise, traditional readers of the Bible have shunned the sting of the myth because it deals with the perennial temptation of human beings in every age, namely, to lust for infinite knowledge in order to become "like God" (3:5). When they read the myth literally, they are relieved to find that it is not their own problem but, rather, the problem of some ancient characters for whom they are in no way responsible.

When Jews and Christians—Roman Catholic or Protestant—take the story of the Garden of Eden literally and not as a myth, they indulge in an easy evasion in face of the existential ambiguities of our nature in our own time. Because it is a myth, the story of the Garden threatens our self-adulation and our sense of security.

Far from being antifeminist, the storyteller was a theologian who unabashedly admired womanhood. To be sure, according to the story, man was created first, woman second, but this order did not indicate a movement of descent from superiority to inferiority. Rather, it pointed to man as incomplete without woman. The myth intended to suggest dramatically that man, without woman, is existentially alone.

Man's Existential Loneliness

The ancient mentality, especially Hebraic, considered aloneness as the negation of authentic living, for true life is not individual but corporate and social. The Hebrew word translated as "alone" (Gen. 2:18) carries an overtone of separation and even of alienation. Human beings live only insofar as they are related within their environment to partners with whom

9

they share mutuality and complementariness. Animals do not fulfill the requirement of true partnership.

Whether the myth implied at some early stage of development a prohibition of zoophilia is not clearly indicated, but such an interpretation is not impossible. More likely, the storyteller was polemizing against the worship of a deified earth, the Earth Mother. In Hebrew the word *adam,* "man," is related to the feminine word *adamah,* which means not "woman" but "fertile soil." Agrarian activities in the ancient Near East as well as in other parts of the world were, in effect, known as the art of husbandry. Consciously or unconsciously, the tilling of the soil was deemed an act of religious and sexual love. In some of the Semitic languages, including Hebrew, the semantic field of the idea for "plowing" embraces the sense of beginning, deflowering, defiling, raping, and being a sinner. The Hebrew tribes who had infiltrated from the desert into the fertile lands inevitably faced the problem of coping with agriculture. Israel in Canaan became acquainted with the protoscientific methods of inducing the fertility of the soil. Agriculture entailed a ritual of atonement and propitiation. The semi-nomads who became farmers had to learn from the Canaanites how to pacify and enlist the divine powers of the land. Their idolatry proceeded from economic necessity. The notion of *adamah,* "soil," remained ambiguous for a long time. In the myth of the Garden, however, the *adamah* was not divine nor could it be an erotic partner for the *adam,* who thus was literally left "to the loneliness of himself" (Gen. 2:18a).

The theological judgment is forthright: "It is not good for man to be alone." In the subsequent story the fate of Cain is to remain a wanderer and a foreigner "over the face of the *adamah*" (Gen. 4:12–26).

Woman as Savior

The myth of the Garden presents the creation of the woman as a gift for the completion and perfection of the human realm of being. Man receives woman as his true mate, his companion, even as the provider of his existential succor (Gen. 2:18b).

Many readers believe that the word "helper," which modern translations generally substitute for the traditional "an help" (KJV), suggests the idea of a retainer, an employee, domestic help, or again, a mother's or a teacher's helper. The Hebrew word, however, evokes an entirely different notion. The verb *'azar,* from which the noun *'ezer* derives, means "to succor" (at the existential level of being), "to save from extremity," "to deliver from death." In some other Semitic languages the cognate describes the action of someone who gives water to a person dying of thirst or who places a tourniquet on the arm of a bleeding man, thereby saving his life. In one of its verbal forms it sometimes refers to a person who offers testimony in a law court and thus provides grounds for the defendant's exculpation and acquittal. Far from being a subordinated or menial servant, woman is the savior of man.

Outside of this passage, the word *'ezer* applies only to God himself. He is the giver of succor, "the helper of Israel in time of distress" (Deut. 33:7; Pss. 33:20; 115:9).

If there is no helper, there is no hope, no salvation, no health, no peace, no life. The woman brings out of the man and to the man the totality of existence. She comes as if he had cried out, "Help! Help!" No subservient maiden is she.

Since the creation of woman is placed in the context of the rejection of the animals as fitting companions (Gen. 2:20), Yahweh Elohim declares that he will make for man someone who will deliver him from the distress of his solitude. The usual rendering "[a help] meet for him" (KJV), or "[a helper] fit for him" (RSV), attempts to explicate the Hebrew term *lenegdo,* literally, "for what is in front of him." Some commentators have inferred from the physical imagery of the expression that the woman was merely a sexual mate of the man, especially in view of the preceding details on the animals.

The sexual meaning is certainly implied by the whole narrative. At the same time, the noun *neged,* "that which is conspicuous, in front of, in full sight of," possesses a whole range of ideas, which include vigor, courage, efficiency, adventurousness, and presence. A *nagid* is a ruler or a prince. The verbal root *nagad,* "to go ahead," suggests achievement, pioneering, risk and deliberate thrust into the unknown. Significantly, in one of its voices the same verb means "to tell," "to declare," "to communicate," "to narrate," "to make known," "to expound," "to reveal," "to disclose." Using this same verb, singers will say that the firmament celebrates God's handiwork (Ps. 19:1).

The myth of the creation of woman points to a presence of attuning, equal to man and adequate for him. In addition to providing him with a deliverance from the void of alienation, it encompasses the whole of human potentiality. Woman is for man the savior from his void and the mate prepared to respond to his ongoingness.

An Aesthetic and Lasting Mystery

The creation of woman remains for man a mystery. "Yahweh Elohim caused a deep sleep [*tardemah*] to fall upon the man" (Gen. 2:21). *Tardemah* is no ordinary sleep. It is far more than a deep sleep. It is, rather, the stunning prodrome and effect of a revelatory dread or trance, when the stream of consciousness is arrested, immobilized, as mystics have often experienced. The Greek translators of pre-Christian times (Septuagint) well understood this nuance, for they used here the word "ecstasy." Likewise, in a *tardemah* (Gen. 15:12), Abraham received his vision of a covenant for him and his descendants (15:18).

Far from being a misogynist, the designer of the myth of the Garden displays his own sense of wonder in the presence of this extraordinary creature, woman. The motif of the so-called rib has been widely used to justify the view that woman is anatomically dependent upon man. Depth psychologists and others have speculated at length on "Adam's rib." We do not know what the word *ṣelach* meant in the language of the Yahwist singers. The reading "rib" merely follows the tradition inaugurated by the Greek translators. The Hebrew word is never used elsewhere in the Bible to describe a part of the human body. As in Akkadian, it means a terrace on the side of a valley, the architectural supports or side chambers of the temple, the shell of the ark. While there is uncertainty about its etymology, the word may well be derived from another root (written in a similar but different way in Arabic, yet with identical letters in Hebrew) which means "to skip," "to dance acrobatically," "to limp," and also, "to survive." In his wrestling with the angel, Jacob is hit in the groin, and he limps; the seat of his vitality has been impaired. What tradition calls "the rib" may have been understood in a sexual sense by early audiences. We must confess our ignorance.

In any case, the woman was "built," and not simply "made." The myth explicitly insists upon the mode of her creation. While the man was "molded" out of the finest clay (Gen. 2:7), the woman is compared to a work of the architectural arts (2:22a). In the ancient Near East during the Bronze Age, architecture necessitated, as much as today, a whole concentration of scientific, technological, and aesthetic faculties. The builders of the pyramids were not only astronomers and mathematicians; they also knew how to transfer accurately into several dimensions their extremely minute measurements. It is a marvel how the angles of the gigantic pyramids meet precisely at their summits from quadrilateral sides.

Different but similar comments could be made for Canaanite city walls and gates that have been unearthed by archeologists. Even semi-nomads were able to appreciate the art of erecting monuments. It follows that the use of the verb "to build" for the woman implies an intellectual and aesthetic appreciation of her body, the equilibrium of her forms, and the volumes and proportions of her figure. More than physical harmonies are at stake here, however. It may well be that the distinction between the relative endurance of the female and the ephemerality of the male is also evoked. An attractive although, of course, undemonstrated hypothesis is that the myth intended to hint at a hidden truth. Like clay, mortal man is "molded" for today. Like basalt or marble, the woman is "built" for tomorrow. The verb implies beauty, stability, and durability.

The Totality of Love

The woman comes to the man, not the contrary. When the story tells that God takes the initiative by introducing the woman to the man, the pro-feminine character of the myth appears in its most surprising relief. "And [God] caused the woman to come toward the man" (Gen. 2:22b). The verb used is often found in a sexual sense and always refers to the advances of the male toward the female, with the further connotation of entering and penetrating. Such is not the case here. The man is sexually as well as existentially unawakened. We may, perhaps, detect in this phrase, instead of a trace of male chauvinism, a touch of satirical humor at the expense of phallic aggressivity.

Until this moment, the "man" or "human being" *(ha-adam),* who had been alone and was existentially unaware, is now truly becoming "man" *(ha-ish),* the husband, the mate and the partner of the woman *(ha-ishshah).*

> This time! This one [feminine pronoun] is bone of
>   my bones and flesh of my flesh.
> This one [feminine] shall be called 'woman' [*ishshah*],
>   for she was indeed extracted from 'man' [*ish*].
> (Gen. 2:23)

The narrator indulges in a bit of fanciful etymology for the purpose of wit, a folkloric practice found elsewhere in the epics of the early Hebrews, the pre-Islamic Arabs and still among present-day *Beduin.* Actually the word for man as husband *(îsh)* derives from the idea of marching ahead *(awash)* in order to blaze a trail into the unknown, while the word for woman as wife *(ishshah)* comes from the image of delicateness and elegance *(anash).* By producing the assonance *îsh-ishshah,* the storyteller may well have intended to show at the same time both the differentiation of functions and the oneness of man-and-woman, husband-and-wife, in a new community of exchange, in a reciprocity of needs, in a mutuality of responsible concerns. The antique narrative thus points to ideal monogamy. And this is exactly what Jesus saw here (Matt. 19:5; Mark 10:8).

The expressions "bone of my bones" and "flesh of my flesh" refer to a totality of relationship, not just to a physical, anatomical, biological resemblance or near identity. The polarity of bone–flesh designates not so much opposites as the whole spectrum of human characteristics, from strength (bone) to weakness (flesh). There is no antagonism between man (strong) and woman (weak), as traditional commentators thought they had discerned between husband and wife. On the contrary, the story shows a complex admixture of both power and weakness within each sex.

Moreover, a relation described by the metaphor of the same "bones and flesh" does not refer only to a corporeal rapport, as if sexuality were limited to genital union. Whenever it reaches the apex of mutual consummation, sexual union is the symbol of a fully exchanged play and an inclusive solidarity of purpose. When the northern tribes of Israel (ethnically quite unrelated to the hybrid tribe of Judah), in the eleventh century B.C., came to Hebron in order to make David their king, they said, "Behold, we are your bones and your flesh" (2 Sam. 5:1). They were not referring to a blood kinship. To the contrary, they spoke of a psychic bond of covenant loyalty, and they made to David a politico-religious commitment. A similar conclusion arises from several parallel uses of the same expression. In the myth of the Garden, the man acknowledges not only the discovery of sexual union and the sublimity of its consummation, but also the completeness of his moral and spiritual solidarity with the woman and its consequences of responsibility in time and of fidelity in duration. Although the terminology is not explicit, the storyteller is here expatiating upon the wholly embracing power of love. The man and the woman are united in a love that is at once sacramentally manifested and sacramentally deepened by sexual union. It involves all levels of psychic and social well-being as well as psychic and social existence.

Such a covenantal bond of unity, which is not identification since it respects the differences between the sexes, overcomes and eventually conquers the violence and the enmity inherent in that differentiation. Interpreters have not paid sufficient attention to the force of the phrase, "she will be called woman because she was *violently* extracted out of man" (Gen. 2:23b). The verb is used in an intensive voice and means far more than "taken out." It conveys the undoubted qualification of abruptness, forcefulness, even of violence. Sexual separation between male and female is viewed as a tearing-apart of wholeness, the violation of a harmony disrupted with the direst of risks and with the possibility of fateful consequences. The Hebrew myth may have preserved at this point an extremely ancient Northwest Semitic belief that, through the Phoenicians and the proto-Socratic philosophers of Asia Minor, may have influenced Plato's notion of primeval androgyny.

In the Genesis story the allusion is obscure, but it may indeed permit the conjecture that sexual love, with its existential demand for perennial happiness, is meant to establish the fullness of humanity, the healing of wounds, the bridging of apartness.

Here again we find no implication of woman's inferiority to man. Rather, when they were expelled from the Garden, we may perceive an anticipation of the hostility between the sexes and even the faint insinuation of a pathos that literature and history have recorded in abundance and that has arisen from the experience of misunderstanding and competition between man and woman.

Precedence of "Maritality"
over Male Filiality

The story of man's and woman's creation in the ancient myth of the Garden concludes with a unique and astonishing statement:

> Therefore the man will abandon his father and his mother and cleave to his woman. (Gen. 2:24)

In the ancient Near Eastern and most other cultures, patriarchal lineage prevailed in such a way that the primary bond of solidarity was the duty of a man toward his ancestors in general and to his progenitors in particular. To honor one's father and mother was the most sacred obligation of social responsibility (Exod. 20:12; Deut. 5:16). By dramatic contrast, the Yahwist theologian scandalously upsets, even shockingly reverses, this deep-rooted principle of tribal morality.

Against the cultures of his environment, the Hebrew mythmaker declares unambiguously that man's first loyalty is to his woman. Man must *abandon* his father and mother. The Hebrew verb 'azab means not only "to depart from" but also "to forsake," "to drop and leave" in the sense of deliberately putting oneself away from idols or from pagan deities. It is also the word used by the prophets and the psalmists when they daringly state that Yahweh will forsake his own people. The poet of Psalm 22 composed an exceptionally poignant lament. Making no confession of sinfulness, he found divine absence entirely unjustifiable, even inexplicable, and therefore asked: *"Eli, Eli lammah 'azabtani"*—"My God, my God, why hast thou abandoned me?" The Gospels place this first verse of Psalm 22 on the lips of Jesus on the cross, slightly misquoting the Hebrew phrase by interpolating the Aramaic verb for "abandon," namely, *sabachtani*. The abandon is total, the framework of existence annihilated. In a similar manner, the myth of the Garden enjoins man to abandon his parents in favor of his wife. His lineage is subjected to his marriage. The impact of this feature should not be missed. The phrase acts as a setting for the completion of the thought, "and he will cling to his woman" (Gen. 2:24).

Just as the verb "to forsake" implies the breaking of a covenant, so also the verb "to cleave" designates its maintenance, not only with outward respect for the commitment but also with the inner compulsion of love. The Deuteronomic style favors this notion whenever it refers to the covenant between Yahweh and Israel, especially from the latter's point of view: Israel is asked to *cleave* to Yahweh, *forsaking* all other gods (Deut. 10:20; 11:22; 13:4; I Kings 11:2; Josh. 23:8). The imagery is originally that of clinging, sticking, remaining physically close, as girdle to loin, as skin to flesh and flesh to bone. While the moral connotation of friendship is included (Ruth 1:4), the erotic embrace of man and wife, in the myth, is both the sign and the source of the bond that keeps them together.

Such a vivid meaning is confirmed by the final line of the archaic poem, "And they shall be one flesh" (Gen. 2:24c). Literally, "they shall become one flesh." The Hebrew nuance, not usually conveyed in the English translations, indicates that this state of "unicarnation"—if one may employ a neo-logism—results from a process of development that deepens in intensity and strengthens itself with the passage of time instead of dissipating like a straw fire. Indeed, through their individual selves, the man and the woman are creating by their union a new reality of beingness. The "one flesh" refers to sexual concourse and psychological concurrence, in the full sense of the conjunction of bodies and of minds, at once through *erōs* and *agapē*. Sexual love is *erōs* and *agapē* together. It implies a psychic as well as a physiological gift of loyalty and exchange.

Paradigm of Covenantal Mutuality

The ramifications of the text, viewed within the semantic field of the Hebraic theology of the covenant, invite an almost inevitable conclusion. The Yahwist's myth of the creation of man and woman likens the lasting tie that attaches man and woman, to the historical alliance of Yahweh with his people. The Pauline school, ten or eleven centuries later, was expounding the theological implications of the early creation myth when it compared Christian marriage to the mystical union of Christ with his bride, the church of God (Eph. 5:31).

One will also observe that in the myth of the Garden, the reality of love between man and woman is not primarily related to the problem of procreation, if at all. The view of some interpreters, according to which the man and the woman become one flesh in the flesh of their children, is not warranted by the text. Love, at all its levels, is regarded for its own sake. The myth breathes an atmosphere of unabashed sensuality. There is no puritanical or ascetic disparagement of sexuality. The story contains not the slightest hint of moral or cultic impurity. There is the distinct absence of any statement concerning legal uncleanliness of genital secretions, sexual abstinence at sacred times or during menstruation, need for ritual cleansing, or moral atoning or purification for an act considered as ritually impure or sinful. The coming together of the couple is the healthy fulfilling of the Creator's intention, without shadow or qualification. Against the view which still prevails in many sections of Jewry and Christendom, there is no sin in the sexual urge or activity as such.

Finally, the poem of man's recognition of woman, and his commitment to her, undoubtedly reflects an experiential testimony. The man and the woman are already sexually aware, and their love has been consummated *before* the story continues with the eating of the forbidden fruit (Genesis 3). The man and the woman know the significance of "one flesh," *unicarnation*. The meaning of the subsequent act of eating the fruit, which is subsequent to the act of love, cannot therefore be identified with the discovery of sexuality, nor does the prohibition aim at keeping the man and the woman apart. Such a view, unfortunately made popular by the church fathers and the medieval schoolmen, is wholly unjustified by the ancient myth of the Garden.

One should not conclude, however, that the biblical dynamics of manhood and womanhood impose heterosexual marriage as the only form of human fulfillment. Zoophilia appears to be rejected as a subhuman and therefore degrading practice, because sexuality implies the totality of human exchange—physical, mental, moral and spiritual. Homosexuality is not a concern of the myth, either in favor or in opposition. Neither is the problem of the single sex nor of the celibate vocation, whether for secular or for entirely religious reasons. Scripture, in other of its parts, may offer some hints of enlightenment on these questions.

In summary, woman represents the supreme act of creation. She saves man from cosmic and metaphysical loneliness. She is implicitly compared to the divine helper in a *situation limite*. She is not a menial, but the queen of the created order. Yet more amazing, the bond between the man and the woman takes precedence over the most important sociological ties in the ancient world. It outranks the duty of a son to his father and mother. "Maritality" displaces patriarchal filiality.

The first characteristic of humanness is a covenant of sexual mutuality. The human couple is thus presented as the paradigm of theological loyalty.

Now comes the serpent.

Chapter 2

The Lure of Infinity

The second part of the myth of the Garden of Eden is notorious in several ways. It is generally called the Story of the Fall of Man. Some people find the divine prohibition against the eating of the fruit of the tree of knowledge bizarre, if not immoral: why should the Lord God prevent knowledge of good and evil? Most others charge the woman with the role of seductress. These views are incorrect.

Snake Worship

The nudity and innocence of the man and the woman (Gen. 2:25) constitute the link between Part One (Creation) and Part Two (Temptation). The storyteller pointedly insisted that the man *(ha-adam)* and his woman *(ha-ishshah)* were both naked, and they were ashamed neither of themselves nor of each other. This feature clearly confirms the idea implied by the lyrical song of delight which man intones when he discovers woman (2:23–24) with its climactic ending on "one flesh." They live in freedom from modesty, shame, and fear. They enjoy their sexuality and they trust each other. There is no impediment, physical or psychological, separating them. There is no barrier, no concealment.

Implicitly, however, the storyteller wants his audience to reflect on the equivalence between sexual modesty and the awareness of guilt arising from concealment and distrust, either between human beings or between humanity and God.

The conclusion to the first part of the myth (Gen. 2:25) constitutes also a transition to the second part: "Now the serpent was [rather, had been for a long time] more subtle than any of the animals of the fields which Yahweh Elohim had made" (3:1). As it often happens in folkloric style, the narrator plays on the assonances of unrelated terms. The word 'arôm, "naked," is used in the plural form 'arummîm (2:25) along with the word 'arûm, "subtle" (3:1). The intention is to create an unexpected association of ideas. The narrator wants his audience to think that the serpent is not only the most subtle but also the most naked of all animals.

The ancient Near Eastern world in general and Canaanite culture in particular were haunted by serpent *(ophis)* cults. The archeological evidence is that ophiolatry abounded in all the cities of the Fertile Crescent, including Jerusalem. The serpent was related to the worship of the Earth Mother goddess because it can stand erect from the ground, has neither fur nor pelt, and its head strangely resembles the phallus. Some of its species are venomous and produce terror. The serpent is, par excellence, the symbol of virility.

Not only the poor farmers, eager for the success of their crops and cattle breeding, but also the high officials, the princes and the royal family itself would capitulate before the Canaanite practices of worshipping the powers of fertility through sexual rites. This is amply attested by the biblical record itself. David's purchase of Araunah's threshing floor at the Canaanite "Rock of Zion," just above the city of Jerusalem, for a sacred site on which to set up the ark of Yahweh indicates that he was quite eclectic in his religious observances. When Solomon built a temple on the site of the sacred rock a few years later (ca. 975-950 B.C.), through the skills of a Tyrian architect, the way was opened in high circles as well as among the masses for tolerating a surviving form of Canaanite worship side by side with the adoration of Yahweh, the God of Israel.

The nation as a whole soon yielded to the fascination of the nature cults. In spite of three or four short-lived reforms in the course of the following four centuries, the temple in Jerusalem was the center of practices aiming at pleasing Asherah, later called Ashtoreth, the Holy Mother—the Earth Goddess—and enlisting her services for the prosperity of the land. All the features mentioned in the books of Kings support the same conclusion: the adoration of Yahweh as the sun deity, erotic ceremonial performed by the queen mothers of Judah, snake worship, techniques of divination through astrology and through male homosexuality.

In some of the ancient Near Eastern myths, like that of Adapa, the serpent is the life-giver and healer. In the eighth century B.C., King Hezekiah destroyed *Nechushtan,* a cultic object representing the sacred snake (2 Kings 18:4; cf. Num. 21:4–9).

Magical Use of Sexuality

Centuries before Amos and the other great prophets of the eighth century B.C., the Yahwist liturgists recited the myth of Eden at the sanctuaries of Israel and Judah because they had discerned the dangers in the worship of sun, sex, and serpent. They knew that such cults were related to the magical distortion of religion common to the whole of mankind. Magical techniques imply that divine service and even deeds of morality are tools of manipulation for enlisting divine power. From the time of Moses and the exodus out of Egyptian slavery, on the contrary, the faith of the ancient Hebrews considered life and prosperity on earth as a gracious gift offered by a transcendent and free deity. Worship was an act of thanksgiving. By contrast, the fertility cults of the ancient Near East centered on the marriage ceremonial between the male element of life, related to phenomena of the sky (sunshine, thunderstorm, dew, and rain) and the female element, associated with Mother Earth (germination of seeds in the soil and fertility of animals). To compromise with the Canaanite sacred methods of agriculture was correctly judged by the Yahwists and the great prophets as the negation of Hebrew faith.

It was not sexual activity and sexual pleasure as such that the theologians of Yahweh opposed, but the magical use of sexuality.

The North West Semitic religionists communed with the forces of nature. During the celebration of seasonal feasts related to solstice and equinox, and thus to the cycles of reproduction and growth in vegetation and animal husbandry, they entered into harmony with the cosmos in a way that later Judaism and Christendom have tried to repress. This repressiveness constitutes one of the factors leading, in synagogue and church, to the traditional dichotomy between a pure spirit and an impure flesh.

The Attempt to Grasp Infinity

The early Yahwists did not view sexuality as a source of corruption, but they objected to inducing physio-psychological *ecstasis* through heterosexual and homosexual union in a ceremonial of fertility and through physio-psychological techniques of oracular divination. When sexual trance becomes confused with divine ecstasy, the latter is thereby placed at the disposal of human initiative, autonomy, and fulfillment. Divine transcendence is thus reduced to anthropocentric endeavor, and the godhead becomes an instrument enslaved by mankind.

In addition, humanity's forceful entrance into the realm of the divine introduces within the transcendental character of God a cosmic sexuality. Divine beingness is sexually differentiated into male and female deities. Polytheism is inherent in fertility cults. The rites of hierogamy on earth reflect the mystery of divine eroticism in heaven. While attuning themselves to the rhythms of nature, human beings in effect achieve the illusion of animating and energizing divine life. Consequently they believe that they become the center of the universe.

In view of the cultural ambience that overwhelmed Israel in the land of Canaan, one may easily understand why the mention of the serpent at the core of the Garden myth irresistibly evoked the most fearful and also the most inebriating experience of the North West Semitic religionists. The mere mention of the serpent intimated, through the physio-psychological rites of sexual consummation, a sensorial mysticism in which finite human beings felt identified with the infinite.

In the final and present stage of the story, there is no trace of a cosmic fight between the Creator and the primeval serpent. The myths of creation abounding elsewhere in the literatures of mankind almost always present the creation of heaven and earth as a divine combat between order and the aggressive forces of chaos. The principle of disorder receives various names, such as the Dragon, Leviathan, or the Sea Serpent. In the Genesis myth, on the contrary, the storyteller declares that the serpent was merely one of the creatures of the field. His intention is clear. Let no worshiper of Yahweh for a moment believe that the dark forces of earth or ocean belong to a cosmic enemy of Yahweh, eternally threatening him and eternally menacing the security of men and women. The Garden myth "defuses" the pagan fears about the instability of the world and proclaims the omnipotence and the uniqueness of God.

Yet, by rejecting cosmic dualism and thereby affirming the absolute power of Yahweh, the mythmaker unwittingly produced the problem of evil, which has plagued Jewish and Christian theologians ever since. How can the creating God, who is good and all-powerful at the same time, allow the presence of an "evil impulse" (Gen. 6:5) within human nature, as it is symbolized by the serpent in the Garden?

The storyteller was not, however, a metaphysical philosopher but a liturgist and preacher polemizing against the lure of infinity in the Canaanite cults. He did not face intellectually the scandal of psychological evil in the context of a good creation. Rather, he confronted as an apologist the seduction that the wonders of sun, moon, soil and sex exercised, spell-like, upon the men and women of Israel in the land of Canaan. Subjected at once to the fascination of the sexual urge, on the one hand, and to the quest for existential survival and eternal immortality, on the other, worshipers of Yahweh were sorely tempted to follow Canaanite religion and to indulge in the fulfillment of their supreme desire: to know and to possess infinity.

This interpretation, suggested by the motif of the serpent, receives ample confirmation from the presence of another motif: the eating of the forbidden fruit.

The Tree of Absolute Knowledge

Contrary to the rabbinical and patristic opinions and the gratuitous conjectures of most depth psychologists as well as of many feminists, the woman in the Garden is presented in a sympathetic and even admiring manner. Not the man, but the woman is endowed with intellectual perceptiveness, aesthetic flair and, above all, mystical propensities. She inquires, hesitates, argues, ponders, before she finally and—it seems—reluctantly yields. In contrast, the man acts without protest and he succumbs at once. He is silent and passive. The woman is a sophisticated being. The man acts like a brute.

It is possible that the traditional chanting in the synagogue services during the early centuries and the High Middle Ages conveyed at this point the humor of the situation. The sentence on the eating of the fruit (Gen. 3:6) receives in the Hebrew manuscripts an unexpected punctuation. Everywhere else in the Bible the scribes have divided verses more or less equally in two halves, thereby indicating a short pause for breathing, no doubt, thus recording the usage of the cantors. Yet, this is the way the scribes have divided the fateful phrases:

And when the woman saw that the tree was good for food, pleasant to the eyes, and a tree to be desired to make one wise, she took of the fruit thereof, and did eat, and gave also unto her man with her, (3:6a)

and-he-ate [in Hebrew, *wattakol*]. (3:6b)

The two "halves" (!) are entirely disproportionate. The effect was dramatic. Hesitation and pondering in many words followed by the man's action—in a single word.

What was it the woman ate and gave to her husband? First of all, it was not an apple. This notorious error comes from the medieval Western church, where the Latin words *malum,* "evil," and *malum (maleum?),* "apple," were heard as a sly pun, impossible in the Hebrew original.

Second, it is commonly believed that the eating of the forbidden fruit means the performing of the sexual act. The dialogue between the serpent and the woman has nothing to do with the sexual act as such. It is strictly theological. Even if one argues that the first consequence of the eating is the discovery of sexual modesty, one should not conclude that the man and the woman enjoyed for the first time, and as an act of rebellion, the experience of sexual consummation. It is impossible to maintain that the God who offers to man a woman as his true partner, in all the senses of the term, and, indeed, as his existential deliverer and savior, would also forbid them from loving one another sexually and from discovering the oneness of their flesh. Moreover, such an interpretation would imply that sexual happiness is the prerogative of God, not of man. Finally, it has been seen that the first part of the Garden myth clearly describes the discovery of manhood and womanhood as the revelation of sexual ecstasy. Sexual concourse and the eating of the fruit are entirely distinct.

The eating of the forbidden fruit is presented as an existential revolt. Temptation develops slowly. The serpent's suggestion is involved and also subtle. It plants a doubt within the woman's mind concerning the intentions of the deity toward his creatures. It aims at transforming trust into distrust. It plainly intimates that God is not a generous provider but a capricious tyrant. "Yes, but . . . is it possible that God would have said, 'Ye shall not eat of any tree of the garden?' " (Gen. 3:1b).

The dialogue between the serpent and the woman has been going on for a long time before the audience is permitted to hear this "Yes, but . . . " The Hebrew expression represents a stylistic device common to the folkloric art of narration (and now revived in screen, radio, and television fade-in and fade-out). The blatant misstatement uttered by the serpent leads the woman to reestablish the simple truth. No, she replies. God has not said that. He said we might. But "as for the fruit of the tree which is in the midst of the garden, he said, 'Ye shall not eat, not even touch it!' " (Gen. 3:2–3).

It is now the woman's turn to exaggerate, for in the earlier dialogue between God and the man, at which the woman, incidentally, was not present, no mention has been made about the prohibition of touching. This detail suggests a hint of the narrator's affectionate regard for the woman. She reacts with the innocence of a child facing a similar situation.

The tempter becomes more perfidious, for he seeks to undermine the woman's confidence not only in the trust, but also in the truthfulness of God. Playing on the double meaning of the Hebrew phrase, "surely thou shalt die" (Gen. 2:17), the serpent retorts to the woman, "No, thou shalt not surely die," or, perhaps, as the syntactic construction of the phrase permits the reading, "No, thou shalt not die at once," or even, "No, thou shalt not die forever" (3:4).

The tempter does not lie outrightly. He mixes doubt with ambiguity. And, of course, the audience knows that the eating of the fruit did not immediately bring about the death of man and woman. The serpent merely implies that death is a remote possibility, undeserving of serious consideration. In effect, he makes the woman reason about human mortality and he conceals from her the realm of grace, which might bring immortality. Man and woman are mortal. God is eternal. The fruit of the tree of knowledge, so the serpent claims, will erase this awful distinction.

The woman is childlike and theologically alert. She is quick to imagine the mirage of self-deification and wants to "be like God." Her desire is to leave the human condition and snatch equality with the divine. The serpent's explanation is clear:

> For God knows that in the day ye eat thereof,
>   then your eyes shall be opened,
>   and ye shall be like God, knowing all!
> (3:5b)

Other examples in which the expression "good and evil" and especially "to know good and evil" appears elsewhere in the Hebrew Bible (a dozen times) always refer to the entire field of potential knowledge. "Good and evil" means "from the best to the worst." The tree of knowledge in the myth of the Garden does not suggest moral conscience, since the couple are able, before they eat, to distinguish between the permissible and the forbidden; nor does it allude to the rationality of the mind, nor to analytic consciousness. The context implies that man and woman already possess all these faculties as creatures. The fruit of the tree gives something more because it will enable man and woman to eat of the tree of life and live forever (3:22). It is on account of this absolute knowledge leading to infinity of time and not as a retribution for disobedience that the couple is expelled from the Garden of Eden (3:24a).

A Lust for Self-Deification

The story of the temptation of man and woman is not an allegory but a parable. An allegory, let it be recalled, is a rhetorical form in which every detail contains a hidden meaning that requires decoding, as it were. On the contrary, a parable is a story that makes one or two major points and it is ornamented with accessory features for producing *couleur locale,* thus stimulating dramatic expectation and sustaining the audience's curiosity. Analysis of Genesis 2:46—3:24 in comparison with the literatures of the ancient Near East shows that the form of this myth as we know it represents a long historical development. Mythological strands of various origins have coalesced in the course of time through the contributions of many generations of Hebrew rhapsodists.

One should, then, beware of deriving from the story a theological statement about divine envy or divine irresponsibility, which would radically contradict the picture of God represented by the early traditions of Moses, the oracles of the great prophets and the liturgical poetry of the psalmists. The narrator wished simply to show the religious situation of humankind. He depicted the sin of hubris par excellence as a lust for self-deification. He is concerned not with the being of God but with the psychology of human temptation toward self-sufficiency.

The myth of the Garden constitutes a shrewd indictment of all forms of cults that use religion as a technique for seeking power over death. Such cults attempt in vain to extend human finitude into the realm of eternity. The original intention of the myth was to polemize against the fascination of the fertility mysteries of Canaan. Human beings, through sexual rites, thought that they experienced sensually the ecstasy of being "like God." The eating of the forbidden fruit does not signify the act of sexual love. Rather, it symbolizes the religious use of sexuality as a means of reaching the power of infinity. One may thus see why, as a result of eating, man and woman make the discovery of their sexual shame. In their passion for obtaining absolute knowledge, they find out that they are naked. The ludicrous manufacture of fig-leaf girdles—not of rhubarb or of other large leaves—adds a further touch of satirical mockery, especially when it is remembered that figs and fig leaves played a part in the fertility rites of the ancient Near East.

No misogyny should be ascribed to the divine curses. Man receives as harsh a treatment as woman. They both are condemned to labor and toil. Once taken from the earth, they will return to the earth. As the French say, "Le terrien vient de la terre et retourne à la terre." What is not often observed is that the man, to the end, is no gentleman, for he "passes the buck" onto the beautiful mate whom he had previously acclaimed in the lyrical praise of passion. By implication, he even accuses the Creator: "The woman whom thou gavest me, she . . ." Likewise, the woman objectifies her sense of guilt and, just as her man, disclaims any sense of responsibility, but she devises a new phrase for it: "The snake beguiled me" (Gen. 3:13).

Self-assertion means estrangement. Sexual shame has become the sign of estrangement between man and woman as well as between human beings and God. Sexuality itself becomes vitiated by the human thirst for infinity.

In a sense, the ritualism or the moralism of the modern synagogue and church, which paradoxically has taken the place, among secular humanists as well as in religious circles, of the old mystery cults, represents also the attempt to make man self-sufficient and the master of his destiny. Ritual acts and moral virtue tend to become techniques for man-initiated salvation.

Without suspecting it and surely without wishing to do so, Jean-Jacques Rousseau, at the height of the Age of the Enlightenment, made a profound comment on what has become the clue to the subjectivism of contemporary literature and mores, when he wrote in the *Confession of the Savoyard Priest:*

> Conscience, conscience, divine instinct,
> immortal and celestial voice,
> infallible judge of good and evil,
> which makes man similar to God!

As a precursor of Romanticism, Jean-Jacques Rousseau followed the traditional and mistaken meaning of the tree of knowledge when he exalted the moral powers of human beings. At the same time, he dimly perceived that the use of morality as a substitute for a humble response to grace represents the ultimate idolatry.

Whenever man and woman "work out their own salvation" in either a religious or a secular distortion of Judaic and Christian faith, the myth of the Garden is reenacted and proved to be "a true and lively myth," the indictment of all forms of mercantile religiosity and of technological cultures.

This dark picture of the human situation represented a polemic against the shallow religiosity that flourished during the nationalism and the self-congratulatory mood of the Davidic and Solomonic times. The myth of the Garden (Genesis 2 and 3) is now prefaced with the entirely different picture of the creation of male and female "in the image of God" (Gen. 1:27). It is an error to think that this image was lost with the expulsion from the Garden. The image of God is not a "quality" or a "talent." It represents a *mode* of creation that lifts humankind from the level of animality.

The analysis of biblical dynamics, based upon the careful recognition of cultural differences between two independent stories now juxtaposed in spite of the centuries that originally separated them (ca. 950 and 550 B.C.), liberates the contemporary reader of the Holy Scripture from a long-ingrained and mistaken belief in an original sin that would be transmitted through heredity by "the seed of Adam," or by the stain of sexual delight when love is expressed in the flesh.

The myth of the Garden, far from declaring the realm of sexuality corrupt and corrupting, exalts its significance and its goodness. Sexual union fulfills manhood and womanhood, provided it be within the framework of transcendental recognition. Human beings respond to their creatureliness when they freely enjoy the existential opportunity for sexual love without deluding themselves into believing that they may thereby become the center of the universe.

In its naive and picturesque style, the story directs our attention to a mode of being where "Eden" is indeed "delight" (one possible meaning of the Hebrew word). This delight may well signify the embodiment of human happiness in mortal existence, and therefore become a symbol of grace.

In its biblical context, which covers a dozen centuries, the myth of the Garden does not describe original sin or a vitiation of human nature. Still less does it indicate a flaw inherited from "our first parents" through the act of procreation, more particularly through the male seed. The belief in the monogeniture of the whole of humankind through a historical couple, Adam and Eve, represents a willful and obstinate confusion on the part of modern fundamentalists, whether Roman Catholic or Protestant, between the idea of *chronos,* which designates clock or calendar time, and that of *kairos,* which means the opportune moment, independent of the categories of past, present, and future. To look at the myths of creation in Genesis as records of past events is to ignore *kairos.* The purpose of the narrators was not to describe the origins of the human race but to pinpoint the present predicament of the human situation. In the early traditions of the myth of the Garden, man and woman, as yet unnamed, are not chronologically "the first couple": they are symbols of everyman and everywoman. The "time" is not "then" but "now" *(kairos).* The ancient narrative is a true myth: "It has never happened, but it happens every day." We cannot relegate Adam and Eve to the distant past unless we unconsciously wish to exculpate ourselves. We are unaware of our eagerness to dull the "bite" of the myth whenever we take it literally. Fundamentalists simply show that they unconsciously fear being Adam and Eve. To transform the myth into a historical event is to deny that we are all subject to the existential limitations of sin and mortality.

Man and woman, united in love, fall apart through their distrust of God, and therefore of one another. The man *(ha-adam)* and the woman *(ha-ishshah)* of the myth become Adam and Eve only when they are estranged, not merely from themselves but also, and foremost, from their God. The loss of the dimension of transcendence results in spoiling harmony between the sexes.

This somber view of human love does not, however, permeate the early Hebrew Epic, nor does it fit the poetry of the Song of Songs, the purpose of which was to polemize against one of the curses hurled at the woman as she was being expelled from Eden: "Thy desire shall be for thy man, and he shall rule over thee" (Gen. 3:16cd).

Chapter 3

The *Erōs-Agapē* Continuum

The word "erotic" is commonly associated with sexual desire and pleasure. Such an understanding is only partially correct. The word *erōs* designates the whole of the human urge to go beyond the self. It covers not only the sexual aspect of the human wish to live fully but also the thirst for knowledge, scientific curiosity, aesthetic endeavor, religious instinct and an obscure longing for life beyond death. It is from this broad perspective that one may include sexuality within the whole realm of *erōs*.

By contrast, the word *agapē*, so we have been told, ignores the aggrandizement of the self and is concerned with the welfare of "the other." As many writers insist, it designates the altruistic movement of the *psychē*, a love which may go as far as self-sacrifice. Not a few theologians have made fashionable this contrast between *erōs* and *agapē*. Classical Greek usage of the two words does not justify it. Nor does modern psychology. An intermeshing of emotions and motivations—pleasure given is pleasure received—basically characterizes the human being. Indeed, the Bible knows that true *erōs* is *agapē*.

Furthermore, many people still believe that Scripture reflects an antisexual bias. The rabbis and the church fathers, in Roman and Byzantine times, appealed to biblical texts to bolster their views on the ritual stain or the moral impurity of sexual desire and activity. However, they disregarded the complexity of biblical literature, the inner tensions that provoked the growth of that literature, and the sometimes concealed line that went from the historical Moses to Jesus. In fact, the Bible is the first literary monument of the ancient world—classical Orient and classical antiquity—that fully knows romantic love. It is genuinely romantic love, because the unifying stream of Scripture knows woman neither as a slave nor as the tyrant of man. The popular idea that the passion of love as a motif of literature began in the Middle Ages with the troubadours does not take into account the early traditions of the Hebrew Epic, the Song of Songs, or the Egyptian love poetry.

Human Love in the Hebrew Epic

In spite of many vagaries, which short-lived reforms did not successfully eradicate, the Hebrews in the ancient Near East, an uprooted group at once ethnic and religious, were looking for the fulfillment of an ancient dream—that of a united humanity (Gen. 12:1–3). Emerging from the patriarchal societies of the Fertile Crescent at the dawn of recorded history, the Abrahamic clan placed the relation between male and female within a new perspective.

The epic of the patriarchs (Genesis 12—50) represents the slow transmission of oral traditions that were recited around the campfires and later on the threshing floors and sanctuaries of the land of Canaan. This process lasted six or seven centuries. Eventually the various strands of the national epic were edited together and they received their final form in early Judaism after the exile in Babylon (587–538 B.C.).

Each of these traditions evolved as a blend of ancestral memories, based on actual events, and of moral or religious teachings that sought to offer models of behavior, individual and collective, for new generations.

The stories of Abraham and Sarah, of Isaac and Rebekah, of Jacob and Rachel aimed at depicting dynamics of social relations and moral meanderings. In later times, the people remembered them as paradigms of conduct. Biblical scholars, however, do not often stress that these tales picture couples in love.

Marriage was a juridical and economic institution, the primary purpose of which was the procreation of children and the stability of the nuclear family. In the ancient Near East as well as in Israel generally, woman was considered to be the property of her father or of the other males in her native family until she passed on to the ownership of a husband.

The customs and rituals pertaining to Hebrew marriage and its juridical aspect are not the concern of this study. This inquiry seeks to isolate the consciousness of love between man and woman. Such a subject has not received the attention it deserves. The astounding fact is that in spite of the patriarchal system that dominated the Middle Eastern culture, the ancestresses of the Hebrew nation—Sarah, Rebekah, Rachel—were presented as heroines of valor, of courage, and of wit. Endowed with superior talents, they commanded the full respect of the men who surrounded them. More than this, the intimacy that bound them to their husbands and their husbands to them transcended the juridical aspect of the institution of marriage. The secret of this transcendence was mutual love as an emotion of lasting significance that meshed with a continuity of the allegiance.

This fact is the more remarkable when one observes that the patriarchal traditions of Genesis do not glamorize the morality of the heroes: Abraham, the father of the faith, is portrayed as a liar, and he shamelessly sends to the desert his slave Hagar and their son Ishmael. The name of Jacob, the patronym of Israel, is "the Supplanter," *Ya^cakob*, who kicked his twin in their mother's womb and subsequently became a thief.

The women do not always fare better morally. The rivalry of Sarah and Hagar, the scheming of Rebekah in her old age, the jealousy of Leah and

Rachel are not conveniently forgotten. The insistence upon the spirituality of love between man and woman that pervades these traditions is thus the more astonishing.

It appears from the literary evidence so far available from archeological discoveries that the clan of Abraham was indeed exceptional. Its religious vision embraced the goal of a united humanity (Gen. 12:1–3). It also stressed the dignity of womanhood.

Scholars have suggested that Abraham the Hebrew was related either ethnically or culturally to the Hurrians, who had settled down in northern Mesopotamia at the end of the Early Bronze Age and who apparently practiced matrilinear succession. This conjecture has not been demonstrated.

The narrators of the Hebrew Epic have taken great pains to enhance the characters of its heroines. Above all the others, the tale of Rebekah's epiphany before the solitary Isaac (Genesis 24) has always elicited admiration. Few novellas rival the biblical story, nor do they excel it, not even that of Ulysses discovering Nausicaa in the Odyssey.

Although the Genesis traditions develop primarily a religious theme to show how the ancestors of the nation responded to their new faith, the teller of the story of Rebekah and Isaac emphasizes two motifs which set the Yahwist's ideal of womanhood and manhood apart from attitudes prevalent in the ancient world: the woman's freedom of decision and the couple's love for one another. It is true that the chief purpose of the tale is to illustrate the loyalty of Abraham to Yahweh—the God who called him to leave his home—and his fear of religious corruption through intermarriage with pagans. This double concern has been a recurrent theme throughout the history of Judaism from biblical times to this day. Endogamy (marriage within tribe or clan parentage) thus reflects a practical need to preserve a certain standard of religious behavior and also to maintain the purity of the race.

The narrative presents Abraham thrown into grave anxiety lest his son marry a daughter of the Canaanites among whom he sojourns. He therefore sends Eliezer, his trusted servant, to fetch for that son a wife of his own kin from Mesopotamia. The coincidences are recounted as providential—a characteristic typical of religious folklore. The whole story unfolds itself according to a divine plan. The damsel was not only endowed with beauty but also with social graces going beyond the nomadic customs of hospitality. Eliezer met her at the well and asked for merely "a sip" of water rather than for "a drink." This nuance is usually lost in modern translations. Not only did the young woman offer the elderly stranger enough water for his refreshment but she also went down to the well repeatedly in order to bring up sufficient water for his ten thirsty camels—a feat of endurance and generosity.

Far more than this, Rebekah was to reveal in the course of the novella a liberty of choice that must have startled Middle Easterners in the second millennium B.C. Her family fully respected her power of decision. Here is a unique example, for that time and place, of the highest view of womanhood. Rebekah was not a part of the family chattel. She was a person in her own right.

The final feature is even more remarkable. When the young man and woman at last discover one another, the tale has reached a psychological point of forceful simplicity, hardly ever paralleled in the literature of the ancient Near East or in classical antiquity.

> And Isaac brought her to his mother Sarah's tent, and took Rebekah; and she became his wife, and he loved her. And Isaac was comforted after his mother's death. (Gen. 24:67)

It is not generally noted that the Hebrew verb translated "and-he-loved-her" (a single word in the original) meant not only "and he made love to her" but also "and he was in love with her." The verb "to love" is susceptible in Hebrew of two different pronunciations, which the synagogue cantors and the Jewish scribes of the early Middle Ages have scrupulously preserved as two distinct vocalizations. One is that of an "active" voice, which in this word emphasizes the erotic aspect of the relationship. The other is that of the "stative" voice, which designates a state of duration, with an element of continuity in time, appropriate for expressing a lasting sentiment rather than a temporary emotion or sensation. The Hebrew manuscripts indicate the stative pronunciation.

One should not, however, conclude that Isaac's love for Rebekah was "spiritual" rather than carnal. Such a language, which has no biblical foundation, implies a divorce between spirit and flesh, which has spoiled sexuality among Christians as well as Jews for centuries.

The context of the story indicates that Isaac and Rebekah enjoyed sexual delights together. Another strain of the tradition pictures them as engaged in sex play (Gen. 26:8), but their *erōs* was so deep that it should be described as *agapē*. After many centuries, the Hellenistic Jews who translated the narrative of this mutuality of love rendered the Hebrew verb "to love" with the Greek *agapein* (Gen. 24:67c, LXX). Still later, Jerome used the Latin *dilexit*, a verb that implies that there cannot be sexual delight unless it be shared by the two lovers.

In the post-Freudian era, interpreters may speculate on the peculiar character of the bridegroom. Looking at another layer of the story, one might point out that Isaac was still a celibate at the age of forty (Gen. 25:20). He thus appears to have been a "mamma's boy." Such a conclusion, it is sometimes maintained, is confirmed by the curious detail of the marriage's consummation after Isaac took his bride to his mother's tent and by the even more unexpected touch, "And Isaac was comforted after his mother's death" (24:67c). To determine the age of a folkloric hero by juxtaposing heterogeneous traditions now meshed together by a redactor is at best precarious. In the earliest traditions, Isaac may well have been a youth at the time of his wedding. Moreover, references to his mother's tent and to her death reflect the storyteller's intention to hint at the delicacy of his hero's feelings. It would be anachronistic to read into these features modern ideas which have come to light only through contemporary discoveries of depth psychology.

It would be equally wrong, on account of another unusual detail, to view Isaac as a "sissy." Just before Rebekah's arrival he had gone to the fields at eventide in order "to meditate" (Gen. 24:63). By including this detail, the narrator wished to insist upon the spirituality of Isaac's character. The usual diversions of semi-nomads were, of course, more likely to be hunting or violent sports and games than meditations in solitude.

Such features bring the portrait of Isaac into a special light. Could it be, on the part of the ancient Hebrew rhapsodists, that the purpose of these features was to heighten the young woman's attractiveness? She was able at once to enrapture a solitary man who still mourned his departed mother. Like the woman in the myth of Eden, she cured her mate of the meaninglessness of existence. The style is terse. No explicit description of love-making or love-feeling should be expected, but intensity of previous loneliness, as always, creates intensity in subsequent embrace or attachment. "All real living is meeting," wrote Martin Buber. "Existence cannot be possessed, but only shared in."

Isaac is redeemed from solitariness by a woman. To the perennial question, What is love? the novella replies with another question, which poets have repeatedly asked from time immemorial:

> Is it a reattainment of our centre,
> A core of trustful innocence come home to?[2]

While a theology of love between man and woman is not present in this ancient episode of the Hebrew Epic, its later formulation finds here its roots. The psychological astuteness of the narrator indicates an intellectual sensibility which was not missed by the sapiential poets of subsequent ages.

There are other mentions of genuine romance between a man and a woman among the ancient Hebrews. Most of them reflect the legal aspect of marriage with its implication of political and economic negotiations between ethnic and rival groups, and therefore of male dominance, since the bride is usually selected by the bridegroom's father or male guardians. The subjection and humiliation of the females are not usually told. In addition, some of the stories of marriage entail the shabby consequences of business deals and, as in the case of Abraham and Jacob, who were polygamists, the sorry development of female jealousy. Narrators often insist, however, upon the quality of lasting, mutual devotion that unites the couples. The love of

Jacob for Rachel is succinctly and convincingly told with its element of wonder:

Jacob served seven years for Rachel, and they seemed unto him but a few days for the love he had for her. (Gen. 29:20)

It is this love that makes the story of her untimely death in childbirth exceptionally poignant.

In a more startling manner, the episode traditionally called the ravishment of Dinah (Genesis 34) presents itself in a way that compels balance of judgment. The story is told from the standpoint of Israel's facing the danger of pagan corruption, and thus it transcends the social issue of endogamy versus exogamy (marriage within or without the clan or tribe respectively). It also entails male dominance, complicated by the tribal and religious pride of Jacob's sons, who had been deeply offended by the young man's action. Shechem, who kidnapped Dinah, a daughter of Jacob, was the son of the local prince, Hamor, a foreigner and therefore the worshiper of other gods.

And Dinah, the daughter of Leah, which she bare unto Jacob, went out to see the daughters of the land. And when Shechem, the son of Hamor the Hivite, prince of the country, saw her, he kidnapped her, and lay with her, and dishonored her. (Gen. 34:1–2)

This is not a simple anecdote illustrating male brutality enacted by an alien religionist. The sequence of the action introduces a rather unexpected note. Shechem was caught by his own feeling, and the young woman apparently responded to his initial violence.

But his soul clave unto Dinah, the daughter of Jacob, and he loved the damsel, and he spoke to the heart of the young woman. (34:3)

The pronunciation of the Hebrew verb for "love," as indicated in the manuscripts, supports the Greek translation which recognized in this instance the reality of *agapē*. This interpretation is, moreover, confirmed by the language of the subsequent development. For Hamor said to Jacob and to Dinah's brothers, who were indignant at Shechem's act:

The soul of my son Shechem is profoundly attached to your daughter. I pray you give her to him to wife. (34:8)

Although the political repercussions of the event led for a time to violence between the two ethnic groups, the narrator still insists that the young man continued to find "delight" in the young woman (34:19). This is not an ordinary rape. Dinah's response is not explicitly told, but it is clear that such "delight" could not be sustained without a reciprocity of passionate devotion.

While the legal and political aspects of marriage as an institution in ancient Hebraism conform to the political mores, high regard for womanhood is celebrated in such stories as the idyll between Isaac and Rebekah, the lifelong romance between Jacob and Rachel and even, through the eventual paradox of an *agapē* which permeates *erōs*, in the dark story of Dinah and Shechem.

Interpretations of the Song of Songs

More surprising and shattering to old prejudices is the poetic sequence wrongly known as the Song of Solomon. Such an attribution is bizarre, for this king was a callous spendthrift, a religious opportunist, and a cynical womanizer, who collected wives and concubines by the hundreds. Nevertheless, he acquired a reputation for wisdom because he attracted to his court artists and poets who belonged to the international intelligentsia. To his editorship were ascribed a number of writings, which on this account could enter the list of sacred books. That the Song of Songs, meaning "the Song par Excellence," would have found its way into the Hebrew canon constitutes in itself a paradox. Rabbis and church fathers, followed by medieval schoolmen and some pious Jews and Christians to this day, have interpreted this masterpiece of erotic poetry as an allegory of the love of God for Israel or of the love of Jesus Christ for his bride, the church. This spiritual interpretation was later applied to the Virgin Mary and, still later, to divine love for individual souls. That the Song probably was canonized on account of its interpretation as an allegory does not constrain the modern reader. It is difficult today to imagine that the original poet or editor had in mind the love of Yahweh for his bride, Israel, in spite of the fact that mystics in all cultures are prone to use sexual metaphors in order to describe their spiritual ecstasies.

It may be stressed that the imagery of the Song includes so many concrete allusions to the anatomy and physiology of the sexes and to the delights of erotic love, with precise references to the senses of touch, smell, taste, sight, and hearing, that the original poet could hardly have accumulated these motifs for a "spiritual" purpose. In addition, the book is devoid of any moral, historical, ritual, or theological statements of the type abounding elsewhere in the Hebrew Bible. Isolated attempts to find in this poetic sequence allusions to the covenant, the desert, and other motifs of the Hebraic faith have not been successful. Scholarly consensus looks at the Song of Songs as a lyrical poem about two young lovers. Here, however, agreement ceases. What is its date, its purpose, the milieu in which it arose, the occasion for which it was composed and the audience to which it was first addressed? Answers to these questions are important for a study of manhood and womanhood in Scripture, for upon them depends the meaning of love that the Song of Songs portrays.

The problems of date, composition, and genre are interrelated. The presence of the loanword *pardes*, "orchard" (Song 4:13), which was used in the

Persian language and from which is derived, through the Greek equivalent, the word "paradise," does not necessarily indicate a postexilic date, when Jews in Palestine or in the Diaspora lived under the jurisdiction of Persian governors. The word may well have been of ancient origin and entered several languages of the Fertile Crescent, including Hebrew, at a relatively early time.

The allusion to the beauty of Tirzah and Jerusalem (Song 6:4) as the twin capitals of the divided kingdoms during the ninth century B.C., before North Israel moved its administrative city from Tirzah to Samaria (ca. 850 B.C.), cannot be used as a definitive argument for an early date, since in most cultures poetic imagery tends to preserve the memories of ancient sites and events.

The several references to the geography of northern regions like Lebanon does not favor a North Israel over a Judah environment, for these references are counterbalanced by mentions of southern places such as the springs of Engedi, above the Dead Sea. Furthermore, the mysterious "daughters of Jerusalem" are addressed directly no less than six times.

The unity and occasion for the composition of the poem are also a matter of unresolved debate. Were the love dialogues and love soliloquies originally wedding songs, similar to the folk genre of the *wasf*, the bawdy song which is standard fare at nuptial festivities in Syria and other Near Eastern countries? Or was the poem a homogeneous literary piece? Was it destined to be acted by two singers and a chorus? Could it then be considered a play with a plot, in which a country lass prefers her shepherd to the glamor of a royal suitor? Efforts to discover dramatic action, with a knot and a denouement, have been contradictory and thus mutually defeating.

Far from being a secular and homely piece of entertainment, is it possible, then, that the Song represents the literary survival of a liturgy of "hierogamy" or sacred marriage between king and priestess at the occasion of the vernal equinox? Its vocabulary of flora and fauna and also its sexual terminology are common to those of several descriptions of sacred-sexual rites preserved in the ancient Near Eastern literature. Nevertheless, the Song does not concern itself with the renewal of fertility in fields, animals, and human beings. No hint whatever can be found that would identify the two lovers as sacerdotal partners, sacramentally incarnating the sun god and a deified earth or any other deity of the ancient pantheons.

According to a recently proposed variation of the cultic theory, the Song would reflect banquets and sexual orgies in which the ruling classes of both Israel and Judah indulged at the occasion of funerals and which were condemned by the Great Prophets like Amos (6:4–7), Isaiah (28:7–8) and Jeremiah (16:6–8). It has been claimed, for example, that the mention of myrrh, spices, honey, wine, and milk in a single verse (5:1) followed by the unexpected, indeed startlingly open, invitation "Eat, friends, drink, be intoxicated with love!" (5:1ef) are the same features as those of funerary rites and sacrificial meals of the Fertile Crescent, even as late as in the Roman times, especially at Palmyra.

It is further pointed out that the well-known verse that stands in climactic position toward the end of the poem,

> Love is as strong as death,
> And passion as cruel as the grave
> (8:6)

clinches the demonstration that the Song was composed for funeral banquets.

These arguments are tenuous. Spices and choice food or drink are served at all festive occasions, including weddings and holy days. The enjoyment of fragrant herbs and honey is clearly used here as an image of sexual delight. The Hebrew text suggests that the so-called open invitation in fact addresses itself exclusively to the young couple:

> Eat, friends, and drink:
> Drink deeply, O ye lovers!
> (5:1ef)

The translation of the last word, *dudim*, as "lovers" is preferable to that as "sexual delights," for it refers to human beings by progressive-synonymous parallelism in response to *re'im*, "friends" (cf. ancient versions and medieval Jewish commentators, especially Rashbam, Ibn Ezra, Rashi).

The theme of love, both at times of erotic summit and in the haunting months of jealousy or rejection, does not need a funeral ceremony to summon the thought of death and of the underworld. Do not the French pointedly call the moment of consummation *la petite mort*? Furthermore, the famous aphorism on death (Song 8:6), within its contextual allusions to lasting time and commitment to the future, contains ontological reverberations. It includes the implicit questions What is "to be"? Who am I? Who art thou?

All conjectures on a precise occasion or date of the Song are in some way deficient. While the hypothesis of a wedding entertainment has much in its favor, it fails against two observations. On the one hand, wedding songs and farces played at marriage parties always include an exhortation to procreate and the hope for a large and prosperous family. This motif is absent from the Song. On the other hand, wedding songs such as the *waṣf* genre in the modern Middle East are disjunct and seemingly haphazard, impromptu collections. The Hebrew poem, on the contrary, far from being a casual anthology of unconnected love lyrics, presents a tight structure through striking parallels of motifs that are repeated in identical or reverse order, and through a number of other rhetorical features that imply a superb unity of composition.

Structure and Unity

Several schemes of structure have been proposed in recent times, but all of these have required the reordering of poetic lines and sometimes entire groups of verses. There is no manuscript evidence to support such a tampering with the text. The following proposal, on the contrary, respects in all its details the traditional Hebrew text and does not necessitate the slightest alteration.

An elucidation of the structure of the Song of Songs is significant, for it brings to light the unity of the poem, the movement of its moods and the purpose of its composition. As it may be seen from table 1, the poem is divisible into seven parts, which correspond to each other in an intricate and modulated way, with parallel motifs that are repeated in identical sequence or in identically reverse order (chiasmus). Such peculiarities can scarcely be accidental.

1. Prelude and Reverie (1:2—2:6) This part is sung by the young woman alone. The prelude and reverie are echoed at the end of the Song of Songs by a reverie and postlude, sung in a dialogical exchange by each lover in turn (8:6–14), but the woman has the first and last words. This feature is extraordinary, in contrast to the patriarchal mores. It may reflect an Egyptian influence.

The reverie is a lyrical soliloquy that expresses the woman's emotion of secret longing and also her nostalgia as she remembers previous trysts. She appeals to "the daughters of Jerusalem," a chorus of young girls who are addressed only when the woman is separated from her lover (1:5; 2:7; 3:5; 5:8; 5:16) or when he is asleep following the afterplay (8:4).

In the course of this reverie, the woman recites to herself the litany of praises that her lover has presumably whispered to her in a prior rendezvous. These praises enumerate her charms (neck, breasts, lilies; 1:10—2:2), and the same litany will reappear on the lover's lips during the first tryst (4:4–16) and during the second (in reverse order; 7:1–9). A similar litany of the young man's charms will be sung by the woman in the course of her second dream (lilies, loins, whole self; 5:11–16).

2. The First Dream (2:7—3:5) Having fallen asleep, the young woman hears in a dream the voice of her lover. She imagines him at her door, seeking to enter and to reach her. Suddenly, the pleasant phantasm turns into a nightmare. Her lover has disappeared. She vainly attempts to find him through the city streets until she is mocked and threatened by the watchmen.

3. The First Tryst (3:6—5:1) When the two lovers eventually meet, the description of their night of love includes three motifs, each of which

Table 1 — Structure of the Song of Songs

1. *Prelude and Reverie* (1:2—2:6)
        O daughters of Jerusalem! (1:5)
His left hand (2:6)

          2. *First Dream* (2:7—3:5)
        O daughters of Jerusalem! (2:7)
My beloved is mine
  And I am his (2:16)
        O daughters of Jerusalem! (3:5)

                  3. *First Tryst* (3:6—5:1)
                  Who is this? (3:6)

          4. *Second Dream* (5:2—6:3)
        O daughters of Jerusalem! (5:8)
        O daughters of Jerusalem! (5:16)
I am my beloved's
  And my beloved is mine (6:3)

                  5. *Second Tryst* (6:4—7:9)
                  Who is this? (6:10)

          6. *Commitment* (7:10—8:5)
I am my beloved's,
  And his desire is for me (7:10)
His left hand (8:3)
        O daughters of Jerusalem! (8:4)

7. *Reverie and Postlude* (8:6–14)

This structural analysis requires no rearrangement of the text. Verse numbering in the Hebrew text differs from that of the English versions as follows: English 6:13—7:13 = Hebrew 7:1–14.

contains three elements (see table 2). In the first motif, (a) the youth's question heralds the arrival of the woman as a natural wonder:

> Who is this coming up from the wilderness
>   Like a column of smoke?
>   (3:6)

He then (b) compares her power to Solomon's sixty bodyguards (3:7) and (c) expostulates on the woman's beauty (4:1a). The last element introduces the second motif (4:1b–7), with its threefold sequence: (a) neck (4:4a), (b) breasts (4:5), and (c) euphemistically, "lilies" (4:5).[3]

Table 2 — Parallel Motifs

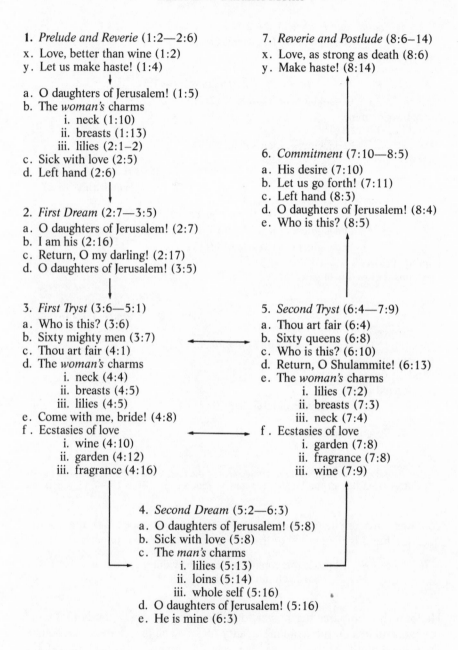

1. *Prelude and Reverie* (1:2—2:6)
x. Love, better than wine (1:2)
y. Let us make haste! (1:4)

a. O daughters of Jerusalem! (1:5)
b. The *woman's* charms
   i. neck (1:10)
   ii. breasts (1:13)
   iii. lilies (2:1–2)
c. Sick with love (2:5)
d. Left hand (2:6)

2. *First Dream* (2:7—3:5)
a. O daughters of Jerusalem! (2:7)
b. I am his (2:16)
c. Return, O my darling! (2:17)
d. O daughters of Jerusalem! (3:5)

3. *First Tryst* (3:6—5:1)
a. Who is this? (3:6)
b. Sixty mighty men (3:7)
c. Thou art fair (4:1)
d. The *woman's* charms
   i. neck (4:4)
   ii. breasts (4:5)
   iii. lilies (4:5)
e. Come with me, bride! (4:8)
f. Ecstasies of love
   i. wine (4:10)
   ii. garden (4:12)
   iii. fragrance (4:16)

7. *Reverie and Postlude* (8:6–14)
x. Love, as strong as death (8:6)
y. Make haste! (8:14)

6. *Commitment* (7:10—8:5)
a. His desire (7:10)
b. Let us go forth! (7:11)
c. Left hand (8:3)
d. O daughters of Jerusalem! (8:4)
e. Who is this? (8:5)

5. *Second Tryst* (6:4—7:9)
a. Thou art fair (6:4)
b. Sixty queens (6:8)
c. Who is this? (6:10)
d. Return, O Shulammite! (6:13)
e. The *woman's* charms
   i. lilies (7:2)
   ii. breasts (7:3)
   iii. neck (7:4)
f. Ecstasies of love
   i. garden (7:8)
   ii. fragrance (7:8)
   iii. wine (7:9)

4. *Second Dream* (5:2—6:3)
a. O daughters of Jerusalem! (5:8)
b. Sick with love (5:8)
c. The *man's* charms
   i. lilies (5:13)
   ii. loins (5:14)
   iii. whole self (5:16)
d. O daughters of Jerusalem! (5:16)
e. He is mine (6:3)

With the lover's begging, "Come, O bride!" (4:8), the third motif introduces the description of the ecstasies of love, within a threefold imagery of wine, garden, and fragrance (4:10–16), in correspondence with the three distinct sensations of taste, sight, and smell.

While the Song of Songs as a whole gives prominence to the young woman's depiction of her own sensuality, it is the young man who concludes the account of the first tryst with a rapturous cry, at the threshold of their love consummation (5:1abcd). With reticence, the poem fades out in order to veil from outsiders the moment of utmost intimacy, while the chorus intones:

> Eat, O friends, and drink!
> Drink deeply, O lovers!
> (5:1ef)

4. The Second Dream (5:2—6:3)   Once again, the young woman goes to sleep, and her second dream parallels the first. She hears the voice of her lover, who vainly knocks at her door. When she opens it, he is gone. She desperately calls him in the night and goes out to search the city for him. This time the watchmen find her and beat her. They even take away her mantle. She thus adjures the "daughters of Jerusalem" (5:8a; 5:16d) almost exactly as in her initial reverie (1:5) and in her first dream (2:7—3:5). Their questioning about the qualities of her lover prompts her recital of the litany, this time not of her own charms but of his, in a mirror reflection of her previous recital now adapted to the male sex (5:10–16).

5. The Second Tryst (6:4—7:9)   As it may be expected, the second tryst parallels the first but adds an element of psychological progression. In a sequence forming another chiasmus with the first sequence, the youth expatiates once more upon the beauty of the young woman (6:4). He compares her not to "sixty mighty men" but to "sixty queens," and he is led a second time to inquire her true identity: "Who is this?" (6:10; cf. 3:6). He knows her, but this rhetorical question reflects his feeling of utter newness in the rediscovery of her mysterious selfhood.

At the beginning of the first tryst, he had asked, possibly alluding to the Hebraic epic of the Sinai wanderings:

> Who is this [woman], coming up from the wilderness
> Like a column of smoke?
> (3:6)

Moved by the recollection of her ardor and perhaps anticipating even greater heights, he has now modified the first query, and he asks in cosmic terms:

> Who is this [woman], looking forth like the dawn,
> As fair as the moon, as bright as the sun,
> As terrible as the great constellations?
>
> (6:10)

The lines which follow evoke delights in euphemistic metaphors:

> I went down to the nut orchard . . .
> To see . . . whether the pomegranates were in bloom.
>
> (6:11)

Because it is not possible to determine whether the verbs are in the masculine or in the feminine, one may conjecture that the strophe was intended to be sung as a duet by both lovers.

The obscure phrase in the last verse—"I do not know myself" (6:12a)—may refer to a swooning or a state of trance. This interpretation finds support in the summons, apparently sung by the chorus, with a fourfold emphasis summoning the woman to "return" to reality:

> Return, return, O Shulammite,
> Return, return, that we may look at thee in rapture!
>
> (6:13ab)

The urgency of this plea may be justified by the woman's preceding cry, which could be rendered not as "I do not know myself [any longer]" but as "I do not know whether I am alive!" (6:12a). Was it the lovers' transports that threw the woman into a trance from which she had to be brought back?

The final question presents another problem of interpretation:

> Why should you [plural] gaze in rapture upon the Shulammite
> As upon a sword dancer?
>
> (6:13cd)[4]

Is this question a rebuke that the lover addresses to the chorus for insisting upon the woman's return to her senses? Or is it merely a literal explanation of the fact that she has disappeared from view and needs to be brought back to the stage center in full sight of the audience?

The meaning of the name "Shulammite" is a riddle. While many suggestions have been put forward in the course of the centuries, none is convincing. A most likely conjecture is to consider this name as the Hebrew equivalent of the Akkadian *Shulmanitu*, one of the appellations of Ishtar, goddess of war and of love. While the dawn, the moon, the sun, and the great constellations were deified in the ancient Near Eastern cultures, one may easily understand that the climax of the same strophe would identify that young woman with a female deity personifying the tenderness and the violence of passion.

At any rate, still united, the couple renew their dialogue. Once more the lover intones the litany of the woman's charms with its threefold metaphor in chiasmus (lilies, breasts, neck, 7:2b–4a). Like the first, the second tryst ends with yet another description of the ecstasies of love, in a slightly modified imagery of garden, fragrance, and wine (7:8–9).

6. Commitment (7:10—8:5) The woman is now fulfilled and confident. A third time, she confesses her conviction of the solidity of the bond linking her to her man, but with an unexpected and startling difference (see table 1).[5]

In the course of her initial reverie she had averred, "My darling is mine and I am his" (2:16). At the end of her first dream the simple repetition of the same awareness led her merely to exchange subject and object, as if to stress the reciprocity of possession: "I am my darling's and his desire is toward me" (7:10). The Hebrew word *teshuqah* is unusual for expressing "sexual desire." Its presence in this context reveals one of the main purposes of the Song of Songs: to present aesthetically and choreographically a woman's polemic against the malediction of Eve at the end of the myth of the Garden. It will be recalled that the ancient Genesis story concludes with a double curse of the woman: pain in childbirth and submissiveness to her man:

> Thy desire [*teshuqah*] shall be toward thy man,
> And he shall rule over thee.
>
> (Gen. 3:16cd)

In a dramatic reversal of roles, the woman of the Song of Songs finds in the present economy of existence an equilibrium of rapport between manhood and womanhood. Her lover's longing for her continues to move in her direction, and his desire toward her is accompanied by the virtue of loyalty.[6]

Although the heroine of the Song refrains from adding, "and I shall rule over him" (cf. Gen. 3:16d), she knows that while her man is not submitted to her, he is nonetheless subjugated by his drive toward her, and that such a movement will not abate. Beside the evocation of two encounters which include peaks of mutual happiness, this psychological climax now crowns the lyrical sequence.

The aftermath includes pathos as well as light-hearted playfulness. "Let us go out early to the vineyards!" (7:12). It also contains the fanciful wishes, games with mandrakes (7:13), the fantasy of incestuous dallying (8:1), and the need to restore the exhausted lover with spiced wine and pomegranate juice (8:2). Above all, let the daughters of Jerusalem refrain from awakening him! (8:4b). It is easy to recognize the folkloric motif common to all erotic poetry and humorously called *le repos du guerrier*.

7. Reverie and Postlude (8:6–14) A new reverie, unlike the initial one, leads in calmness to the contemplation of a secure future (8:6–14). Some words and images present a number of obscurities, but one aspect of this final part is certain. The young woman is more than ever the central character.

a. The chorus sings for the last time and renews the quest for the disclosure of her identity, repeating the lover's wonderment concerning her true being (8:5; cf. 3:6 and 6:10). The question is significantly offered, however, for it is asked by observers of the lyrical action, who notice the serenity of the couple walking in close embrace:

> Who is this [woman], coming up from the wilderness,
> Leaning upon her darling?
>
> (8:5ab)

b. The young woman once more addresses her man, reminding him that it was she who had aroused him in his mother's house (8:5cd). This may be an indication that she had taken the initiative for this idyll.

c. She now looks toward the future and begs to receive a sign of his commitment to a lasting companionship. What is love without a future? The seal is the symbol of an official document, binding heads of state to heads of state or ambassadors to their sovereigns and conversely:

> Set me as a seal upon thy heart,
> As a seal upon thy arm.
>
> (8:6ab)

She knows that the full meaning of *erōs* is the mutual engagement of *agapē*, "till death do us part."

> For love is as strong as death,
> Passion as cruel as the grave.
>
> (8:6cd)

The reality of love is always bound to the fear of death. The experience of *erōs* evokes in most cultures the anticipation of *thanatos*. It conveys a dimension of completeness which overpowers the forces of human mortality and even of cosmic destruction, by fire or by flood (8:6–7). It also depreciates human wealth, symbol of man's acquisitive accumulation of property in the face of death (8:11–12).

d. At the end of their love-play, the two lovers dovetail a concatenation of songs. They both imagine the coming of "their" little sister (8:8–9). Still playfully, the young woman reflects upon her feminine responsibility for bringing well-being, health, and growth in mutual comprehension. *Shalom,* "peace," is the great harmony that is the secret of "corporateness."

> Then, I was in his eyes
> As one who brings out peace.
>
> (8:10cd)

This last expression, *kemoṣeet shalôm,* "as one who brings out peace," may well provide a clue to the meaning of the mysterious name *Shulammite* (6:13), a word of the same derivation. It may also offer an assonantal transition to the young man's last musing on his own superiority over Solomon (in Hebrew, *Shelomoh;* 8:11–12).

e. As in musical divertissement and ballets of many cultures, the end is heralded in a low key, like an artistic return to banal reality. This device is akin to *le retour au calme,* "the return of calm," at the conclusion of Greek and Shakespearean tragedies.

(1) The youth begs his lass to sing a closing song for the benefit of his friends:

> O thou that dwellest in the gardens,
> My companions are ready to listen to thy voice.
> (8:13)

(2) To this invitation she replies, but only for his private hearing,

> Make haste, my darling, and be like a gazelle
> Or a young stag upon the hills of spices!
> (8:14)

Wistfulness, melancholy, even apprehension, color this entreaty. Although the injunction "Make haste!" forms an *inclusio poetica* that echoes the call of the prelude, "Draw me after thee, let us make haste!" (1:4), the Hebrew verbs and their syntactic functions are different. In the prelude, the young woman invites her swain "to race," "to run" with her. In the postlude, on the contrary, she bids him "to flee." Is he then in danger? From what menace should he escape?

The end of the poem is swift, leaving the audience tantalized, in suspense.

A Musical Masque of Love

Many features of the Song of Songs have been omitted from the foregoing analysis of its poetic structure. The metaphors of flora and fauna, in particular, and the several allusions to Solomon, which are introduced with a rare sophistication of rhetorical symmetry, contribute subtly to the progression of mood and the deepening of the emotions. Enough has been presented, however, to indicate a coherence of composition which provides a key to the purpose of the poem.

Since no dramatic plot can be derived from the text, the "theatrical theory" in the conventional Western sense should be abandoned. Nevertheless, it may still be that the Song was intended as a musical and highly literary piece of *divertissement.* It should then be called, without anachronism, *A Musical Masque of Love.*

During the divided monarchy (ca. 922–587 B.C.), the wisdom circles of the Jerusalem royal court provided the princes with artistic works designed for entertainment at events of secular festivity. Before it was written down

45

as a book, the Song of Songs may well have been an "oral script" for an evening of court diversion, with acting singers and a female chorus, "the daughters of Jerusalem." In most ages and climes, the line of differentiation between poet, musician, and dancer is often not clear. In ancient cultures poetic speech was always modulated, even cantillated, with instrumental accompaniment, passing imperceptibly into a spectacle of stance, gesture, and movement, with dance steps and figures.

For a long time scholars have proposed that the Song, preserved as it was in the third canon of the Hebrew Bible, the "Hagiographs" or "Writings," belonged, like Job, Proverbs, and Ecclesiastes, to the wisdom literature. The sages of Israel and Judah were the intellectuals and artists of the nation. Their books have many features in common. Their vocabulary reveals a wide acquaintance with the geography, flora, fauna, and poetry of the Fertile Crescent and Egypt. They do not stress—they even ignore—the specifically Hebraic themes that are found in the first two canons of the Bible (Torah or Pentateuch, and the Prophets). They sometimes use the language of covenant, temple, cult, law, and morals, but they are more interested in a broad humanism than in a strictly ethnic and religious nationalism. Their authors and editors were members of a cultural elite that overcame the barriers of language and cult. Parts of the Book of Proverbs, for example, have been directly or indirectly translated from the Egyptian Wisdom of Amen-em-opet, older by several centuries than the time of the Hebraic collection.

The Song is a secular poem of love. If its language is influenced by cultic usage, either pagan or Israelite, it does not place human *erōs* within the perspective of divine love. Although it once refers to "the flame of Yah" (8:6f), this expression does not actually allude to deity, for it represents a conventional idiom meaning "a vehement flame." Its secular character does not, however, preclude a purpose that has theological dimensions.

Against Eden's Curse

The Song of Songs testifies to the pluralistic aspect of Hebraic culture. It celebrates erotic love, and it is entirely devoid of legal, juridical, ritual, and moralistic considerations.

1. The poet ascribes to the young woman a status equal to that of the young man, perhaps even a psychological awareness and a sensitivity superior to his. The poet concentrates his aesthetic interest on her. The Song represents in a musical and possibly choreographic mode a woman's passion for her lover, not the man's "seduction" of a woman, as in the traditional pattern of patriarchal societies. In this Masque of Love it is the woman who initiates the lyrical action. She seeks her absent lover, she dreams and is anxious about him, even to the final verse of the entire poem. She expatiates upon her feeling. She ascribes to his love for her a magnificence and a pathos that she draws from her distinctly feminine experience. The imagery of the garden and of the fountains suffuses the whole poem. It displays a

concentration of physiological and psychological observations that converge on female rather than on male sexuality.

2. While the lyrical action slowly unfolds toward the hope of a relationship of lasting mutuality, and while the words for "fiancée" or "bride" are freely used by the young man, there is no allusion whatever to the legal aspect of marriage, to procreation, or to the institution of the family.

3. The poem avoids any direct allusion to the tragedies of history, the sinfulness of human nature, the corruption of social justice, or the enigma of natural disorders. However, it is aware of the realities of city life: the night watchmen harass the young woman, at least in her dream. Furthermore, the concluding association of love with death implies the dark mentality of the ancient Near East on evil in the world, an unstable and uncosmetic "cosmos":

> Primeval waters cannot quench love,
> Neither can floods drown it.
>
> (8:7)

This awareness does not presume a terror of natural phenomena. It simply states that love is endowed with a quality of transcendence akin to an eternity that overcomes the temporality of the universe.

In the Song of Songs the act of love becomes a sacramental gesture that prolongs, enhances, and seals the psychological emotion that precedes it and leads to its consummation. It is a sacramental gesture because it is truly "a means of grace." This grace, if not divine, is at least human. The woman is hailed as "one who brings peace." It may be human, but it is endowed with the virtue of a beyondness that may overcome the fear of mortality.

Here are a man and a woman whose love isolates them from the responsibilities and therefore from the anguishes of history, so that they may portray in art form this most intimate mystery of human existence. Not only do they enjoy the sexual byplay but also they hold within their horizon the subtle game of mutual discovery, the flowing into "the other," the manifold delays of trysting, the agonies of separation, the thrills of reunion, the almost unbearable heights and depths of consummation. They even hint at the fear of love's eventual transmutation by what Racine called "Time's irreparable outrage."

The poet was aware of a future for lovers. This future may not last beyond death—the statement on the primeval waters that cannot quench love is ambiguous—but it at least begs for a temporal dimension of existence upon the earth that looks beyond the fragility and the mortality of nature.

Love in this poem is not, however, to be called "romantic," in the literary and tragic sense that it inevitably leads to an untimely and violent separation. Nor is *erōs* a tool for provoking a mystical fusion with infinity. It needs religious language for its formulation, but this does not mean that it implies the sacralization of sexuality. Erotic love is not a substitute for religion; neither is it a magical ritual.

The Song remains in a profound way open-ended. It permits the thought that when this man and this woman grow old, the approach of death will only feed their hope upon their exquisite common memories. They may, in effect, anticipate many poets who in their youth have imagined their future recollections. Without anachronism, these two lovers will say to one another:

> And so, as kinsmen met at night,
> We talked between the room,
> Until the moss had reached our lips
> And covered up our names.[7]

It is possible that the sensual and emotional intensity of the second tryst led to a physio-psychological experience of ecstasy. The young woman, at least, may have passed through a momentary eclipse of consciousness. She may have faced the risk, in retrospect, that this eclipse might create the illusion of a finitude melting into infinity. Nevertheless, the poem as a whole celebrates the playful and therefore the healthy, not in any way pathological, aspect of *erōs*. In the end, the woman is called "the Shulammite," but also "one who brings out peace, health and serenity" (cf. the threefold meaning of the Hebrew word *shalôm*). The refusal to avoid extremes and the refusal to avoid skidding over the edge of consciousness—the negation of being—are found in many other artistic expressions of the erotic emotion, but they are absent from the Song. Here love does not lead to a flirtation with death. It blossoms forth into a greater appreciation of living. It may well use the sense of the inevitability of death but only as the expectation of a natural phenomenon, and it does so in order to stress the solidity, the durability, the obstinate tenacity, and perhaps even the supra-temporality of love.

The encounter through this kind of *erōs*, which is *agapē*, uses *thanatos* as a comparison and defines at once its finality and its relativity. It is a sacramental gesture, because it not only makes all senses and feelings more acute but also evokes eternity. Its memory sharpens the light. The deprivation of the lover's presence renders nature at once more beautiful—and stark. The expectation of the beloved's return transforms time into an ascent to the summit, with its dizziness, and where the light dazzles and then shimmers, but always glows.

A further point needs to be stressed. The poet of the Song of Songs is not embarrassed by the pleasure of the two lovers. There is no shame, no sin of the flesh as such, and carnal love is celebrated in terms of wonderment beyond the limitation of natural phenomena.

While several metaphors in the poem carry echoes of the covenant between Yahweh and Israel, there is no hint that human love is justified only if it is made official by a sociological institution, but its outcome, in the course of time, is colored by an existential appreciation of manhood and womanhood in the context of the universe. This universe is not empty, for it reveals a purposeful creation. The poet knows the strange alchemy which allies *erōs* to *agapē*. No genuine enjoyment of sexual communion and no sexual abandon is possible without a hidden or an open commitment. The mutual gift, between two lovers, implies a loyalty of life-long devotion. *Erōs* is not transmuted or sublimated into *agapē,* for authentic *erōs* includes *agapē* and it overcomes the fear of separation in death.

The Song redresses lyrically the prejudice of male dominance and of female subjection that the myth of the Garden of Eden in its final redaction construed as the poisonous fruit of religious pride, the desire to break the bonds of finitude, and the lust to triumph over mortal finality. It not only affirms the possibility of human happiness in the conciliation of womanhood and manhood but also intimates that mortality in the light of love becomes a metaphor of life.

Chapter 4

The Gender of God

Can we maintain today that the God of the ancient Hebrews was a male deity? Why is the name Yahweh masculine? Can we still call God "Our Father"? Why not pray to "Our Mother"? Are there not feminine as well as masculine dimensions within the divine reality?

These questions have been legitimately asked in recent times. It appears, however, that many of those who formulated them ignored the uniqueness of Hebraic faith. The religion of ancient Israel differed from the other religions of the classical Near East and Mediterranean antiquity in several aspects, the chief of which was its affirmation of divine transcendence over nature. The Yahwists, the psalmists, the prophets and the sages never identified their God with nature. This is the reason for which they never thought in terms of divine sexuality. God for them was neither male nor female. Unlike the Jerusalem priests, however, who presided over the birth of Judaism in the fifth century B.C., they were not afraid of human sexuality, but they knew that sexuality could not be a mode of communion with the divine.

At the same time, the religious language of ancient Israel was derived, of course, from human experience. Therefore, it ascribed to God feminine as well as masculine characteristics.

In order to grasp the use of feminine and masculine connotation in biblical faith, one must look at three areas: first, the theological metaphor of human love; second, maternal semantics and the Mother Goddess; and third, paternal tyranny and divine fatherhood.

Human Love as Theological Metaphor

Both the Hebrew epic and the Song of Songs present a rare ideal of human love. The stories of Genesis do not conceal the moral problems of envy or even hate that pertain to polygamy and concubinage. At the same time, the idylls of Isaac with Rebekah and of Jacob with Rachel link the mystery of sexual attraction to a profound and lasting sentiment: the mutuality of love. The Song of Songs goes further than the Hebrew epic, for it gives to the woman a preeminence in the initiation and the depth of *erōs* against the

51

threat of *thanatos* and confers upon the temporality of sexual consummation a quality of endurance that may even surmount the scandal of mortality.

This rare ideal of human love permitted the ancient Yahwists to describe the bond that united, but never identified, Israel with Yahweh. They looked upon that bond as a covenant, a lasting agreement comparable to that of a marriage between a man and a woman.

The word "covenant" did not mean "testament" in the modern sense, a "last will" directing bequests of goods and properties after death. The Hebrew word *berit,* which the Greek-speaking Jews of Alexandria in the third century B.C. rendered as *diathēkē,* was eventually translated by Jerome with the Latin word *testamentum.* Hence, the traditional titles Old Testament and New Testament. This wording is legitimate only when one remembers that *testamentum* referred to a solemn testimony, the proclamation made before witnesses of a contract between two parties engaging themselves to become partners for a specific enterprise or purpose.

The evolution of the word "testament" in modern times is similar to the corruption of the verb "to protest," which originally meant "to testify" and not "to contest." The name Protestantism has acquired a negative sense on account of its adversaries. It derives from the expression *Protestati sumus,* "We solemnly proclaim and testify." In like manner, the word "covenant" implies an engagement *attested* before witnesses.

The Hebrews probably received the practice of covenant-making from the Hittite rulers in Asia Minor as early as the third millennium B.C. These potentates established covenants or contracts with their vassals who administered the provinces of their empires. The religious leaders of Israel, however, adopted the ritual of covenant between Yahweh and Israel in the light not of relation of master and servant but of the link of loyal love between man and woman.

Prophets found in the mutuality of attraction and obligation, which most of them experienced in marriage, the symbol of a lasting relationship. For them the covenant between Yahweh and Israel was like a marriage across the centuries. They used the imagery of marital love as a figure of religious behavior enduring *in time.* They maintained that Yahweh and Israel were engaged to one another, committed to one another in loyalty, the obligation of love.

As early as 751 B.C., the prophet Amos of Tekoa, in southern Judah, alluded to the beauty, the youthfulness, the innocence, the expectancy of the nation, when he called it with the bridal title "the virgin Israel" (Amos 5:2). The conjugal symbolism was implied by the proclamation of exclusive chosenness, when Amos, speaking in the first person singular, in the name of Yahweh, declared, "You only have I known from among all the families of the earth" (3:2).

The idea of election, which is usually misunderstood by the modern temper, is meaningless without the engagement of love, with its demands of reciprocity. Israel was Israel only provided that she live up to the responsibilities of her unique privilege: "to do justice, to love mercy, to walk humbly with [her] God" (Mic. 6:8) and to be "a light to the nations" (Isa. 49:6).

The motif of conjugal symbolism persisted throughout the extraordinary succession of those fearless critics of the regime, "the goodly fellowship of the prophets." They loved their country as much as they loved their God. Through a double transference of passionate attachment, of Yahweh for Israel, and of theirs for the same, they spoke of "the beloved one," "the fiancée," "the bride of Yahweh," "the virgin Israel."

Isaiah of Jerusalem, who had probably heard Amos in his early years, compared the covenant bond to that of a vintner and his vineyard (Isa. 5:1–7). The import of this metaphor may not easily be grasped by modern urbanites or even by farmers, but vintners everywhere will at once sense the deep pathos of endless care and expectancy that the Palestinian winegrowers felt, as toward the ideal woman of their hearth and bed, while their vineyards were at the mercy of spring frost, summer insects, drought, or marauders.

In the last years of Judah, at the end of the seventh century, Jeremiah of Anathoth still spoke of the joy that Yahweh felt toward Israel, as an engaged youth for his fiancée (Jer. 2:2). Even during the exile in Babylon, when reasonable hopes for a renewal of life at home were dashed, when two-thirds of the population had died in the siege of Jerusalem by fire, sword, starvation, thirst, and epidemics, when the few survivors of that ordeal had been forcibly marched a thousand miles down to the malarial marshes of the Persian Gulf in southern Mesopotamia, an anonymous poet of the Isaianic school rallied his coreligionists by announcing the new era, beyond the meaningless torments of their history. This is what he said:

> As the bridegroom rejoices over the bride,
> So shall your God rejoice over you.
> (Isa. 62:5)

These poets followed the daring model that the prophet Hosea of Benjamin had proposed in about 745 B.C. His words were "acted out" in his life. It is not possible to ascertain the sequence of cause and effect if we attempt to discern the mode of the prophet's inspiration. Did Hosea marry a woman in order to portray the bond of love between Yahweh and Israel? Or was it, on the contrary, through his own marital experience that he gained an insight into the pathetic dimensions of divine love? The first chapter of his book, which may reflect a later view of his biography—a sort of re-created "memory of things past"—tells of his marriage and divorce. The third chapter contains the autobiographical story of the prophet's new marriage or remarriage. In a concrete sermon he obeyed the divine command to portray the future relation of Yahweh with his people.

Inserted between these two stories, the second chapter explains the theological significance of the symbolism. The first part looks back at the first chapter and justifies the divorce (Hos. 2:1–13). The second part anticipates the theological meaning of the second marriage (2:14–23).

In the account of the first marriage (1:2–9), the woman is named Gomer, which probably meant "one who brings fulfillment." She is described as *bat-Diblayim,* not "daughter of Diblayim" (as traditional versions rendered it), but "of elegant figure" (cf. one of the many Arabic synonyms for "breasts"). The usual translation of *eshet-zenûnîm,* "woman of harlotry," mistakenly implies that Gomer was already a street prostitute when he married her, but the Hebrew suggests only that she was "potentially promiscuous" (1:2).

The story of Hosea's marriage and his theological proclamation could not be understood by his contemporaries unless love between men and women was generally known, at least ideally, as a passion of mutual devotion.

That love, for Hosea, was not a casual affair but implied a lasting bond of trust in each other is made clear by the prophet's expectation of the future.

Whether the third chapter describes a remarriage or a new marriage is not told. What is significant is that Israel will look at her God in a way that will discard forever the idea of a master-and-slave relationship. In other words, the new bride will not be the instrument, the property, the possessed thing of her husband. The polemical intent cannot be missed. It is directed against both the ancient Near Eastern conception of marriage and the attraction of Canaanite Baalism.

> In that day, says Yahweh,
>   Thou wilt call me "My man" [*îshî*],
> And no longer wilt thou call me "My owner" [*ba'alî*].
>   (2:16)

The word "my man," *îshî,* echoes directly the story of the creation of woman in the myth of the Garden (Gen. 2:23). The word "my owner" or "my master," *ba'alî,* not only refers to the worship of the Canaanite "lords" or "owners" of the fields, the *baalim,* but also attacks the male sexist idea of marriage as a contract of ownership through which a woman is nothing more than the property of a man. Israel, like the ideal bride in the ideal marriage, will not look at her God as if she were the slave of her master, but she will enjoy with him the status of partner and trusted friend.

Hosea provides a remarkable anticipation of the Johannine notion of divine-human friendship that makes Jesus say to his disciples, "No longer do I call you slaves ... but I have called you friends" (John 15:15). The announcement of a bright future for Israel as the new bride is predicated upon the mode of God's approach to the new covenant. The response of Israel to Yahweh will be similar to that of a loving, self-giving husband. The words used by the prophet carry two levels of speech implicit in the metaphor of human love:

> And Yahweh said to me: Again go,
> Love a woman who is beloved of her lover and an adulteress;
> Even as Yahweh loves the people of Israel,
> Though they turn to other gods and love raisin cakes.
>
> (Hos. 3:1)

Such a story could not be comprehended by the mentality of the time unless the notion of love as a *giving-of-the-self,* the sacrifice of one's own interest for the sake of another, was psychologically accessible to the average member of the population.

As it has been seen already, there were several Hebrew synonyms to express the ideas of to love, to embrace, to cherish, and the like. The most current of these was the verb *ahab* or *aheb,* "to love." Depending upon the pronunciation, such an idea was susceptible of two related but different senses. The so-called active pronunciation, *ahab,* referred to the act of love, without an implication of duration in time. The so-called stative pronunciation, *aheb,* referred to a state of being, with the connotation of a lasting sentiment. The first has been correctly translated by the Septuagint in Hellenistic times with words related to *erōs,* whereas the second was rendered with words related to *agapē.* The difference between the two meanings does not correspond to a dualism between body and soul, one carnal and sexual, the other "purely spiritual." The distinction lies, rather, in the source and purpose of the emotional involvement toward the other person. According to the first meaning, the agent of love in the active form of the verb is self-centered, seeking pleasure for its own sake. The Septuagint understood the linguistic particularity represented by the two pronunciations of the same verb *ahab* or *aheb.* They saw, for example, that when Solomon "loved many foreign women," the verb indicated lustful and casual encounters. Therefore, they paraphrased accurately, "Now Solomon was a womanizer [*philogunaios*]" (1 Kings 11:1).

The Greek translators of Hosea's autobiographic account of his second marriage discerned the deeper implications of the stative way in which the verb *aheb* was pronounced. Thus, they rendered the phrase "Again go, love a woman" (Hos. 3:1) with the verb from which derives the well-known noun *agapē:* Eti poreuthēti kai agapēson gunaka.

The love of God for the new Israel was portrayed by the love of the prophet for his bride. This kind of love is true love, for it is purposefully centered upon the beloved.

Thus, the heart of biblical faith, from Hebraism to Christianity, may be found in the trust that "God first loved us" (1 John 4:19). The demands of love are, however, immense. Human behavior depends not on pragmatic morality based upon self-interest but on the response to divine love. Repentance cannot be a mercantile method of courting providential favor. It flows from a response to the divine lover (Hos. 3:5; 2:21–23). Worship and ethics are the manifestations of gratitude, and human gratitude is the response to divine grace.

In Hebraism, theological semantics are predicated upon the metaphor of human love projected into the divine dimensions. This metaphor becomes the clue to the Hebraic understanding of history, looking backward to the wilderness and forward to the messianic age.

The use of the metaphor of conjugal love is not, however, exclusive of other rhetorical devices. Israel was not always compared to a bride. The imagery of son, daughter, or child was almost as current among the prophets as that of wife. Hosea himself, in the middle of the eighth century, could picture the pathos of a frustrated deity not only under the scandalous image of a deceived husband (1:2–7; 2:13), but also in the equally scandalous image of parental love which finds only rebuttal. According to the mentality of the time, the spectacle of a powerless father was as shocking as that of a village cuckold. Significantly, the description of this parental failure, ascribed to God, is borrowed from the combined experience of maternal and paternal anxiety.

> When Israel was a child, I loved him,
>   And I called them out of Egypt.
> The more I called them,
>   The more they went away from me.
>   (11:1–2a)

The theme of rebellious children appears among other prophets, Isaiah of Jerusalem in particular, but Hosea's language is perhaps the most revealing example of paternal sorrow in the face of filial revolt.

It has been suggested that while his wife was away, pursuing her lovers and leaving young children unattended at home, Hosea himself took over the tasks that in those days were certainly the exclusive responsibility and prerogative of a mother.

> Yet it was I who taught Ephraim how to walk.
>   I took him up in my arms;
>   But they did not know that I healed them.
> I led them with human bands,
>   With bands of love,[8]
> And I became to them as one who lifts a nursling against the cheek,
>   And then I stooped down to feed them.
>   (11:3–4)

The entire past of the history of Israel was thus presented as the story of a maternal as well as a paternal God, whose tender care was spurned by a rebellious child. Having assumed toward his own sons and daughter the role of a mother, the prophet described God, by implication, with the semantics of motherhood.

Hosea went still further. The drama of divine judgment against Israel in revolt was going to be radically altered into a glorious mystery of reconciliation. The symbolism of the children's names, as presented in the story of the first marriage, pointed to the severance of the covenant bond between Yahweh and Israel. The little daughter, for example, abandoned by her mother, was called *Lo-ruchamah,* "The One for Whom There Is No Motherly Compassion." Later on, the picture of historical renewal for Israel includes this promise, which brings together the verb and the proper name:

> In that day, says Yahweh,
>   I will answer the heavens,
>
> . . . .
> And I will have motherly compassion for Lo-ruchamah.
> (2:21, 23)

The idea of motherly compassion together with that of grace constitutes the paramount aspect of divinity among the ancient Yahwists, the prophets, the psalmists, and the sages. Like the word for "grace" *(chen),* the word for "compassion" *(rachmim)* is related to the sensations and emotions of motherhood. The whole creedal sweep of ancient Israel and early Judaism is articulated upon the trust in "the Lord God who is compassionate *(rachum)* and gracious *(channun)."* This is true from the early traditions concerning Moses (Exod. 34:6) down to the time of Nehemiah in the Persian period (Neh. 9:17). The verb *rachem,* "to be compassionate," appeared already in the literature of Ugarit, a city of North West Semites who were culturally the ancestors of the Phoenicians and the Canaanites. It is also found in classical Akkadian *(rēmu),* and it has survived in classical and modern Arabic.

Several years ago, the author heard a Ru'alla *sheikh* use the Arabic verb in a context of maternal suffering. When this *Bedu* was asked to explain the eerie shrieks of the she-camels, he replied merely with the verb, "they yearn," and he employed the Arabic cognate of the Hebrew verb *chanan.* In their agony of bereavement, because their young had been forcibly weaned and taken away from them for the purpose of early training, the mother camels would moan loudly all night long, sometimes mutilating and starving themselves. "To be gracious" was originally for a mother to suffer pain and longing for the fruit of her womb. When God was presented as "gracious," the connotation of maternal grief could hardly be missed by people alert to the affinities of sound and meaning.

The word *rachmim,* "compassion," represents the so-called plural of majesty of the anatomical term *rechem,* "uterus" or "womb." It would be shortsighted to propose that the Hebrews alone among the ancient Semites were aware of the maternal metaphor when they used such a term. Like the word for "grace," which originally had meant "maternal yearning," the verb "to be compassionate" was related to the word "uterus" not only in Hebrew but also in other Semitic languages, especially in Ugaritic and Akkadian.

In most cases, the metaphor of the womb was no longer live in the minds of the Hebrew poets who spoke of divine mercy. A man like Joseph was said to have been moved at the sight of his brother Benjamin, because, the story went, his compassion *(rachmim)* was stirred toward his brother (Gen. 44:30). However, the prophets and other Hebrew poets show contextually that they were conscious of the feminine aspect of the metaphor.

Although Jeremiah lived in Judah a century after the destruction of the Kingdom of Israel, he could not believe that the special affinity that had linked Yahweh to Ephraim (Israel) had come to nought. He expected that the dispersed survivors (now known as the lost tribes) would be gathered in the new era. The oracle opens with a comparison between Yahweh and a human father:

> I am a father to Israel,
> And Ephraim is my firstborn.
> (Jer. 31:9)

The image of fatherhood is, however, soon modified by the evocation of Rachel weeping for her children in Ramah (31:15), and the finale allows the divine emotion of motherly compassion to overcome the masculine style that had appeared at the beginning:

> Is Ephraim my dear son?
> Is he my darling child?
> For as often as I speak against him,
> I do remember him still.
> Therefore my inner parts long for him;
> I will surely show him the compassion of the womb, says Yahweh.
> (31:20)

The shift of gender in the imagery of the divine attitude leads to a similar change of gender in the imagery of the human predicament. Israel is no longer compared to a son, but becomes the daughter of Yahweh:

> Return, O virgin Israel,
> . . . .
> How long will you waver, O faithless daughter?
> (31:21, 22a)

An enigmatic line concludes the whole poem:

> For Yahweh has created a new thing on the earth:
> The female will embrace the he-man!
> (31:22b)

Biblical scholars, who until recently were almost exclusively males, have puzzled over this line. Many of them eased their bewilderment by declaring it a marginal addition. There is no manuscript basis for such a conjecture. The interpretation is still open to doubt. In all probability, Jeremiah was proclaiming that in the future economy of history, the relation between the sexes will be completely new. Only the verb "to create," *bara,* suggesting cosmic amplitude (cf. Gen. 1:1), may fittingly characterize it. The woman of the reborn humanity will not only equal the man *(îsh),* but she will also take the initiative. "The female will embrace [even] the he-man *(geber)."*

The sexual overtone of the phrase should not be ignored. The woman is actually designated by the word "female" *(neqebah),* and the man is not just the husband of the myth of the Garden (Gen. 2:23) but the physical specimen of high virility, who is aware of his sexual potency and of his valor in danger. The word *geber,* "he-man," is only one step below the superlative of the same root, *gibbôr,* which means "hero in battle."

Thus, the last line of the Jeremianic oracle, unexpected as it may be for timid exegetes, polemizes against the traditional prevalence of woman's subservience. There may well be a hidden connection between the prophet's theology, which employs a masculine and a feminine comparison for his description of God, and his prefiguration of a different form of sexuality in the world to come.

Toward the end of the exile, a new generation of Judahite survivors in Lower Mesopotamia heard Second Isaiah express the certainty of his hope in the future restoration of Yahweh's remnant. He was so sure of the advent of a new world that he presented the activity of God as a fait accompli:

> Yahweh has comforted his people,
> And upon the afflicted he shows his motherly compassion.
> (Isa. 49:13)

So vivid was the metaphor in the poet's mind that he asked a rhetorical question. To those who complained of divine forgetfulness he retorted:

> Can a woman forget her suckling infant,
> That she should have no compassion
> For the child of her womb?
> (49:15)

At other times, the image of the womb was no longer live, and it was used for a father as well as for a mother. Thus, the psalmist would affirm:

> As a father shows compassions of the womb to his children,
> So Yahweh shows compassions of the womb to those who fear him.
> (Ps. 103:13)

Although spoken of in the masculine gender, Yahweh was endowed with the moral characteristics of both fatherhood and motherhood.

Maternal Semantics and the Mother Goddess

The Hebrew poets knew that the gender of God involved the moral attributes of both fatherhood and motherhood. Why, then, did they still speak of God in the masculine gender? The question is the more urgent since modern exegetes have often pointed out the feminine dimensions of divinity in the faith of ancient Israel. Several writers of today, however, seem to be unaware of the specificity of Hebraic faith. They appeal to the studies of C. G. Jung, E. Neumann, and others on the Great Goddess of classical antiquity, while they misread or ignore the biblical evidence. They confuse monotheism and pantheism. They are unaware of the meaning of transcendence. They do not see that the worldwide myth of the Great Goddess represents a deification of Nature with a capital *N*, in its two primary manifestations: life and death, sexuality and mortality, *erōs* and *thanatos*. Hebraic literature shows that attempts to revive the notion of a feminine deity are based upon a serious confusion between divine transcendence (the distinctive feature of Hebraic faith) and natural immanence (the basis of ancient paganism and its secular, modern equivalent).

It is this confusion that permeates traditional mysticism of whatever form—Jewish, Christian, or Muslim. This mysticism is alien to the radical stringency of the Hebraic theologians. Indeed, they knew the feminine aspect of the divine. Why is it, then, that they never called their God "Mother"? The answer is that they reacted against the allurement of the Mother Goddess cult because they somehow sensed the difference between true divinity and deified nature.

Dwellers of the hinterland, like the Canaanites, who lived in the mountains, worshiped the female deity as Mother Earth. Mesopotamians, who dealt with the tidal floods of the Indian Ocean, or the Phoenicians, who lived on the coast of the Mediterranean and became seafarers as far as Gibraltar and beyond, adored Mother Ocean, or the Female Abyss.

The cult of the Mother Goddess exercised a sexual fascination of the deepest kind. It lulled human beings into communing with the cycles of nature. As it has already been seen in the myth of the Garden, the cult of the Mother Goddess succeeded in merging the sexual drive with the thirst for religious ecstasy and the need for economic security. It offered an overwhelming thrill with physio-psychological effects. The rituals it proposed led to sexual fulfillment, metaphysical satisfaction, and the hope of success in agriculture, viticulture, and animal husbandry. They gratified basic instincts, for they combined erotic pleasure with religious delight, as well as with an escape from the dread of hunger and thirst. They answered human desires at all levels of expectation.

The prophets opposed the Canaanite rituals because they found them incompatible with the religion of Yahweh. Their faith, issuing from the visions of Abraham and Moses, was so thoroughly theocentric that they could not admit the possibility of a fusion between the divine and the natural realms—vegetal, animal, or human. This fusion is the perennial characteristic of religious sexuality, even of the sexually sublimated forms of mysticism in Judaism, Christianity, Islam, and Eastern religions. The prophets' polemic against the worship of the Mother Goddess resulted from their clear opposition to any human manipulation, by magical deeds or sexual trance, of the forces of life in nature. However, the prophets did not oppose sexuality as such. They fought the use of sexuality as a tool of power over the forces of the deified principle of fertility.

Mother Earth was, in effect, the sexual playmate and workmate of the agrarian Canaanite. Fertility rituals brought together the mysteries of the germination of the seed in the soil and the procreation of offspring in woman and female animals. The collective memory inherited from neolithic agriculturists molded the Israelite mentality, from princes to peasants. They believed that conception and childbearing were a form of fertility linked to the mysterious power of the irrigated soil.

Hierogamy was a ritual intercourse between a holy man and women in a temple. Restricted to the seasonal feasts of the equinox and solstice, it celebrated the death and rebirth of vegetation. It led at sacred times to sexual orgies "on every high hill and under every terebinth" or "green tree" in the sacred groves (1 Kings 14:23).

North West Semitic philology points to the pre-Hebraic antiquity of these archetypal beliefs. Since the Terra Mater was the true wife of the Canaanite and Israelite-Judahite farmers, the Hebrew language, originally a dialectical variation of Canaanite, has preserved echoes of this myth of the divine earth. A cluster of verbs derived from the various roots that in the Hebrew are spelled with identical letters *(chalal)* means "to bore, to pierce, to wound, to plow, to rape, to deflower, to defile, to pollute, to begin, to feel guilty." The several Hebrew verbs did not derive from a single stem, but they became associated in pronunciation and even identified in spelling. To begin plowing was, in a deep sense, to rape the earth.

The queens of Judah seem to have played a special role in the hierogamic ritual of the Jerusalem temple. With only two exceptions, their names were always given in the regnal lists of the Davidic monarchy (922-587 B.C.). The title of *Gebirah*, "She-Woman," assigned to the queen mother, designated a sacerdotal function and the sacramental aspect of the monarchic succession. The worship of Asherah, the Mother Goddess, dominated the religious practices of court and populace alike. The widespread presence of statuettes of Asherah, discovered by archeologists, indicates that the cult of the female deity flourished everywhere in Palestine, even during the monarchic period of Israel and Judah.

The reformations that a few kings (Asa, Jehoshaphat, Hezekiah, and Josiah) attempted in the course of three and a half centuries did not succeed in preventing, for more than a few years at a time (1 Kings 14:23–24; 15:12; 22:43–46; 2 Kings 23:4–8), the coalescence of the allegiance to Yahweh with the cult of the Mother Goddess.

The recurrent presence of male homosexuals, as well as the evidence of snake and sun worship, point to the belief that the rock of Zion was the navel of the earth. Delphi and other Greek sanctuaries made similar claims and were centers of adoration for Gea, the Terra Mater, before they became associated with other deities of the Hellenistic pantheon, such as Dionysus and Apollo. In Jerusalem the power of the devotion to the feminine principle, with its magico-mystical consequences, maintained its grip upon princes and the masses at least until the destruction of the temple by the Babylonians in 587 B.C. It persisted sporadically in Palestine during and after the exile.

The love of agriculturists for the Mother Goddess apparently cast a spell upon the people of Judah not only on account of its hedonic and self-gratifying eroticism, but also because it responded to sadomasochistic urges and included barbarous practices such as self-mutilation and human sacrifice. Mother Earth was at once the beneficent and the terrible goddess. She gave birth and also swallowed her children. The deified earth was both life and death. The underworld, to which the sacred rock of Zion was directly linked, presented the constant and ultimate threat. Mortality was as powerful a force as fertility. *Erōs* could not be separated from *thanatos*.

Even after the beginning of the exile, when Jeremiah escaped the net of the Babylonian army and found refuge in the Nile delta instead of being taken captive to Lower Mesopotamia, the Judahites who surrounded him revealed the disarray of their faith. Jeremiah observed among them a new manifestation of devotion to the feminine principle. Just as the contemporaries of Hosea in Benjamin, two hundred years previously, had indulged in the sacramental food of sexual rites, which they called "raisin cakes" (Hos. 3:1), so the women of nascent Judaism in Egypt were "baking cakes to the Queen of Heaven" (Jer. 44:15–23). From the Semitic Asherah to the Egyptian Isis the step was small, and the underlying motivation remained the same. In the presence of the unknown, human temptation has always been to blur the line between magic and religion and to perform rites aimed at controlling the powers of life and death.

The prophets and other Hebrew poets ascribed to Yahweh the moral characteristics of human motherhood, but they never deified the feminine reality. It is this radical distinction that has escaped the notice of most anthropologists and psychologists who have written in modern times on the "gender of God" in the literature of the Bible.

Paternal Tyranny and Divine Fatherhood

Even when this oft-ignored fact of history—the Hebraic opposition to the myth of the Mother Goddess—is taken into consideration, the questions may still be asked: Why is God, in the biblical literature, always designated as "he"? And how is it that both the synagogue and the church came to invoke "him" as "Our Father"?

It is no secret that the notion of fatherhood has tended, in our epoch, to be viewed in an unfavorable light. This cultural development may be ascribed to a number of unrelated factors. One of them, particularly in the Anglo-Saxon world, is the loss of authority that paternal tyrants have incurred. Reaction to paternal tyranny has led in the twentieth century to a deterioration of fatherhood in the nuclear family. Manifestations of this trend are current in literature, especially in popular novels and plays, and they also, in a debased fashion, penetrate popular advertising, which tends to portray fathers as little more than naive morons. Another factor is the restlessness of young people when their adolescence is unnaturally prolonged by schooling and economic circumstances.

The decisive factor in this cultural change is the influence of depth psychology. From the autobiographical memories of Freud's and Jung's early years, it is clear that their treatments of the biblical God have been marred by their own emotional reactions to paternal authoritarianism. In different ways both Freud and Jung have read into the literature of the Old Testament theories which have no exegetical foundation.

Freud has presented the origin of Hebraic monotheism as a peculiar symptom of the Oedipus complex amplified to the ethnic scale. Borrowing the views of Ernst Sellin, he postulated that during the wandering in the wilderness, after the exodus from Egypt, the Hebrews rebelled against the tyranny of Moses and murdered him. Although Sellin's hypothesis is not substantiated by the biblical documents and has been completely rejected by scholars, Freud accepted it blithely because it fitted his psychoanalytical conclusion of hostility to the father figure. He theorized that the memory of this national trauma—the murder of Moses—was repressed in later generations, and this repression produced in Israel an unbearable sense of guilt, which the prophets at a later age exploited as they promoted a highly ethical religion.

In his *Answer to Job*, Jung chose to emphasize exclusively the dark side of the Hebraic divinity. In Yahweh he saw a capricious power, which he called "revolting" to the modern mind. Offering a correction to the traditional Christian doctrine of the Trinity, he proposed a "Quaternity," in which the feminine principle, represented by the virgin Mary, would qualify and even contradict the paternal tyranny presumably implied by Hebraic monotheism. Apparently, he never discussed or appreciated the many instances of love and forgiveness that the poetry of ancient Israel ascribed to Yahweh.

In particular, Jung failed to see that the poem of Job (Job 3:1—4:6) was to be distinguished from the ancient folktale of foreign and probably Edomitic origin (Job 1:1—2:23; 42:7–17), which was used only as a setting for the theological discussion, written seven centuries later. Unlike the archaic folktale, the poem did not present the deity as a barbarous and vindictive idol. Jung overlooked the wistfulness of Yahweh's questioning Job from the whirlwind. He did not see that Job, in the poetic dialogue, was the mouthpiece of human pride, not unlike that of man in the myth of the

Garden. He failed to discern the purpose of the poet, which was to point out human arrogance in judging the Deity and especially in imposing, as Job's friends did, standards of human morality upon a supramoral divinity.

In its whole sweep, the masculine gender of the biblical literature by which God is designated does not at all signify that the Hebrews considered Yahweh as a deity with male genitals. Likewise, the motif of divine fatherhood, which was used most sparingly, never implied that Yahweh was a progenitor in the sexual sense.

Language is a cultural phenomenon not easily adapted to revolutionary change, especially in the realm of religion. When twentieth-century usage speaks of the "rising and setting of the sun," almost everyone knows today that this geocentric figure of speech dates from another era. Yet, it persists. Similarly, when the ancient Hebrews spoke of God as "El," they preserved inevitably the terminology of an obsolete past, but they were aware of the radically new meaning they gave to the name for divinity.

Their ancestors were ethnically and culturally related to the Proto-Phoenicians or Proto-Canaanites of the second millennium B.C. The epic traditions of Genesis remembered that these ancestors had come from "Ur in the Chaldees," and that they had sojourned for a time in Haran, a region of northwestern Mesopotamia contiguous with Syria-Aram (Gen. 11:31–32).

When the Israelite farmer offered to Yahweh the first fruit of his harvest, he would recite a liturgical creed, "My father was a wandering Aramean exhausted from hunger and thirst" (Deut. 26:5). Every Yahwist was aware of that distant past, when his fathers had worshiped "other gods" (Josh. 24:2). The Ugaritic texts (fourteenth to thirteenth centuries B.C.) preserved fragments of the myths that described some of those other gods. The people of Ugarit, on the Mediterranean coast of northern Lebanon, placed above all other divinities in their pantheon the god El. As early as the fourteenth century B.C., they told how El had emasculated his own father, *Shamem*, the sky god, for the sake of his wronged mother Arts, the Goddess Earth, and how El had then ravished his own sisters.

The theme of patricide and incest, common to the mythologies of many cultures, was significant among the pagan ancestors of Israel. Here is, then, a startling irony: Freud's use of the Oedipus complex to explain the rise of Hebraic monotheism, merely according to the gratuitous conjecture of Sellin, precisely fails to explain the specificity of the Hebraic faith, although it fits quite well the religions of the ancient Near East and Egypt.

The tradition is unanimous. The epic of Abraham insists upon the theological rupture that the Hebrews and their eventual successors, the Israelites and Judahites, and then the Jews of the Persian period, have constantly remembered as the distinctive feature of their religious particularity. As depicted in the story of the call of Abraham (Gen. 12:1–3), the Hebrews broke away from the mythological beliefs of their predecessors. They preserved the hitherto proper name El, but they demythologized its connotation of a male athlete affirming his selfhood by sexual violence. They transformed the word *El* from denominative designation to generic naming. This means that the proper name El became a common noun signifying "God." They remembered also that, under the influence of Moses, they came to worship that God under a new proper name, *Yahweh* (Exod. 3:1–15).

For the Hebrews El was not "the progenitor of gods and men," as he had been for the people of Ugarit in the Bronze Age. El was Yahweh, "the One who causes to be whatever he causes to be" (Exod. 3:14).[9] The imagery of creation is expressed here in a surprisingly modern abstraction, which links the idea of God to the notion of the maker of all things, but never of a father in the sense of a physiological procreator.

Thus, the grammatical gender for God was inherited from an obsolete stage of the language. Having preserved the word *El* as a masculine noun, the Hebrews applied the masculine gender to the designation of the Deity without any implication of sexual maleness.

It was probably on account of their radical departure from the mythological past of the ancient Near East that the Hebrews avoided at first the habit of naming Yahweh as Father. The monarchs of many archaic cultures, including those of the Fertile Crescent and Egypt, were actually boasting of their divine origins when they spoke of some god as their father. On the contrary, the people of Israel used the word, but they did so very infrequently, in order to compare the closeness of their relationship with Yahweh to that of human children with their own father. In every instance, the comparison had to do not with the act of procreation but with the growth of a living, loving, and protecting father.

In the relatively ancient poem known as the Song of Moses, now incorporated into the Book of Deuteronomy, Yahweh was for the first time in the preserved literature of ancient Israel presented as Father, but the context shows without doubt that the use of the word is metaphorical:

> Do you thus requite Yahweh,
> O foolish people, and unwise?
> Is he not thy Father that has redeemed thee?
> Has he not made thee and established thee?
> (Deut. 32:6)

The allusion is to the historic event of the exodus, in which Israel saw the "birth" of its national existence in history.

A similar allusion is found in the dynastic oracle concerning David:

> I will be his Father,
> And he shall be my son.
> (2 Sam. 7:14)

The emphasis lies on adoption and nurture, not on procreation. The rhetorical trope may reflect the style of the covenant treaties between a suzerain and his vassal, as found in the Hittite documents of an earlier age. In the same fashion, the Enthronement Psalm, which was probably composed for a king of Judah, descendant of David, most easily placed in the mouth of the new monarch the prayer:

> Thou art my Father, my God,
> And the Rock of my salvation.
> (Ps. 89:26)

The few examples in which Yahweh is compared to a human father point not to a mythology of divine ancestry but to a symbolical formulation of history. As Hosea, the eighth-century prophet from Benjamin, had done, Jeremiah a century later compared Israel to a son (Jer. 3:4), but the context shows that the people's rebellion is also expressed in the language of marital infidelity.

> I had thought that thou wouldst call me "My Father,"
> And that thou wouldst never separate thyself from me.
> But, as a woman who betrays her lover,
> Thus the house of Israel has betrayed me.
>
> (3:19, 20)

Of course, the image of divine fatherhood implies not only protection and nurture but also tutoring, which is disciplinary guidance, so that Israel may walk "in a straight path" (31:9). The image of fatherhood keeps in equilibrium power and grace, justice and mercy.

When the exiled in Babylon invoked Yahweh's help, they said, "Thou, O Yahweh, art our Father," but they added in the same breath an unmistakable reference to their national emergence from Egyptian slavery: "Our Redeemer, from of old, is thy name" (Isa. 63:16).

Throughout the history of salvation, from the exodus, when God acted out the marvels of nature, to the exile, when he hid himself with the intent to chide but not abandon, the same metaphor was summoned in the light of a concept of time that was more than past *(chronos)* because it offered a fresh opportunity *(kairos)* to start again. Divine fatherhood entails the affirmation of a purpose.

Biblical interpreters have not stressed that the notion of divine fatherhood is inseparable from a theology of time.

Every one of the few allusions to God as Father in the Hebrew Bible connotes the vision of a human father who carries in his arms a helpless infant and later a rebellious child, so that this child may mature into full adulthood.

The comparison of Yahweh to a human father eventually became associated with a theology of creation, which moved from a cosmic perspective first to a national consciousness and eventually to an individual awareness of personal communion.

O Yahweh, thou art our Father,
   We are the clay, and thou art the potter;
We are, all of us, the work of thy hand.
                 (Isa. 64:8)

Originally applied to a collective reality, that is, to the people chosen "to be a light to the nations," the metaphor of fatherhood underwent a subtle transformation when individual piety used it to express a pain of spiritual loneliness made more horrible by the memory of a divine intimacy now past.

The word "father" is not explicitly used in the "Psalm of Dereliction" (Ps. 22), but the poet who cried out, "My God, my God, why hast thou forsaken me?" (22:1) dwelt upon the thought that the same God had acted at his birth as a surrogate father:

Yet, thou art he who took me from the womb;
   Thou didst make me trust upon my mother's breasts;
I was cast upon thee as soon as I was born,
   And from my mother's bosom thou hast been my God!
                 (22:9–10)

Even in the midst of a meaningless existence and with the prospect of his proximate and unjust mortality, the poetic hero of Job is able to bring together the motifs of fatherhood and creation. On the one hand, he protests against the God who permitted him to live at birth (3:3–19). On the other hand, with the sublime contradictoriness of a man whose faith persists in spite of chaos, he appeals to the love that an artist always nurses for the masterpiece he has created:

Remember that thou hast made me of clay:
   Wilt thou turn me to dust again?
               (10:9)

The Hebraic experience of creatureliness coincides with its psychological consciousness of spiritual filiality.

For the prophets and the other poets of the Old Testament, divine fatherhood was a metaphor used for a theology of transcendence that never accepted the impassibility or the detachment of a pseudophilosophical deism.

Matriarchy and the Fatherhood
of God

Biblical faith has been attacked on the ground that the notion of divine fatherhood is inevitably associated with a patriarchal system of society that oppresses womanhood. Moreover, some readers of the Bible have charged that the same notion of divine fatherhood, far from being a metaphor of compassionate protection and nurture, shows the survival of a mythology of cruelty, as demonstrated by the story of the sacrifice of Isaac (Gen. 22:1–16).

It has also been maintained in recent years that matriarchy, originally related to the moon cult, favored the worship of a maternal deity that promoted a societal system true to nature because it was based on the normal attachment of mother and child. At the same time, it has been asserted that the religion of Yahweh reflected a patriarchal sexism predicated upon an abstract and antinatural principle of ethics, the father-son relationship, which in turn produced the male enslavement of females. Such views are not substantiated by facts.

Lunar worship is not the necessary mark of matriarchy, nor are solar rites and beliefs the concomitants of patriarchy. In spite of the folkloric linking of woman's menstruation with the lunar "month" and of woman's three ages (virginity, maternity, and postmenopausal sterility) with the three phases of the moon (waxing, full, and waning), lunar myths are not the symptoms of maternal religions. Although the ancestors of the Abrahamite clan may have been moon worshipers, no inference is to be drawn from such a possibility since the moon cults are typical of nomadic, pastoral societies, in which both sexes tend to be complementary to each other with equality of respective rights and responsibilities. It is, rather, the agrarian mode of existence that concerns itself with the fertility of the soil, favors the worship of Terra Mater, and is inclined to consider women as mere chattel on a par with beasts of burden.

The opposition of the Yahwists and the prophets to the fertility cults was not the result of a patriarchal polemic against matriarchy. It stemmed from a unique awareness of divine transcendence over the forces of nature and of the cultic corruption that menaced Israel in the land.

The use of the story of the sacrifice of Isaac as evidence of a mythology of divine cruelty, on account of its implied belief in a God who was at once creator and destroyer, may be construed from some rabbinical legends, but it does not rest upon the exegesis of the text.

Having become the recipient of a vision that led him to expect the mission of his posterity in the future history of mankind, Abraham, the model of faith, is confronted with the ultimate threat and horror which may torment a father:

> Take thy son, thy only son, him thou lovest, Isaac,
> And go to the land of Moriyyah,
> And give him up there in a fiery sacrifice.
> (Gen. 22:2)

The language is charged with all the pathos of fathers who have conformed for millenniums to this barbarous ritual. It is not Yahweh who is portrayed here as the brutal destroyer of hope. To the contrary, the story combats the agrarian rites of the neolithic cultures which lingered among the West Semites of the Fertile Crescent as well as in the pre-Hellenic societies of the Mediterranean world.

The emotion of the teller of the folk story is unmistakable. He knows that faith means total devotion. He also intimates that the God who conceals himself is a true God, whereas the deification of nature represents the projection of self-interest. The sign of pure religion, like that of Job in the ancient folk tale (Job 1:9), lies in love at all costs. The clue is to be found at the end of the story with its substitution of a ram for the child.

Martin Luther was a lifelong prey to spiritual testing and therefore to trials and temptations *(Anfechtungen)*. His comment on this text shows that he sensed the subtle interaction that unites the pathos of the human father with the pathos of God.

> The father raised his knife, the boy did not wince. The angel cried, "Abraham! Abraham!" See how divine majesty is at hand in the hour of death. We say, "In the midst of life we die." God answers, "Nay, in the midst of death we live." *(Weimar Ausgabe* 43.220 ff., trans. R. H. Bainton)

The Hebraic theologian who told this Genesis tale understood the deeper meaning of the notion of divine fatherhood.

The presence of Yahweh was elusive. His protection was never at man's command. It did not depend upon moral behavior or the correctness of cultic rituals. Nevertheless, while condemned, Israel never felt ultimately alienated, abandoned, forlorn.

The language of Israel's faith renders totally irrelevant the modern charges of male sexism in the biblical notion of God. On account of Israel's inheritance from a mythological past, which was repudiated and replaced by a theology of time, the theological language of the Bible speaks of God in the masculine gender. Yet, one cannot dismiss the God of the prophets and of the psalmists as a puppet of paternalism.

Those who wish to go "beyond God the Father" may be inspired by legitimate intentions, such as that of liberating oppressed womanhood from a patriarchal culture, but they have misread the biblical evidence and ignored its dynamic tensility. They have seen in the metaphor of divine fatherhood an expression of moralistic or ritualistic tyranny, which was not typical Hebraism but was current only among the Jerusalem priests who founded Judaism. They did not pay attention to the stress of prophets and psalmists on fatherhood as metaphor of grace and motherly compassion.

The prophetic and psalmodic theology of fatherhood dismisses as an egregious error the popular conception of a mercantile God who rewards and punishes, in an oversimplification of providence.

With the passing of the Persian and Hellenistic centuries, as the memory of the national past became more intensely colored with the urgency of a hope in the advent of a new world, the metaphor of divine fatherhood became associated with the notion of the end time. The view of *chronos* as the calendar structure of past, present, and future became eventually for Jesus of Nazareth the time of opportunity, *kairos*. The time is now.

As it will be seen in chapter 8, the various interpretations of Jesus in the early church were in large part predicated upon a new theology of fatherhood, which, in turn, involved a novel interpretation of sonship. In early Christianity, the notion of fatherhood is inescapably bound to the notion of the son who goes willingly to his sacrificial death.

The old North West Semitic deity El, "the Father of Years," was the mythical parallel, on the coast of Lebanon, to the pre-Hellenic god Chronos. The Freudian conjecture on the psychological significance of the Oedipus myth, with its emphasis on the motif of patricide, may apply to the North West Semitic culture from which the Hebrews emerged and against which they rebelled. It does not bring any light on the Yahwistic faith.

The prophets promoted religious equality between men and women. It was nascent Judaism in its priestly form that debased the religious status of womanhood with its legal strictures on sexual purity and the new meaning it conferred upon the rite of circumcision.

Circumcised Male
and Pollutant Female

The birth of Judaism in Babylon, during the sixth century B.C., constitutes one of the wonders of ancient history. Phoenicians, Lebanese, Syrians, and other ethnic groups were deported to Mesopotamia besides the inhabitants of Jerusalem. They were eventually assimilated within the Babylonian Empire, but the Judahites became the Jews.[10]

Under the influence of the prophet Ezekiel, the descendants of the Jerusalem priests in Babylonian exile assumed a major role in the formation of Judaism. They provided a complex system of ritual acts that molded the lives of all men and women at every moment of their drab existence. It was the daily ceremonial of separating the sacred from the profane, the pure from the impure, that kept the community distinct from its environment, maintained its sense of identity, and reminded its members both of their heritage and of their mission in history.

Ritual gestures included the realm of sexuality. A new significance was conferred upon the ancient rite of circumcision. No longer a puberty rite, it became the sign of the covenant, administered to a male infant. Thus, the female participated in the community of Israel not by herself alone, but only through her relation with the male as daughter, wife, or mother. Likewise, a new legal emphasis was laid upon the rites of purification from the "impurity" of menstruation and childbirth, thus promoting a cultic disbalance between the male, "son of the covenant," and the "pollutant" female.

Ezekiel and the Pentateuch

Ezekiel was a disciple of Jeremiah, but he belonged to a family of priests from Jerusalem. Passionately attached to the myth of Zion as the center of the world, he called Jerusalem the navel of the earth (Ezek. 38:12). Taken to Lower Mesopotamia after the first deportation (598 B.C.), he had a vision of the end (587 B.C.) and "saw" that the glory of Yahweh had left the temple when the Babylonian armies profaned the sanctuary. The memory of this vision haunted him for the remainder of his life in the impure land of exile. He believed that Zion would someday be restored in a renewed earth.

To keep alive the faith of the other deportees he convinced them that the catastrophes that had destroyed the kingdom of Judah resulted from a just retribution for the nation's guilt. He stirred the hopes of his fellow Judah-ites—the nascent Jews—by preparing a blueprint for "holy living" in the new Jerusalem.

In the meantime, he revived and in some cases initiated a number of practices destined to govern the behavior of every man and woman. Ritual gestures are extremely significant in times of spiritual disarray. They support by repetition and habit a certain type of living, an attitude that constantly promotes reverence for the holy. They undergird and exteriorize inner faith. They become a celebration of life in all its moments. For uprooted minorities they assuage the sense of nostalgia and they galvanize the will to wait for tomorrow.

> Oh, longing for places that were not
> Cherished enough in that fleeting hour!
> How I long to make good from afar
> The forgotten gesture, the additional act.[11]

Rainer Maria Rilke articulated in these lines the feeling of loss and of need for sacred places, as well as the desire to find them again. Ezekiel not only made "good from afar the forgotten gesture" but also proposed "the additional act" for expiating guilt and regaining a daily awe, with the holy in the midst of an impure land. He inspired his priestly colleagues and his disciples to continue his work of legal codification. Rules of cultic, civil, criminal, and constitutional jurisdiction were assembled, amplified, edited, and published, together with the epic traditions of the Hebrew ancestors on the "genesis" of the world, the election of Israel, and the exodus. The earlier codes were incorporated in the larger unit. Because the Jewish exiles in Babylon felt they were living in the desert of history, waiting to enter again the promised land, this finished product was placed in the aura of Moses, the new legislation was presented as the revelation of Yahweh at Sinai, and the model of the new temple was described as the elaborate tabernacle of the wilderness. The whole literary monument was eventually written down on five scrolls, to be placed in five clay vases (in Greek, *penta teuchē*). It is known today as the Law of Moses *(Torah)*, or Pentateuch.

Ezekiel had been particularly obsessed by the sexual aberrances that had been perpetrated in the temple of Jerusalem during the monarchy. He used a much cruder language than that of his predecessors, the prophets of the eighth and seventh centuries, to condemn the sexual manifestations of idolatry (Ezekiel 8 and 23, especially).

Princes and masses alike had been lured for most of three centuries by the cult of the Mother Goddess, thus vitiating the allegiance demanded by the God of the ancient Yahwists. In spite of a few short-lived reforms between 922 and 587 B.C., the temple of Jerusalem had been contaminated by ophiolatry and heliolatry, by sacred orgies related to the cycles of the seasons, and by the activities of male homosexual diviners, the ceremonial weeping for Tammuz (the dying and rising god of fertility), and the veneration of an idol called the image of pleasure (Ezek. 8:3). The priests of the nascent Jewish community during the exile were determined to reform the ritual drastically. It is on account of an overreaction against pagan rites of sexuality that the Priestly Code, which now forms the framework of the Pentateuch, ascribed for the first time a theological significance to the ancient rite of male circumcision and stressed officially the cultic impurity of sexual secretions.

Circumcision as Covenant Rite

The rite of male circumcision goes back to the Stone Age. The Hebrews apparently perpetuated an earlier practice inherited from their North West Semitic predecessors. For the performance of the operation they still used flint blades, evidence of its neolithic origin (Josh. 5:3; cf. Exod. 4:25). Until the sixth century B.C., when the Jerusalem priests in exile attributed for the first time a theological significance to the age-old rite of circumcision (Gen. 17:9–14, 21; Exod. 12:48; Lev. 12:3; Josh. 5:2–7), it had been part of the mores for centuries as a matter of course. No literary document of an earlier period permits us to infer a religious justification of the practice.

The Code of the Covenant (Exod. 20:22—23:25), which incorporates some of the legislation of Israel from the eleventh to the ninth centuries, ignores the rite entirely.

Many explanations for the ablation of the male foreskin have been proposed, from Herodotus, Philo of Alexandria and the postbiblical rabbis to modern anthropologists. It has been said that the practice indicated tribal markings in some patriarchal societies, or that it constituted a puberty *rite de passage,* testing an adolescent's endurance to pain or preparing him for sexual intercourse, with the purpose of enhancing or, on the contrary, of reducing sexual pleasure.[12] Others have suggested that the ablation of the foreskin facilitated physical cleanliness or prevented phimosis and paraphimosis. Still others have looked upon it as a sacrificial substitute for emasculation, supposedly practiced in prehistoric times as a gesture of total dedication to the Mother Goddess. Still others have viewed the rite as an attempt to sacralize procreative power, or as a token of humiliation and subjection for slaves and war prisoners. None of these conjectures is susceptible of demonstration.

There is reason to believe that in Egypt and in Israel circumcision was at first a puberty rite.[13] A relief sculpture in a Saqqarah tomb of the Sixth Dynasty (twenty-sixth to twenty-first centuries B.C.) suggests that ancient Egyptians were circumcised at the onset of adolescence. In the Hebrew tongue, inherited from the proto-Canaanites, the word *choten,* "father-in-law (of the bridegroom)," literally means "circumciser."

The isolated fragment of an archaic tradition now incorporated in Israel's national epic represents Moses as "a bridegroom of blood" (Exod. 4:24–

26). Such a folkloric memory confirms the antiquity of an association between circumcision and marriage.

> On the way [from Midian back to Egypt], Yahweh met Moses at the campsite and sought to kill him. Thereupon Zipporah [Moses' wife] took a flint blade and cut off her son's foreskin, and touched [Moses' genitals] with it, and she said, "Surely thou art to me a bridegroom of blood!" Then [Yahweh] left him alone. She said "bridegroom of blood" on account of circumcision. (Exod. 4:24–26)

Modern readers have frequently been offended by this story. They maintain that it ascribes a capricious and cruel character to the Deity, and they are prone to use it in order to disparage Old Testament faith as opposed to that of the New Testament. Such an attitude ironically reveals a static view of the canon of Scripture. Traditions of the fathers were recited over many generations. They came from a number of unrelated sources. Many of them may have been remembered only for the sake of preserving the past. Others may have been incorporated into the national epic whenever the storytellers aimed at instruction by means of narration.

Not unlike the story of Jacob fighting all night long with the spirit of the ford in the canyon of the Jabbok river (Gen. 32:24–32), this tale evokes an atmosphere of darkness and terror. Was the intention of the narrator to convey the impression that an uncircumcised Moses was running a mortal danger? Did Zipporah, Jethro's daughter, a Midianite woman, perform a gesture of apotropaic magic in order to ward off evil? Was the circumcision of her son "vicarious" since she touched her husband's genitals with the bloody foreskin of her freshly mutilated child? Was there in this tale an attempt to show the shift from prenuptial to infant circumcision? Answers are all conjectural.

In a similar vein, the gory tradition of Dinah and the uncircumcised Hivites of Shechem supports the view that the ritual of circumcision constituted a requirement preliminary to marriage (Gen. 34:24–25).

As the Israelite tribesmen infiltrated the land of Canaan (twelfth to eleventh centuries B.C.), they did not find themselves, in this respect, different from the foreigners they encountered. They knew that Moabites, Edomites, Ammonites, and later, Arabs were also circumcised (Jer. 9: 25–26).

That the ritual was taken for granted is clear from the use of the word "uncircumcised" as a term of contempt for the Philistines, in the times of the judges and of Samuel, and for other enemies, as late as the prophet Ezekiel in the sixth century B.C. The same prophet, who initiated the theological significance of ancient rituals as substitutes for the temple ceremonies that could not be performed in a foreign land, never mentioned circumcision.

Modern observers have often noted the traumatic effects produced by foreskin ablation among pubescent Arab boys.[14] Was it on account of a similar dread of its psychological aftermath that the Hebrews, at some moment in their history, lowered the age of the mutilation from adolescence to early infancy? Again, there is no literary basis for an answer.

Jeremiah knew that some of Israel's neighbors, including the Egyptians, also practiced circumcision. He clearly placed the integrity of the will and the consecration of the inner being above "the circumcision of the flesh" (9:25–26). With all his prophetic predecessors, he attributed to the total dedication of the inner self and the courage for intellectual lucidity an overwhelming and sufficient importance that made the outward act of ritual alone superfluous. Like the preachers of the reformation led by Josiah (621 B.C.), he admonished: "Circumcise yourselves to Yahweh, remove the foreskins of your heart" (Jer. 4:4; cf. Deut. 10:16; 30:6).

The deuteronomists and Jeremiah did not believe in the sacrosanctity of circumcision as a ritual gesture. They appealed to the powers of decision, the faculty of volition—a meaning subsumed by the Hebrew word for "heart"—and they deemed the psychological roots of the human character to be far more important than any outward symbol. They used ablation of the foreskin as a metaphor of openness to the word of Yahweh (Jer. 6:10).

At the same time, it is possible that some contemporaries of Jeremiah began to associate the rite with access to membership in the covenant people. Those who spoke of the circumcision of the heart also stressed the love of God for the fathers and their descendants. They singled out Israel as elected "above all peoples" (Deut. 10:15–16).

One or two generations later, the deportees of Judah in Lower Mesopotamia were thrown into an alien environment. Passionately eager to maintain the consciousness of their identity, they came to reflect upon the theological dimension of their own distinctiveness. As the Babylonians did not practice circumcision, the Jerusalem priests in exile easily exalted the ancient gesture of foreskin ablation, together with the observance of a weekly Sabbath, as the sign of their belonging to the covenant.

For the first time, they introduced into the legislation of the community, in both the form of a narrative and the style of jurisprudence, the explanation that male circumcision signified membership in the people of God. They ascribed the origin of the rite to a revelation of Yahweh to Abraham and noted that it was performed not only on his son Isaac, ancestor of Israel, but also on his son Ishmael, ancestor of the Arabs. Apparently no contradiction was found between this fact and the interpretation of circumcision as the mark of the Hebrew covenant.

And God said to Abraham, "And as for thee, thou shalt keep my covenant, and thy seed after thee throughout their generations. This is my covenant which you [plural] will keep between me and you [plural] and thy seed after thee. Every male among you shall be circumcised. And you shall circumcise the flesh of your foreskins, and it shall be the sign of the covenant between me and you." (Gen. 17:9–11)

The pronoun "it" in the last sentence of verse 11 is grammatically ambiguous. Does the mark of the covenant reside in the act of ablation, or is it contained in the severed foreskin itself, and therefore does the sign appear in the absence of the foreskin? Circumcision may well have been viewed as a sacramental act of renunciation of the self, as the offering of a gift, the devotion of one's entire being to the Deity.

It is also possible that the sign was not related to a mutilation of the flesh as such, but showed an unconscious reminiscence of the archaic expression "cutting of a covenant." The Hebrew idiom for "to make a covenant" was "to cut a covenant"—possibly an allusion to the slaughtering of an animal that accompanied the formal act of agreement. There is no evidence, however, that the biblical writers ever associated the ritual of circumcision with a sacrificial enactment of a contract.

By ascribing to the ancient ritual of male circumcision a theological significance, the priests inevitably stressed, intentionally or not, a *religious* distinction between men and women. At least, they contributed to the development of a new masculine consciousness as cultically different from the feminine self-awareness.

Males were raised to the level of "sons of the covenant." They bore the mark of the covenant in their flesh. The link between them and divinity was intimate, direct, and not susceptible of being undone. It placed the burden of devotion to God less on the dynamics of faith than on the peculiarity of flesh and of sex. As a consequence, females were further removed from the cultic realities of divine presence. They were not directly or immediately "marked" in their bodies as men were. They belonged to the covenant people indirectly through the mediation of their men, by physiological descent, by marriage, or by the birthing of sons. The process may have exalted their social position as daughters, wives, and mothers, but it lowered their cultic status as indirect participants in the divine election.

Together with the theological justification of circumcision, the legislation on sexual purity, which the exilic priests officially rendered authoritative and placed in the context of divine holiness, appears to have accelerated the trend toward cultic discrimination against womanhood.

Laws of Sexual Purity

The legislation on cultic purity, especially in the realm of sexual relations, is found chiefly in the Book of Leviticus. Compiled in the sixth century B.C. by Ezekiel's disciples, this legislation made official certain rules that had appeared in earlier codes, and also introduced new regulations, which were for the first time presented as the revelation of a holy God. Some of the ancient practices were folkloric customs that had survived from prehistoric ages. Others apparently represented priestly measures of a stringent character. They may have been intended to help Israel resist the temptation of practicing Canaanite magic. Thus, the love of neighbor (Lev. 19:18), which in later times received an importance second only to that of the love of God (Luke 10:27), appeared in a commandment followed by prohibitions against several kinds of ritual mixtures, such as those of cattle breeds, textiles, and garden seeds (Lev. 19:19). This last admixture alluded to the planting of the gardens of Tammuz, or Adonis, in which different botanical species were cultivated together in a clay pot as a ritual gesture aimed at insuring the fertility of fields and animals.

Inasmuch as sexual interdictions were listed side by side with the prohibition from sacrificing children by fire (Lev. 18:6–23; see v. 21), it appears that the laws directed against various kinds of incest, male homosexuality, transvestism, and bestiality (15:19–33) fell into the same category of over-reaction to idolatrous worship. At the same time, heterosexual monogamy was, by the sixth century, taken for granted.

For generations the Yahwist theologians had recited at festivals the story of the Garden of Eden. There, man and woman formed "one flesh" (Gen. 2:24). When the Jerusalem priests in exile legislated on marital intercourse, they did not need to include the institution of marriage. Nevertheless, immersed as they were in the culture of international wisdom, they told anew, on a cosmic scale, the story of creation and proclaimed that God had created human beings as "male and female" (Gen. 1:27). They were, also, intent upon asserting the distinctiveness of the chosen people. In their fear of the Canaanite folkloric practices that had prevailed until the fall of Jerusalem in 587 B.C., they promulgated rules for the ritual cleansing of sexual secretions for both males and females (Lev. 15:1–33). Consequently, they stressed far more the ritual contamination of a bleeding woman than that of a man. A menstruating woman was declared unclean, and any person or object coming into contact with her became likewise cultically impure.

Sexual intimacy with a menstruating woman was strictly forbidden (Lev. 18:19). The penalty for the breach of this prohibition was drastic. Both the man and the woman who had violated it were to be "cut off from among their people" (20:18). This expression meant either excommunication or, euphemistically, capital punishment. In all probability, the origin of the prohibition lay in the priests' revulsion against some pagan ritual that involved the magical use of menstrual blood.

From the most remote antiquity, women with an issue of blood were excused from normal activities, but no law excluded them from the direct worship of Yahweh. It was told in the national epic that Rachel had tricked her own father Laban when he tried to find his family gods, which Jacob had stolen. As Laban was searching Rachel's tent, she refused to rise, having concealed those idols beneath her, and claimed she was "in the way of women" (Gen. 32:35). Laban respected her rights, but he was not in any way made unclean by contact with other objects in the tent which his daughter had obviously touched. A woman was known to be "pollutant" only in the priestly laws of a later age.

There was no provision anywhere, in the early legislation, in the code of Deuteronomy, in the historical records of Judges, Samuel and Kings, or in the prophetic and psalmodic poetry, for subjecting women to the rules of menstrual impurity.

The Jerusalem priests in exile also revealed their antifeminine bias by placing under the sanction of divine holiness a legislation concerning the validity of women's vows (Num. 30:1–15). While a man, according to this legislation, might never break his word, an unmarried or a married woman's vow could be annulled by her father or her husband, respectively (30:5, 8, 12, 15).

The priestly regulations on the impurity of woman for several weeks following childbirth (Lev. 12:2–5) call for similar observations. Again, the origin of these laws probably lay in the prehistoric dread of female blood. The antifeminine bias was even increased by the female sex of the newborn child. If the infant was male, the mother remained in a state of ritual impurity for thirty-three days after his circumcision. If the infant was female, the mother's time of "confinement" was longer.

> She shall not touch any hallowed thing, nor come into the sanctuary, until the days of her purifying are completed. But if she bears a female child, then she shall be unclean two weeks, as in her menstruation; and she shall continue in the blood of her purifying for sixty-six days. (Lev. 15:25–30)

In the spiritual chaos of the Babylonian exile, the Jerusalem priests sought to prepare a new age and to prevent the recurrence of Canaanite syncretism, but several of the archaic practices that they codified in the name of the God of Moses placed women in a state of religious inferiority to men and may have even insidiously penetrated the feminine consciousness with a sense of guilt that had nothing to do with moral behavior.

Women in Ancient Hebraism

The emergence of Judaism in the sixth century B.C. carried into the religious sphere the social and political stringencies of a patriarchal system inherited from Near Eastern culture. Throughout the centuries that preceded the exile and the birth of Judaism, Hebrew faith had involved men and women equally. Some women even occupied in the memory of the nation a place of prominence. They were known for their religious innovativeness, their daring and courage, their authority and influence.

At the time of the exodus from Egypt, when the people had barely escaped death from the pursuing Egyptian army or the engulfing tide of the sea, it was Miriam, "a prophetess," who sang the first hymn of thanksgiving in the history of Hebrew psalmody (Exod. 15:20–21).

To be sure, the final edition of the Pentateuch shows that Moses had first led the people in the singing of a long poem of gratitude and praise (Exod. 15:1–8). However, literary and form-critical analysis definitely reveals that this poem, while relatively ancient, bears marks of an age much later than that of the exodus in the thirteenth century B.C. It rehearses the history of the conquest of the land down to the time of the Philistines, during the period of the judges, and it even refers anachronistically to the erection of a sanctuary "on [God's] own mountain" (15:17), hence in the reign of Solomon (tenth century B.C.).

With its wild accent and its elliptical style, the Song of Miriam gives all the signs of high antiquity. This archaic passage is significant, for it incorporates the first Hebraic example of a Psalm of Thanksgiving *(Todah)*. A woman was credited with composing a Hebrew paean, but this victory hymn did not extol the achievement of male warriors. No exploit of men in battle was praised. To the contrary, the female singers expressed their gratitude to Yahweh. Miriam's Song is a manifestation of this peculiar ability of the Hebraic faith to discern a divine dimension in the unexpected gift. Without human work or merit, God's grace in saving was immediate, yet immense, and its impact shattering. Life instead of death!

Miriam and her brother Aaron complained to Moses "on account of the Cushite woman he had married" (Num. 12:1). The ground of the complaint is obscure, for the thread of thought immediately shifts from this marital issue to another theme. Miriam questioned Moses on the authority of all three of them to speak in the name of God. She asked, "Has Yahweh spoken only through Moses? Has he not spoken also through us *[gam–banû]?"* (Num. 12:2).

This was a rhetorical question. It expected a positive answer and did not intend to elicit a discussion. Miriam assumed that the opinion implied by her question was not subject to contradiction. She dared to challenge the prerogatives of Moses. The final editors of the Pentateuch apparently included this story in their epic of the desert wanderings in order to exalt the uniqueness of Moses (12:3–8). They stressed at length Miriam's presumption and her punishment for it (12:9–15). In their view, there was little doubt that a woman, even a sister of the national hero, did not have the right to share the prophetic office with him. Although Aaron was associated with Miriam in the introduction to the narrative (v. 1), it was Miriam alone who spoke and Miriam alone who suffered the retribution.

A small detail deserves notice. Miriam was summoned to the tent of meeting, together with the two men Moses and Aaron. One may presume that in the early tradition, a woman was not suspected of cultic impurity (vv. 4–5), or the idea of cultic impurity had not arisen in the mind of the storyteller.

Embedded in the priestly description of the way in which the desert tabernacle was manufactured, a fleeting reference to an earlier and different tradition is found concerning the tent of meeting. This canvas structure is not to be confused with the ark or with the tabernacle. It did not shelter any cultic object. It was empty, but it was used to conceal Moses from the public gaze when he entered into private dialogue with Yahweh, talking "face to face" (Exod. 33:9, 11).

Unrelated to the priestly context, an ancient fragment provides a valuable testimony on the cultic freedom of women:

> He [Bazalel] made the bronze laver and its bronze base from the mirrors of the ministering women, who ministered at the door of the tent of meeting. (Exod. 38:8)

This is a startling statement. Certain women exercised a specific function at the door of this archaic symbol of divine presence among the Hebrews. There was no question of women's cultic purity or impurity.

Like Miriam, Deborah was remembered as "the prophetess." She lived at the time of the judges, during the slow infiltration of the land of Canaan. Invading Israel formed then a loose confederation of social units that looked for their diverse interests more than for a united cause. At a time of national crisis, when some Canaanite rulers threatened the very existence of the Hebrew tribes, Deborah rallied most of them and summoned a military ruler, Barak, from the far north to take command of the situation (Judges 4:1–24). The Song of Deborah (Judges 5:1–31), one of the early poems of the national epic, celebrates her exploits as well as those of her appointed captain. Nothing much is known about her, except that "she sat" (ceremonially and juridically) under a sacred palm tree in the central mountain range of Ephraim, between Ramah and Bethel, and that "people came to her" (4:5). Her religious and political authority was such that she was able to overcome the apathy or the parochialism of some of the more independent tribes. Her appointee Barak was able to defeat the Canaanite coalition.

It seems that the word "prophetess" designated an official profession related to the proclamation of Yahweh's will. No restriction of cultic purity prevented a woman from occupying such a position of religious and national eminence. After the settlement of the tribes within the land of Canaan, a cryptic allusion to the misbehavior of the sons of Eli, the priest in residence at the temple of Shiloh, confirms the professional status of women dedicated to the service of the sanctuary. It was charged that Eli's sons "lay with the women who ministered at the entrance of the tent of meeting" (1 Sam. 2:22). The words used in both stories (Exod. 3:8 and 1 Sam. 2:22) are identical. The Hebrew verb for "to minister" *(tsaba)* implies the idea of a draft for military service. Who those female ministers were, what exactly they performed at the entrance to the tent of meeting, is not told. Apparently, female ministers served side by side with male personnel, since the men worked in the tent of meeting "with their families" (Num. 4:22, 24).

Even more significant is the tradition concerning Hannah, the mother of Samuel (1 Sam. 1:9–18), at the sanctuary of Shiloh. She did not in any way enjoy a cultic status, and she may therefore have been considered, in anachronistic language, a plain laywoman. Yet, she had access to the temple without incurring any suspicion of cultic impurity. Having accompanied her husband Elkanah to the open court surrounding the temple, she participated in the yearly sacrifice. After the sacrificial meal, she went up to the shrine itself to pray, for "she was deeply distressed" on account of her lack of children. The text is unambiguous: "She continued praying in the presence of Yahweh" (1 Sam. 1:12). About forty Hebrew manuscripts read "toward Yahweh" rather than "in the presence of Yahweh." Was this a scribal attempt, many centuries later, to alter the picture of a woman who possessed the right of access to the temple and lived in direct and intimate communion with the Deity? Did she pray "before" Yahweh or from afar "toward" the entrance of the temple?

The most eloquent witness on the religious prerogatives of women before the exile is offered by a detail in the narrative of Josiah's reformation in 621 B.C. (2 Kings 22:1–20). This narrative points to an event of unique significance in the history of Western civilization, for it marks the origin of the notion of a sacred scripture for Judaism, about to be born, and later for Christianity, and eventually for Islam. A woman played the central role in this momentous development in the history of three major religions of mankind.

Just as Miriam may be remembered for having been the first psalmist and Deborah for having been the heroine of the first Hebrew epic poem, so Huldah, who, like them, was called "the prophetess," should be hailed as the certifier of the first Bible. The wife of a certain Shallum, son of Tikvah, son of Harkas, keeper of the wardrobe, therefore an aristocratic court and temple official, Huldah was a cultic functionary in her own right. As prophetess she was a temple diviner, and her gift of speaking on behalf of Yahweh was recognized by the highest circles of government.

The story tells that a scroll that had been found in the basement of the temple was presented to King Josiah as "the book of the law." The royal secretary read it aloud to the monarch. Profoundly impressed, Josiah remained apparently in a state of suspended doubt concerning the authenticity of this *torah* (which modern scholars have identified with the central part of the Book of Deuteronomy, chaps. 12:1—26:11).

The king summoned his chief counselors, saying, "Go, inquire of Yahweh for me, and for the people, and for all Judah, concerning the words of the book that has been found" (2 Kings 22:13). With no mention of debate, hesitation, or delay of any kind, the story states that the royal advisors simply consulted Huldah as a matter of course. She *was* the prophetess. Her authority was unquestioned. And her reply was couched in the traditional form of prophetic oracle: "Thus says Yahweh, the God of Israel, tell the man who sent you to me . . ." (22:15). It is not impossible that her choice of the mere word "the man" instead of a title of honor, or at least of protocol, for the ruler of the land reflects the old tension between monarchy and Yahwism, but this conjecture is not demonstrable. In any event, many scholars question the exactitude of the report. Whether strictly historical or not, the narrative is extremely important for the purpose of this analysis. A seemingly incidental feature acquires a landmark value for Judaism at its birth in the sixth century B.C., precisely at a time when women were being denied cultic status on a footing of equality with men.

The royal delegation to Huldah included the inner cabinet, so to speak, of the royal government. A woman's oracle was requested. The woman responded, and her word was accepted forthwith. Hindsight shows that at that instant the living Word of prophets was needed to authenticate the written Word of the scribes. The nucleus of a code of law, from which emerged the whole Pentateuch and eventually the four canons of Scripture (Torah, Prophets, Writings, and New Testament) was declared legitimate, sacred, and authoritative. The Bible was still far from complete, but the inception of a Sacred Scripture had taken place through the intermediary of Huldah, a woman. The canonical process, that slow evolution of a literary development pointing to a standard or norm for faith and moral order, had begun.

The foregoing data are admittedly scant. Nevertheless, they show that women fulfilled an active and decisive role, with dramatic consequences, in the religious life of ancient Hebraism and in pre-exilic Judah during a half dozen centuries. There may have been other women, who for one reason or another have not been remembered in the written record. The impact of these few women, however, upon the modern understanding of the female status in the Hebrew religion, before the exile, is inescapable. There was no law excluding women from cultic service on the basis of ritual impurity. There was no evidence of a formal distinction between men and women in the realm of worship.

To be sure, it must be added that there was no female priesthood in Yahwism. It will nonetheless be observed that the function of a priest before the exile was quite different from the sacerdotal offices in Egyptian and Near Eastern religions, or from the sacred and mediatory status which priesthood later acquired in Judaism and in patristic Christendom.

In the early days, and even in the time of the monarchy until the fall of Jerusalem to the Babylonians, a priest was the keeper of the shrine. His duties were varied and important, but they were not sacramentally mediatory between God and human beings. A priest was the chief treasurer and caretaker of the edifice and grounds, the manager of doorkeepers and maintenance personnel, the master of festal ceremonies, and the memorialist as well as the teacher of both liturgy and legal precedents in civil and criminal legislation. He did not offer sacrifices on the behalf of others, unless delegated to do so as a convenience for kings and other prominent members of the court. He was not the dispenser of divine reality to the congregation, not even the intercessor or the mouthpiece on behalf of praying and worshiping individuals.

A distinction between what may be called anachronistically clergy and laity should not be read into the national epic or other literary records of the pre-exilic era. The priests of Jerusalem were royal functionaries. As hereditary members of the royal government they mirrored a male-oriented system of political society. There was no religious reason for having women in a priesthood that was not a clergy but a department of state administration. The absence of women from the Jerusalem priesthood did not result from theological considerations or ritual exclusion.

It is true that the early legislation on the religious festivals, which went back to the time of the judges, appears at first sight to have ignored women in religious ceremonies. "Three times a year shall all your males appear before Yahweh Elohim" (Exod. 23:17; 34:23; Deut. 16:16). We need to understand the situation concretely. At a time of the seasonal peak for agricultural activities, women were not expected to substitute, or stand in, for the male farmers: a husband could not be excused from religious obligations. He had to take time off in order to worship Yahweh, even when he should otherwise have been at work in the fields. During the early years of the exploitation of the soil in Canaan, an act of worship sanctified at the local shrines the activities of agriculture. Plowing, harvesting, threshing, and grape or olive pressing constituted, in effect, religious acts. In addition, "all males" meant the entire family. During the centuries preceding the exile, when sacrifices were sacramental meals involving women, as illustrated by the story of Hannah (1 Sam. 1:3–18), the note that dominated worship, oft repeated in the code of Deuteronomy, was not that of atonement for guilt, as it was in Judaism after the exile, but on the contrary, good cheer in communion with the Lord of the harvest. This rejoicing in the presence of Yahweh involved the whole household.

> You shall rejoice in your feast, you and your son and daughter, your manservant and your maidservant, the Levite, the sojourner, the fatherless, and the widow, who are within your walled villages. (Deut. 16:14)

Married women did not have to be explicitly listed. They were there as wives, mothers, and hostesses for the whole family and its retainers. The mention of "the Levite," that is to say, "the priest" (who belonged to the tribe of Levi), among domestic help and the poor confirms the lack of distinction between clergy and laity.

Women in Early Judaism

The situation was drastically different after the exile. In the so-called Restoration era (sixth century B.C.), most of the descendants of the Judahites who had been deported to Lower Mesopotamia by the Babylonians had, by their own preference, remained or even spread abroad elsewhere in the eastern Mediterranean world. They prospered under the Persian imperial regime, and the great majority of them elected to settle in their newly adopted lands. They formed the Jewry of the *Golah,* "Dispersion," or the Diaspora of Hellenistic times. The few Jews who returned to Jerusalem were those who had been thoroughly imbued with the spirit of Ezekiel and his priestly school. They deserve to be called the first Zionists, but of a strictly cultic character. The main purpose of their return was to rebuild the temple on the sacred rock of Zion. They offered sacrifices of atonement for the national guilt, and sang lamentations. In effect, the "Restoration" should be called a "Sacerdotal Innovation."

Little is known of the precarious existence of the first Zionists apart from the extreme difficulties they met in the land of their ancestors. Inspired by Zerubbabel and the prophets Haggai and Zechariah, they raised on a modest scale the ruins of Solomon's edifice. The second temple was consecrated almost twenty years after the return of the first group of exiles (515 B.C.). Some of the descendants of the Judahites who had managed to escape the net of Nebuchadnezzar's army in 587 B.C. had remained in caves and on deserted steppes. They continued after the exile to practice pagan rites "under terebinth and green trees" (Isa. 57:3–13; 65:1–7, 11–15; 66:17).

During the reign of the Persian emperor Artaxerxes I (probably in 458 B.C.), the priest Ezra came back from the east. He sought to impose a strict application of the Torah—the now completed edition of the Pentateuch. An exacting search for racial purity and a fear of ritual corruption by foreigners led him to compel the Jerusalem Jews to repudiate their foreign wives (Ezra 10:1–5, 10–19). It seems that the scarcity of Jewish women among those who had first returned from exile had led the Zionists, even their priests and Levites (now a lower class of clerics, descendants of the provincial priests who had been dispossessed by Josiah's reform), to marry women from "the peoples of the land."

A few years later (in either 445 or 432 B.C.) Nehemiah was appointed by the Persian imperial government to be the Jewish governor of the province. He returned to Jerusalem especially to rebuild the city walls. He was of the same rigorist persuasion as Ezra, but he appears to have been slightly less intolerant on the matter of mixed marriages. Whereas Ezra had apparently obtained from the males of the Jerusalem congregation a solemn oath to put away the foreign women they had married (Ezra 10:5, 17) and even "their children" (10:44), Nehemiah was satisfied with a promise that in the future Jewish fathers would not allow their sons and daughters to marry foreigners (Neh. 13:23–27).

Little is known of Jewish wives during that critical period. Since the Restoration community was dominated by the rigorist party, they were probably forced to accept the horrors of family disruption. Ritual purity overpowered humaneness. Sectarian religion was capable of becoming inhuman.

It is worth noting that a certain Jewish woman known as Noadiah, the prophetess, as well as "the rest of the prophets," opposed Nehemiah's reform. Nothing else is clear about her or them. Nehemiah merely listed in his diary "those who wanted to make me afraid" (Neh. 6:14). Did Noadiah the prophetess and the rest of the prophets actively protest Nehemiah's exclusivism on mixed marriages? Or were there other issues prompting their hostility to the governor? It seems that a woman readily took the lead in upholding standards of broad humanity and especially in defending female dignity against the inhumanity of a concern for ritual purity that destroyed family cohesion and trampled over the realities of love, loyalty, and marriage commitment.

The romance of Ruth, the Moabitess, made at that time its own contribution to the problem of womanhood in a male-dominated society. While the origins of the Book of Ruth are ancient, there is little doubt that its final edition and its introduction within the growing collection of the Sacred Scripture came about during the Persian period, precisely at a time when Judaism in Zion faced the issue of sexual relations with foreign neighbors—Edomites, Moabites, and others. One cannot affirm with certainty that the book was published as a polemical tract in opposition to the priestly exclusivism that inspired the reforms of Ezra and Nehemiah. At the same time its heroine, Ruth, was a foreign woman, furthermore a Moabitess. For generations the Moabites had been traditional enemies of Israel. Ruth was presented as a model of faith in Yahweh and a direct ancestress of King David. As this romance became widely known during the Persian era and the book was eventually canonized, its influence could not fail to promote respect for womanhood, independent of race or nationality.

During the Maccabean crisis and the upheaval that followed, two feminine figures, Esther and Judith, inflamed the folk imagination with their courage. However, their acts of heroism were not exactly inspired by the visions of the prophets or by the worldwide outlook of the sages.

A reactionary attitude toward the dangers of cultural dilution is always the product of religious uncertainty. Sectarian rigidity reveals doubt and the fear of tolerance. Erotic fascination with the agrarian rituals of the ancient Near East still appealed so powerfully to the Jewish community that the maintenance of faith in a transcendent deity, always free from human manipulation, demanded an even more powerful safeguard. The legal regulations of the priestly school were intended to obviate the danger that pagan rites presented to a genuine theology of transcendence. They succeeded in preserving Jewish distinctiveness, but at a heavy price. Distinctiveness produced ethnic separatism, closed sectarianism, and male sexism.

The theological significance ascribed to the rite of male circumcision and the dread of ritual impurity represented by sexual secretions, especially those of the female, contributed to the cultic degradation of womanhood. In the old days, woman worshiped on a footing of equality with man. After the exile, woman was relegated to the status of a second-class religionist. It was only through man that she had access to the holy.

At some time during the era of the second temple, a women's court, distinct from that of the men, was erected on the eastern terrace of the temple, beyond the men's court. Thus, women were kept at a distance from the sanctuary itself. This form of sexual discrimination has survived in most synagogues to this day. It explains in part the ambiguity of early Christianity concerning the place of women in the church and their exclusion from priesthood in traditional denominations of Christendom.

Sacred gestures surround, embrace, and to a certain extent, determine or at least order every instant of daily existence. They may have a beneficial effect on pedagogy and therapy in times of national crisis and personal disarray. They may be legitimate, even urgently needed, when they support an open religion and an open morality. They may nurture an attitude of expectancy toward the grace of God. They sometimes provide a mode of intimacy with the holy for occasions of daily living. They tend, however, to become egocentric substitutes for the inner dedication of the self to the Deity. This dedication stands at the core of prophetic faith. Moreover, ritual gestures may divert attention from the taking of moral responsibility toward others. In extreme cases they may become tyrannical manifestations of an unconscious recourse to magic. John Donne spoke unambiguously of "ritual and ceremonial, which are the subsidies of religion." In the *Bridge of San Luis Rey*, Thornton Wilder wrote of Doña Maria, Marquesa de Montmayor: "For what she had lost of religion as faith she had replaced with religion as magic."

Both morality and ritual fall into moralism and ritualism when ethical virtue and cultic obedience are used insidiously as tools of pressure upon divine freedom. This is particularly true when moralism and ritualism separate men from women and sectarians from all outsiders, in Christendom as well as in Jewry.

Adolescent Judaism was too complex and diverse a religious phenomenon to be reduced to priestly Zionism. Not only the Book of Ruth but also the Book of Jonah presented the most daring overture to the world when they proclaimed that divine mercy embraced the whole of mankind. This universal embrace appeared in the personified figure of the Hebrew *Chokmah* and, later, in the Hellenistic *Sophia*, "Feminine Wisdom."

The Play of Wisdom

The figure of "Wisdom at play" is unexpected. The word "wisdom" evokes a virtue of prudence, deliberation, and solemnity. *Sophia*, "wisdom," which brought forth *philosophia*, "the love of wisdom," makes one think of the hieratic portrait of a Byzantine empress rather than of a dancing girl.

Play, on the contrary, summons memories of an enjoyment devoid of care. Play suggests the freedom of a child, the gaiety of a game, and the preludes to amorous delight. A tragedy or a comedy is called a play because the highly complex labor of theatrical art is concealed to create total involvement. Play is pleasure and it is also pleasure in make-believe, in aesthetic emotion, including dance and ritual.

The figure of "Feminine Wisdom at play" (Prov. 8:22–31), incongruous as it may seem, should be considered the pivot of Scripture, the motif that, more than any other, leads from the Old Testament to the New. It is also the point of bifurcation between Judaism and Christianity.

Far more significant for the purpose of this inquiry on the biblical theology of manhood and womanhood, the figure of Wisdom at play reveals the reciprocity of the masculine and feminine in divinity as well as in humanity. It uncovers a structure of mutuality that binds theology and anthropology. It informs the human image of divinity and the divine expectation of humanity. It offers a new basis for sexual ethics. It transcends male and female pride and stirs in men and women the incentive to be fully human.

The Ecumenical Outlook

Biblical scholars are beginning to give serious attention to the wisdom literature (Job, Proverbs, Ecclesiastes, Ecclesiasticus or Sirach, and the so-called Wisdom of Solomon). The Hebrew word for wisdom *(chokmah)* and its Greek or Latin equivalents *(sophia, sapientia)* should be considered as a semantic "umbrella" covering diverse and sometimes contradictory realities. Among the early Hebrews as well as in the other ethnic groups of the ancient Near East, a "wise man" could be a skilled artisan, a navigator, or an architect. A "wise woman" designated a midwife—compare the French *sage-femme*—or one of a queen's ladies-in-waiting.

The terms "wise man" and "wise woman" were applied to individuals who, at campfires or at city gates, entertained with stories and fables they garnered from international folklore. They refined pithy sayings, proverbs, maxims, epigrams, riddles, and satires, wittily reflecting their candid observations on the successes and failures of human existence.

The wise generally promoted a utilitarian and prudential morality. With no apparent interest in sanctuaries, feasts, and ceremonies, the early Hebrew sages did not polemize against the cult; they were simply not preoccupied with formal religion. Many of the sages, however, manifested a quiet and steady faith, but their God was not especially the Lord of the covenant and of the chosen people. They went so far as to maintain that "the beginning of wisdom is the fear of Yahweh." Yet, they did not relate this fear, that is to say, the awesome love of deity, to legal, ritual, national, or racial particularism. Their sense of the greatness of Yahweh colored their reactions to human existence, but the source of their knowledge was the accumulated experience of the ages, selected and interpreted in the light of their own empirical observations. They displayed a broad interest in the welfare of humanity, without cultic, linguistic, or ethnic distinction. Their outlook might be described as religious humanism, international and even interracial—genuinely ecumenical.[15]

Early Wisdom and Woman

It will be recalled that the first psalmist was a woman—Miriam, the sister of Moses—and that the earliest prophets were females: again Miriam, and later, Deborah. In a similar and striking way, the first Hebrew sages, at least those who left concrete memories in the national heritage, were women.

Abigail of Carmel did not receive the explicit title of a wise woman (*chakamah*), but she was known as a woman of good sense, intelligence and insight (*sekel*; 1 Sam. 25:3). In the stylized story preserved in the Davidic *epos*, her husband bore the name of Nabal. This unlikely appellation may have been a derogatory surname, for the noun *nabal* means "fool," the antithesis of "wise." By implication Abigail is presented as a model of wisdom. She impressed the young David, at that time a guerrilla leader pursued by King Saul. Nabal conveniently died, and David married Abigail, the wise counselor from Carmel.

The anonymous wise woman from Tekoa, in the south, proved to be, like Abigail, an astute politician (2 Sam. 14:1–20). Some years later, another woman of wisdom, from the town of Abel, in the far north, counseled one of David's captains during a political crisis (2 Sam. 20:13–22). Folk wisdom, at the dawn of the monarchy, was thus represented by women from the whole length of the land.

Solomon acquired in the course of time a legendary reputation for wisdom. The Book of Kings remembered him as a literary and musical artist, who composed proverbs, enigmas, and songs (1 Kings 4:29–34). Scribes were the wise men who taught young princes at the court of Jerusalem for almost three centuries. They preserved the ideal of folk wisdom for social justice and showed a steady interest in the duties and the virtues of monarchs. In the eighth century, King Hezekiah initiated the collections of maxims that expanded after many years into the present Book of Proverbs (cf. Prov. 25:1—29:27).

Since the court intelligentsia was composed of men surrounded by men, one might expect that their proverbs would have mirrored an attitude of male sexism. There is none. The royal sages seldom spoke of women, although at times they distributed praise or blame on wives. Some of them complained about contentious women at home (Prov. 19:13; 21:9; 27:15–16), who brought shame upon their households (12:4b). Others, on the contrary, commended wives for their intelligence or insight, and even dared to affirm that "a discerningly astute woman *(maskelet)* comes from Yahweh" (19:14). The word *maskelet* is related to the word *sekel,* "understanding," with which the story of David described Abigail (1 Sam. 25:3). However, the maxim on the astute woman went far beyond the secular mood that prevailed in early folk wisdom, for it praised such a woman as coming "from Yahweh." The phrase is elliptical, but stunning. It assimilated a woman of intelligence or insight to a messenger from the Deity. A messenger *(mal'ak)* from Yahweh was indeed "an angel."

One of the proverbs went so far as to commend the woman of courage as "the crown of her husband" (Prov. 12:4a). This is high tribute, for the word *chayil,* "strength of character," "courage," was traditionally applied to a hero of military valor. To call such a woman the crown of her husband ascribed to her heroic quality.

While the wise lauded womanhood, their perspective remained, of course, that of males (Prov. 18:22), even when one of them in a beautiful and deservedly famous poem (31:10–31) traced the portrait of the ideal wife.

The folk tale of Job, the man of Uz, originated in an Edomitic town, now Khirbet el- 'Iş, fifty-five miles south-southeast of the Dead Sea. The land of Edom enjoyed wide celebrity for wisdom (1 Kings 4:30–34; Jer. 49:7; Baruch 3:22–23). The Jobian tale may have been recited among the folk storytellers as early as the time of Samuel and Saul in the eleventh century B.C.

In the face of her husband's agony, Job's wife advised him bluntly to "curse God and die" (Job 2:9), and he rebuked her as "one of the female fools." Whether this detail reflects the misogyny of an Oriental society remains open to debate. It is quite possible that this woman was so moved by her husband's mental and physical pain, for which no issue but death appeared possible, that she proposed to him a theological form of euthanasia: "Curse God and die!" Blasphemy was believed to cause instant death.

The end of this foreign folk tale contains an exceptional feature, which stands out from the male-dominated cultures of the ancient Near East. After

89

Job recovers his health, his new daughters are listed by name, whereas his new sons remain anonymous (Job 42:13–14). Pointedly, the sapiential narrator added that the daughters of Job were fairer than all the other women of the land and that "their father gave them inheritance among their brothers" (42:15). Such a procedure was unparalleled in the literature of ancient Israel.

In the social and cultic vacuum of the deportation to Babylon (598 and 587 B.C.), folkloric and court wisdom as well as secular and religious wisdom coalesced. The Zionist community of the second temple was ruled by a legal code of behavior inspired by the priestly disciples of Ezekiel. It was enforced by Ezra and Nehemiah. The Jewish sages, successors of the ancient wise, appear to have held woman in high esteem, completely free from the prohibitions of cultic impurity. Was it in reaction to the grossly male one-sidedness of the divorce legislation (Deut. 24:1–4) that the Book of Proverbs never alludes to the repudiation of wives, even of those with a quarrelsome temper, and that it also ignores the rejection of foreign wives, which the priest Ezra imposed?

The first part of the Book of Proverbs (chaps. 1—9), generally considered to be later than the early folk wisdom or court wisdom, contains singular advice to husbands. They are enjoined to respect utmost marital loyalty.

> Drink waters from thy own cistern,
> And running water from thy own spring.
> Should thy fountains overflow on the street,
> And thy water brooks on the public squares?
> (5:15–16)

Unabashed candor for the sharing of carnal delights leads this sapiential poet to continue in a lyrical style familiar to the Egyptian love singers:

> Let thy fountain be blessed,
> And have joy from the woman of thy youth,
> The hind of many loves, the gazelle with gracious favors!
> Let her breasts inebriate thee at all times,
> Her love constantly ravish thee!
> For why shouldst thou be ravished by a stranger,
> And embrace the bosom of another woman?
> (5:18–20)

The language is not remote from that of the Song of Songs. In both poems the intensity of passion implicitly raises the ancient commandment against adultery from its economic and male unilateralness to the level of mutual devotion between man and woman.

The Inaccessibility of
Divine Wisdom

It is not possible to ascertain the date at which the Jerusalem sages or their Jewish postexilic successors began to think of Wisdom no longer merely as a human virtue of prudence and sagacity but as a mytho-poetic figure, a Feminine Person, associated with the Deity.

When the suffering of the early Jews demanded a moral explanation, an unknown poet used the ancient folk tale of Job as a springboard for discussing, not the problem of evil, but the meaning of pure faith. He trusted in a God who stood above the human ideas of good and evil. To judge the motives of the Deity was, for this poet, an intellectual form of idolatry. He thought that the human idea of a just God corresponded to a man-made idol. The true God escapes the neat mercantilism that prudential wisdom ascribed to Yahweh whenever it declared that sin was punished and virtue rewarded.

At the end of the discussion between Job and his three friends (Job 3:1—27:23), the poet provided for a musical interlude, during which a chorus sang a hymn on the inaccessibility of Wisdom (28:1–28).

While the priests prescribed a rigid code of cultic purity and the royal sages held that success and prosperity represented a divine reward for moral virtue, the prophet Jeremiah understood that God was not bound by human achievements (Jer. 8:8–9; 9:23–24). As a disciple of Jeremiah, the Jobian poet faced the task of strengthening the faith of his fellow sufferers, who could not reconcile their belief in the justice of God with their unexplainable misery. Yet, this poet knew that the wisdom of men was too often a source of egocentricity. It was on account of his egocentric pride that Job grieved, once he had seen with his own eyes, so to speak, that the Holy Sovereign of nature was also intimately concerned with the plight of every creature (Job 42:1–6).

Like Jeremiah, the Jobian poet discerned a divine kind of wisdom. "Yahweh, the true God" (Jer. 10:10) manifested that very wisdom in the harmonies and the wonders of the universe. Jeremiah had chanted:

> It is he who made the earth by his power,
> Who established the world by his wisdom,
> And by his intelligence stretched out the heavens.
> (10:12)

Similarly, the Jobian poet included in his libretto a hymn on the Wisdom of God. Because the language of this hymn was hovering ambivalently between the style of abstraction and the concreteness of feminine personification, it inaugurated in Judaism a new form of theological discourse. It went a step beyond the imagery of motherhood, familiar to prophets and psalmists, and it did so without running the risk of compromising Hebraic monotheism with the pagan myth of the Mother Goddess.

The first strophe (Job 28:1–11) describes the success of human technology. The daring and industry of *homo faber* enable him to exploit the distant riches of the earth. Startlingly, the refrain asks:

> But where shall wisdom be found,
>   And where is the lode of intelligence?
> Mortal man is ignorant of her way:
>   She shall not be found in the land of the living.
>   (28:12–13)

The second strophe (28:14–19) deals with the efforts of *homo religiosus*. Kings and priests accumulate treasures of gold and precious gems for the houses of worship, through which the piety of princes and masses alike seeks to obtain power over the forces of the Abyss *(Tehom)* and of the Primal Sea *(Yam)*, thus to insure the safety of the human habitat. Cultic beliefs and rituals may lull human fears of cosmic evil in the outer spaces of stable earth:

> But wisdom, where does she come from,
>   And where is it, the lode of intelligence?
>   (28:20.)

The wording of the second refrain introduces a subtle variation on the nonspatiality of divine wisdom. It forms a transition with the third strophe (28:22–28). While the Abyss *(Tehom)* and the Primal Sea *(Yam)* had confessed that Wisdom did not reside with them, the Utter Depths *(Abaddon)* and Death *(Mot)* admit that they have heard of her fame (v. 22). The Great Unknown that binds existential time is as foreign to Wisdom as the immensities of the universe, which limit existential space. This thematic shift ushers in a dramatic contrast constituting the raison d'être of the entire hymn, and forms its climax as well as its justification:

> Elohim! He is the one who grasps the way of wisdom,
>   And it is he who knows her residence.
> For it is he who looks at the extremities of the earth,
>   [whenever] he gives their élan to the winds
>   And metes out the waters by measure,
> Makes a schedule for the rains
>   And a path for the flash of lightning.
> At that instant, he sees her and celebrates her;
>   He embraces and penetrates her.
>   (vv. 23–27)

Poetic style is always ambiguous. The Hebrew words are susceptible of more than a single meaning. Traditional translators have refrained from suggesting in the final distich the possibility of a sexual imagery. For example, the reading of the King James Version favors an abstraction:

> Then did he see it, and declare it;
>   He prepared it, yea, and searched it out.
>   (v. 27)

And the New English Bible paraphrases the line in figurative speech:

> Even then he saw wisdom and took stock of it,
> He considered it and fathomed its very depths.

These attempts and others like them seek to render the literal meaning of the Hebrew words. Yet, the allusions to the Abyss, the Primal Sea, the Utter Depths, and Death belong to Oriental mytho-poetic thinking. In a similar manner, Behemoth and Leviathan are found elsewhere in the poem of Job (3:8; 40:15—41:34). Commentators who insist that mythical reminiscences are absent from the Hymn on Wisdom ignore the presence of these demonic personifications of cosmic evil. Like them, Wisdom, in the feminine gender, becomes a living figure. Furthermore, the verbs depicting Elohim's relation with her are loaded with erotic connotations.

The poet never intended to hint at a sexual act between a god and a goddess, such as those portrayed and enacted at the feasts of the ancient Near Eastern rituals. He went beyond the stories of a marriage between a divine heaven and a divine earth. Through his experience of human love, he was able to stimulate the imagination of his audience with the association of a sublimated intimacy between the Creator and Wisdom. The description of Wisdom as a feminine figure implied on the part of the hymnist a delicate and high view of womanhood.

Many scholars believe that the last line of the poem was added by a conventional scribe, for it contradicts the tenor of the preceding themes.

> Then [Elohim] said to man,
> Behold, wisdom is the fear of the Lord:
> To shun evil, this is intelligence!
> (v. 28)

The poem as a whole declares that man is unable to obtain Wisdom, for she remains an exalted companion of the Creator. The use of *Adonay,* "the Lord," may reflect an orthodox attitude and perhaps a later hand. At the same time, one should observe that this final phrase may well continue the central truth of the hymn. Like the woman of man's dreams, the object of his longing forever unfulfilled, or *la princesse lointaine* of medieval lyrics, Wisdom remains always beyond human grasp. So also moral perfection and "the shunning of evil."

Just as *homo faber* and *homo religiosus* delude themselves when they try to become wise, *homo moralis* vainly flatters himself into believing that he is able to avoid evil behavior and evil thought. Man always remains short of communion with Wisdom. The avoidance of malevolence is not within his attainment. In a similar fashion, "the fear of Adonay" designates far more than conventional piety. It means an absolute commitment, the gift of self, the abandoning of egocentric interests for the sake of the pure love of the divine. Let it be noted that "the fear of Adonay" is not equated with "the beginning of wisdom," as elsewhere in the sapiential sayings. Rather, the fear of the Lord, which is the fear of total devotion to that Lord, is Wisdom in her wholeness and fullness of being. In one word, humanity is not capable of divinity.

According to this interpretation, Wisdom comes close to the reality that Aeschylus called the awful grace of God. Such a grace is received and accepted. It is not sought, obtained, or merited. It knows the fallacy of salvation by works. It always remains outside human manufacture, human achievement, and human obedience to law, either cultic or moral. The poem is an indictment of all forms of perfectionism, of sacramental or moralistic Pelagianism.

By including the Hymn on Wisdom in the poetic drama of Job, the poet of his school started a radically different trend in the theology of exilic and postexilic Judaism.

While the priests, by their rigid system of cultic and legal separatism, sharpened the distinction between men and women as well as between Jews and non-Jews, the Jobian circle stressed the theme of a feminine-masculine dialogue at the heart of divinity. They provided a transition from wisdom as a self-centered moral virtue to Wisdom as a self-giving bounty. They blazed a trail through the maze of ethnic and religious exclusivism toward a united, intersexual, interracial, and intercultic view of mankind.

The Play of Wisdom in
Yahweh's Presence

With the poem on "Wisdom Playing at Creation" (Prov. 8:22–31), the theology of the feminine entered a new phase. First, it linked the belief in masculine order with the idea of feminine harmonies. Second, it introduced the notion of play within the serious, even solemn, eventually tragic, notion of God. Third, it enhanced the search for an intermediary agent between the transcending Sovereign of nature, in an atmosphere of fiercely monotheistic defensiveness, and human creatures, lonesome in their cosmic solitude and in their historical confusion. Fourth, it promoted this search for mediation in the context not of a masculine go-between, but of a feminine mediatrix, projecting thereby the human experience of womanhood onto the screen of divinity. Fifth, and finally, it displayed a perspective of human universalism, beyond the ideology of a particular covenant, election, or people, capable of embracing within one sweep "all the families of the earth" (Gen. 12:1–3).

This extraordinary poem assumes the rhetorical form of an aretalogy. The use of this term is not entirely adequate, for it applies traditionally to the rhetorical form of divine self-praise. The goddesses of Oriental pantheons in their speeches of revelation often introduce themselves with such phrases as "I am Ishtar of Arbela" (Mesopotamia), and "I am Isis" (valley of the Nile). The self-asseverating form had, however, been used in Israel for a long time. The stories of divine visitations to the patriarchs, to Moses or to the prophets prefaced Yahweh's summons by such formulas, and the familiar phrase "I am Yahweh thy God who brought thee out of the house of the slaves" became the initial declaration of Israel's cardinal beliefs.

In a startlingly new way, it is now a feminine figure who uses this language: "I am Wisdom, Prudence is my mate!" (Prov. 8:12a). The entire sequence is made of three poems. They may not have come originally from the same artist, but the singer who brought them together aimed at a progression of thought that should not be overlooked. First, Wisdom calls (Prov. 8:1–11); second, she extols her virtues (8:12–21); and third, she discloses her double mission, with divinity and with humanity (8:22–31).

The first poem boldly contrasts Wisdom with the "strange woman" who invites men in public places:

> Is not Wisdom calling
>   And intelligence crying aloud?
> On prominent heights beside the main roads,
>   Is she not standing at street corners?
> Before the gates that lead to the city,
>   Beside the main portals, does she not give her voice?
> To you, O men, I call,
>   My voice addresses itself to mankind.
>   (8:1–4)

Traditional exegetes believe that this invitation was modeled after the spectacle of male teachers who recruited students on urban thoroughfares. There is no evidence that Judahite educators before the exile or Jewish pedagogues in the Persian era resorted to such practices. It was much later, in Alexandria and other Hellenistic towns that Greek Stoics, Epicureans, Cynics and Sophists publicly urged youths to enroll in their schools.

More likely, this vivid evocation of Wisdom as a woman calling to men was the antithetical counterpart of street prostitutes, sacred or secular, who sought to seduce potential clients. In the immediately preceding sequence, a sage warned against the lures of the professional courtesan and of the casual adulteress (Prov. 7:4–27). On the contrary, this master instructed young men of his school of scribes and high functionaries of the state:

> Say to Wisdom, Thou art my sister!
>   And call Intelligence, my intimate friend!
> This will preserve thee from the loose woman,
>   And from the strange female with smooth words!
>   (7:4–5)

Unlike the prostitute, who proposes death-dealing illusions of love, Wisdom offers the life-giving virtues that enable princes to govern with insight, justice, and nobility. This is the gist of the second poem (8:12–21). Not only does Wisdom have access to knowledge and insight (8:12b) but she also dispenses the qualities of statesmanship, counsel, skill, and a keen sense of civic rights.

> By me kings do reign,
>> And rulers decree what is just.
> By me princes govern,
>> And nobles judge the earth.
>> (8:15–16)

The first two poems of this sequence, "Wisdom's Call" and "Wisdom's Virtues," may well have echoed subtly the hymn on the inaccessibility of Wisdom, used as a chorus in the dramatic dialogue of Job (Job 28:1–27). Here as well as there, specific allusions are made to silver, gold, coral jewels (Prov. 8:10–11), green gold, red gold, and refined silver (Prov. 8:19; cf. Job 28:15–19).

While the Wisdom of the Jobian hymn was wholly beyond human reach, the Wisdom of these poems enters into the life of the future spiritual elite of the nation, feeds its members with her fruits, endows them with her treasures (Prov. 8:19, 21).

Contrary to the seductress beckoning at the city gates, Wisdom offers an intimacy of exchange that is comparable to a genuine love uniting a man and a woman:

> I love those who love me;
>> Those who passionately seek me will find me.
>> (8:17)

Nevertheless, the prudential humanism of the earlier Wisdom survives. The second poem reflects the rarefied atmosphere of an exclusive school for students of privileged classes. Wisdom is no longer conceived as a virtue to be acquired but is now conceived as a subtle figure to be desired for her own sake. She is the dispenser of riches and prosperity to those who seek her out.

Entirely different is the third poem (8:22–31), in which Wisdom presents herself as the "Playmate of the Divine Architect."

8:22 Yahweh acquired me, the first of his activity,
      Prelude to his masterworks of old.
  23 From ancient times I was anointed,[16]
      From the beginning, the first days of the earth.

  24 When the Abysses were not yet, I was conceived,
      Even before the fountains of the Deep came to be,
  25 Before the mountains were secured within their bases,
      Ahead of the hills I was brought forth;
  26 At a time when he had not yet made the earth or space,
      Or even the first of the cosmic dust.

  27 I was there when he prepared the heavens,
      When he drew a circle on the face of the Abyss,
  28 When he filled the clouds with the waters of above,
      And the springs of the Abyss gushed forth,

29 When he assigned a code to the Sea,
    That the waters should not trespass [the word of] his mouth,
    And when he traced the foundations of the earth.

30 Then I was at the side of him, the architect,[17]
    Then I was [his] delights day after day,
    Playing in his presence at all times.
31 Playing in the whole span of his earth,
    And [now] my delights are with the children of men.

It is clear that in this poem Wisdom portrays herself as the daughter of Yahweh. In spite of the belief in the uniqueness of God, so fiercely defended in early Judaism, mytho-poetic thinking on the corporate character of Yahweh survived throughout all periods of biblical history. Godhead was viewed as a collective personality.

The myth of the sons of God seducing the daughters of men (Gen. 6:1–2) found its echo in allusions to "the assembly of God" or "the divine council" (Ps. 82:1), the sons of Elohim (Job 1:6; 2:1), and the sons of El (Job 38:7). "The messenger of Yahweh" who spoke to patriarchs and heroes of an early age (Gen. 16:7) was the forerunner of the angels and archangels of Persian and Hellenistic Judaism.

In the poem on "Wisdom at Play," the self-appraising heroine refers to her divine origin when she makes the claim: "He begot me," "I was conceived," and "I was brought forth" (Prov. 8:22, 24, 25). Did the poet intend to present these words as figures of speech only? Or did he attempt to suggest, without falling into a crass polytheism, that the transpersonality of God could best be imagined as a community of work and play?

The poet did not set forth a pantheon with genealogies of gods and goddesses pursuing their love affairs or their internecine fights. Such stories (theogonies, theogamies, and theomachies) were common to Oriental and Greco-Roman myths, which describe the adventures of the so-called Immortals. Nevertheless, he wishes to picture Wisdom with such an apprehensible vividness that he used, consciously or not, the language of the Egyptian, Mesopotamian, or North West Semitic mythologies. At the same time, he succeeded in avoiding the suggestion of a mythological fancy derived from human immorality. His depiction of Wisdom, playing in the presence of the Creator, hovered beyond the merely intellectual notion of a divine attribute and the purely emotional image of a human experience. Hebrew poets were the recipients of a most unusual gift: their vocation was to probe into the transcendent and to summon the invisible and to make it available in some way for human contemplation. They knew how to evoke the vision of the inner eye.

Wisdom's function was not to build. Her mission was to entertain the divine masterworker. She was not even holding a blueprint for the world-to-be. She did not prefigure Practical Reason with a Plan. She did not act as a Muse with an Idea.

The ancient translators probably found the motif of Wisdom at play before God incongruous and perhaps even blasphemous. Was such levity compatible with holiness? The Septuagint either paraphrased or else had at its disposal a Hebrew textual tradition quite different from that which later prevailed in the medieval synagogue:

> I was with him, harmonizing [or, fitting together]
> I was the one in whom he delighted,
> I was gladdened by his presence,
> When he finished the world and was pleased with it,
> And when he was pleased with the sons of men.
>
> (Prov. 8:30–31, LXX)

Traditional English versions may claim that they follow the Hebrew text, but they render "playing" by "rejoicing," a seemingly more pious word. Yet, all the occurrences of the verb in biblical Hebrew mean either "playing," as children making merry with toys and games among themselves, or "playing musical instruments" and "dancing" (1 Sam. 18:7; 2 Sam. 6:5). A psalmist even sang of Yahweh's having created Leviathan to "play with him" (Ps. 104:26). With a slightly different spelling, the same verb is used of "love-playing" as in the story of Isaac and Rebekah (Gen. 26:8).

There is little doubt that the poet intended to show that Wisdom's playing gave to the Creator "great delights."[18] Other heavenly beings are described elsewhere "acclaiming" the cosmic Artist:

> When the morning stars sang together,
> And all the sons of God shouted Hurrah!
>
> (Job 38:7)

Wisdom did more than that. Her play produced great delights in God.

The choice of the word *sha'ashu'im,* "great delights," is significant, for it indicates extreme pleasure in love, either in the love of Yahweh for his chosen people (Isa. 5:7; Jer. 31:20) or the love of the psalmist for the divine law (Ps. 119:24). Its root, *sh'',* in the intensive voice, *pilpel,* evokes the image of a rhythmic sliding or gliding, a movement back and forth. In other Semitic languages, it suggests caressing and sporting.

The poet then uses again the same word for indicating a reverse direction of the relationship. Wisdom not only produces delights in God; she also feels great delights in herself "with the children of Adam" (Prov. 8:31). The key word is "delights" as the link between God and humanity. Wisdom stands at the center of a new community that gathers God and man. The delights she gives to God are the delights she receives from the children of men. Through her playing at creation, Wisdom becomes the mediatrix between the Creator and his creatures. Play becomes the bridge between the Sovereign of the universe and lonely man. The Hebrew word used here for "man" is *adam.* It is not certain that the expression should be rendered "sons of Adam," for the text does not explicitly show that the poet was thinking of the Genesis myth of the Garden. Nevertheless, in the context of cosmic creation, the children of men clearly signify the whole of humanity, male and female, the totality of humankind. The poet does not breathe the restrictive atmosphere of the covenant. The orbit of his perception is the world, and the delights of Wisdom embrace all human beings.

Toward a Theology of Mediation

The implications of the poem on Wisdom at play before the Creator are far-reaching. The God of Moses could not be identified with the forces of fertility in nature. Nonetheless, Yahweh was not remote from his chosen people. Acts of worship and sacred space at the shrine, together with the sacerdotal sexuality of kings, made the proximity of God an almost sacramental reality. Through the cult, the worshipers participated in the divine.

With the end of the monarchy, the loss of the land, the destruction of the Jerusalem temple, and the exile among foreign nations, a traumatic blow was struck at the traditional faith of Israel. The Judahite survivors, namely, the first Jews, labored in a spiritual void. They maintained their trust in Yahweh, but they did so at the cost of a religious revolution, for better and for worse.

The travails of Job, far more than his physical misfortune, resulted from his total isolation from the God of his childhood. The primal cry of his agony was, "Where might I find him?" (Job 23:3). Like Israel, Job looked desperately for a way of access to the divine. He asked in vain for a go-between, an intermediary, a conciliator "who would place his hands on the shoulders of both God and man and bring them together" (Job 9:33). Like Job, his young friend Elihu dreamed of "an angel," or "an interpreter," or even "a mediator" who might have feminine, indeed, motherly compassion on man (33:22–24). There was none. God remained out of man's reach, just like Wisdom in the Jobian chorus (28:1–28).

The poetic drama ended with a "whirlwind" intervention by the Creator (38:1—42:6), comparable to the wonders of the divine appearances on Mount Sinai (Exod. 19:16–18) or to the secret visions of the prophets. But such were the privileges of the few, in the desert of solitude. What about the common man and woman? Those privileges never last. They only taste of ephemerality. Moreover, God's presence through the covenant ritual had become God's absence from history.

Nascent Judaism offered a cultic solution to the problem of divine remoteness. The descendants of the Jerusalem priests, disciples of Ezekiel, proposed a sacramental mode of mediation between God and man. In many ways, the sacred status of the high priest—the newly devised sovereign pontiff—took the place of the Davidic king. Under the prototype of Aaron, which dominated the Zionist community from the time of the Persian centuries until the final destruction of the temple in A.D. 70, the high priest or supreme pontiff provided an answer to the religious vacuum. The high priest stood at the pinnacle of the sacerdotal college. The so-called successor of Aaron, after the exile, fulfilled the mediating function of the Davidic king, who was no more. He was the vicar of God on earth. Like Aaron and like David, the high priest was "anointed," in Hebrew *ha-mashiach,* the sacramental messiah.

The apocalyptists, successors of the prophets, presented an entirely different cure for the human predicament of cosmic solitude. Revising the ancient liturgies of the royal enthronement ceremonies (Isa. 9:2–7; 11:1–9; Ps. 110:1–7), the apocalyptists revived the notion of the Davidic monarch, who also was "the anointed one," *ha-mashiach,* but they projected the advent of this Son of David into a future always postponed until the end of time. Periodically, eschatological fever erupted into a new manifestation of hope. Popular Judaism lived for centuries on the strength of this hope.

Both the myth of the high priest and the myth of the Messiah-to-come exacerbated the separatism, the exclusivism, the sectarian character of the Jewish community. Defensiveness against pagan assimilation led to a white-hot but socially divisive notion of messianism. Whether men and women rallied around a high priest, known as *an* anointed one (*a* Messiah) in history, or expected the envoy of God, known as *the* Anointed One (*the* Messiah) coming at the end of time, both attitudes still belonged to a restrictive economy of males, the circumcised sons of the covenant. The high priest of the terrestrial hierarchy and the Davidic Messiah of the world-to-come represented projections of male consciousness within a national perspective.

The poet of "Wisdom at Play" provided a third solution to the theological conundrum of a transcendence gone into the orbit of divinity and removed from the horrors of the human condition. Within a community of male sexists, the poet offered the feminine figure of Wisdom as the delighted and delightful go-between who would reunite God and humanity. Although this sage belonged to an ethnic minority that was sometimes oppressed and always discriminated against by the imperial powers of the Persian era, he proclaimed a Wisdom available to all human beings, who would transmit to them a common standard of morality, a common way of life, and a common path of access to a common God.

Like the narrators of Ruth and Jonah, the poet of "Wisdom at Play" exploded the restrictiveness of physiological or cultic ethnicity. He also eradicated the illusion and the pride of male superiority.

The poet of "Wisdom at Play" fulfilled another task. Perhaps under the direct or indirect influence of the Egyptian sages, he probably knew the speculations on Maat, the goddess of natural harmonies and playful order.[19] He was the forerunner of an alliance between religion and culture, worship and the arts, theology and philosophy, faith and science.

Like a psalmist of the first temple or the Jobian poet of the whirlwind, the hymnist of "Wisdom at Play" intended to convey a sense of intellectual aesthetics—the beauty of thinking and the pleasure of learning. He discerned the theological vocation of those who pondered the mystery of the universe. He portrayed Wisdom as the feminine principle in both contemplation and reason. He perceived the thrill of seeking not only the *good* in human behavior but also the *true* in the cosmic equilibrium and the *beautiful* in natural harmonies. For him, as for the poets of Psalm 104 and of Job 38:1—42:6, the maker of the world was the supreme artist. Like them, he exclaimed lyrically upon the wonders of nature. But he went beyond them. As suspense built up in his audience while he was showing Wisdom at play, singing and dancing before Yahweh, he suddenly brought in the utterly unexpected vision of the same Wisdom, hitherto the playmate of God, now one who delights also in human creatures.

Playful Wisdom is more than the mediatrix of Presence. She lays the ground for union between pure faith, that is, the selfless adoration of God, and pure science as well as philosophy, that is, the selfless pursuit of truth for its own sake.

Creation as such does not reveal itself.[20] It is Wisdom at play who becomes the mode of revelation. There is no religion without intellectual integrity in scientific research. There is no philosophy or science without a sense of transcendence. There is no humanism without the exacting demands of theism. Human thirst for knowledge is the twin of Wisdom's playfulness in the presence of the Creator. It is in communion with Wisdom, at once transcendent and immanent, that philosophy, science, art, and religion find their ultimate unity. The passion for social justice, the search for truth, and all the arts receive their meaning only in the celebration of the God who upholds heaven and earth in their course.

The anthologist who collected the various pieces that now form the first part of the Book of Proverbs (chaps. 1—9) placed immediately after the poem on "Wisdom at Play" three poetic sequences that developed the more conventional pictures of Wisdom as the *Teacher* of life (8:32–36), Wisdom as the *Hostess* at her banquet (9:1–12), and in final contrast, *Woman Folly,* who is seductive but knows no shame and whose guests eventually fall into the bottomless pit (9:13–18).

As the circles of the sages moved on from the Persian to the Hellenistic era, the feminine figure of Wisdom became the ambiguous *Sophia.*

Chapter 7

From *Sophia* to *Logos*

In the course of six or seven generations, Judaism emerged from its feverish infancy and became a full-fledged adult. Under the relatively enlightened policy of the Persian administration, many Jews preferred not to return to Palestine and remained in various provinces of the Empire. They spread all over the Eastern Mediterranean lands. Some prospered and responded to the overtures of a cosmopolitan *oikoumenē*. Soon after the death of Alexander the Great (323 B.C.), even the Zionists of restored Jerusalem welcomed the intellectual alertness of Hellenistic culture. The descendants of the early Jewish sages continued to compose poems in praise of Wisdom, calling men to her and instructing them in the right way to live. Transformations did occur, however. Toward the end of the third century B.C., the teaching of an erudite sage, Jesus son of Sirach (ben Sirach), by his speculations on Wisdom led to the Hellenistic Jewish views on *Sophia* and eventually to the Christian interpretation of Jesus of Nazareth as *Logos* made flesh, in the prologue to the Gospel of John.

Wisdom and the *Erōs-Agapē* Continuum

While the prophets and the psalmists of Judah, during the monarchy, had described the bond of Yahweh to Israel as a marriage of love, there were in the early days very few expressions of the love for God by individuals. By contrast, the circles of the sages sang Wisdom's invitation in terms of love. Unlike the street women who offered inducements to men, Wisdom was not in any way portrayed as a sacred or secular prostitute. Nevertheless, it was she who invited men to come to her (Prov. 2:4). The movement of communion between the divine and the human was not man-initiated.

Response to Wisdom could not be ignored, and just as her call was expressed in terms of seduction, so also the part to be played by man suggested similar overtones of erotic embrace.

> She is a tree of life to those who grasp her,
> And those who hold her tight are made happy.
> (Prov. 3:18)

Sexual imagery became at times yet more explicit. The dialectic reciprocity of the union between Wisdom and man belittled the traditional prerogative of the male and conferred upon the female partner a distinctive superiority through her power to give: True *erōs* means *agapē*. The female aspect of the Wisdom imagery shows the self-giving love of Wisdom for human beings.

> Do not abandon her, and she will keep thee safe.
> Love her, and she will stand guard over thee.
>
> . . . .
> Cherish her,[21] and she will exalt thee.
> She will give thee glory when thou wilt embrace her.
> She will place a garland of grace upon thy head,
> And crown thee with wonder and magnificence.
>
> (Prov. 4:6, 8–9)

The charge of male chauvinism that, at first glance, might be advanced against these lines, on the grounds that only a man could have imagined them, must be softened into a more balanced view. The poet could hardly have thought out in such terms the benefits of divine Wisdom to mankind if he had not first experienced the mutual give-and-take between true lovers. The psychology of manhood and womanhood has become one of the sources of a theology of grace. Metaphysical equilibrium from the good received at the same instant the good is offered reflects the highest awareness of love chemistry within the human couple. There is no hint at a brutish image of a man raping a woman or seducing her for merely selfish purposes. Rather, the temper of this sapiential advice is lifted to a plane of paramystical emotion, in which the experience of ecstasy, in an *erōs* that is *agapē*, becomes the mode of evoking a thrill of religious communion. The human experience of mutuality in the act of love was sublimated into a new grasp of the exchange between Wisdom and man. The *erōs-agapē* continuum that underlies the style of this exhortation may well echo from afar the myth of the Egyptian Isis or of the Mesopotamian Ishtar without their fertility rites.

An approach to God through Wisdom prefigures the Hebraeo-Christian theology of grace rather than a Jewish praxis of law and ritual observance. "We love him because he first loved us."

The Love of Wisdom in Ben Sirach

Two or more centuries after the completion of the Book of Proverbs, Jesus ben Sirach developed the theme of the *erōs-agapē* exchange in a longer poem on "Loving Wisdom" (Sir. 51:13–22). Until recent times, this lyrical piece was known only through the Greek version of the Septuagint. Fragments of a parallel text in Hebrew were discovered around the turn of the twentieth century in the attic or storeroom *(genizah)* of a Cairo synagogue. This text seems to have been translated back into Hebrew from a Greek version. In one of the Dead Sea Scrolls, unearthed in the middle fifties of this century, the poem appeared in what is probably an early copy of the original text. A few scholars believe that Ben Sirach quoted this acrostic poem on the love of Wisdom[22] rather than composed it. A survey of the entire book shows that he wrote over many years and gathered widely different reflections. He may have been the originator of this rather eccentric meditation upon his love for Wisdom.

A comparison between the traditional Septuagint version and the Qumran Hebrew text immediately indicates that the Greek translators produced a somewhat pompous and toned-down paraphrase fit for the pious, perhaps as a homily in a synagogue school. Here is an English rendering of the Greek translation:

Sir. 51:

13   When I was still a youth before I wandered,
        I sought wisdom openly in my prayer;

14   Before the temple I prayed about it,
        And to the end I shall continue to seek it out.

15   In its flower, as the grapes ripen,
        It has been the delight of my heart.
        My foot has trod in a straight line,
        Ever since my adolescence I have followed it.

16   Scarcely had I inclined my ear before I made a move toward it,
        And much education did I get for myself!

17   I made steady progress in it;
        To my wisdom-giver I shall render glory.

18   For I firmly resolved to enact it,
        And I ardently desired the good,
        So that I might never be put to shame.

19   My soul grappled with it,
        And in the practice of the Law I was exacting.[23]

        I spread out my hand to heaven,
        And I was able to imagine its unknowable [aspects].

20   I drove my soul straight to it.
        And in purification rites I found it.
        I got an understanding with it from the start;
        Therefore, I shall never be abandoned.

21   My deepest heart was moved to look for it;
        Therefore, I have obtained a most precious treasure.

The Hebrew text of the Qumran scroll presents a different and far bolder treatment.[24] It reveals a passionate desire, painted in sexual terms, to possess Wisdom, a female lover.

11QPs[a], XXI

11   I was an adolescent, before I could go astray,
            And then I sought her.
        She came to me, seeking [me],
            And I examined her on all sides.

12	Even as blossoms fall while grapes ripen And gladden the heart,
13	So my foot went straight forward. From puberty on I have known her.
14	Scarcely had I inclined my ear Than in abundance I found [her] seductive words,

15	She came to me as one who gives suck,
	  And to my teacher I gave my manhood.
	I resolved to make love [to her].
	  I burned for pleasure
	  And I would not turn back.

16	I heated up my desire for her, And I did not take a rest.
	I sustained my desire for her, And on her heights I did not neglect [her].
17	I let loose my hand, And I pierced her nakedness.

The differences between the Hebrew and the Greek are obvious. In the text copied at Qumran, the Jerusalem sage did not refrain from expressing his love for Wisdom in a style inspired by the human experience of desire, pursuit, and consummation. The picture of his exaltation upon communing deeply and at length with Wisdom implies a high view of the love that unites man and woman. Unlike the misogynist author of Qoheleth (Ecclesiastes), Jesus son of Sirach thought of Wisdom—whether he quoted an ancient poem or composed the poem himself—as the initiator of his intimacy with her. He compared it to the courtship of a woman by an adolescent youth, but it was the woman who made the first advances. While the probable interpretation of line 11b, "She came to me, seeking [me]," is uncertain, it fits the whole context. The seeker of wisdom knows that the movement of pleasure, together with the transfer of learning and well-being, goes from Wisdom to him, not from him to her. He receives love from her, and at the same time he offers her his virility. Elsewhere, Jesus son of Sirach wrote of the ideal union of Wisdom with the sage, "She welcomed him as the bride of his youth" (15:2–8). The same thought was already present in the poetry of his predecessors (Prov. 5:18–19).

The *erōs-agapē* continuum of the relationship between Wisdom and man recalls the lyric effusions in the Song of Songs. There, woman is placed on a pedestal and granted the better share. Anticipating the mystics of a later age, Jesus son of Sirach might have said to Wisdom, "I would not have sought thee, hadst thou not already found me."

Wisdom and Zion

Another poem of Ben Sirach (Sir. 24:3–22) praises the feminine aspect of the Creator. Although its structure is patterned after the canticle of "Wisdom at Play" (Prov. 8:22–31), its themes bear many more differences from, than similarities to, those of the earlier piece. The Hebrew text has not been preserved, and the Greek translation, probably made by Ben Sirach's grandson in about 180 B.C., may well have softened and even sanitized the pungency of the original. Here, Wisdom sings her own praises in the four strophic movements:

i

Sir. 24:

3	I came out from the mouth of the Most High,
	And like a vapor I covered the earth.
4	In the highest heaven I sojourned for a time,
	And my throne stood above the pillar of cloud.
5	The vault of heaven I circled alone,
	And on the depths of the abysses I walked.
6	Over the waves of the sea and in the whole of the earth
	And over every people and nation I held sway.
7	Among all these I looked for a resting place:
	In whose country might I ever settle?

In the first part of his book, Ben Sirach had confessed that the Lord himself had spread Wisdom as a gift to "all flesh." Perhaps with qualifying restriction the sage added that the Lord granted Wisdom to "all those who loved him" (Sir. 1:10). Later on, however, his purpose was to show not at all that Wisdom embraced the whole of mankind but that a sense of particularity motivated and limited her cosmic search. Heaven is her point of departure, but her travels upon the earth reveal her desire to choose "a resting place." This word points to the theology of the cultic presence in Zion (cf. Ps. 132:13).

Still open to a universal outreach, but in the sense of a religious form of cultural imperialism, Ben Sirach's Wisdom centered herself upon the sacred congregation in Jerusalem, the chosen people obedient to the law, and not upon the whole wideness of humanity. In the end, Ben Sirach identified Wisdom with the Torah, the full-fledged written law of the second temple.

While the canticle of "Wisdom at Play" (Prov. 8:22–31) might be called a sober aretalogy, that is to say, a self-appraisal of Wisdom as the mediatrix between the Creator and all the children of mankind, Ben Sirach's poem is quite different. Its preface presents an unabashedly self-congratulatory eulogy, displaying a plethora of Oriental hyperboles.

> Wisdom proclaims her own praises:
> In the midst of her own people she glorifies herself,
> In the assembly of the Most High she opens her mouth,
> She glorifies herself before his omnipotence!
> (Sir. 24:1–2)

The third-person description soon makes room for a first-person display:

ii

Sir. 24:

8   Then, the fashioner of all things issued my orders,
     And my maker decreed where to pitch my tent,
     And he said, Pitch thy tent in Jacob.
     And in Israel place thy inheritance!
9   From antiquity, from the beginning, he created me,
     And forever I shall remain [there].
10   In the holy tent I ministered in his presence,
     And thus I came to be settled in Zion,
11   In the beloved city, his inheritance,
     And in Jerusalem, the seat of my authority.

As in the earlier poem, Wisdom was created "from the beginning" and she remains an intermediary between heaven and earth, but her mediating function is restricted to linking the celestial abode with the shrine of Jerusalem, "the beloved city." There is no authority *(exousia)* for Wisdom, unless it conforms to the priestly system centered in Zion, "Jerusalem, the seat of my authority."

iii

Sir. 24:

12   I have taken root in a glorified nation,
     And in the estate of the Lord, in his inheritance.
13   I have grown tall like a cedar in Lebanon,
     Like a cypress on the slopes of Mt. Hermon.
14   I have grown tall like a palm tree in En-gedi,
     Like purple hydrangeas in Jericho,
     Like a green olive tree in the Shephelah,
     Like a sycamore in the waters.
15   I exhale a fragrance,
     I give a scent like choice myrrh,
     Like galbanum, unguent, and balsam,
     Like the smoke of incense in the tabernacle.

The exalted stature of Wisdom is directly related to her intimacy with the privileged nation, which in turn is identified with the Lord's estate or inheritance. It is in this ground that the roots of Wisdom take their subsistence. The benefits bestowed by her are as inebriating as the most precious perfumes, and the esthetics of fragrance point to a sensual spirituality typical of most religions, including the traditional Eastern and Western churches. The long list of comparisons is framed by the cultic theme, which appears in both the first distich, with "the estate of the Lord" (v. 12) and in the last, with "the smoke of incense in the tabernacle" (v. 15). Has the feminine personification of Wisdom now been forgotten? Not at all, as her invitation speech, in the fourth and final strophe soon shows, with its transition from fragrance to taste, from playmate to mother and from tree to fruit.

iv

16 I, myself, have deployed my branches like a terebinth,
    My branches are full of glory and grace.
17 I, myself, like a vine have I spread shoots with elegant tendrils,
    And my blossoms ripen in beautiful and magnificent fruit.
[18] [I, myself, I am the mother of the most beautiful love,
    And of fear, and of knowledge, and of the holy hope.
    I give myself to all my children,
    To all those who have been chosen by him.]²⁵
19 Come to me, you who desire me,
    And take your fill of my fruits,
20 For the taste of me remains sweeter than honey,
    The possession of me is more delicious than the honeycomb.
21 Those who eat me will hunger for more,
    And those who drink me will yet thirst.
22 Whoever listens to me will never be put to shame,
    And those who act within me will never fall into sin.

Jesus ben Sirach was clearly pleased with his aretalogy. He loved Wisdom and could easily indulge in the lack of modesty that he lent to her. Did not the glorification of her virtues reflect upon the privileged status of her own people, the chosen race? As if there lingered a doubt concerning the satisfaction that the Jerusalem sage derived from the pampering of his sapiential mistress, duly naturalized and Zionized, he felt the need to add his own slightly ponderous comment:

All this, it is the book of the covenant of God Most High,
The Law which Moses prescribed for us
To become the inheritance of the assemblies of Jacob.
(v. 23)

Ben Sirach came to believe that the sway of divine Wisdom was restricted. Was this belief coexistent with a rather severe, debasing, and possibly hostile view of womanhood? It is clear that for him the feminine figure of Wisdom was no longer the mediatrix of divinity to the whole of humanity. Unambiguously, he considered her to be the channel of a two-way communication between God and Israel only. As in Ezekiel and in the priestly school, which sought to prepare the return to Zion after the exile, foreigners were to be excluded. The word for "nations," *goyim,* acquired the sense of "pagans." Might it be that women also would suffer from the sectarian spirit of cultic and legal Judaism? Or was Ben Sirach's misogyny merely coincidental to his theology?

The Book of Ecclesiasticus (Ben Sirach) contains the reflections of the Jerusalem sage on many topics, including the behavior of the sexes. On the one hand, Ben Sirach condemns "the man who lusts after his own flesh" (a possible allusion to narcissism, homosexuality, or incest; Sir. 23:16c), and he also rejects "the man who passes by his own marriage bed" (23:18a). On the other hand, he is also aware of "the really good wife" (26:1–3), her "grace" and her "accomplishments" (26:13–26). On balance, however, he is far more interested in the unfaithful woman. He is upset by the spectacle of the adulteress, and he lists various examples of disagreeable and even harmful women, without concealing his prejudices (23:22–37; 25:13–26; 26:10–12).

Still more ominously, Ben Sirach found in the myth of the Garden (Gen. 3:23) the justification for what amounts to a clear case of theological misogyny.

> Woman is at the origin of sin,
> And it is on account of her that we must all die.
> (Sir. 25:24)

Although the apostle Paul generally held Adam responsible for sin and mortality (Rom. 5:12; 1 Cor. 15:21–22), the Pauline school issued misogynist statements that culminated in an interpretation of the same myth of the Garden quite similar to that of Ben Sirach: "Adam was not deceived, but the woman was deceived and became a transgressor" (1 Tim. 2:14; cf. vv. 11–13). This accusation was somewhat softened by a tribute to woman as mother (v. 15).

In Ben Sirach, divine Wisdom no longer embraced the *oikoumenē* of the world but dealt directly and exclusively with the covenant people, who presumably obeyed the law of Moses.

A sectarian theology led to a closed rather than to an open morality. Culturally based and oriented, such a closed morality, enunciated by males, throws upon the female the responsibility for the existential burden of guilt and death.

The data accumulated by anthropologists and historians of comparative religion suggest that misogyny is frequently coincidental with either an idealization or a disparagement of woman. The well-documented attitude of looking upon woman as virginal goddess or as whore may have influenced the thinking of Jesus ben Sirach, as in later times it contributed to the growth of Mariology among Byzantine and, then, medieval Christians. The love of divine Wisdom as the perfect mistress is psychologically and culturally compatible with the ascribing of the dread of guilt and death to womanhood in general. Woman becomes man's escape from his existential predicament.

The Hellenistic *Sophia*

With the Book of the Wisdom of Solomon, originally written in Greek and preserved in the Septuagint Bible, the feminine personification of Wisdom has considerably evolved. The Hebrew *Chokmah* is now the Hellenistic *Sophia*. The author of the Book of Wisdom presents himself as King Solomon, but he lived in the Jewish intellectual circles of Alexandria probably during the first half of the first century B.C. Although in many ways faithful to his Hebraic heritage, he reveals exposure to Hellenistic philosophy. His contribution to the history of Jewish thinking, similar to that of Jesus ben Sirach, constitutes a remarkable link between the canticle on "Wisdom at Play" (Prov. 8:22–31) and the Christian hymn on the "*Logos* Made Flesh*,*" which is now preserved in the prologue to the Gospel of John (1:1–14). His debts to the ancient sages include those to the more recent Ben Sirach. However, unlike the Jerusalem sage of the late third century B.C., this Hellenistic Jew never identified Wisdom with the law (Torah), nor did he link her exclusively with the chosen people. On the contrary, he stressed the cosmic function of Wisdom. While the earlier poem on "Wisdom at Play" had presented her as the mythical daughter of the Creator, who entertained God but did not actually participate in the making of the universe, and while Ben Sirach had looked upon her as an admiring spectator, who wandered over the world until she found "rest" in Zion, the Hellenistic poet depicted her as the actual "artificer" of the world.

No longer the divine player and entertainer, nor, again, the specialized agent for the divine election of a special people, Wisdom was now the full partner of the God who creates. In this Hellenistic document, "King Solomon" proudly declares:

> I have known the whole of reality, concealed or evident,
> For Wisdom, the lady-artisan of the universe, taught me
> (Wis. 7:21–22)

Furthermore, Wisdom is now linked with the Spirit, for a long time viewed as an actor at the making of the world (Gen. 1:2). This praise of cosmic Wisdom describes the qualities of the Spirit in a crescendo of seven triads with a total of twenty-one epithets, which rise from the level of the human mind to that of the divine sphere. They were possibly amplified from the Isaianic picture of the sevenfold Spirit of the Davidic Messiah (Isa. 11:2–3a).

Wis. 7:
22b   There is indeed a Spirit in [Wisdom],
        Intelligent, holy, unique,
        Multiple, subtle, mobile,
        Lucid, stainless, clear,
        Inalterable, loving good, diligent,
23   Autonomous, beneficent, philanthropic,
        Firm, assured, tranquil,
        Able to enact, able to oversee, and able
            to penetrate all spirits,
        The intelligent, the pure, and the most subtle.
24   Thus, Wisdom is more mobile than any movement;
        On account of her purity she passes through
        and permeates all things.

25   She is the effulgence of the power of God,
          A pure irradiation of the glory of the Almighty.

This spectacular display of vocabulary shows acquaintance with Greek and Hellenistic philosophers, such as Anaxagoras, Aristotle, Diogenes of Apollonia, Epictetus, and even Posidonius (135–50 B.C.). The pattern of twenty-one expressions may be not only a multiplication of the hebdomad in the Isaianic hymn on the Davidic Messiah, who receives a sevenfold spirit, but also the echo of a Mithraic liturgy. Unlike the Wisdom of Ben Sirach, identified with the Mosaic law and restricting her concern to the covenant people, the Hellenistic-Jewish *Sophia* is open to the whole of mankind. King Solomon, the mouthpiece of this Jewish philosopher, invites all the kings of the earth and their counselors to listen to her and to understand her (6:1–11). *Sophia* is not pictured in more abstract terms than was the *Chokmah* of the earlier sages, but her personification continues to nourish the imagination of the Alexandrian poet.

As in the aretalogy of "Wisdom at Play" (Prov. 8:22–31), *Sophia* embraces all those who receive her. More especially, she brings them together as the beloved friends of God (Wis. 7:27). However, like Ben Sirach in the Qumran recension of his poem on "Loving Wisdom" (Sir. 51:13–21), this philosopher unhesitatingly uses erotic language to portray his figure of Wisdom:

I have loved her and pursued her ever since my youth,
    And I sought to make her my bride,
    And I became a lover *(erastes)* of her beauty.
                  (Wis. 8:2)

The interplay from Wisdom to God and from Wisdom to mankind, which was suggested in the earlier poem of "Wisdom at Play" by the double movement of Wisdom's objective and subjective delights (Prov. 8:31), is now reflected in a more clearly delineated sketch.

First, Wisdom is symbiotic with the Divine:

She confers glory upon her noble birth
    by her life-sharing *(symbiosis)* with God,
And the Master of all has loved her.
                  (Wis. 8:3)

Indeed, she is now viewed as a "mystical initiate *(mustis)* into the science of God" (8:4). The word is borrowed from the mystery cults of the Hellenistic religions. Through their esoteric sects men and women participated in the divine Being and attained immortality.

Second, the life-sharing *(symbiosis)*, which the poet readily ascribed to Wisdom's participation in divinity, was eventually transferred to his own sapiential passion:

> I determined, then, to take her to live with me *(symbiosis),*
> Knowing that she would be my counselor in happiness
> And my comfort in anxiety and sorrow.
>
> (8:9)

It appears that the poet was close to becoming an intellectual mystic, for whom the line of distinction between infinity and finitude is obliterated, and union becomes fusion between subject and object. Nonetheless, despite the repeated use of the word *symbiosis,* the poet has not trespassed the ground of communion in love, which, however intense and complete it may be, is not to be confused with mystical identification.

Under Hellenistic influence, the author of the Wisdom of Solomon introduced within the theological thinking of Hellenistic Judaism the belief in the immortality of the soul (2:23; 3:1–9; 4:7–14; 5:15–16). It was his union with Wisdom that helped him to overcome his fear of death: "Through her I shall have immortality" (8:13a).

With both nostalgia and longing he lingered on the metaphor of his marriage with Wisdom as a *symbiosis* between husband and wife:

> Going to my house, I shall find rest in her,
> For our coming together has no bitter taste,
> And her life-sharing *(symbiosis)* has no pain, no grief.
>
> (8:16)

Coming to one's home and finding rest in Wisdom became for this poet the best way to express hope for life beyond death—a transposition of the love that binds two human beings and confers upon both of them a sense of overcoming the ravages of time and of exploding the shackles of existential finitude.

Unlike Ben Sirach, the author of the Wisdom of Solomon maintained a universal vision. To be sure, he stressed the story of the exodus (Wis. 10:15—19:17) as a warning against the risks of idolatry and political oppression. He feared the philosophical and mystical speculations of Alexandria, but he never identified *Sophia* with *Nomos* (the Torah), nor did he associate her with the temple cult of Jerusalem. He was interested neither in legal observances nor in rites of exclusivism but in personal and universal access to the divine. For him Wisdom was not, however, a substitute for communion with God himself. She was still a true mediatrix, in the same manner as in the ancient canticle of "Wisdom at Play" (Prov. 8:22–31):

> It is [God] who is the roadguide of Wisdom,
> And the reformer of the sages.
>
> (Wis. 7:15cd)

The poetic parallelism that he employs hints also at a conjunction between *Sophia* and the Word *(Logos).*

> God made all things through his Word [*Logos*],
> And with his Wisdom he equipped and garnished man.
> (9:1b–2a)

Logos was not, of course, for him the philosophical "reason" of the Middle Platonists or even less of Philo, the later mystical philosopher of Alexandria. Rather, for this theological poet of the early first century B.C., *Logos,* very much akin to *Sophia,* could be hailed with the ancient Hebrew prophets and sages as the agent of God creating harmonious beauty out of chaos (Gen. 1:2) or history (Isa. 40:8b).

The theological poet of the Wisdom of Solomon went a step further when he asserted, "It is [God] who gave me an exact knowledge *(gnōsis)* of those who exist" (7:17a). Yet, this knowledge was not the esoteric *gnōsis* that the later Gnostics, both Jewish and Christian, claimed to acquire from an identification of divine Wisdom with their faith *(Pistis Sophia).*

In the early days of the church, some of the Gnostics presented a serious threat to the free and open preaching of the Gospel to all human beings, for they restricted their secret knowledge *(gnōsis)* to the initiates. It was most probably to avoid a confusion with Gnostic mysticism that the prologue of the Fourth Gospel, although clearly presenting Jesus as the incarnation of *Sophia,* prefers to proclaim him as "the Word *(Logos)* made flesh" (John 1:14).

Jesus and Wisdom

The word "Christianity" is in some respects a misnomer. In order to speak of Jesus as "the Christ," the early church, by a semantic tour de force, had to empty from the Hebrew word *mashiach,* "messiah," "anointed one" (in Greek, *christos*), its militaristic, nationalistic, avenging connotation. It had to pour into it an entirely different meaning borrowed from the song of the Suffering Servant (Isa. 52:13—53:12).

The mindless crowds and even some of the early disciples thought of Jesus as a political leader, endowed with the wondrous powers of heaven, who would deliver Israel from Rome, their hated enemy. It is said that the crowds, one day, wanted to crown him king. Jesus rejected such a view. While he may have associated himself with the agent of God who would come at the end of time, and while he accepted the title Son of Man—a title probably borrowed from Daniel through Enoch and the popular literature of the era—he firmly refused to be called *Mashiach,* "Messiah."

After the execution of Jesus as King of the Jews, the men and women who proclaimed his life beyond the grave and his continued presence among them remembered that he had brought God close to them with instantaneous conviction, in a wholly original way. They believed in the unique quality of his person. They felt his magnetism and his selflessness. In his utter humaneness they perceived the reflection of the infinite. Through his words, acts, gestures, and attitudes they sensed the power of a maternal compassion that the ancient prophets and psalmists had detected in Yahweh. He disclosed to them the holy in a shattering, yet intimate and comforting, manner. Women as well as men felt liberated, forgiven, healed, and renewed. No wonder that they saw in him far more than a teacher of wisdom. They thought that they had lived with divine Wisdom in the flesh.

The sayings of Jesus that have been preserved in the Gospels of Matthew and Luke (these "sayings" being commonly known as *Logia*, or *Q*, from the German word *Quelle*, "[special] source") indicate a thorough familiarity with the literature of wisdom. That Jesus was at first held to be a sage is easily understandable, since he borrowed rhetorical forms from the sapiential circles of ancient Israel and early Judaism. Such forms included the parable, the thematic chiasmus ("No one can serve two masters; either . . . or . . .") and especially the beatitude. This exclamatory exhortation, not to be confused with the priestly blessing, was found in Job, Proverbs, and the wisdom poems of the Psalter. Such a rhetorical form began not with the passive participle *baruk*, "blessed," but with a strange word, *'ashrê*, in Greek, *makarios*, traditionally rendered "blessed" or "happy," but which really defies translation in modern languages and means, in effect, "the ongoingness of . . ." The beatitude connotes the idea of a dynamic movement toward an always distant goal, the exhilaration of a leader who goes ahead on uncharted paths and is able to convince others to follow. It admirably fits the sapiential affirmation of life, which Jesus completely endorsed in his devotion to the oppressed minority of his milieu—women, the poor, the so-called sinners (i.e., Jews who did not observe in all its details the law of Moses), Samaritans, and all foreigners.

Another layer of the same *Logia*, possibly representing a later stage of the Christian tradition concerning Jesus, includes startling statements that implicitly identify him with personified Wisdom herself.

In the sequence of denunciation of scribes and Pharisees, according to the Matthean version of *Logia* Jesus declared:

> On account of this, behold! It is I who send you prophets and wisemen and scribes, and you will kill some of them. . . . Amen, I say to you. All this will happen against this brood! (Matt. 23:34–36)

The parallel account in Luke places almost identical words in the mouth of personified *Sophia:*

> This is why also the Wisdom of God has said, I shall send them prophets. . . . Yes, I say to you, [their blood] will be claimed from this brood! (Luke 11:49–51)

The first Gospel also contains an extraordinary passage in which Jesus prays, proclaims, and then invites people to come to him. This threefold structure, its language, and its thought are all borrowed, directly or indirectly, from the Wisdom of Jesus son of Sirach.

i
The Prayer of Thanksgiving
I return grace and thanks, O Father. . . .
(Matt. 11:25–26; cf. Sir. 51:1–10)

ii
The Proclamation
. . . All things have been turned over to me. . . .
(Matt. 11:27; cf. Sir. 51:13–22)

iii
The Invitation
Come unto me, all ye that labor and are heavy laden,
and I shall give you rest.
Take my yoke upon you and learn of me. . . .
(Matt. 11:28–29; cf. Sir. 51:26–27)

Most notable is the similarity with Ben Sirach's admonition, "Put your neck under the yoke" (51:26), ". . . Come unto me, ye who are unlearned. . . ." (v. 23), and the old sage's confession, "I have found myself much rest" (v. 27).

The Johannine *Logos*

The prologue to the Gospel of John offers perhaps the most astonishing illustration of the influence that the theology of feminine Wisdom played upon the attempt by the early church to define the indefinable in the person of Jesus. The hymn that is now incorporated in the prologue of John celebrates the appearance of Jesus in history in terms of "the *Logos* made flesh" (John 1:14), but the entire movement of the poem is patterned after the praise of Wisdom by Jesus son of Sirach. There is no doubt that the Johannine theologian identified the masculine *Logos* with the feminine *Sophia*. Jesus was for him *Sophia-Logos* made flesh. He proposed, in other words, a theological androgyny of Jesus.

To show the thematic lineage of John from Sirach, one might read the text thus:

i

John 1:
1   In the beginning was [Sophia],
       And [Sophia] was in the presence of God,
       And [Sophia] was God.
2   [She] was in the beginning in the presence of God.

ii

3   All things came into being through [her],
       And apart from [her] nothing came into being,
4   In [her] was life,
       And this life was the light of men.

5   The light shines in the darkness,
         And the darkness did not conquer [her].

6-9   . . . .

iii

10   [She] was in the world,
         And through [her] the world came into being,
         But the world did not acknowledge [her].

11   [She] came into [her] own,
         But [her] own did not receive [her].

12   Yet all those who received [her]
         [She] empowered to become children of God;

13   . . . .

iv

14   And [Sophia] became flesh,
         And [she] pitched [her] tent among us,
         And we have seen [her] glory,
         The glory of an only [Daughter] from [her] Father,
         Filled with grace and truthfulness;

15   . . . .

16   And from [her] plenitude
         We have all received grace upon grace.

Among the many parallels that have been discovered between the Johannine prologue and the Wisdom of Jesus son of Sirach, the following may be listed: Like *Sophia,* the *Logos* stands in the presence of God (John 1:1, Sir. 1:1), is anterior to the created world (John 1:1; Sir. 1:4), shares in the creative act (John 1:3; Sir. 24:5–6), gives life to the universe and light to mankind (John 1:4; Sir. 1:9–10), pitches a tent among human beings (John 1:14; Sir. 24:4, 8bc, 10), offers them a vision of glory (John 1:14; Sir. 24:16–17; 43:1), and confers on them grace upon grace (John 1:16; Sir. 24:16).

While the similarity between the two texts is beyond dispute, the difference is of capital importance, because it marks the root of separation between Judaism and Christianity. In Ben Sirach, Wisdom finds her residence in Zion, in the midst of the chosen people. In John, the *Logos* "tents" in the man Jesus, and "his own" have rejected him. Moreover, in Ben Sirach, Wisdom is identified with *Torah,* "the law of Moses," the strict observance of which bears fruit in grace. In John, the *Logos* transcends legal obedience in offering "grace," according to its "gratuitous" meaning of free gift, undeserved and unearned. The *Logos* takes the place of *nomos,* "law."

As the addendum to the hymn shows (John 1:17–18), the Johannine poet radically altered the theological intermeshing of grace with law. This addendum, which at first sight appears to be a non sequitur, actually polemizes against Ben Sirach's identification of Wisdom with law, repudiates it and offers in its stead the theological dynamics of pure grace, the love which is gratuitous, unearned, and unmerited.

John 1:

17 For the Law was given to Moses,
   Grace and truthfulness come through Jesus Christ.

18 No one has ever seen God;
   It is the Son, the Only One,
   Who is [going] into the Father's bosom;
   It is that One who interpreted [him].

The word *kolpos,* "bosom," is found many times in classical Greek literature as well as in the Septuagint to mean "a mother's womb." It boldly ascribes to God an explicitly paternal and implicitly maternal significance. The metaphors of human sexuality are clearly transcended in a manner quite similar to the prophetic and psalmodic style that compared the Deity to both a human father and to a human mother. The directional object "into the Father's bosom," with its Greek preposition of movement alludes to the Johannine theme of the death of Jesus: not a curse, but a glorification.

The teaching function of Wisdom, broadly stressed in the Book of Proverbs, has dictated the choice of the unusual verb *exegoumai,* "to interpret" (hence the word "exegesis"), for succinctly depicting the function of Jesus in history. The primary meaning of the verb is "to lead, to guide step by step [toward understanding]," hence, "to explain," "to disclose," and "to reveal." The notion of *Sophia* still adorns the semantic background of the hymn to its very end.

It is most probable, as some recent scholars have suggested, that the Johannine writer substituted in the hymn he quoted the notion of *Logos,* a masculine word, for the feminine term *Sophia.* He had to do so on account of the dangerous trend of Christian Gnosticism in the second and subsequent generations of the church. Some of the Gnostics spoke of *Sophia* as "the sister of Jesus," or represented her as an androgynous figure in a way that recalled Athena, the classical Greek goddess of wisdom. Sectarian eccentrics even depicted Jesus in carnal terms. They portrayed him as kissing Mary Magdalene on the lips.[26] On the contrary, others "spiritualized" his earthly being as a mere appearance of humanity (Docetism). The Nag Hammadi documents, together with the other apocryphal gospels, show that the Gnostics of the second and third centuries A.D. associated their esoteric Knowledge *(Gnōsis)* with Grace *(Charis,* whom they called the feminine Silence or the Mother of all), Wisdom *(Sophia),* Intelligence *(Epinoia),* and other mystico-philosophical entities.

As gnostic speculations on Jesus began to circulate among the churches of the Roman Empire, the word *Sophia* lent itself to theological confusion. *Sophia* and *Logos* were becoming synonymous. The ancient prophets, psalmists, and sages had associated the divine Word with the creation of the world. Both Jesus son of Sirach and the author of the Wisdom of Solomon, among others, had placed *Sophia* and *Logos* in close parallel. The two realities were interchangeable.

Since the Johannine evangelist hailed the man Jesus as "the only-begotten son of the Father," it was obviously impossible for him to speak of Jesus as the incarnation of feminine *Sophia*. That Jesus belonged to the male sex was a datum of history, which could not be altered. At the same time, the maleness of Jesus in his human condition did not imply a sexual one-sidedness within the transexistential figure that he came to assume for the Christian community after his death. This is perhaps the main reason that the word "androgyny" is not appropriate for describing the plenitude of his image.

As in some medieval lyrics and in modern dialogues like those of Paul Valéry and Samuel Beckett, two aspects of one person appear as distinct but complementary beings, who interact, "interthink" and "interfeel" with one another. In the genuine embrace of lovers for whom *erōs* and *agapē* are indissoluble, the awareness of sexual differentiation remains, but it is con-ducive to a rhythmic exchange of functions and roles. True lovers give or receive, usually receive as they give. Dual surrender moderates the urge to be either dominating or submissive. A new being is born not necessarily the flesh of a child but unmistakably in the emergence of a corporateness that defies time and existential finitude.

The processes of religious inspiration and of theological revelation are obscure. They vary with individuals and with cultural eras. Is there no correspondence between the lyrical language of the sages in their poems on "Wisdom at Play" and "Love for Wisdom" and in their Wisdom aretalogies, on the one hand, and their own introspective responses to womanhood, on the other? Conversely, does not the kind of God one really trusts affect the ethics of human love?

For the sages of early Judaism, the metaphors of the masculine and the feminine were metaphors that conveyed divine interplay.

Wisdom wakes up to the wonders of creation and, in turn, she celebrates the orchestrator of cosmic harmonies. Wisdom is not unlike the lover who whispers at the height of passion:

> Du. Ich will dich in den Wassern wecken!
> Du. Ich will dich aus den Sternen schweissen!
> Du. Ich will dich von dem Irdnen lecken. . . .
>
> Thou. I want to awaken thee in the waters!
> Thou. I want to smelt thee out of the stars!
> Thou. I want to kiss thee from the earth. . . .[27]

When a biblical theology of manhood and womanhood arises from a study of the Hebraic motif of Wisdom as it leads to the Christian motif of the *Logos* made flesh, several consequences emerge. (1) History obtains mean-ing as it is liberated from legal and ethnic exclusivism. (2) Nature is no longer deified as in classical religions, nor is it abused and exploited as in secular technology. Ecology, like sexual ethics and international morality, springs from theology. (3) Invention dances before power, and justice is tempered by the delights of intelligence, while reason is unshackled by imagination. Art, science, philosophy, and religion do not coalesce; they weave patterns of mutual penetration. A synthesis of aspirations and disciplines is possible for the whole of the human endeavor.

When *Logos* becomes the other side of *Sophia* and when both form a new alloy within a human being—Jesus of Nazareth—the expectations of the great prophets of Israel are made concrete not only for a new heaven tomorrow but also for a new earth today. In this perspective, man and woman are reconciled, nations and races aspire to a coordination of responsibility for the welfare of "all the families of the earth" (Gen. 12:1–3).

The attitude of Jesus toward women and pagans reflected his understanding of God, Father and Mother of all. The ethics of his behavior mirrored his theology. The nexus between these two—between his behavior and his theology—now requires special attention.

Chapter 8

Jesus, Woman,
and the Fatherhood of God

Women in the time of Jesus shared in the plight of men's dread of the Roman occupation forces. In addition, they suffered from barbarous discrimination from their own men, fathers and husbands, on account of the ritual laws of sacerdotal Judaism.

How is it, then, that women followed Jesus on a footing of equality with men, that Jesus defended them in flagrant violation of the Torah, and that he would even teach them, along with men, to address God as "Our Father"? Might it be that the meaning Jesus conferred on divine fatherhood was directly responsible for his unprecedented revolt against the patriarchal mores of his environment?

Womanhood in Ritual Judaism

The religious and social predicament of Jewish women in Palestine during the first century A.D. is not amply documented by contemporary sources, but the oral traditions that were preserved in the slightly later Mishnah, the Talmud, and other rabbinic literature have received validity, by consensus of Jewish scholars, for the period in question—the years before the end of the Second Commonwealth (A.D. 70). The religious and legal status of women had been given its official stamp in the final edition of the Pentateuch (ca. 397 B.C.), which became known in its entirety as the Law of Moses, or Torah. Orthodox Judaism came to look upon its text as divinely dictated.

On account of the days and weeks of their ritual impurity ascribed to menstrual and postpartum bleeding, women were excluded from public participation in the services of the Lord. The temple of Jerusalem segregated them in a women's court, and the synagogues in a women's gallery. In later times, interpreters of the law explained the impurity restrictions not as demeaning women's dignity but, on the contrary, as protecting their freedom from connubial duties at home and from religious obligation in places of worship.

The social consequences of these religious stipulations were stringent. Daughters were their fathers' property until puberty, the onset of which was officially placed at not later than twelve and a half years. Marriage was arranged by the fathers, and it occurred either before or at about that time.

Brides immediately passed into the ownership of their husbands. The prerogative of repudiation belonged to men alone.

A wife bred and nursed her master's offspring, fed and clothed her household. Her numerous duties included the washing of her husband's feet and hands. She had no legal power of decision on the marriage of her own children. Polygamy and concubinage were permissible, although economic considerations rendered such practices infrequent.

It was unseemly for a woman to receive a secular or a religious education, especially knowledge of the Torah. Notable exceptions in later centuries included the maidservants of Rabbi Judah and the wife of Rabbi Meir. A writer of the rabbinical period declared that it was better to burn the holy scrolls than to teach them to a woman. Furthermore, women were forbidden even to teach the Torah at home. In judiciary courts women were generally not allowed to testify. Some legislatures based this prohibition on the story of Sarah, whose veracity had been questioned (Gen. 18:15). (One should, perhaps, not ask whether Abraham's own lies made him a model of reliability.)

With few exceptions, especially among the wealthy and the ruling classes, women were not supposed to be seen in the city streets. If they went out of their master's house, they had to wear a double veil, and as a rule, they were prohibited from speaking with strangers.[28]

It is, of course, legitimate to infer from comparison with other patriarchal and polygamous societies that Jewish women, already in the time of Jesus, may very well have obtained through subtle means the ability to influence, even dominate their menfolk at home, fathers as well as husbands. This cultural phenomenon has been widely observed among Muslim women and others in polygamic societies.

When relevant evidence is sifted and appraised, it must be concluded that woman's religious rank and religious privileges in Palestine at the time of Jesus were just a bit superior to those of slaves in Greco-Roman societies.

Who, then, were the women following Jesus on the roads of Galilee, Samaria, and Judea? Did they not run the risk of being treated as tramps, campfollowers, or in modern lingo, "groupies"?

The Women Who Followed Jesus

By the standards of Palestine at that time, the conversations of Jesus with women, and his words and his attitudes concerning them were revolutionary.

The historicity of the oral traditions on these matters can hardly be challenged. The details of the Gospel narratives in general were part of an elaborate composition—artistic works of literature—which often reflected the problems of the early church up to the third and fourth generation. After the middle of the first century A.D., less than thirty years after the death of Jesus, Christian communities were becoming more and more men-oriented.

At least, they institutionally evolved male-dominated hierarchies. How could the Gospel writers have invented stories or sayings that placed women in such full light and conferred upon them such prominence unless these had been solidly based upon eye-observed and ear-witnessed testimonies?

The picture of Jesus as he traveled on the roads of Palestine with the Twelve and with many women is recounted by Luke alone. Far more than the other Gospel writers, the third evangelist insists upon the concern of Jesus for those who are oppressed or excluded from the "respectable" elements of society: the poor, the sick, the maimed, the mentally unstable, women and children, foreigners, and the so-called sinners, that is, those Jews who were not strict observers of the Torah.

> And it came to pass, soon afterwards, that he went about through cities and villages, preaching and bringing the good tidings of the kingdom of God, and with him the twelve, and certain women who had been healed of evil spirits and infirmities, Mary that was called Magdalene, from whom seven demons had gone out, and Joanna, the wife of Chouza, Herod's steward, and Susanna, and *many others* [italics added], who ministered unto them of their substance. (Luke 8:1–3)

Some of these women, perhaps all of them, had independent means. The detail according to which they contributed "of their substance," *ek tōn huparchontōn autais,* appears to contradict the mores of the times. Women were not free, as a rule, to dispose of their property, which technically belonged to their husbands or fell under their fathers' jurisdiction. There were of course notable exceptions in aristocratic and influential families. It is conceivable that the women who followed Jesus enjoyed the use of private incomes, like Mary Magdalene, or that they belonged to the privileged classes of society, like Joanna, wife of Chouza, a man who managed the estates of Herod Antipas, tetrarch of Galilee and Perea.

Some commentators have identified Chouza with "the royal official" who begged Jesus at Capernaum to heal his son (John 4:46–54). This hypothesis is not improbable, for the wife of a high functionary at the court of Herod Antipas would not likely have traveled about unless she had her husband's concurrence. If Chouza was, indeed, "the man who put his trust in the word Jesus had spoken" (John 4:50), Joanna was the mother, or at least the stepmother, of a boy Jesus had healed. In any case, like Mary Magdalene, she had been cured of some ailment by Jesus.

Nothing is known about Susanna or the "many other women" who attached themselves to Jesus for various reasons. They assisted their master and his twelve disciples with "their substance" and presumably helped the community with their work. They were not, however, merely menial assistants, preparing food and shelter.

It is possible that the usual rendering of the word *huparchonta,* "substance, resources, goods, or means," represents on the part of traditional interpreters an unconscious assumption of male sexism. In classical,

Hellenistic, and especially in Septuagintal Greek, the meaning of the word covers a wide range of ideas and objects. It might signify "initiative," "talents," or "potentialities," as well as "real beings." Such an interpretation would indicate that the Lukan understanding of the women's contributions was quite different from that of Mark (15:41) or of Matthew (27:55). These two writers said that the women who watched the crucifixion from afar were those who had simply attended Jesus and his disciples in his ministry. Even Jerome's rendering is open to this exegesis, for the word he used (in Luke 8:3), *facultates,* might also refer to potentialities and talents other than material resources. The breadth of the semantic parameter in Luke's statement is not to be overlooked. It does suggest that the women followers of Jesus were not just the prototypes of the modern female assistants who, according to the vernacular, provide men with "coffee and doughnuts." Mary Magdalene and the other women were probably contributing to the well-being of Jesus not only their wealth but also their cultural, intellectual, and spiritual gifts. They belonged to the inner circle as fully as the Twelve did. They listened to the words of Jesus and shared with the men the mysterious power of his presence. They were liberated Jewish women, but this fact does not at all imply that they were "free" or "easy" women.

The Sexuality of Jesus

According to the available evidence of the earliest traditions, which are strikingly at variance with the anti-Christian polemics of a later age or with the eccentric fantasies of the Gnostic gospels, Jesus was known to have stood beyond sexual affection, intimacy, or attachment. To maintain that he was married because all rabbis mentioned in the Jewish literature of the second and third centuries A.D. were married (except one, the object of much amazement) is to commit a triple error.

The first is an error of historical anachronism, for there was no rabbi, in the technical sense of the word, at the time of Jesus. The appellation "rabbi" given him in several passages of the Gospels meant simply "my teacher," without the later connotation of a synagogal or didactic function and status.

The second error lies in the failure to observe that while the mother, brothers, and sisters of Jesus are known to the ancient oral tradition and in the written gospels, no mention is ever made of a wife. This argument, admittedly *e silentio,* is nonetheless significant, for the nascent church paid a great deal of attention to the family of Jesus, and especially to Mary and the women who were said to have been present at his execution or at the empty tomb.

The third error is one of psychological insensitivity to his ascetic training. Allusions to his prolonged periods of fasting and reminiscences of his nocturnal watches in solitude devoted to prayer strongly support the view that he was both celibate and chaste.

Not that Jesus erected celibacy as a requirement of discipleship, even in the light of his belief that the world was soon coming to an end. Nevertheless, the mystery of his sexual life remains entire.

In any event, there was no promiscuity among his followers. His enemies never brought against him, against the Twelve, nor against the women who accompanied them on their travels, the charge of sexual immorality.

The words attributed to him tend to show that, like John the Baptist, of whom he had been for a time the disciple, Jesus chose a life of singleness. It was said that he transferred to "all those who [did] the will of [his] Father in heaven" (Matt. 12:15 and par.) the allegiance to his immediate family. From this family the mention of a wife is conspicuously absent.

The bonds uniting Jesus to his disciples, male and female, transcend the ties of his heredity, consanguinity, or connubiality. Moreover, his utter respect for women as well as for men was eloquently made evident by the words of Oriental hyperbole that the Sermon on the Mount ascribed to him:

I say unto you that every one that looks on a woman to lust after her has committed adultery with her already in his heart. (Matt. 5:28)

The opposition of Jesus to divorce, in flagrant violation of the law of Moses (Deut. 24:1–4), showed that he upheld the dignity of womanhood. He knew that legislation on divorce was almost uniformly one-sided in favor of husbands, and that it revealed "the hardness of their hearts" (Matt. 19:3–12 and par.). His opposition to divorce was motivated by his support of women's liberation. It certainly did not justify the rise of a new legalism. Through a sad irony, several denominations of Christendom, as it is well known, prefer to condemn divorce on any grounds. This absolutism, which in some churches leads to the hypocritical casuistry of permitting marriage "annulment" or "dissolution," clearly violates "the mind of Christ." These denominations, whether Greek, Roman, or Anglican, manifest sectarian myopia and artificiality rather than the humaneness that is the mark of the truly universal church.

That Jesus did not flaunt celibacy, chastity, or virginity as the ideal of manhood and womanhood, even in times of eschatological fever, must be stressed without ambiguity. However, Jesus recognized the rights of individuals to abide by their own ideals of conduct and to refuse sexual commitment. Such a refusal might have been justified only as a sign of the belief in the imminence of the new world. This is the probable meaning of the cryptic phrase:

There are eunuchs that made themselves eunuchs for the sake of the kingdom of heaven. He that is able to receive it, let him receive it. (Matt. 19:12)

This saying, of course, did not signify the barbarian acts of self-emasculation that the Asia Minor devotees of the goddess Attis, in a state of religious frenzy, would practice at the time of their initiation. For Jesus, freedom of choice remains entire. Only an abusive exegesis would find in his words a basis for imposing the medieval practice of priestly celibacy.

From all available evidence, it must be said that the attitude of Jesus toward women and men might be described as a direct, unfettered candor. Not only those women who had benefited from his therapeutic gifts but also "many other women" who presumably had always been, like the Twelve, in normal health belonged to the inner circle of the Jesus community.

Wisdom's Vindication in Womanhood

It was immediately after the scene of the anointing of Jesus at the house of the Pharisee (Luke 7:36–50) that Luke referred to the many women (8:2) who accompanied him and the Twelve on their journeys. In view of this sequence, ancient and modern interpreters have often identified Mary Magdalene, the prominent figure in the story of the women following Jesus, with the unnamed woman in the account of his anointing. Probably for this reason the Mary Magdalene legend in piety, literature, drama and iconography to this day induces the popular illusion that she was a repented prostitute. There are no grounds whatever for looking upon Mary Magdalene as a notorious sinner.

The story of the anointing was most likely intended to illustrate the proverbial saying: "And Wisdom is vindicated in all her children" (Luke 7:35). The third evangelist well understood the breadth and the depth of sapiential theology. Divine Wisdom seeks all men and women without discrimination of sex, race, nation, ritual purity, or moral virtue.

By using verse 35 as a transitional epigraph to the story that follows, Luke wanted to explain this proverbial saying with the sketch of a woman's utter devotion for Jesus and with the parable of the two debtors. The evangelist suggests that all human beings are Wisdom's children whenever they *vindicate* her in their openness to her unconditional outreach of love.

The woman who anointed Jesus with the priceless perfume has often been identified not only with Mary Magdalene but also with Mary of Bethany. In the other three Gospels, the incident at the Pharisee's house is ignored, and Mary of Bethany anoints Jesus just before his arrest.

The Gospel writers clearly consider this scene as a foreboding sign of the death and burial of Jesus (Matt. 26:12; Mark 14:8; and par.). The setting is also that of a meal, held this time in the house of a man called Simon (Matt. 26:6; Mark 14:3). The similarity of settings may be the evidence of a conflict in the oral traditions concerning a single event, although the possibility of two different scenes should not be discounted. In the Lukan story, the street woman is presented as "a sinner." Surely, such a charge cannot be made against Mary of Bethany, unless the word "sinner" implied merely a liberal attitude toward the observance of the Torah (cf. Luke 6:32–33; 24:7; Gal. 2:15; cf. also 1 Macc. 2:44). Nevertheless, the host said reprovingly, "If that man were a prophet [some manuscripts read, "the prophet"], he would know who is clinging to him" (Luke 7:39; cf. John 20:17). The Greek verb, here translated "to cling," has a dual meaning, or perhaps two different verbs are spelled with the same letters, for it sometimes meant "to attach, to lock, to knot, to embrace, to have intimate relations with" and at other times meant "to light a fire." It suggests far more than an elusive caress—rather, a clasping and continuous *étreinte*. It is, of course, possible that the Pharisee used a hyperbolic term, so common in Oriental speech, simply to signify his distaste for the scene. In any case, Jesus knew the law. He was aware of breaking it by accepting the woman's caresses and by not rebuking her or even thrusting her roughly away from himself. He deliberately made matters more offensive by the words he addressed to the Pharisee, his host. He contrasted her attentions to the Pharisee's disregard for the traditional gestures of hospitality. This detailed enumeration must have been quite displeasing and even insulting to a pious man. How could a self-righteous scholar accept being compared disparagingly to a woman of uncertain reputation? First, Jesus replied, she was moved to express her grief. Second, she washed his feet with her tears. Third, she dried his feet with her hair (a notoriously erotic act). Fourth, she had not ceased kissing his feet tenderly *(katephilei;* Luke 7:38; cf. 7:45). The Greek verb, which rendered an original Aramaic or Hebrew word, appears in Xenophon and Plutarch in the sense of sexual intimacy.

Even if the strictures of legal uncleanness through bodily contact with a woman were to be disregarded, this woman's display of amorous affection was bound to induce among the bystanders a feeling of utmost embarrassment. It has been said that humor is the reaction of sudden exposure to the incongruous. The obscene (literally, that theatrical action which should be banned from stage-center to off-scene) is also sudden exposure to the incongruous, and its aim may sometimes be to sharpen the attention and compel objection.

By acting and speaking as he did, Jesus not only upheld the dignity of womanhood in a male-dominated society but he also punctured moralistic prejudices based on appearances. Moreover, he revealed the contrary and complementary aspects of his character: he was at once courageous and self-composed. He was able to withstand both the hostility of his adversaries and the malaise of his friends. He had outgrown the stringencies of his upbringing. A truly liberated man, he was free from a judgmental rejection of human beings who did not conform to the religious strictures of their environment. He applied to Scripture an interpretive principle of equilibrium, with a liberty which was not libertinism, because he had perceived human qualities beyond the vagaries of nonconformity. He moved serenely and firmly from the sacred of religiosity to the holy of humaneness. His reliance upon God emboldened him to reason out accepted mores and to oppose them in the name of humanity. Like Hosea, Jeremiah, and Second

Isaiah, he was continually sensitive to the foibles and the crimes of a mindless society. He looked upon human beings as individual persons. He did not tag them according to economic status, social class, race, nationality, religious persuasion, sectarian allegiance, or sex. A woman, just as a man, was a creature of God.

The only discrimination he allowed was based upon a single criterion. He said of the woman, "She loved much" (Luke 7:47). The Greek phrase *ēgapēsen polu* reflects the old Hebraic notion of *agapē,* which does not imply a kind of spiritual emotion opposed to *erōs*, but designates a psychological movement of love as gift of self, the overcoming of egocentricity, the outgoingness of one's concern for another person and for the sake of that person's benefit.

Jesus freed himself from the cultic legislation on the ritual impurity of bodily contacts because he looked at all human beings in the context of a theology of creation. Women, like men, were God's children, toiling, suffering, erring, sinning, still hoping and waiting "for the manifestation of glory." While the original Aramaic phrase is not known for certain, the Greek for "much," *polu*, most probably renders the Hebraic idea of "excellence," *me'od*. This word is generally used as an adverb, but it appears as a noun in the first commandment of Israel's creed, "Thou shalt love the Lord thy God ... with all thy might" (*me'od*; Deut. 6:5), that is to say, with the whole of thy "muchness," thy *élan vital,* the outgoing aggrandizement of thy personality, thy potential for excellence.

Jesus discerned in the woman the treasures of her potentiality for changing her ways. She had been moved to give her wholeness. Through genuine love and at the risk of being misjudged, she accepted her responsibility. Jesus saw in her act the occasion for a parable of social coherence and betterment (Luke 7:41–43).

Akin to this theme is the answer of Jesus to Martha, the busy hostess, who complained that her sister Mary was not assuming her share of the household chores while listening to the words of their guest. This answer has become famous, but its meaning is obscure.

> Martha, Martha, thou art anxious and troubled about many things; but one thing is needful: and Mary has chosen the better part, which shall not be taken away from her. (Luke 10:41–42)

It is probably against the background of woman's status in Judaism at that time that this saying is to be appraised. Surely, Jesus was not approving sloth, nor extolling unconcern for the labor and the plight of others when a woman desired to broaden her spiritual and intellectual horizon. He considered Mary's eagerness to be as legitimate as her homemaking obligations. The mores of her milieu stifled her cultural and even her religious potentialities. In reaction to the religious oppression of women, Jesus did not exaggerate when he suggested that Mary "had chosen the better part."

The Violation of the Torah

The fearless nonconformism of Jesus appears in another scene reported in all three Synoptics (Matt. 9:18–26; Mark 5:35–43; Luke 8:40–56). In the midst of this scene is incorporated the healing of a woman with an issue of blood (Mark 5:25–34; Luke 8:43–48). One of the administrators of a local synagogue in Galilee, a man named Jairus, came to Jesus because his twelve-year-old daughter was dying. The story is told with suspense. It is interrupted by another, unrelated incident, the healing of an older woman. When Jesus arrived at the house of Jairus, ritual wailing indicated that the girl was beyond cure. According to Luke's pointed statement, when Jesus insisted that she was only asleep, "they laughed him to scorn, knowing that she was dead." A pious Jew might have avoided any direct contact with the body of a sick person, let alone with a corpse, but, the text adds, "taking the child by the hand, [Jesus] said to her, *Talitha qumi;* which is, being interpreted, 'Little girl, I say to thee, arise!'" Once again, this narrative illustrates the freedom of Jesus vis-à-vis the legal prohibitions on ritual uncleanness. In addition, he shows his concern for a young female. The tone of his voice may well have been remembered in the early church as one of unusual tenderness, for the phrase he pronounced was preserved in the original Aramaic, as if a witness had heard it directly spoken, with its own inflection, which defied translation into Greek.

Inserted within this episode is the incident of the woman "who had an issue of blood for twelve years." In spite of her ritual uncleanness, of which she was certainly aware, the woman touched the robe of Jesus from the back. Again, the Greek verb, as in the Lukan story of the anointing by a street woman, means more than merely "touched." It means "grasped" or "clung to." Matthew and Luke specifically say "the fringe of his garment." This probably refers to the hem of the square mantle with tassels of three white threads and one hyacinth-blue thread at each end of its four corners, worn only by the most pious Jews. If this interpretation is correct, the robe worn by Jesus indicated the strictness of his upbringing in sharp contrast to the boldness of his beliefs. When the woman tugged at the tassels of that garment, he was aware that "power had gone out from [him]" (Mark 5:30). The text stresses this feature, but no word may be construed as implying that he felt and resisted contact with a ritually impure woman. To the contrary, the episode ends with a theological twist of the first magnitude. Jesus declared in effect that it was not a pseudo-magical gesture of physical closeness that brought about her cure. He immediately lifted the level of discourse from the crass culture of superstition to the lofty area of divine and human relationship: "Daughter, thy faith has made thee whole" (Mark 5:34).

The Greek verb, "to make whole," *sōzein,* has a wide range of meanings, from "preserving from danger" or "saving from death" to "conferring life."

In the Septuagint translation of the Hebrew Bible it is used for about sixteen different Hebrew ideas, from "succoring in existential risk of nonbeing" to "giving peace and health," the growth of wholeness within the self and the community *(shalem)*. The exact Aramaic verb used by Jesus is, of course, unknown, but we may be sure that he had refrained from any rebuke, preferring to speak of a reality that far outshone the mere negativity of an ailment. The woman was now reconciled to herself, reinstated within her own community. She had become a new being, a full-fledged daughter of God.

A similar meaning emerges from a similar story, about the healing of a woman crippled for eighteen years, reported by Luke alone (13:10–17). It possesses an added connotation. Jesus took the initiative and pointedly directed the attention of the bystanders to the woman as woman. He singled her out of the crowd, called her, and said to her, "Woman, thou art loosed from thy infirmity" (13:12). The indignation of the synagogue ruler, since it was the day of the Sabbath, led Jesus to compel the audience to reflect when he asked the rhetorical question: Should not this woman, "being a daughter of Abraham," be healed, even on the Sabbath? The emphasis could not be missed. The Jews prided themselves on being "the sons of Abraham." Are not women on the same footing of privilege? Are not the females of the covenant at least the equals of the males? A hidden irony was bound to prick the consciences of the pious, whose eagerness to fulfill the Law had made them blind to their male-sexist arrogance. This is the closest Jesus came to protesting the theological meaning of exclusion, which was attached to the ritual of male circumcision.

Sexual Sin and Male Pride

The story of the encounter between Jesus and the Pharisees over the fate of an adulteress (John 8:3–11) is not found in the more ancient manuscripts. It may have been added to the Gospel of John in the second century A.D. The matter of its authorship, however, does not cast a reasonable doubt over the genuineness of the episode. Its point is akin to that of other scenes in which the attitude of Jesus toward womanhood is being questioned, not only by his contemporary enemies but also by moralists within the church. This unique story brings with it a distinctive note, for it deals not only with a legal question but also with a sensitive issue in the realm of sexual ethics.

On the surface, the accusers of the woman are unequivocally right. "Now, in the law, Moses ordered that such women be stoned." This is a clear reference to a well-known clause in the code of Deuteronomy (22:21–22). Yet, that clause calls for the stoning of both the man and the woman caught in adultery, which is viewed as a capital offense against the woman's husband. Here, neither the husband nor the lover is mentioned. It is a case of unilateral, antifemale sexism.

Jesus knows that the strict religionists who brought the woman to him were attempting to entrap him. Either Jesus would uphold the law and recommend stoning the woman, in which event he would get into trouble with the Roman authorities (since the Jewish court was not permitted to carry out capital punishment), or else he would flagrantly flout the most sacred fountain of Jewish conduct, public or private.

At once Jesus lifted the case at hand from the level of legal discussion to that of psychological analysis, and—let it be stressed—not of the character of the guilty woman but of her male accusers' self-awareness and true motivation. This shift enabled Jesus to introduce the theological issue of *existential* sinfulness in contrast to illegal acts that might be catalogued as sins. The distinction was evidently not familiar to his audience.

What is the existential situation of mankind, of men as well as of women? Sexual irregularity, infringement of a right, affront to man's honor, violation of the mores of a particular society, breach of ethics? Jesus did not for a moment deny their reality nor the urgency of the situation, but he placed a distinctly sinful woman in the larger context of sinful humanity. She belonged in his eyes to the same category as that of men who are seemingly perfect, scrupulously observant of the law. For Jesus, legal righteousness could not be isolated from complex oneness with the human family. Such oneness was in turn based upon common creatureliness. He affirmed the solidarity of the human race. This is the meaning of original sin. The vitiation of virtue through self-centeredness was never far from the myth of the Garden. It is the plight of every man and of every woman. The crimes of Abraham or Jacob were not slurred over. Moses himself had died in solitariness, the victim of his heroic pride. To achieve any moral act is to run the risk of believing in self-sufficiency. Judgment of others, especially in the realm of sexuality, is the inability to distinguish, in most cases, between lust and love, viewed from the perspective of a virtuous status, with its concomitant of arrogance and perhaps greed. One cannot really condemn the sexual irregularities of others without placing them in the larger context of social injustice and pride.

Jesus did not, however, condemn those who condemned. As was his wont, he urged them quietly, indirectly, to think for themselves beyond the letter of a code, to reflect upon their own inner lives, to probe the secret wounds or the scars of the past.

The woman was prostrate on the ground. Society had abased her into shame. She had lost her dignity, her self-respect. She was in dread of losing her life. Jesus seemed to agree with her accusers, but another kind of truth shone in a bright light. "He that is without sin among you, let him be the first to cast a stone at her!" Now, a true miracle happened. The virtuous men departed, one by one. Some manuscripts add, "convicted by their own conscience *(suneidēsis).*" *Suneidēsis* is a word found in the wisdom literature (Wis. 17:11) and in the letters of Paul (2 Cor. 4:2). It was also familiar to Hellenistic philosophers. The comment of the narrator shrewdly exteriorizes the attitude of Jesus. The inner voice of fairness toward all human beings, men or women, transcends inherited prejudices, the pull of custom, and even the dictates of the law that was deemed to be divinely ordained.

Jesus did not condemn the woman, but he added, "Sin no more!" The woman was placed on her own. Her response reflected the grace manifested to her. Moral behavior depends upon the acceptance of a gratuitous gift. This woman becomes the exemplar of a recipiency that tempers character into a fine metal—into the will to act constructively.

The Samaritan Woman as Apostle

Like the Lukan story of the anointing of Jesus by a streetwalker, the Johannine episode of the Samaritan woman at Jacob's well (John 4:4–42) is found in only one Gospel. While the scene was probably composed as a liturgical piece for the service of worship in some Christian church, probably at Ephesus, toward the end of the first century A.D., it gives all the signs of having been based upon a historical event.

Samaritans descended from a mixed breed of Israelites who had escaped Assyrian deportation at the collapse of Samaria in the Northern Kingdom (722 B.C.). They were in part the remnant of the so-called Lost Tribes. Their daughters intermarried with war veterans from Mesopotamia and Media whom Nineveh had resettled in the land of Samaria (2 Kings 17:24–41). After the exile of Judah in Babylon and the construction of the second temple (519–515 B.C.), the Samaritans published their own Pentateuch, written in the Northern dialect of Hebrew, and they worshiped in a temple built upon Mt. Garizim, above Shechem, in the central mountain range. A high priest from Jerusalem burnt this sanctuary in 128 B.C. For the Jews of the Roman period a Samaritan was a religious dissident, as well as a hybrid, accursed half brother.

In a Jerusalem regulation of A.D. 65–66, Jews were warned that Samaritan women were "menstruants from the cradle," that is to say, ritually impure at all times.

The disciples who surprised Jesus in conversation with a Samaritan woman at the well were amazed that he talked with a religious heretic, but they mentioned only the fact that he spoke with a female, alone (John 4:27). They knew the gross impropriety of this encounter (cf. Sir. 9:1–9; Pirqe Aboth 1:5; Babylonian Talmud, Tractate Erubin, 53b). As in the Lukan story of the anointing by a woman of the street, Jesus did not hesitate to violate the moral standards and the religious restrictions of his milieu in order to affirm his reverence for womanhood. He knew the equality of both sexes under his God.

The Fourth Gospel, even more than the Synoptics, reveals some of the problems faced by Christian communities in the first, second, and perhaps third generations. Toward the end of the first century A.D., the word "apostle" tended to acquire a technical meaning. It led to the ecclesiastical notion of the apostolic college. This new meaning of the word "apostle" was anachronistically read back into the time of Jesus. It is from this perverted telescoping of language that the still later notion of apostolic succession arose. As is well known, the notion remains to this day one source of deep divisions among the various denominations of Christendom. It is also in part responsible for the exclusion of women from the Greek, Roman, and Anglican priesthood.

The Fourth Gospel insists upon the primary meaning of the word "apostle," which is simply "someone sent," "an envoy," "a messenger." The word did not originally designate an individual in any way sacramentally or ontologically set apart. There was no apostolic college in the early church. The Johannine evangelist is concerned with the spread of the good news. As elsewhere, Jesus is presented as the one who "sends" harvesters (John 4:38; cf. Matt. 9:37–38). The Greek verb *apostellein* does not mean "to make an apostle" in the later sense given it by the patristic church, but "to send into the fields." The Samaritan woman was one of the first gospel bearers and evangelists. While the noun is not applied to her, it is correct to state that John considered her an apostle.

"She went to the town, and said to the people, 'Come and see. . .' " (John 4:28–29). It was her testimony that transformed her fellow citizens. "Now, many of the Samaritans who lived in that town turned their trust toward [Jesus] on account of the woman's word" (4:39). The Fourth Gospel inserted these words of Jesus to his disciples just before a startling conclusion to an equally startling episode, but the evangelist did not do this through a casual juxtaposition of bits and pieces culled from oral tradition:

> Myself, I have *sent* you [italics added]
> To harvest for that for which you have not worked.
> (4:38)

The verb "to send," *apostellein* or *pempein,* underlines the nontechnical sense of the noun "apostle," *apostolos,* in John. The woman from Samaria was indeed an apostle, in the primary sense of a missionary, an ambassador, a deputy.

Mary Magdalene, Midwife
to Christianity

In a similar way the Johannine Gospel ascribes to Mary Magdalene the status of a bearer of good news. The early church remembered her in a unique way among the women who surrounded Jesus. She appears prominently in all four Gospels, and several of the apocryphal gospels even go beyond restraint in praising her superiority not only over women but also over the men who were revered among the first artisans of the church.

The name of Mary Magdalene is mentioned more often than the names of the other women and men who followed Jesus. Hagiographers, artists, poets, dramatists, and littérateurs to this day have been fascinated by her alleged ill repute, although the canonical Gospels simply state that Jesus had expelled seven demons from her ("demons" being a contemporary way of describing emotional or mental impediments). The significance of Mary Magdalene for the early church arises especially from the momentous scene on the first day of the week after the crucifixion.

The disciples had scattered in frustration and dismay. With minor variations, the oral tradition now preserved in the four Gospels speaks of women going "very early" to the place of burial on the morning after the Sabbath and becoming there the recipients of an angelic visit.

In the sixties of the first century A.D., Mark told how "amazed" these women were to see "a young man" in resplendent whiteness, who bade them not to be afraid, for Jesus would precede them to Galilee. There, he promised, they would see him. He also commanded them to inform the disciples "and Peter." But the women fled in terror and said nothing to anyone (Mark 16:1–8). The postscript now appended to the Markan Gospel and not found in the earlier manuscripts relates how Jesus, alive, appeared to Mary Magdalene, but how the disciples disbelieved her report (16:10–11).

About twenty years later, the Gospel of Matthew also mentioned an angelic vision but stated that Mary Magdalene and the other women did convey the message to the disciples. Thereupon, the text continues, "Behold, Jesus met them, saying, All hail!" (Matt. 28:8–9). Luke, at about the same time (A.D. 80–85), specifically named Joanna as one of the "other women" who accompanied Mary Magdalene to the tomb. She had been listed previously in the same Gospel as the wife of a high functionary in the court of Herod Antipas (Luke 24:10; cf. 8:3). Unlike Matthew, Luke withheld the account of the appearance of Jesus to the disciples for a later occasion (24:36–43), just after the story of the two otherwise unknown men on the road to Emmaus (vv. 13–35).

It was only toward the end of the first century (A.D. 95–97) that the Johannine evangelist sounded a distinctive note. In a sketch drawn with restraint, he told how Mary Magdalene, alone, went to the sepulchre "when it was yet dark" (John 20:1). Seeing that the stone had been taken away, she rushed back to Simon Peter and the other disciple "whom Jesus loved" (20:2). In their turn, the two men ran to the tomb and discovered that it was empty. Peter apparently remained unconvinced while the other disciple "saw and believed" (v. 8).

At this point, the Johannine writer introduced one of the most exquisite prose poems in the literature of all time. Mary Magdalene, standing outside the sepulchre in tears, was comforted by two angels. Constricted by anguish, she said to them, "They have taken away my Lord, and I know not where they have laid him" (v. 13). At that instant, she turned back and saw Jesus, standing. She thought it was the gardener, until he said, "Mary." And she replied, "Rabboni!"—a term of endearment with the possessive, "My dearest master!"

Recognition is indicated only by the exchange of the words. With this chasteness of elocution, John reaches the summit of the storytelling art of religious sensibility. He at once conceals and reveals the depth of pathos, the tenderness of the bond, the passionate relief, the rock-bottom unshakableness of expectation.

Sixty or seventy years after the death of Jesus, in about A.D. 95 or 97, the church at Ephesus in Asia Minor—probably the milieu in which the Johannine author was writing—dared to propose its own version of the birth of Christianity. The accent differed from that of the Roman church (Mark and Luke) or of the Antioch community (Matthew). The many features at variance from Gospel to Gospel indicate graphically that a long process of retelling and literary amplification took place among the Christians of the first three generations. Even toward the end of the century, when an aura of institutional reverence surrounded the Twelve, neither the Synoptics nor the Johannine accounts attempted to conceal the unbelief that assailed the original male circle.

By contrast, there were the women, with the Magdalene at their head, who came out in the limelight. They—the women, not the men—were the first recipients of the new vision.

Mary of Nazareth was remembered in the Lukan Gospel of the infancy, as the tabernacle of the Most High, with the babe in her womb, the first daughter of the new economy related to the advent of the man Jesus in history. But Mary of Magdala remained in the golden legend the midwife of Christianity.

It would be an egregious misapprehension of the birth of the church to question its historical reality. The faith in the resurrection created Christianity. Nevertheless, the nature of the event that produced this faith escapes the rigors of modern investigation.

The traditions on the empty tomb are probably late. They were ignored by the apostle Paul in the middle of the century (1 Cor. 15:3–8). His list of the appearances of the living Lord differs from those of the Gospels. He never mentioned the part played by Mary Magdalene and the other women. It is, then, the more astonishing that, in an increasingly male-oriented church, the role of Mary Magdalene would have been affirmed without ambiguity by the evangelists. For centuries, Magdalen devotion outshone Marian piety. This fact by itself constitutes a singular testimony of the reverence in which Jesus held womanhood at the dawn of Christianity.

One should view with caution modern comparisons between the motif of the women at the tomb and the lament rituals of the vernal feast in the religions of the ancient Near East and classical Greco-Roman antiquity. It is, of course, possible that memories of those ancient rites played a part in the liturgical appeal of the Mary Magdalene legend in the early church. However, those memories differ markedly from the Christian proclamation of the living Lord, with its revolutionary implications of sexual, social, and national equality.

In the Mesopotamian epic of Gilgamesh, a harlot anoints the dead hero with fragrant oil and still weeps for him. But she is not liberated from her social abasement.

The Canaanite epic of Baal at Ugarit calls for the reenactment of the goddess Anat's gruesome search for the dead god. Her heart is like that of a cow looking for her calf, said the poem. But the myth and its ritual remain static, devoid of consequences in the realm of social justice within history.

Similar comments apply to the lament of Isis for Osiris in Egypt, or of the Judahite women for Tammuz (Adonis) in the temple of Jerusalem at the time of Ezekiel (Ezek. 8:14). Even the young woman in the Song of Songs searches anxiously for her absent lover, yet remains a world apart from Mary Magdalene. In the words of Rabanus Maurus, the ninth-century theologian of Mainz and Tours, Mary Magdalene became "an apostle to the apostles."

Similarities between Mary of Magdala in the garden and the ancient Near Eastern myth of women searching for the dead lover remain peripheral and chiefly stylistic. They point to the survival of words and gestures in the literary imagination of a regional culture. They do not account for the thrust of the Johannine story and its attempt to spell out the presence of the holy in human life. At the same time, the storyteller sharpens the aim of his story. He endows Mary Magdalene with the mission to transmit a message. She is bidden to proclaim the Word.

At the beginning and at the end of his Gospel, the Johannine writer implicitly conferred the status of apostleship upon two women, the woman of Samaria at Jacob's well and the woman from Magdala in the garden.

Just as the alien sectarians of Shechem placed their trust in Jesus through the word of a woman, so also the dispirited and disbelieving disciples were brought to a new hope, not through the perceptiveness of their own devotion to their master but through the witness of a woman, Mary Magdalene.

The Samaritans and the disciples were brought to a new economy of historical existence and to a new mode of being by the female agent of the holy.

Peter and the other disciples had not believed that Jesus could be alive after his death, but Mary Magdalene's simple word was "I have seen the Lord." It was she who had received from the living man of God the commission to proclaim the good tidings. She was the mediatrix of a new divine reality that somehow was attached to the man Jesus, beyond his death.

In the presence of the transcendent person of the God-like Being, the Magdalene is not rejected. To the contrary, she is commissioned. Yet, the holy always requires distance, a withdrawal from propinquity: "Do not touch me!" (John 20:17). The now-famous phrase *noli me tangere* translates a Greek sentence, *mē mou haptou,* which in turn presupposes in the Septuagint usage the well-known Hebrew verb *dabeq,* "to attach oneself, to cleave to, to embrace." The words actually mean "Do not cling to me!" They imply far more than casual touching. They refer to the clasping and holding of the flesh of a lover. The Johannine theologian at this juncture intimates the marginal abyss that separates the divine from the human while preserving the bond between them. The presence of God is always elusive, but its proximity does not deceive. Mary's embrace, like the embrace of Jesus' feet in the Lukan story of the anointing (the same Greek word is used in both narratives), suggests the mystical attempt to arrest time.

As in the vocation scenes of Moses and the prophets, from Amos to Isaiah and Jeremiah, the woman from Magdala was asked to keep her distance. As in the scene of the burning bush, the flame that does not consume itself becomes the sign of an immanence that is never diluted into a merely human emotion. The holy remains the holy. "Do not cling to me!"

Nevertheless, the restraining of the communion immediately precedes an order to act: "Go to my brothers and say to them. . . ." Like Moses and the prophets of Israel, Mary Magdalene received a commission. She was now the mouthpiece of the living Lord. She had become an apostle, in the original meaning of the word.[29]

Jesus and the Fatherhood of God

There is a final feature in these stories of the two female "apostles"—the Samaritan and the Magdalene. Reverence for womanhood, in violation of the religious strictures of the environment, goes hand in hand, contextually, with a daring and an original apprehension of the fatherhood of God. This fact has generally been ignored by commentators.

Concluding his words to the Samaritan woman at Jacob's well, Jesus said:

> Believe me, woman. The hour comes
> When you will worship the Father
> Neither on this mountain nor in Jerusalem.
>
> . . . .
>
> For the hour comes and is now here
> When true worshipers will worship
> The Father in spirit and in truth.
>
> . . . .
>
> And it is such worshipers
> That the Father seeks. . . .
>
> (John 4:21, 23)

The context brings together "the will of Him who sent" Jesus (John 4:34), the woman, the "sending" ("apostolate"), and the naming of God as the Father.

Likewise, when Mary Magdalene is "sent" to the brothers of Jesus, namely, to his disciples (John 20:17b; cf. v. 18a), she receives a specific message to transmit:

> Say to them, I ascend to my Father and your Father,
> To my God and your God.
>
> (v. 17b)

Is the naming of God "my Father" in the context of "sending" a female witness as an "apostle" a mere coincidence? Or is there a thematic link in the Johannine theology, or indeed, in the whole spectrum of the thinking of Jesus and the primitive church, between womanhood and divine fatherhood?

Words used to designate God are almost always inherited from earlier cultures. Some contemporary Christians, men as well as women, oppose the language of divine fatherhood as "sexist." It is true that the name Father as an appellation of God came from the ancient Near Eastern myth of a male deity, "progenitor of the gods." While Israel repudiated the sexual character of divinity and spoke of Yahweh in terms of creation rather than of procreation, reverence for the Hebrew "fathers" maintained an affinity between religious language and a patriarchal form of society.

The Jerusalem priests reacted to the cult of the Mother Goddess, and their fear of the fertility cults largely presided over the birth of Judaism during the exile in Babylon. Stressing ritual purity and circumcision, the priests officially subjected women to men in the realm of religion.

Against the institutional Judaism of his time, Jesus upheld the humanity, the dignity, and the equality of womanhood. The name Father, which he favored as a designation of God, paradoxically reflected his radical overthrow of patriarchy. Jesus intended a metaphorical name that meant not mastery over slaves, nor tyranny over women and children, but on the contrary, tenderness and care and responsibility for the growth of a new family. Moreover, the notion of divine fatherhood did not at all mean for Jesus the physiological bond of paternity with its repressed archetype of oedipal rebellion, which depth psychology and anthropology have emphasized in our time. For him the name Father evoked a transcendence voluntarily curbed by self-immolation.

The God who is compared to a father is, like a mother, the protector and the feeder, the one who tutors and nurtures, receives and forgives, supports and comforts, in order to lead from infancy to adulthood.

As an assiduous reader of the Hebrew Bible, Jesus appears to have placed the prophets and psalmists on a par with the Torah (Pentateuch). The Gospels report that he frequently quoted from, or alluded to, the Books of Deuteronomy, Isaiah, and the Psalms. He found in them metaphors of God that evoked both a paternal and a maternal relationship. Such a language corresponded closely to the requisites of his own faith. Yahweh carried

138

Israel from Egypt "as a father carries his son" when the child is tired (Deut. 1:31). Like a mother, Yahweh loved his son, taught him to walk, took him in his arms, caressed his cheek, and fed him (Hos. 11:1–4). The prophets discerned a remarkable parallel between their understanding of God's care for Israel and their own experience of parental responsibilities. They emphasized the coalescence rather than the separation of parental roles within the family. Like a mother who will not forget the child of her womb, God will not forget Zion (Isa. 49:15). The lapses of his people in history are compared to the ingratitude of a child to both father and mother, "the Rock who has begotten [them] and . . . the God who has given [them] birth" (Deut. 32:18). It is on account of the stirrings of the divine womb that a criminal hopes to be forgiven (Ps. 51:1 [Heb. 3]).

A minute analysis of the four Gospels has shown that the early Christians tended, as time went by, to mention more frequently the name Father when they reported the words of Jesus. The number of occurrences, which rose from four in the earliest Gospel (Mark) to fifteen in Luke, forty-nine in Matthew, and one hundred nine in John, indicates a theological development in the early church.

At the same time, there is little doubt that Jesus dared to call God *Abba,* "Dear Father." This Aramaic term of endearment was common on the lips of young children when they spoke to their own fathers. Both Mark (14:36) and the apostle Paul (Rom. 8:15; Gal. 4:6) preserved the name in its original tongue, although they were writing in Greek. It seems that the contemporaries of Jesus hardly ever used it for God, probably because it had a connotation of familiarity that would have appeared disrespectful for the divine. Jesus adopted the word *Abba* precisely because it implied the surrender of mature adults and their return in utter confidence to the simplicity, destitution, and complete dependency of childhood.

When proud men and women call God Father, they give up their claim to anthropocentric independence. They descend from a vaguely religious humanism or from a cold, philosophical deism, to the genuine humility of infancy. Divine fatherhood, for Jesus, meant the renunciation of hubris and the return to innocence. He symbolically declared that only little children would inherit the kingdom of God.

To rely upon God as Father did not mean a blind obedience to infinite power. Rather, it implied resistance to "the lure of infinity." To pray, "Our Father," was to admit at once theological childhood and ethical sisterhood as well as brotherhood within God's family. For Jesus, divine forgiveness was inseparable from mutual respect and reconciliation among human beings, black and white, rich and poor, Easterners and Westerners, male and female.

To pray, "Our Father," was to insert the self into the end of time and to participate in the divine realm. The invocation "Our Father" immediately commands a threefold request: first, that God's name, Father, be manifested as holy to the entire world; second, that his realm come, thereby affirming the advent of a new creation; and third, that his will be done, on earth now as it is done in the divine sphere. To affirm the fatherhood of God is to affirm the certainty of this advent, with a foretaste of his presence.

The prophets had compared the love of Yahweh for Israel to the tenderness of a father and a mother toward their offspring. Jesus pursued this comparison, but he did more than that. While the prophets looked for a time when Israel would call Yahweh "my Father," Jesus brought the hope to present reality. A poetic metaphor for God tomorrow had become the name for God today.

The parable of the prodigal son should be called the parable of the two rebellious sons. It depicts the father of two children; the younger had revolted and returned, making no claims and relying on his father's love (Luke 15:18); and the elder had remained at home but actually revolted, arguing on the grounds of merit and of self-righteousness (vv. 29–30). The father received the one as well as the other when he said, "All that is mine is thine" (v. 31).

The attitude of Jesus toward men and women corresponded to a theology of paternal and maternal interaction. Nowhere is this more dramatically expressed than in the exclamation that Matthew and Luke have reported when Jesus looked upon the holy city:

> Jerusalem, Jerusalem, that kills the prophets,
>   And stones those who are sent to thee!
> How often would I have gathered thy children together
>   As a mother bird gathers her little ones under her wings,
>   But you would not!
>   (Matt. 23:37; cf. Luke 13:34)

The usual translation, "as a hen gathers her brood," is due to Jerome's rendering, *"quemadmodum gallina congregat pullos suos,"* but the Greek does not suggest the imagery of a barnyard, and the word *nossia* does not mean "chicks, little chickens," but designates the "brood" of any ornithological species. With two exceptions, in Xenophon and Aeschylus, the word *ornis,* commonly found in Homer, Sophocles, Aristophanes, and others, refers to a wild bird. The comparison may well be a distant echo of the feminine imagery that the Hebrew poets of the deeds of Yahweh used when they praised the Lord of history for his motherly nurture of Israel throughout the ages. They likened the Lord to the Egyptian mother bird who teaches her young how to fly, supports them when they fail or risk falling. The Egyptian vulture often appears in the iconography of the goddess Isis, whose wings either protect or stimulate, empower, enable, and encourage. Yahweh succored his people

> Like a vulture that stirs up her nest,

That flutters over her young,
Spreading out her wings in order to catch them,
Bearing them on her pinions.

(Deut. 32:11)

The Hebrew theologians of healing history *(Heilsgeschichte)* spoke of their God not only as a protector and a provider but also as a teacher who brought them to maturity. The verb *racheph,* in the intensive active, "to flutter," is the same as that found in the Wisdom account of the creation of the world (Gen. 1:2), which the Jerusalem priests in exile adopted for their interpretation of the Sabbath as a sacrament of communion with the creator of the world and of human beings "as male and female" (vv. 26–27).

The word *racheph* alludes not to brooding, as traditional interpreters have mistakenly believed, but rather to nurturing toward adulthood, teaching the young how to fly by themselves and to become mature.

The familiar phrases in which it was told that the children of God take refuge in the shadow of his wings (Pss. 17:8; 36:7 [Heb. 8]; 57:1 [Heb. 2]; 61:4 [Heb. 5]; 63:7 [Heb. 8]; 91:4) should not distract from the dynamic meaning of the mother-bird imagery. In the Wisdom account of creation (Gen. 1:1—2:4a), it is the Spirit of God (a feminine word) that "flutters," *(racheph),* over the face of the abyssal waters (Gen. 1:2). Among the early Christians, the Spirit of God was still represented "in bodily form, as a dove" (Matt. 3:16; Mark 1:10; Luke 3:22).

In the lament over Jerusalem, the attempt to gather the children as a mother bird gathers her little ones together has a threefold purpose: to bring out of danger toward an effectual refuge, to create the social harmony that is the cement of a genuine community, and finally, to stir up and energize for action.

The children of Jerusalem, "the city that kills the prophets . . . would not" be gathered (Matt. 23:37). If this saying goes back to the earliest levels of the gospel tradition, it shows that Jesus, on the one hand, conceived of fatherhood under the imagery of motherhood, and on the other hand, would not separate his faith in a maternal-paternal God from the awful reality of his children's rebellion. Jesus may even have gone a step further when he implied in this lament over Jerusalem an identification between himself and the prophets, on the one side, and, on the other, compared himself to a mother bird who fails.

As Paul Ricoeur has pointed out in his essay "Fatherhood, from Phantasm to Symbol," Hegel spoke of "the religious representation" as the figurative form of the self-manifestation of the Absolute. A "manifestation" inevitably modifies "the Absolute" through self-imposed limitations within historical relativity.

God as Father is no longer simply a transcendent deity, who exercises his lofty power and remains detached from the weaknesses and the tragedies of the human condition. God is the self-offering Spirit, who shares in the suffering and even in the death of humanity. The impending death of Jesus prefigures the true fatherhood of God, a God who immolates himself for the sake of his children.

The apostle Paul accurately translated the teaching of Jesus on divine fatherhood as he wrote:

> When we cry *Abba,* Father, it is the Spirit himself who bears witness to our spirit that we are children of God. (Rom. 8:15b–16)

To call God "Father" is to recognize his sovereignty in weakness, never in the sense of tyranny but always in that of identification.

In praying to "Our Father," the disciples of Jesus, like Paul, "share in the agonies of Christ." Women as well as men become the children of the Most High. The acceptance of their filiation becomes the secret of their emancipation.

How, then, could the theologians of the early church, Paul at their head, hesitate as they did on the issue of sexual equality, and indulge in equivocations and ambiguities that have plagued the church to this day?

Chapter 9

Men and Women
in the Infant Church

Women played a prominent part in the birth of Christianity. Had not Jesus reversed the trend of ritual discrimination among his female and male followers? Was it not a woman, Mary Magdalene, who had rallied his disheartened disciples after the crucifixion? Yet, it was the men who eventually assumed administrative, sacramental, and teaching authority in the growing church.

Sociological structures of male domination in the synagogues of Palestine and the Diaspora strongly militated against women in the life of the early Christian communities. In most instances, these communities arose within a synagogal environment.

At the same time, there are clear indications in the literature of early Christianity that women assumed a vital role in the spread of the gospel from Jerusalem to Asia, Greece, and Rome.

Men and Women in the
Jerusalem Church

When the Book of Acts was published, about fifty years after Pentecost, the word "apostle" had already acquired a technical sense that soon received an aura of sanctity. *Apostolos* originally meant "envoy" or "mouthpiece," "someone sent" to speak for another. Jesus belonged to a group of religious eschatologists who were brought up on the popular apocalypses, from Daniel to Enoch. He expected that the kingdom of God would soon put the horrors of the present world to an end, and he knew that time was short.

The views that Jesus held on the quality of God's advent were not, however, in the least militaristic and nationalistic. His concept of the kingdom was in sharp conflict with the notions entertained by the majority of his fellow Jews. On account of both the urgency of time and the fact that his people misunderstood the nature of God's kingdom, he sent his close friends ahead of him on the roads of Galilee, Samaria, and Judea to spread the "good news" of genuine liberation—not from Rome but from sinfulness. The oral tradition of the early church, which soon became Greek-speaking, called these envoys *apostoloi*. In view of the Jewish mores, Jesus could not have sent women envoys with the men of his inner circle. Moreover, the literary evidence in the Gospels, the Book of Acts, and the letters of Paul shows that Jesus did not have in mind an apostolic college, endowed with a hierarchic status, confined to twelve males who would transmit a hieratic, pseudo-magical power to successors through some ritual gesture. The idea of male apostolic succession represents an anachronistic delusion of a later age.

When the Lukan editor of the Book of Acts described the earliest Christian community in Jerusalem after the ascension, the disciples who had surrounded Jesus during his ministry and who had come back together again through their faith in his resurrection were known as the apostles. The Lukan editor carefully gave their names (Acts 1:13) and reported the first speech of Peter to his "brothers" (vv. 15–22). Yet, between these two details, he inserted an astonishing observation:

> All of these with one accord devoted themselves to prayer, together with the women, and Mary the mother of Jesus, and with his brothers. (Acts 1:14)

"The women" were obviously those who had followed Jesus on the roads of Galilee during his ministry. The mention of "Mary the mother of Jesus" and "his brothers" is entirely unexpected.

The Synoptics as well as the Fourth Gospel suggest that Jesus maintained a distance between his family and himself. It was no doubt on account of the shortness of time before the end of the world that he urged his followers to forego their obligations of filial loyalty in favor of a new allegiance to God.

One of his would-be disciples hesitated in the face of this demand. To that man Jesus said: "Let the dead bury their dead, but go thou and publish abroad the kingdom of God!" (Luke 9:60). In reaction to the principle of patriarchal loyalty, Jesus spoke of God as the true Father. In effect, he was opposing the belief in the chosen race. The fathers passed into second place. At times, he even expressed this drastic reevaluation in the style of Oriental hyperbole: "If any man comes to me and does not hate his own father and mother, and wife and children, and brothers and sisters, yea, his own life also, he cannot be my disciple" (Luke 14:26; cf. Matt. 10:37–38). In Hebrew and other Semitic languages, the verb "to hate" could be used to express a comparison in priorities rather than to indicate a blunt antithesis to love.

The story of Jesus at the age of twelve, reported in Luke 2:41–51, and the scene of the wedding at Cana, found in John 2:1–11, indirectly confirm this attitude.

In the former story, the boy Jesus had stayed behind instead of returning home to Nazareth with his parents. When at last they found him in the temple, his mother said: "Son, why hast thou thus dealt with us? Behold, thy father and I sought thee sorrowing." But he replied: "How is it that you sought me? Knew you not that I must be in my Father's house?" (Luke 2:48–49).

In the scene at Cana, Mary shows her pride in her already famous son as they both attend a wedding party. She apparently tried to force his hand at performing wonders, and her expectations were in the end vindicated. Nevertheless, at first he rebuked her, saying, "Woman, what hast thou to do with me? My hour has not yet come!" (John 2:4). While this reply did not indicate a lack of respect, its tone was somewhat stern and perhaps even abrupt. The Aramaic idiom behind the Greek translation suggests an attitude of noncooperation.

Some early Christian traditions did not represent Jesus as a typical Jewish son. His reverence for his father and mother did not take precedence over his devotion to the Sovereign Lord he called Father. His total gift to the God of universal tenderness led him to place human bonds, even the closest, on the level of relativity.

Entirely congruent with this understanding was the "hard" saying of Jesus that Luke alone preserved:

A certain woman out of the multitude lifted up her voice, and said to him, Blessed is the womb that bare thee and the breasts which thou didst suck. But he said, Yea, rather, blessed are they that hear the word of God, and keep it. (Luke 11:27–28)

The woman's exclamation gave Jesus an opportunity to affirm the greatness of his mother. Unawares, this woman was initiating an ideological trend that eventually led to a full-blown Mariology. Jesus, on the contrary, seized the occasion to stress the primacy of prophetic religion and to declare anew the duty of a white-hot dedication to the Word of God. He may also have detected in the woman's outburst a sentimental tribute to his own personality. True to his self-effacing habit, he immediately reversed the direction of the remark and used it to call attention not to himself but to the demands of his gospel.

In view of the comparative detachment that Jesus exhibited toward his mother and the other members of his family, it is significant that the editor of the Book of Acts pointedly mentioned not only "the women" but also "Mary the mother of Jesus" in his notice concerning the earliest Jerusalem church. It was not, however, on the part of the Lukan editor the sign of an early tendency to exalt the figure of Mary. Rather, this detail corresponds to the healthy attitude that, throughout the two volumes of his opus, the writer traditionally known as Luke maintained toward women in general.

The Magnificat and Radical Feminism

History and literature have shown for a long time, and depth psychology has lately confirmed, that misogyny in its various manifestations, including the puffing of the male ego, has led men to look at women either as goddesses or whores but not as real persons on a footing of equal partnership and complementariness. The male fear of woman is probably responsible for the patriarchal systems that entailed her oppression or submission. This fear may also explain the male tendency to reject her and to place her outside of "decent" society, either as mere instrument of male lust or, on the contrary, as ideal figure of inaccessibility and adoration, untainted by familiarity or abuse—the ever-virgin and the mother-sister. This paradoxical dichotomy in man's unconscious notion of womanhood has played a part in the growth of the cult of Mary as the new Eve, in both the Eastern and the Western churches.

The author of the Lukan Gospel is not in the slightest a victim of this syndrome of female opposites. More than any other evangelist, he shows his interest in authentic womanhood and he does so in sympathetic and balanced terms, beginning with the infancy narrative.

The Lukan story of the annunciation and nativity differs markedly from that of Matthew. The latter concentrates attention on the figure of Joseph, while the former places Mary in the center of the entire picture of the nativity and infancy. This characteristic conforms to the special concern for women in the rest of Luke's Gospel and also in the Book of Acts. In each volume of this single work a constant stress is laid upon the downtrodden members of society—the pagans, the poor, and women.

While Luke was ostensibly engaged in describing the birth of Jesus, he offered incidentally a sketch of Mary, the first daughter of the church. He did so with an exquisite delicacy and an emotional restraint not excelled elsewhere in the early Christian literature.

The salient features of Mary's portrait are hinted at throughout Luke's narrative of the infancy, but they all converge in the Magnificat (Luke 1:46–55). This short poem is couched in the form of an ancient psalm. It articulates its various themes in such a way as to show the vocation of a woman in the whole context of the *magnalia Dei*, the grand opera of God in history. The context in which it is now placed confers on the strictly Hebraic character of its theme a new meaning: the Magnificat becomes a programmatic model of true woman, from handmaid of the Lord to mother of sorrows, who keeps the faith and brings together adoration and action.

Originally composed in Hebrew within the Jewish sect of "the Poor Ones," *Ebionim* or *'Anawim*, the Magnificat was translated orally into Greek when the church moved abroad from Palestine. Together with the other canticles that are now found in the Lukan narrative of the infancy, it was sung in assemblies at worship, and all of them became part of the Christian liturgy: the Ave Maria (Luke 1:28), the Benedictus (1:67–79), the Gloria in Excelsis (2:13–14), the Nunc Dimittis (2:29–32). Among these, the Magnificat is placed on the lips of a woman.

The poet revealed an intimate knowledge of the Hebrew Bible. He quoted from it or alluded to it twenty-four times in only nine *bicola* (double poetic lines). If, for the purpose of analysis, the Greek text is hypothetically translated into Hebrew, its poetic structure and technique stand out. One discovers in it the symmetry of parallel motifs, the assonances of both consonantal and vocalic sounds, an inner rhythm and a strophic division underlining the movement as well as the growth of its main themes. The Magnificat ranks with the Song of Songs and the poem on "Wisdom at Play" as a masterpiece of lyrical poetry. It would be no accident that these pieces might well have been composed by women. In addition, the Magnificat should be considered as an entire Biblical theology in miniature, viewed from the perspective of a woman.

i

46. My whole being celebrates the grandeur of the Lord,
47.   And my spirit thrills in God my salvation.
48. Because he has looked upon the lowliness of his woman-slave,
      Behold! on this account, all generations shall proclaim my happiness.

ii

49. For the divine hero has done for me great deeds:
      And his name is the Holy One,
50. And his womblike compassion shall be
      From generation to generation toward those who fear him.

iii

51. He has acted out the power of his arm,
      Dispersed the proud into the imagination of their heart,
52. Deposed the potentates from their thrones,
      And exalted the humble.
53. He has filled the hungry with good things,
      And the rich he has dismissed empty-handed.

iv

54. He has upheld his slave boy Israel
      In remembrance of his womblike compassion,
55. As he spoke to our fathers,
      Abraham, and his seed forever.

Detached from its Lukan context and taken as an isolated unit, the Magnificat is entirely true to its Hebraic heritage. It is reminiscent of several hymns, such as the Song of Hannah (1 Sam. 2:1–10) and other poems (e.g., Ps. 35:9), especially the oracles of Second Isaiah (Isa. 41:8–9). As a section in the narrative of the infancy, it assumes a fresh meaning, with a series of theological themes moving from the joy of a young Madonna to the sorrows of a Mater Dolorosa.

The poem falls into four strophes of two bicola each (two double lines) except for the third strophe, which is expanded to three bicola (three double lines). This was obviously a device to show the passion of the singer for social justice, and the intensity of her call for the final revolution.

The first strophe is concerned with praise from the woman-slave of the Lord; the second hints at the theological complex of power and mercy; the third envisions the consequences of this convergence at the end of the world, introducing at the threshold of the nativity the ancient motif of the boy-slave of the Lord.

Thus the whole song progresses from the motif of God to that of Jesus through a theological reflection upon the mission of Israel toward the nations of the world. As in the ancient pieces of the Psalter, the Hebraic aesthetics of singing lend a vehicle to genuine spirituality.

Because the poem is tightly composed, we may expect a priori not only that the key words be strategically situated but also that some of them be repeated in such a way that a new semantic environment will confer upon them an amplified meaning.

In the first strophe, the verb *magnificat*—in Greek, *megalunei*; in Hebrew, *giddelah*—does not mean "magnifies." A human being cannot aggrandize the grandeur of God. The Hebrew verb refers to a liturgical act that exteriorizes feeling in musical and choreographic gesture. Mary *celebrates*. It is not her soul but her "whole being" that is the agent of this celebration. She fleshes out the greatness of God. The Hebrew word *nephesh* designates the totality of the human being in the flesh.

The celebration of divine greatness is echoed and explicated by the second strophe, "Because he has done great things for me" (v. 49a). The poet uses the expression of Israel's creedal traditions, *gedolot*, "great things." This word designates in ancient psalmody the intervention of God in history, the deliverance from Egypt, the foundation of the covenant, the disclosure of Israel's mission to mankind. But this use, which summons up a theological understanding of worldwide history, is soon individualized as it is related to the personality of the singer. The great things of history, the *magnalia Dei*, he has made for *me*, the woman-slave. The great things are no longer the mighty events, the *opus Dei*, the grand opera of the past, epitomized in the phrase often repeated by Israel in the rehearsal of her national memories: "He has delivered us from the house of slaves." Now the great things of history have become invisible and secret. God seems to be powerless in the face of the tyrants of the world, but his power is revealed to those who know how to discern it. "He has looked upon the lowliness of his woman-slave." Since the destruction of the temple, the rape of the land, the exile in Babylon, Israel's faith finds its fruition in the mystery of the man-slave of the Lord, in anticipation of the fourth and final strophe, which declares the sacrality of the future.

The first strophe had already indicated that God is God because he acts in the hidden events of this world. "He has looked upon the humility of his slave-woman." This is particularly a woman's insight, which receives its expression also at the end of the story of the nativity: "And Mary kept all these things, pondering them in her heart" (Luke 2:19).

God now appears to be absent from history. The basis of human faith is no longer the exodus but the cross, and the cross is contained in the mystery of the annunciation. The tragedy of Israel is a *theologia crucis*, a theology of the cross. Israel, the slave of the Lord, now becomes Jesus, the slave boy of the Lord.

Thus it is with her whole being that Mary extols in music and poetry the paradox of Israel's faith. "My soul," in Hebrew, *naphshi*, is far from suggesting the pure and immortal *psychē*, as in Hellenistic philosophy. It is not an ethereal element opposed to an impure flesh. That form of anthropological dualism still poisons our language. On the contrary, the Hebrew *nephesh* designates the fullness of the self, the *erōs*, the drive to extend the self to the utmost, the organic intermingling of what we mistakenly call body and soul, the "psychosomatic" oneness (as we have come to say, using two words to coin a unity). Mary praises God with her flesh alive, her flesh leaping with new life, her womb quickened with the child. Her soul means also her sexual body. The totality of her human reality celebrates in sacramental fashion the grandeur of God. Most white Anglo-Saxon Protestants have lost this knowledge. It is thoroughly Hebrew and Christian to speak of soul food, of soul faith, in the sense of a gut-religion that captures one through and through.

At the same time, the parallelism of the poetic line that follows brings a qualification to the first motif, "And my spirit thrills in God my salvation" (v. 47). Mary sings in the name of the whole of humanity. As the Second Council of the Vatican came to admit, against the Mariological fancy of Pius XII in 1954, Mary is not a figure of theology properly speaking, although this is what some ecclesiastical folklorists, still dreaming of the Middle Ages, continue to maintain in our time. Nor does her presence change the Trinity into a Quaternity, as C. G. Jung naively proposed. Mary is the forerunner of the church, and the church is the people of God. She is the symbol of humankind in process of being saved. She is not in any way the mediatrix of salvation but its first recipient. Like the ancient prophets, she exults in the awareness of her vocation. She jubilates, she gasps, she breathes out ecstasy, she shrieks out her faith.

From the universal church, the singer passes to the intimacy of religious selfhood. Religion flowers in solitariness, even while it eventually becomes a social phenomenon, because it always must express itself through the millenniums of time and the millions of the redeemed. Faith is solitary, but it must transmit itself to others. It becomes social, even collective, when it becomes belief.

Mary is now confiding her secret. She is a prophetess daring to share her intimate jewel. "My spirit thrills!" The word *ruach*, "spirit," refers to a force that overwhelms. It is the breath of the storm. Although the Hebrew word is in the feminine gender, the spirit is comparable to the bull as it jumps in procreative fury. It is a word with a dangerous meaning, designating an ambiguous reality. The singer applies it to herself in a reticent allusion to her private awareness of the annunciation. The angel Gabriel had said to her that the spirit would "come in unto" her and would "overshadow" her (Luke 1:35). The Hebrew word that stands behind the Greek *episkiasei* recalls the "thick darkness," *'araphel* of God's presence on Mount Sinai and also the total obscurity, symbol of his presence, in the innermost room of the Jerusalem sanctuary.

The verb "exults" renders the Hebrew *gîl.* It implies the shriek of delight that may be caused by the intensity of an arrest in the stream of consciousness. Such an arrest may take place in the whirl of a dance, in sexual ecstasy, or especially, in mystical trance, which is its spiritual sublimation. It is the primal scream, the shriek at the propinquity of the ultimate, either of the void or of the godhead.

The theme of exultation must not, however, be confused with that of mystical escape. The singer is not a victim of glossolalia. She expresses herself in sophisticated forms of the rhetorical art. Neither does she support any view of pantheistic identification between infinity and human finiteness. The distinction between object and subject is maintained by the very stress upon her sense of communion with the author of her salvation. Communion with God is not unification with divinity. Religious union is different from mystical identification. Mary exults not in self-loss within the divine but in communion with the God of her liberation. She gives her assent to a theology of history that links forever Christianity to Hebraism.

The first strophe ends with the explosive and all-inclusive invitation: "Behold! On this account, all generations will acknowledge, will proclaim in their own lives, the ongoingness of my well-being" (v. 48b). Such a rendering is admittedly prosaic and didactic. The Hebrew verb concealed behind the Greek *makariousin me* is *ye'ashsheruni.* It comes from a root that does not mean "to give a blessing," "to bless," but instead signifies "to go forward," "to race toward a goal," "to look ahead," and "to lead the way." The notion of "beatitude" represents the culture of Latinity. It implies the passive participle *baruk,* "blessed." On the contrary, the verb used in the Magnificat is that of the wisdom literature and also, incidentally, that of the misnamed "beatitudes" in the Sermon on the Mount. The idea is not static but dynamic. It evokes purposiveness, a moving into becoming. Happiness in Hebraic thought-forms is never individualistic. It is spreading and catching. Happiness is an epidemic of élan vital. One is not happy alone. One cannot be happy unless one makes others happy. For such a powerful reality the word "blessed" is obviously inadequate.

Mary sings, "Behold!" Henceforth, on account of this incredible event, the conception of a child in the humility of service—a willing slavery to the divine goal, the servitude of total adoration—all future generations of mankind will extend, prolong, continue, fertilize, and fructify my happiness! They will, like me, step forward into the unknown territory of time, with the certain vision of the ultimate victory of good over evil. They will participate in my happiness by fulfilling it, by broadening it, by making it immensely real, by fulfilling the call of Israel. In the theology of Second Isaiah, the mission of Israel is to be "a light to the nations, even unto the ends of the earth."

The language of the early Christians at worship borrowed from the poetic idiom of the Psalms and the Prophets. Singing for the church, the mother of Jesus is the model missionary, the model evangelist, the model envoy, the apostle. She is the symbol of the daughter of Zion, delivered from the real-estate complex implicit in the myth of the earth-navel *(omphalos)*. She is freed from the cultic syndrome of a geographical center, which inevitably leads to ethnic exclusivism, whether that of Zion or of Delphi. She inherits the obligation of Israel to be a light to the nations. She inaugurates the universality of the new Jerusalem. She explodes the ritual sectarianism that maintains the myth of a chosen Zion. Mary's womb is the new tabernacle of the desert, not Sinaitic but worldwide, the "thick darkness" of the old innermost room, the earth-wide Holy of Holies. She preaches the ideology of the new temple not built by human hands. In this womb the embryo receives the flow of blood through Mary's own heartbeat. The woman-slave of the Lord, in her humility, has already become the universal family of God.

In the second strophe, God is named *Hag-geber,* "the Potent Man," almost "the Hero." This is an ancient word akin to the name of the angel Gabriel, "God is the Potent One." The Lukan context calls attention to the scene of the annunciation immediately preceding the Magnificat. God's summons may be demanding, but the God who calls is also the God who honors his commitment to his envoys from generation to generation. "And his womblike compassion endures from generation to generation" (v. 50a). The Latin word *misericordia,* from which the English "mercy" is derived, means "an open and destitute heart." It attempts to render the Greek *eleos,* and it is better than the English approximate equivalent of "loyalty" or even the Elizabethan improvisation, "lovingkindness." It stands for a Hebrew term that defies translation. While the Greek *eleos* usually corresponds to the Hebrew *chesed,* which means "covenant loyalty and fidelity," it also reflects the synonyms *chen,* "grace," and *rachmim,* "compassion," which point to the thought-form of divine motherhood. The word *rachmim* stands for the plural of majesty (actually, the superlative) of *rechem,* "uterus." In the language of the Psalms and the Prophets, it means love without restriction or qualification, the longing of the womb for the child it had once carried.

The Hebrew language boldly ascribes the human experience of motherhood to the psychology of God. It compares the deity to a mother who cannot forget the child she has borne. *Kyrie eleison!* "Lord, have mercy!" This phrase is derived from the cry of despair and yet of hope in Psalm 51, where a criminal begs forgiveness and thus appeals to the divine *misericordia.* It also implies the awareness of the universality of human sinfulness. The psalmist and the prophets have sensed that the seat of the human will is desperately wicked (Jer. 17:9). There is no trace of anthropological optimism in the traditions on the patriarchs, for those men are shown to have been liars, thieves, and self-seeking upstarts. Moses, Isaiah, Jeremiah, the Jobian poet, the psalmists and Jesus himself (Mark 10:18; Matt. 16:4) never entertained any illusion concerning the so-called innate goodness of man. Jean-Jacques Rousseau and John Dewey had not yet been born.

Israel, the people of God, ahead of the church, was a common-variety whore. Its dream became a nightmare. The horror of the exile in Babylon had not washed the blood from its hands. *Kyrie eleison!* This is the cry that Mary utters, and it can be heard behind her faith in the *misericordia* of God. It is an appeal to the love of God as the gift of the divine self. It describes strength under the appearance of powerlessness.

The God of Israel never gives up. Deceived and abandoned by his own people, he is put on trial, as in the dramatic trope used by the prophet Micah. There, the Lord is no longer the judge. He has become the defendant, and he asks, "O my people! My people! What have I done against you? . . . Testify against me!" (Mic. 6:3).

Divine pathos culminates in the dance of the sword, which Ezekiel dances as a dance of death or perhaps as a dance that ends in a simulacrum of self-emasculation (Ezek. 21:8–17 [Heb. 13:22]). It also appears in the dirge of the Suffering Servant, beaten to death as the *Agnus Dei,* the Lamb of God (Isa. 52:13—53:12).

One can then understand the Hebraic meaning of fear, so closely breathed after the faith in the *misericordia.* This is not the fear of judgment or of death. It is the fear of adding to the pathos of God. The loyalty of the long-suffering God extends over the passing of time, from generation to generation, for those who fear him because they love him. The fear of God, in Hebraic and Christian theology, comes from apprehensiveness at the prospect of falling short of the divine lover's expectations. It is the anguish of inadequacy before the *misericordia Dei.* It is not the fear of judgment but the fear of love.

The third strophe introduces into Christianity the prophets' passion for social justice and their theological critique of any political system, within Israel or abroad among the nations, that favors the rich at the expense of the poor. The poet is fully aware of Israel's tragedy. The sons and daughters of the liberated slaves have been in their turn enslaving or oppressing brothers and sisters. Mary, like Hannah, is presented as the mother of revolution. In time, the God of the wilderness will "lift the needy from the ash heap and make them sit with the princes" (1 Sam. 2:8). The psychological consequences of social irresponsibility are as devastating as the political and economic upheavals. "He has scattered the proud into the imagination of their hearts" (Luke 1:51b). The wealth accumulated by the proud is actually the symptom of their fear of death, the dread of their final annihilation. The lust to acquire is the sign of the terror of ultimate destitution. Hell is a dead end, and the void.

The fourth and last strophe introduces the Hebraic theme par excellence, which Christianity tends to forget at its own peril. Fidelity to the past should not become the conservation of a fossilized record. The promise to Abraham has teeth: "Go out . . . so that in thee . . . all the families of the earth shall seek one another's welfare" (Gen. 12:1–3). Faithfulness to Scripture is corrupted by scriptural immobilism.

"He has upheld Israel, his slave boy" (v. 54a). This phrase is inspired by Second Isaiah (41:8). Placed in the mouth of Mary, the mother of Jesus, tabernacle of the Most High, the motif of the suffering servant unites Judaism and Christianity: God suffers on Calvary and again through all the holocausts, Christian as well as Jewish, in the course of the ages. The church is the company of those who suffer and still hope for a better world. The barbarians are both without and within the gates. The seed of Abraham is an elite, not of birth but of responsibility, open to all human beings. The Magnificat proclaims the sacrality of the future, the task of the true elite against a static elitism.

Luke's theology of manhood and womanhood manifests itself in both his Gospel and the Book of Acts. At the dawn of the Jerusalem church, Mary, the mother of Jesus, was there, together with the other women who prayed with the disciples, and they waited in hope for the advent of God. The Magnificat stands in the Lukan *opus* as a charter of Christian faith for men and women of all nations. A woman is the theologian of the *Heilsgeschichte,* the history of world healing.

Men and Women in the Greco-Roman Churches

True to his indirect portrait of Mary, the model of the woman of faith, "filled with grace" (Luke 1:28), and the singer of the Magnificat, Luke proceeded to show that women as well as men took part in the growth of the infant church in Palestine and abroad. To be sure, it was a man, Peter, who took the initiative in the midst of his "brethren" (Acts 1:15). Also, the Eleven may have replaced Judas with Matthias, another man (Acts 1:23–26). Again, on the day of Pentecost, Peter's discourse was addressed to the men of Judah (Acts 2:14), and in the Jewish environment where he spoke, women were ignored. Was this, on the part of Peter, the foretaste of what eventually happened in the church of Rome some years later? Caution is required before judgment.

At the festival of *Shabu'ot,* Pentecost, in Jerusalem the audience consisted of men alone (Acts 2:5; cf. v. 14). How was it, then, that so many women soon joined the ranks of the few who had gathered in the upper room at the first hour? Was it not precisely that these few women had spread the good news of their new life by word of mouth from woman to woman, through individual contacts? At any rate, on that day, Peter quoted from the prophet Joel, who had spoken of the outpouring of the Spirit not only upon sons but also upon daughters (Acts 2:17; cf. Joel 2:28–29). As the Christian movement developed, the editor of Acts did not fail to point out that "more than ever believers were added to the Lord, a multitude of both men and women" (5:14). In view of the attitude of official Judaism toward women, who, in most cases, were not even permitted to study the Torah, the Lukan insistence must be understood as the sign of a radical reversal of tradition.

Saul of Tarsus, the fanatic Pharisee, who had been acquiescent to the stoning of Stephen, was said to have "laid waste the church," "entering house after house" in order to drag off "men and women" and to commit them to prison (8:3). In early Christian circles, no distinction of a religious nature was apparently drawn between woman and man.

Again, when Philip preached the gospel to the people of Samaria, the sequence of events is formal: "They were baptized, both men and women" (8:12). Let us picture such scenes, women being publicly baptized by immersion in a stream or in a pool, when, according to the religious mores of the time, women could not go out into the streets without a veil. Once more, the story continues, Saul, "yet breathing threatenings and slaughter against the disciples of the Lord," went to see the high priest and obtained letters for the Damascus synagogues so that "if he found there any of the Way, whether men or women, he might bring them to Jerusalem in chains" (9:1–2).

Meanwhile, at the harbor of Joppa, a certain Tabitha, that is to say in Greek, Dorcas, "Gazelle," remained in the memory of a later generation as a woman "full of good works and acts of love" (v. 36).

When the new faith penetrated Europe, Paul and his attending staff remained some days at Philippi, the leading city of Macedonia. The travel diary used in the Book of Acts states forthrightly, "We went outside the city gate, by the riverside . . . and spoke to the women who had come together" (16:13). One of these was Lydia of Thyatira, a business executive, who conducted an international trade in purple dyes and presumably also in dyed wools and textiles. Her commercial firm was prosperous, supplying several provinces of the Roman Empire. It is significant that the first church in Europe met in the house of a woman, was supported by a woman, and may even have been initially constituted entirely of women. Of Lydia, the Book of Acts offers this concrete detail: "The Lord opened her heart to give heed to what was said by Paul. And when she was baptized, with her household, she besought us, saying, 'If you have judged me to be faithful to the Lord, come to my house and stay.' And she prevailed upon us" (16:14b–15).

When Paul and his companions were jailed and eventually released, it was again in the house of Lydia that they found the shelter of a home (16:40). If Lydia took the risk of extending her hospitality to people who had just been in jail, and thus remained suspect in the eyes of the police, she was indeed a woman of uncommon fortitude and character.

In the large city of Thessalonica Paul and Silas spent three weeks, and the travel diarist stressed once more the importance of women in the earliest congregation of Greece. He referred not only to women but to "leading women," ladies of social standing, who were the cultural pillars of the city (17:4).

The witness reports similarly that among the members of the church in Beroea there were "not a few women of high standing *(euschēmonōn)* as well as men" (17:12). In Athens, Paul's discourse on Mars Hill aroused the skepticism of philosophers. "But some men joined him and believed, among them Dionysius the Areopagite and a woman named Damaris and others with them" (17:34). Damaris was apparently well known in the church at large, for the writer singles her out by name.

In several of his letters Paul sent greetings to the Christians of the various churches to which he wrote, and he always included the men and the women he knew, mentioning them by name. For example, he wanted to send special salutations to Prisca and Aquila, also to Epaenetus, whom he called "my beloved . . . the first convert in Asia for Christ," and a certain Mary, otherwise not identified, except that she had "worked hard" in the Roman congregation. After the names of several men, Paul listed Tryphaena and Tryphosa, the beloved Persis, Julia, Nereus and his sister, whose name the apostle could perhaps not recall, and also Olympas (Rom. 16:1–16). To these should be added Rufus and his mother, also anonymous, whom Paul considered his spiritual mother (16:13). In his letter to the church of Philippi, he named Euodia and Syntyche, two women who must have caused dissension by their opposing views and whom he entreated to reach agreement. He included them lovingly in his high commendation, together with Clement and other co-workers, "whose names," he wrote, "are in the book of life" (Phil. 4:1–3).

One should not forget Nympha, who received the church of Laodicea "in her house" (Col. 4:15). The major manuscripts read "in his house," apparently because the Christian copyists of another age considered Nympha to be a man. However, the reading "her," which is found in minor manuscripts, must have been originally correct, since it could scarcely be explained as the result of an emendation or even of an accidental error committed by monastic scribes in a later age, when misogyny prevailed among copyists of Scripture.

The various comments of Paul on his friends, both men and women, show beyond doubt that he did not insinuate or imply any discrimination against women who occupied responsible positions within the churches they served.

Women Ministers and Apostles

The names of three women mentioned in the list now placed in the manuscripts of the Letter to the Romans deserve further attention. They are Phoebe, Junias, and Prisca, or Priscilla.

The first woman was a *diakonos* of the church at Cenchreae, near Corinth (Rom. 16:1). Most translators call her "a deaconess," but there is no evidence whatever that the ecclesiastical order of deacon or deaconess existed in the middle of the first century A.D. The secular meaning of the Greek word *diakonos* is "servant" or "messenger." It is thus used in Aeschylus, Sophocles, Herodotus, and Clitarchus, as among other writers of the classical Hellenic and Hellenistic periods. In the context of the young church of Jesus Christ, a *diakonos* seems to have been a "minister," man or woman.[30] This is what Paul wrote: "I commend unto you our sister Phoebe, a minister of the church at Cenchreae, that you may receive her in the Lord as it becomes the saints, and that you assist her in whatsoever business she has need of you" (16:1–2).

Of course, if the word *diakonos* does not mean "deaconess" in the institutional sense of the term as in a later age, neither does it refer to a "minister" of the modern Protestant kind, as the English usage of the word suggests. Both interpretations would be equally anachronistic.

At the same time, no precise function, of a hierarchic type, may be ascribed to this word in the earliest generations. Paul designated himself, as well as his co-workers, as a *diakonos* of the gospel, of the new covenant, or simply of Christ. He referred to his work in the church as a *diakonia*, a "ministry" or "service" (Rom. 11:13; 1 Cor. 3:5; 2 Cor. 3:4–6). The meaning of the word was apparently flexible and inclusive, as when Paul, speaking of Stephanas and his household, declares that "they have placed themselves devotedly in the service *(diakonia)* of the saints" (1 Cor. 16:15). He had in mind, quite clearly, both the service of God and the service of the congregation.

It seems, however, that Phoebe exercised a specific "ministry" in the Cenchreae church. She was not solely attending to human welfare. She was also a "servant" of God. Still more extraordinary, she was a *prostatis* of many as well as of Paul. Jerome spoke of her as an assistant! Hence, the modern English versions that identify Phoebe as a helper. This constitutes a mistranslation.

Phoebe was a helper in the sense that the woman in the Yahwist story of creation was a helper for man. As it has been seen above, the Hebrew word *'ozer,* used for the woman in the earlier Genesis myth (Gen. 2:18), meant a rescuer or a succorer of man in his situation of existential extremity. While the word *prostatis* employed by Paul is different from the term *boēthos,* which the Septuagint manuscripts favored for the famous phrase in Genesis, the two Greek nouns are synonymous. A *boēthos* is a warrior who comes to succor another warrior at the utmost crisis of impending death in combat. It is someone who responds to the pathetic cry of "Help! Help!" This sense is well attested in the Hellenic and Hellenistic literatures from Homer to Herodotus, Thucydides, and Xenophon. Likewise, the word *prostatēs* (feminine, *prostatis*) designates some fighter in the thick of battle who courageously "steps forward" to stand in front of a fellow soldier in peril. Phoebe is hailed by Paul as a defender, a protector, who risked her own life in his behalf and for the sake of other Christians in Corinth or its vicinity. Doubtless, like Mary, the mother of John-Mark in Jerusalem (Acts 12:12), like Lydia in Philippi (16:14–15), Nympha in Laodicea (Col. 4:15), and Stephanas in the province of Achaia (1 Cor. 16:15), Phoebe opened her house for the visiting missionaries as well as for the disciples who resided in her town. She gave them both material and religious support. She was a *[diakonos] tēs ecclēsias tēs en Kegchreais,* "a minister of the church which is in Cenchreae," but she did immensely more. In a time of crisis, she saved the lives of Paul and his companions at the risk of her own.[31]

The word *diakonos,* describing Phoebe, was a title that implied a specific function, for it is preceded by the Greek verb "to be" in the present participle, which indicates identification (cf. variations of this syntactic use in John 10:12; 11:49; Acts 18:12).

Just as the word *presbuteros* at that time meant not "priest" but "elder," and the word *episkopos* not "bishop" but "treasurer," "overseer of the funds," so also the word *diakonos* did not mean "deacon" or "deaconess" but "minister," without hierarchical implications.

The second woman in the list of Paul's greetings is Junias. The sentence is exceptional, for Paul writes merely, "Greet Andronikos and Junias, my relatives and my co-prisoners, who are of note among the apostles, who also were in Christ before me" (Rom. 16:7). The gender of the name "Junias" has for a long time been the object of discussion. Many interpreters have admitted that the name was usually feminine but they judged that it here designated a man, probably on account of the masculine gender of the words "relatives," "co-prisoners," and "apostles." Thus, the Revised Standard Version insists that it was a man's name, probably understanding "Junias" as a diminutive of "Junianus," an unambiguously wrong reading. "Greet Andronicus and Junias, my kins*men* and my fellow prisoners; they are *men* of note among the apostles" (italics added). The word "men" is absent from the Greek original, and the masculine gender simply covers both sexes in accordance with common Greek usage.

That Junias, a woman, would be ranked by Paul among "the apostles" is not strange, a priori. The word *apostolos* for Paul participated in the semantic flexibility that it had in the Gospel tradition, where it merely meant "envoys." Paul claimed to be "apostle to the Gentiles." He, of course, did not belong to the original Twelve. He used the term in more than one sense, for he included among the apostles not only himself but also James, the brother of Jesus (1 Cor. 15:7; Gal. 1:19), and possibly also Barnabas (1 Cor. 9:6). Further, he believed that there were "false apostles" (2 Cor. 11:13; 12:11). Such a language unquestionably shows that he applied the term to those who wrongly presumed that they had received of the Lord Christ the vocation to preach the gospel. On the basis of the available evidence, one may say that he never thought of an apostolic college and even less did he conceive of an apostolic succession.

To be an apostle, for Paul, was to possess a charism that was at the highest level of service or ministry *(diakonia)* in the church (1 Cor. 12:28; cf. Eph. 4:11). This does not mean, however, that he considered apostleship the supreme ontological status, at the top of an ecclesiastical hierarchy—a hierarchy that did not yet exist. To hold a contrary opinion is, again, to commit the error of anachronism.

Just as Andronicus, a man, so Junias, a woman, had been converted to the new faith before Paul. They were evangelists of the first hour of the church. Paul salutes both of them without the slightest hint of sexual discrimination.

Prisca is the third name in the list. She requires special treatment, for she was probably a revered teacher in the church and may have been, with the collaboration of Aquila, her husband, the author of the anonymous book called simply "To the Hebrews."

Before we examine the part played by Prisca in the life of the infant church and possibly later in that of the second generation of Christendom, it will be necessary to consider the views of Paul on liberated humanity.

Chapter 10

Paul on Human Liberation

It is chiefly on account of statements from the apostle Paul that male ecclesiastics and theologians throughout the centuries have found a justification for keeping woman submissive at home and silent in church. Today, women are still excluded from the priesthood in the Greek, Roman, and other denominations of Christendom. Until recently, they were not ordained to the Protestant ministry. Even in parishes where the feminine pastorate is officially endorsed, women pastors are not readily acceptable to many members of individual congregations.

Contemporary studies of Paul's theology usually ascribe his ambiguities about the role of women in church to his Pharisaic training. His presumed celibacy is often held to be a symptom of temperamental or cultural misogyny. It is quite possible that on the subject of women the former Saul of Tarsus was only a half-liberated Jew. Nevertheless, his comments dealing with the entire realm of sexuality require scrutiny. Were these comments viewed by Paul himself as universal and perennial principles of morality? Or were they dictated by the concrete and specific situations in the churches to which he was writing, so that they were historically conditioned? These questions do not command ready and obvious answers.

Was Paul a Celibate?

It has often been maintained that Paul was a celibate, but this opinion is by no means certain, nor was it unanimous even during the patristic age, which increasingly praised virginity and celibacy at the expense of marriage. Clement of Alexandria (*Stromata* III.32–33; cf. VI.3) thought that Paul referred to his own wife when he sent greetings to the "dear companion of the same yoke" or "dear yoke-mate" (Phil. 4:3). Eusebius of Caesarea agreed that the apostle was married since he went so far as to comment: "It was not for an advantageous contribution to his own ministry that Paul took his wife with him [on his travels]" (*Ecclesiastical History* III.30).

In one of his letters to the Christians of Corinth that were prompted by recurrent crises and thus should be considered not as formal treatises of theology but as occasional writings, Paul asked pointedly and polemically:

Am I not free: Am I not an apostle? Have I not seen Jesus, our Lord? Are you not my work in the Lord? . . . Have we not the right to eat and drink? . . . Have we not the right to bring with us as wife, sister [in the faith], as other apostles do, and also the brothers of the Lord, and Cephas? Or is it only I, or Barnabas, who should not have the right to be dispensed from working? (1 Cor. 9:1–14)

The sequence of thought is not altogether clear. As it may readily be seen, Paul is writing under deep emotional stress and he refers to several issues at the same time. The rigorist party in the Corinthian parish had accused him of not being an apostle on the same level as Peter (Cephas) and the brothers of Jesus. The meaning of the phrase on "the right to eat and drink" is uncertain. Does Paul defend his freedom to eat and drink with Christians of pagan origin in violation of the Jewish law, or is he claiming the right to eat and drink at the church's expense, without working for his daily sustenance? The latter interpretation is possible, since the apostle compares himself to paid soldiers and laborers who receive wages or some other compensation (vv. 7–9). In any case, he apparently associates himself with the other apostles, who were married, and each of whom was accompanied by "a woman-sister." An *adelphē gunē* designates not a woman who would be considered a "sister," a member of an ecclesiastical order (a totally anachronistic view), but a wife of the same Christian conviction, "sister in the faith."

Paul was not a celibate. As a learned Pharisee and doctor of the law, he certainly was or had been married. Jewish men in general and religious teachers in particular always took a wife, usually doing so at the age of eighteen or twenty. In the entire literature of the rabbinical period, only one formal scholar, a certain Ben Azzai (around A.D. 100) was remembered as celibate. This fact prevented him from being ordained a rabbi. To be sure, the origins of the rabbinate remain obscure, but there is little doubt that a preliminary and somewhat fluid form of the rabbinical institution existed in the middle of the first century A.D.

Although it may be admitted that Saul of Tarsus was married before his conversion, it is possible that he had been separated from a wife who had remained Jewish, or that he was a widower. This conclusion is supported by the words: "I wish that all be as I am. To the nonmarried and to the widows I say it is good for them to remain as I am" (1 Cor. 7:8). The Greek *agamos* means not "celibate" but "no longer married." This is clearly implied by Paul's later distinction between the young woman who is not yet married (*parthenos*) and the older woman no longer married (to whom in classical and Hellenistic Greek the word *agamos* sometimes referred, instead of the more common word *anandros*).

Paul's Ideal of Marriage

Paul's high notion of marriage confirms that he knew intimately, through personal experience, the relation of love that unites husband and wife. Before one accepts the traditional interpretation according to which he allowed marriage only as an accommodation to biological needs and as a remedy for concupiscence, the most notorious passage on this subject requires special discussion. To the colorful and apparently rowdy Corinthians, who had written him questions concerning sexual conduct, he replied: "It is good for a man not to be embraced *(haptesthai)* by a woman. Against the practice of prostitution let every man have his wife and every woman her husband" (1 Cor. 7:1–2). Paul does not say that "man should not touch a woman" or that he should not "have anything to do with women," as ancient and many modern translations wrongly render this passage. Rather, he argues against venal promiscuity. He objects especially to female prostitution for men and male prostitution for women *(porneia),* either in temples or on the street. The usual English renderings of *porneia* as "fornication" or "immorality" are not supported by classical and Hellenistic secular usage.[32]

Paul then proceeds from this general principle to propose a remarkable level of sexual equality in marital union:

> The husband should give to his wife what is her due; likewise the wife to her husband. For the woman has no autonomous freedom over her own body, but the man; likewise, the man has no autonomous freedom over his own body, but the woman. (1 Cor. 7:3–4)

Paul is fully aware of the complex mutuality of love in marriage, and his attitude toward a reciprocity of rights and duties is probably without parallel in classical antiquity.

Against a male-dominated culture, in which man alone possessed the right to sexual satisfaction, the apostle proclaimed unambiguously that woman possesses exactly the same right. He has acquired the knowledge that in married love, with its lasting commitment, a woman's body belongs to her husband, yes, but also conversely. Far more extraordinarily, in contradiction to the Jewish or to the Greco-Roman culture, a man's body belongs to his wife, on a regimen of complete equality. As in the Song of Songs, where *agapē* meets *erōs*, the Pauline view is indeed far-reaching. It reveals, beyond a doubt, a personal experience of sexual delight on the part of the apostle. This delight sees in the act of love not at all the conquest of the female by the male and the more or less reluctant submission of the female to the male but, to the contrary, a double awareness of each mate's needs and desire and a double response to these needs and this desire, without distinction between the rights of each sex. The exegete is permitted to assert that Paul was deeply conscious of the give-and-take in sexual love with respect for mutuality of both sensations and feelings in one's mate. Indeed, Paul was not a celibate. He understood the reciprocity of the gift from lover to lover, without discrimination against the female sex. He concludes in exactly the same vein:

> So do not refuse each other, unless it be by mutual consent, for a limited time,

that you may be occupied in prayer; then come together again, for fear Satan may lead you into temptation by counting upon your want of self-control. (v. 5)

Paul shows himself at this point to be completely liberated from the Jewish legal proscriptions related to the impurity of sexual secretions. He says nothing of requirements either for ritual ablutions or for abstention from sexual union during the woman's period of menstruation.

At the same time, writing to the Christians of Corinth, among some of whom the sexual and religious mystery cults were the fashion, he separates sexual union from prayer. He admits that there is a time for human love and a time for divine love; they may not be confused. For the human couple, there is a time to express love and a time to refrain from the act of love. But, as an intellectual versed in the Hellenistic philosophical tradition,[33] he knows the principle of moderation in all things: *medēn agan,* "nothing too much." He fears excess, either in abstention or in lack of control. Temptation arises from excess, in one direction or the other. The word he uses, *akrasia,* is rare. It appears almost exclusively in Plato, Aristotle, and Xenophon. It indicates "weakness of character."

In addition, Paul recognizes the relativity of his advice: "But I say this only as a verdict of acquittal, not as a prescription" (v. 6). This translation represents a literal rendering of the Greek. Traditional and modern versions are entirely wrong when they translate: "I speak this by permission" (KJV) or, worse, "I say this by way of concession" (RSV and NEB).

Here again, translators have been and still are the passive victims of the Vulgate: "Hoc autem dico secundum indulgentiam." Jerome was apparently showing at this point an emotional fear of sexuality. For the Greek says: "Touto de lego kata suggnômên." The noun *suggnōmē* does not mean *indulgentia,* "permission" or "concession" (except possibly in a single passage of Aristotle (*Nicomachean Ethics.* VI.11.1), but it refers to a verdict of acquittal, of not-guilty, a pardon, or a case of legal dismissal (a *non-lieu*). The verb *suggignōskō* means primarily "to give an opinion." The exegete should always beware of the antisexual bias that unconsciously influenced Jerome and the Western translating habits to this day.

Is there not, however, in the contextual sequence, the hint of an accommodation to the biological urge in Paul's conception of marriage when he states in a passage already considered above with regard to the question of his presumed celibacy:

I say to those who are no longer married and to widows that it is good for them to remain in their condition, as I am. But if they cannot exercise self-control, let them marry. For it is better to marry than to burn. (vv. 8–9)

Most translators and commentators understand that Paul advises marriage as a better alternative than "to be aflame with passion," or "to be consumed with desire." That is not the case.

The verb *purousthai* is used metaphorically only twice in classical Greek (in Aeschylus and in the *Greek Anthology*). It never receives a psychological sense in the Septuagint, where it renders the Hebrew *ṣaraph*, "to burn." Paul alludes to the fire of the Last Judgment.

In other words, the apostle writes that marriage is better than promiscuity and, especially, than prostitution. His thinking at this juncture returns to the beginning of his reply to the Corinthians' questions on sexual morality. He does not advocate marriage as an alternative to celibacy but opposes marriage to the practice of loose morals in the metropolis of Corinth.

It is significant that Paul never justified marriage on the grounds of procreation. Like the poet of the Song of Songs, he was concerned by the ideology of happiness for the couple. The restriction he proposed was most likely due to the eschatological urgency that characterized Christianity at its birth.

The Half-liberated Legalist

Attempts to understand Paul's views of the relations between man and woman in marriage are complicated by the fact that he referred in his letters to concrete situations of localized and ephemeral history. Furthermore, he did not separate clearly the private ethics of marital love from the orderly decorum of public worship. It was in this latter area that the apostle revealed himself as an emancipated Pharisee, to be sure, but also, in some respects, as an only half-liberated legalist.

Discussing the proper attire for prayer in the church assembly, Paul was unable to ignore the problem of a distinction between the two sexes. With "traditions" on his mind (1 Cor. 11:2), he wrote to the Corinthians on another occasion:

> I wish you would remember that the head of every man is Christ, and that the head of the woman is her husband, and that the head of Christ is God. (v. 3)

As in previously noted situations, Paul was not thinking in terms of an ethical principle for all ages. He dealt with the problems of Jewish ritual that lingered within Christianity.

> Any man who prays or prophesies with his head covered dishonors his head, but any woman who prays or prophesies with her head uncovered dishonors her head: it is the same as if she had shaved her head. (vv. 4–5)

The reasons advanced probably reflect the Pharisaic exegesis of the time. "Man was not made for woman, but woman for man" is a clear allusion to the myth of the Garden (Gen. 2:21–23). Paul was arguing within an atmosphere of intense polemics raging in the Corinthian parish. Yet, he proceeded from tradition to liberation, for his final word on the subject appears to have been a corrective to his previous statements:

> For as woman was made for man, so now man is born of woman, and all creatures are from God. (v. 12)

It seems fair to state that Paul sought liberation both from Jewishness and from male sexism, but he did not quite succeed. He strove to be faithful to the theology of creation as it had been taught to him in his Pharisaic days. He could not see that in the myth of the Garden woman was actually presented as the existential deliverer of man, not as a helper in the modern sense of the word. Woman was brought to man as a figurative correspondent of the divine helper. She was created not second, but last, as the crown of the living order. Woman constituted the supreme act of creation. Pharisees did not grasp this dimension.

Biblical hermeneutics, which must preside over a biblical theology of creation, allow us, therefore—indeed, direct us—to consider as preliminary and relative, not absolute, the Pauline proposal to justify his hierarchy of beings: "The head of woman is man." His comment refers to the economy of creation as viewed by a Jew, not to the economy of grace, which, in an entirely different context, led him to declare:

> For through faith, you are all children of God in union with Christ Jesus. Baptized into union with him, you have been clothed into Christ [or, you have put on Christ]. There is neither Jew nor Greek, neither slave nor freeman, neither male nor female, but you are all one and the same in Christ Jesus. (Gal. 3:26–28)

In the Corinthians passage, Paul evidently suffered from theological immaturity. On the one hand, he had seen the fallacy of the rite of circumcision as a principle of covenantal initiation that ipso facto discriminated abusively between Jews and Greeks. On the other hand, he had not seen here what he saw later when he wrote to the Galatians, that circumcision understood as a rite of initiation into the covenant lowers the status of Jewish women vis-à-vis divine presence and divine grace (Gal. 3:28). Thus, as a still half-Jewish cultic theologian, Paul stated in Corinthians that woman is related to Christ through man.

It is possible, of course, that, facing the explosive situation in the Corinthian church, he was careful not to affront abruptly the Jewish-Christian rigorist party. He attempted to appease without antagonizing them further than necessary. More probably, he was sincerely convinced of his fidelity to tradition, although he introduced an element of balance by adding: "For just as woman was taken out of man, man comes into the world through the intermediary of woman, and all come from God" (1 Cor. 11:12).

For centuries commentators have been puzzled by the use of the word "glory" in Paul's discussion: "Man is the image [*eikōn*] and glory [*doxa*] of God, while woman is the glory of man" (v. 7). Apparently, the allusion was not to the ancient myth of the Garden but to the more recent priestly story of creation (Gen: 1:26–27).

Now, Genesis never states that man is the glory of God. Paul spoke, however, of men "who lack the glory of God," *husterountai tēs doxē tou theou*. It is not likely that he would have misquoted either the Hebrew text or the Greek version of Genesis at this point. Yet, he may have remembered the Aramaic Targum for the word "similitude, likeness" (Gen. 1:27), *be-ṣalmah kedeyuqna*, a corruption of the Greek *deigma*, which, in turn, was frequently misspelled in koinē Greek as *dogma*, "opinion," or *doxa*, "glory." According to this most likely interpretation, the idea of woman as the "glory," *doxa*, of man is unjustified, because the idea of man as the glory of God is impossible in the thinking of Paul.

The Voice of Woman in the Church

Despite its great notoriety, the statement about woman's silence in church presents a comparatively unimportant problem. Although the apostle wrote to the Corinthians, "Let women be silent in the assembly!" (1 Cor. 14:34), this peremptory command, like all the others, must be understood in the light of the concrete situation in which it was written.

The Corinthian church was peculiar. It contained eccentric men as well as women, who represented a melting pot of various ethnic and cultural backgrounds. In the wars that had dislocated the Roman Republic, a century before the activity of Paul, the social upheavals attending the rivalry between Mark Antony and Pompey, as well as the feuds that followed the rise of the Empire, led to a chaotic meeting of Eastern and Western cultures.

When Paul alluded to abuses which were to be avoided in the worship services of the Corinthian church (1 Cor. 11:1–12, 31; 14:1–40), it was not through a whim of fancy that he inserted the hymn to love (13:1–13) between his disquisition on spiritual gifts and his consideration of order in the cult. The whole development forms a literary unit and can be captured in a progression of six thoughts: First, the gifts of the Spirit are as diverse as the diversity of ministries (12:1–11); second, the plurality of individual peculiarities does not impair the unity of the church (vv. 12–13), provided, third, that brotherly and sisterly love be viewed above glossolalia (13:1–13); fourth, the search for love must be joined to an aspiration toward the gifts of the Spirit so that in public worship prophesying or inspired preaching may be securely held as superior to a wild speaking in tongues (14:1–25); fifth, let the man who speaks in tongues be silent, for God is not a God of disorder but of peace (14:26–33); sixth, let women likewise refrain from speaking in the assemblies (vv. 34–40).

The apostle does not specifically state that women who are possessed by heavenly tongues must be silent, but the immediate context of verse 35 makes his intention abundantly clear. He refers to female glossolalia exactly as he had previously mentioned male glossolalia (v. 30). Paul's carelessness of style and his failure to be explicit have led to the centuries-long practice of banning women from the Christian pulpit. That Paul never forbade women to preach or pray in public is amply demonstrated by his many references elsewhere to his female co-workers and, indeed, to female "apostles," who, as it has been seen, accompanied him on his missions. The very fact that he recommended that a woman who "prayed or prophesied" have her head covered (1 Cor. 11:5–6) makes this conclusion inevitable.

Just as there were prophetesses in ancient Israel and Judah, that is to say, women who spoke in the name of God, so also there were prophetesses in the early church, as Peter himself indicated when he quoted the oracle of Joel in his discourse at the feast of Pentecost (Acts 2:18). Philip, the evangelist, one of the seven, "had four still unmarried daughters who prophesied" (Acts 21:8–9).

In spite of the hesitations due to his legal upbringing, Paul admitted the equality of women to men, both in marriage and in the church ministry of the Word.

Does this mean that a biblical theology of manhood and womanhood, elaborated through a hermeneutical approach to twelve centuries of tensions, actions, and reactions, from Hebraism to early Christianity, supports and justifies the ordination of women to sacramental priesthood as well as to the pastoral ministry?

The consideration of this question should lead Christendom to reexamine a biblical theology of the sacerdotal service.

The Issue of Homosexuality

In early Judaism and in early Christianity marriage represented mainly a legal contract negotiated between two families for the sake of creating a new family. On the contrary, the myth of the Garden, the Song of Songs, the teaching of Jesus, and the insights of the apostle Paul enable the biblical theologian to suggest that the *erōs-agapē* continuum—namely, the reciprocity of sentiment and of physical communion between husband and wife—stands at the forefront of the ideology of sexual union. Marriage was thereby elevated from a social covenant to a mystery of union between two personalities.

Parental responsibility toward the young, throughout the centuries, remained paramount, as shown by the references of the prophets to childhood, the concern of wisdom literature for the growth of adolescents toward maturity, more especially the extraordinary sense of equality between sisters and brothers exemplified in the Book of Job (42:15), and supremely, the attitude of Jesus toward children, whom he presented as models for adult regeneration. The survival of the Hebraic faith at the time of the exile and the birth of Judaism in 587 B.C., under the most adverse conditions of existence, demonstrates a sharp awareness of the link of love "from generation to generation." Tradition was less a passive attachment to ancestral inheritance than a fierce hope in the future, a lively responsibility toward "a people yet unborn" (Ps. 22:30–31 [Heb. 31–32]). Education as nurture was the fruit of human love.

In addition to the sexual and parental love uniting man and woman, did

Paul accept the validity of intimate friendship between men or between women, particularly when such a friendship implied erotic overtones or manifestations? The question may, at first glance, seem preposterous but it requires scrutiny, for the popular opinion that ascribes to Paul expressions of strictures against "sodomists" and "homosexuals" is based on traditional versions that actually mistranslate the original Greek text.

It is not possible to ascertain whether Paul, a former Pharisee, considered valid the prohibitions of homosexuality found in the Book of Leviticus (18:22; 20:13). As is well known, he was not in any way submissive to the restrictions and prohibitions of the law on cultic impurity. The abrupt condemnations in Leviticus against male transvestism and sexual acts between males[34] were motivated by the fear of the fascination that foreign cults exercised upon Israel and Judah before the exile. Levitical prohibitions of homosexual acts were promulgated within the context of idolatrous practices, together with those on intercourse at times of menstruation, the sacrifices of children by fire to Moloch, as well as the mixing of cattle breed, garden seed, and garment cloth. All these prohibitions were matters not of morality but of cult. Such practices, among others, were magical rites that the Jerusalem priests had fought against more or less unsuccessfully for three centuries and that their descendants, disciples of Ezekiel in the Babylonian exile, sought to eliminate once and for all in the new community of their hope. They therefore objected to them explicitly in their official blueprint for the restoration. The use of the word "abomination," *to'ebah*, which justified the brutal severity of the prohibition against homosexuality (Lev. 18:22; 20:13), shows beyond doubt that this concerned not social ethics but ritual impurity.

The opprobrium attached to homosexuality was motivated by a theological concern for respecting the freedom of God. The intention of the legislators was to keep religion distinct from magic. Humanly initiated acts that aimed at coercing or bending the divine will were understood as signs of idolatry. In all its forms, idolatry reveals a man-centered intention to mobilize the forces of nature for the profit of those who perform such acts. The male prostitutes of the Jerusalem temple were diviners or other cultic professionals attached to the worship of the Mother Goddess, just as the *assinnu*, the *kulu*, the *kurgarû*, and other functionaries of the Babylonian sanctuaries.

In spite of the traditional versions and even of some modern translations that designate these cultic officials as sodomites or pederasts, the Hebrew text called them only "holy men," *qedeshîm* (Deut. 23:17; 1 Kings 14:24; 15:12; 22:46; 2 Kings 23:7) or "dogs" *kelabîm* (Job 36:14). Roman Catholic and Protestant fundamentalists who condemn sodomy as a crime seem not to have looked at the original text of Scripture.

In all probability, Paul had never heard of the designation "sodomite." Quoting the prophet Isaiah he once mentioned Sodom and Gomorrah

(Rom. 9:29) to illustrate the fate of those who are abandoned by God, but he did not allude to any crime of a sexual nature.

Until the first century B.C., Jews did not attribute the notorious disaster of Sodom to a divine punishment for the perpetration of homosexual acts. It was generally assumed that the inhabitants of Sodom had failed to honor the law of hospitality or were guilty of inordinate pride (Ezek. 16: 48–49)[35] and hatred of foreigners (Wis. 19:13).

Since Lot was only a sojourner in Sodom, the elders of the town wanted "to know" the identity of his mysterious guests (Gen. 19:5). Out of some 943 occurrences of the verb "to know" in the entire Bible, only ten of them have a sexual connotation. The Gospel tradition implied contextually that Jesus himself attributed the crime of Sodom to a lack of hospitality. "Whosoever shall not receive you . . . it shall be more tolerable for the land of Sodom and Gomorrah in the day of judgment, than for that city" (Matt. 10:14–15; Luke 10:10–12).

It was only in the folkloric literature of Judaism during the Hasmonean and Roman times that the crime of Sodom was sometimes explained as homosexual acts (Jubilees 16:6; Testament of Naphtali 3:4–5), although it was still attributed by others to the sin of "arrogance" (Jubilees 22:22; 3 Macc. 2:5). However, Philo of Alexander, a contemporary of the apostle Paul, did associate the Sodomites with homosexuality (*Quaestiones et Solutiones in Genesin,* 4:37). On the contrary, the rabbinical literature, even in much later times, ignored the sexual connotation of the crime of Sodom (Sanhedrin 10:3; Pirkê Aboth 5:13).[36]

When Paul wrote to the Roman church of "dishonorable passions" (Rom. 1:26–27), he was concerned not with sexual ethics for Christians but with the repudiation of idolatry among pagans. The decadence of Roman society at this time blurred the line between the sacred and the secular. The sacred prostitution practiced within the temples coexisted with homosexual and heterosexual orgies, which often degenerated into rape and other forms of violence. Surely Paul would not have condoned such abuses. In another allusion to the subject of homosexuality, the apostle was once again concerned by "idolators" (1 Cor. 6:9). Some modern translations unwarrantedly render two Greek words by a single term, "homosexual." The Greek original lists both words in succession: the *malakoi* and the *arsenokoitai,* respectively, "effeminate transvestites" (well-known devotees of the Mother goddess) and "male prostitutes" (functionaries of a mystery cult).

It is not possible to know Paul's attitude on instances of intimate friendship between men or between women, although his extensive knowledge of the Old Testament suggests that he was aware of the idyll that joined in their youth David and Jonathan, as well as the exceptional attachment that linked Ruth and Naomi (Ruth 1:14–18). While the latter relationship must probably be viewed as devoid of erotic overtones, the former presents a different aspect.

David mourned his friend in the most realistic language:

> What pain I feel for thee, Jonathan, my brother!
> I loved thee so!
> Thy love for me was a marvel,
> More wonderful than the love of women.
>
> (2 Sam. 1:26)

The narrator understood the all-shattering quality of this pain and the all-embracing character of this love. Not only from David's elegy but also from other features of the story, the depth of this love is evident. It was told how the "whole being," *nephesh*, of Jonathan was knit to the "whole being," *nephesh*, of David, and it was added that Jonathan loved David as his "whole being," *nephesh* (1 Sam. 18:1–3). It will be recalled that the Hebraic notion of the soul was quite different from its Greek equivalent *(psychē)*, for it was also used as a synonym for the word "flesh," *basar*. The Hebrew word *nephesh* designated an individual person while the word *basar* referred to the communality of the human race.

The erotic aspect of this friendship between David and Jonathan is further demonstrated by its final detail: Jonathan stripped off his own clothes, his armor, even his sword, his bow and his girdle and gave them to David (1 Sam. 18:4).

King Saul was not ignorant of the character of this friendship, for he remarked soon afterward to Jonathan:

> Son of a perverse woman, do I not know that thou hast chosen the son of Jesse for thy shame and for the shame of thy mother's nakedness? (1 Sam. 20:30)

The story of David and Jonathan has nothing in common with the later instances of cultic homosexuality that were condemned by the Levitical code.

That Paul was silent concerning intimate friendships between men or between women constitutes an important element in the current discussion of modern sexual ethics. The apostle's views of personal behavior in all its aspects were predicated on his theology of the new beings.

Man and Woman as New Beings

Because Paul wrote many times of the flesh and of the Spirit and contrasted in human beings the carnal with the spiritual, many readers of the Bible believe that he associated sexuality with sin and the body with evil. This is a misapprehension.

One should remember that the apostle was born into a Hellenistic milieu and that he received a strictly Pharisaic education. It is to be expected that his religious language would reflect both the Greek influence of his time and traces of his upbringing in orthodox Judaism. Furthermore, his conversion to the new faith and, many years later, his preaching of the gospel to communities as varied as those of Galatia in Asia Minor, Corinth in Greece, and Rome forced him to improvise various modes of expression that were not in any way systematic or homogeneous.

It is no wonder that his attitude on relations between the sexes and on the respective places of man and woman within the church would present fluctuations and even inconsistencies.

Modern interpreters have noted that Paul generally addressed his letters to "brothers" and have concluded that he was concerned with men only. However, one should not forget his messages of greeting and frequently of warm affection to many women, at the end of his letters. Moreover, it should be recalled that the former Saul of Tarsus had been brought up in synagogues, where men alone had standing, and that his epistolary style still reflected his Jewish past. In any case, whenever he referred to human beings of either sex, he used the Greek word *anthrōpos*, "man," without distinction of maleness or femaleness. On the contrary, he employed the word *anēr* (genitive, *andros*) for "man" as male, just as he spoke of *gunē*, "woman," in all his comments on sexual ethics.

For Paul, as for Jesus, both man and woman needed to be liberated from the tyranny of the self, from conformity to their environment, and from the sterile pride inherent in blind submission to religious and moral law. This does not mean that he advocated lawlessness. Rather, he knew the mystery of personal growth for those who lived "in Christ." The consequences of this growth were constant and so multidimensional that to live with Christ produced a reorientation of human desires. It dictated fresh decisions. It inspired unprecedented gestures and it directed novel actions in all areas of life, especially in the realm of sexuality.

Like all other aspects of human relations, sexual conduct was for Paul the blossoming of a renovation of the entire self. His view of natural man and woman was without illusion. He knew that persistence in selfhood is never devoid of selfishness, and this is the reason for which he referred again and again to "the flesh" as opposed to the Spirit of God.

By the term *sarx*, "flesh," the first Christian theologian sought to convey not one or the other of its meanings familiar to Hellenistic philosophers, but the Hebrew notion of *basar*, "flesh" in the sense of "mortal communality" in human existence. Such a terminology is utterly bewildering to the modern mind. Like the Hebrew word *basar*, the Greek *sarx*, "flesh," was almost always synonymous with *psychē*, in Hebrew *nephesh*, which did not mean "soul" as an immortal breath but, on the contrary, the individual concreteness of the will to live against all odds, in spite of the egocentric drives during the span of terrestrial time. Hence, for Paul that which is carnal *(sarkikos)* is not different from what he calls the psychical body *(psychikon sōma*; 1 Cor. 15:44). In not altogether successful attempts to avoid compounding confusion, translators usually render *sarkikos* by "natural" (KJV) or by "physical" (RSV) or, again, by "animal" (NEB).

When the apostle referred to the new "beingness" of the man or woman of faith, he used the expression "spiritual body," *pneumatikon sōma* (1 Cor. 15:44). The power of the living Christ renews in those individuals who live in communion with him their bodies of death. In this economy of existence, they are already becoming "spiritual bodies."

To suggest the death of selfishness and the birth of the new being, Paul developed several modes of description. To die and to live again "in Christ" or "with Christ" was for him a way of formulating the process of initiation into a "beingness" that moved within the *erōs-agapē* continuum. Love of others, either in a sexual sense or at the less intimate level of affectionate concern, was based upon a radical transfiguration of self-love.

From his observations of the various churches for which he felt a "feverish" responsibility, as well as from his own experience of the many years spent in solitary reflection following his conversion, Paul knew that a sudden turn or repentance (the *teshubah* of the Prophets, the *metanoia* of the Hellenistic Jews and of the early Christians) was but a prelude to the protracted drama of daily transformation. He expressed this awareness in diverse figures of speech.

For example, Paul favored at times the language of the Greek athlete, who trains himself for winning the prize. New "beingness" is not a datum received once for all. It is only the necessary and traumatic upsetting of amour-propre, which causes a reevaluation of pride and ambition. It permits the beginning of a daily discipline in the "racing" toward an ultimate goal.

At other times, Paul toyed rhetorically with the image of the inner man that is "renewed day by day" (2 Cor. 4:16). He also compared the new being with someone living in "a building from God, not a house made with hands, eternal in the heavens" (2 Cor. 5:1). This line of meditation led him to conclude:

For this we groan, earnestly desiring to be clothed [*ependusasthai*] with our house, which is from heaven. (5:2)

No one should mind that the apostle mixed his metaphors. The eternal "house," or "tent," is like a vestment to replace the outer man and to put on over the inner man.

It was the symbol of "being vested with" an eternal reality that introduced the vision of a united humanity.

As many of you who have been bathed into Christ have put on [*enedusasthe*] Christ, there is neither Jew nor Greek, there is neither bond nor free, there is neither male nor female: for you are all one in Christ Jesus. (Gal. 3:27–28).[37]

Syntactically, these two verses are not articulated together; yet, the meaning shows that they are inseparable. Nevertheless, the latter is often quoted without the former. Only the *erōs-agapē* continuum within the new being in man or woman makes possible the unity of races, classes, and sexes. The key to this unity is the metaphor of vesting the self in Christ.

The apostle was fond of this imagery. He used it in various but similar contexts. He wrote of "putting on the breastplate of faith and love—and for a helmet the hope of salvation" (1 Thess. 5:8). Again, he wrote of "the mortal [who] must put on immortality" (1 Cor. 15:53). Later, he advised the church of Rome "to put on the armor of light," and this prefaced the recommendation "to put on the Lord Jesus Christ" (Rom. 13:12, 14).

These examples show that Paul could use the image of "clothing oneself" with impersonal as well as with personal objects such as Christ or the new being. When he acknowledged that the Galatians had "put on Christ" (Gal. 3:27), he apparently meant that they had engaged in the mysterious process of being transformed by the living presence of the Lord Jesus.

The Septuagint had accustomed him to associate with a vestment such moral virtues as strength and righteousness, or inward qualities like glory and salvation (Isa. 51:9; 52:1; 61:10; Ps. 92:1 [Heb. 93:1]; 103:1 [Heb. 104:1]; Job 8:22). However, Paul's usage probably conformed at this point to secular Hellenistic Greek, especially as it borrowed from the mores of the theater, where actors impersonate specific characters. In a profoundly intellectual and emotional way, true actors become on stage the heroes they portray.[38] Paul could thus describe the transformation of natural man or woman—an egocentric individual—into a Christ-like figure, ready to overcome greed and self-interest, and able to live for the sake of a more inclusive goal in a community of mutual responsibility, of considerate tolerance, and of comprehensive coherence, from the intimacy of marriage and family to the larger circle of the church in its local and universal dimensions.

When Jew and Greek, bond and free, male and female have "put on Christ, they have entered into a mode of osmosis with the spirit of Jesus. They relate inwardly to "the mind of Christ." This phrase does not mean that they imitate literally or reproduce slavishly his acts and mores, but it suggests that in their own capacities and situations they are becoming "new beings." They are therefore liberated from the divisions that separate them from others who are different from them. They have become "one in Christ Jesus."

Some interpreters maintain that for Paul this unity in Christ has abolished differences between Jew and Greek, bond and free, male and female. Thus, they conclude, the apostle had a view, as far as the third element of the triad was concerned, a kind of psychological androgyny, vaguely comparable to the Platonic myth. This view would imply the superfluity of sexual relations, and this would ostensibly have been the reason for which the apostle advised the Corinthians, "It is good for a man not to fasten himself [*haptesthai*] to a woman . . ." (1 Cor. 7:1).

This interpretation ignores other Pauline statements, such as "He that giveth his own virgin daughter in marriage doth well," although the apostle adds, "He that giveth her not . . . doth better" (1 Cor. 7:38). Those exegetes fail to point out that Paul was ambivalent on the subject because he was deeply possessed by the belief in the shortness of time before the return of the Lord in glory. His eschatological breathlessness was also the reason for his opposition to marriage, entirely on practical grounds. This cautionary attitude did not reveal hostility to sexual relations or any phantasm of spiritual androgyny. Paul was animated solely by a pragmatic consideration. He wished that missionaries and other Christians might concentrate their time and energy on the spreading of the gospel. They should not be burdened with family interests. He thought it was better for the unmarried "so to abide, that they may serve the Lord without distraction" (1 Cor. 7:26). This statement can hardly be used as a justification for priestly celibacy since the apostle himself conceded at once that he was giving only his own opinion "in view of the impending distress" (v. 26).

The hypothesis of androgyny for describing the unity envisaged by Paul between male and female is completely out of order. This conclusion can be firmly defended on account of the Greek usage of the word "one," and in consideration of the immediate context.

In classical and Hellenistic Greek the numeral-word "one," *heis,* establishes identity only in such a sequence as "one and the same," *heis kai ho autos* (Homer, Aristotle, et al.). When it appears alone, the numeral-word "one" suggests the unity of coherence, of solidarity, of communion in diversity (Euripides, Xenophon, et al.).

The Pauline phrase amply confirms this latter sense. The apostle took for granted the historical differences between Jews and Greeks. God never rejected his own people Israel (Rom. 11:1). Similarly, Paul accepted as a fact of history, however ignominious, the existence of slavery within the Roman Empire. The modern mind should not lightly pronounce judgments on the mentality of ages gone by. The revolution inherent in the gospel was so enormous that its implications in actual reforms of society *outside* the church were not susceptible of practical enactment nor even of ethical conceptualization. Paul did not suggest to Onesimus that he not go back to his master Philemon but wrote to the latter a moving note on the equality that binds all men who have been clothed in Christ. Slaves and masters within the church were now brothers (Phlm. 12–20).

Likewise, the apostle never thought of nullifying sexual differences, denying biological functions, or promoting a "unisex" view of the human personality. On all three levels of social and economic inequity he stood adamantly for the principle of complete equality, mutuality, and complementariness.

The Hellenistic culture despised the barbarians. The Jews thought of themselves as the chosen ones, looking down upon the *goyim.* In both Judaism and Hellenism, slaves, like wives, were the property of their masters. On the contrary, according to the gospel, which had seized the life and mind of Paul, those who have "put on" Christ are equal. Their historical or physical differences are not annihilated. They become elements of a new coalescence, a hitherto unknown conglomeration of talents, a sublime communality.

Within the organic solidarity of the church, the status of *goyim,* slaves, and women is equalized with that of Jews, masters, and males. All of them belong now to "the offspring of Abraham" (Gal. 3:29). No longer are there oppressors and oppressed. Domination and subordination are excluded from the family of God.

Liberated from the sexual prejudices of both Judaism and Hellenism, man and woman as new beings are free to love one another, as the man and woman in the myth of the Garden or in the Song of Songs, for they "become one flesh" (Gen. 2:24; Matt. 19:5–6 and par.).

At the end of his tergiversations on marriage, motivated in large part by the distresses of the time, the apostle revealed his deepest conviction when he asked, "Art thou bound to a wife? Seek not to be loosed!" (1 Cor. 7:27).

The bond is that complex effluence that does not substitute *agapē* for *erōs* but extends *erōs* into *agapē.* Thus the apostle associated himself with the all-embracing *agapē:*

> Love beareth all things, believeth all things,
> Hopeth all things, endureth all things.
> (1 Cor. 13:7)

The love of man and woman remains finite and never fuses into pantheism. It can be neither narcissistic nor idolatrous, for it unites two beings in adoration—not in the adoration of each other but in the adoration of an absolute reality beyond the "we" into which the human "I" and the human "thou" have been transmuted. To love is to answer a mutual invocation to adore. Hence, in love there is neither an abdication nor an enslavement of one or the other.

Paul's attempt to overcome age-old prejudices concerning manhood and womanhood did not, however, succeed in fully convincing his disciples and followers. Ambiguities persisted and even gained momentum in the second generation of the church.

Chapter 11

The Ambiguities
of the Second Generation

Faith in the living Christ was initiated by a woman, Mary Magdalene. While men like Barnabas and Paul were among the most influential bearers of the gospel and carried it to the centers of the Greco-Roman world, women played a prominent part in many of the new congregations.

The persecution of Christians by Nero (A.D. 64) and the destruction of Jerusalem by Vespasian and Titus (A.D. 70) marked turning points in the history of the church. The first generation of missionaries and converts began to die out at about that time. The new faith became a "tradition" that had to be handed down to a second generation.

It was also during this critical period in the growth of the new movement that the Christian communities definitively broke away from the synagogues. However, many Christians were still exposed to the religious influence of Judaism, now dispersed throughout the Roman Empire, although they dissociated themselves from the political activities of Judaism and especially from its revolt against Rome.

During this new phase in the history of the church (A.D. 65–96), the position of womanhood was theologically and ethically altered. The ambiguities entertained by the second generation of Christian leaders hardened into a male one-sidedness, which excluded women from the governing bodies of the church and eventually produced in the second and subsequent centuries—to this day in the Eastern Orthodox and Roman denominations of Christendom—an all-men ecclesiastical hierarchy.

It was probably on account of this growing tendency to exclude women from the thinking circles as well as from the governance of the church, even as early as in the second generation, that the book called Hebrews—if, indeed, it was composed by a woman—has remained anonymous.

Was Hebrews Written
by a Woman?

When Paul commended his friends at the end of his Letter to the Romans, he listed Prisca ahead of her husband Aquila (16:13). In most manuscripts, the names of the pair come directly after that of Phoebe, at the head of the list:

> Greet Prisca [several manuscripts read "Priscilla"] and Aquila, my co-workers in Christ Jesus, who have for my life laid down their own necks, unto whom not only I give thanks, but also all the churches of the Gentiles. (Rom. 16:3–4)

Quite a tribute! This couple had an ecumenical reputation. They had risked their own lives for the sake of Paul, perhaps during the silversmiths' riot at Ephesus (Acts 19:23–40), perhaps at the time of another crisis.

The names of Prisca and Aquila occur several times in the Book of Acts and in the letters of Paul. Usually they are linked in this order.[39] Thus it would seem that she was more remarkable than her husband. John Chrysostom was conscious of the significance of this detail. Yet, even modern biblical dictionaries often have the entry "Prisca: see Aquila."

Aquila was apparently a Jew who had originally come from the province of Pontus on the Black Sea in Asia Minor (Acts 18:2). For some reason, he went to Rome, where he married Prisca, a Roman woman, who most likely belonged to one of the prominent families of the imperial city.

Eusebius knew of a tradition according to which Peter was the first evangelist to preach in Rome. Jerome affirmed that Peter's initial visit to Rome took place during the reign of Claudius in A.D. 42–43. Was it at that time that Prisca and Aquila adopted the new faith? Other traditions recall that one of Peter's first converts was Cornelius Pudens, a Roman senator, whom the Christians of a later age identified with the Pudens mentioned in the Second Letter to Timothy (4:21).

1. The Pudens Senatorial Family. The hypothesis that relates Prisca to the Pudens family and thus suggests that she was a highborn Roman matron is based upon an exceptional convergence of three independent archeological discoveries.

First, investigations have been conducted in the foundations of the Church of Santa Pudenziana (Pudentia), not far from Santa Maria Maggiore. The brick wall of a private house was uncovered under the foundations of this sanctuary. Pudentia was one of the two daughters of Senator Cornelius Pudens, and both daughters had become martyrs. As a rule, early Roman churches were built above the houses attached to the names of the saints to whom they were dedicated. A second-century tradition, going back to Pius I (ca. A.D. 145), states that it was the house of Pudens in which Peter, Paul, and Mark lived at different times when they were in Rome.

Second, under the floor of the Byzantine Church of Santa Prisca on the Aventine, an inscription on a bronze tablet bearing the date of A.D. 224 was unearthed. This inscription mentions another Roman senator of a family allied to that of the first-century Cornelius Pudens, namely, Caius Marius Pudens Cornelianus. If the house upon which the Church of Santa Prisca now stands was that of Prisca and Aquila—as, on account of the common practice, it is highly probable it was—one may conclude that Prisca was related to the Pudens family.

The third datum in this threefold convergence results from investigations of the Cemetery of Priscilla on the Via Salaria. It has been shown that this catacomb was on the site of a property belonging to the Pudens senatorial family, the Acilii Glabriones, many of whom were consuls and some of whom became Christian. The genealogy of this family, no doubt allied to the Pudens family since they shared the same burial ground, carries the name Priscilla for two of its women: Vera Priscilla and Faustina Priscilla Aciliana.

Admittedly, it cannot be demonstrated in all instances that the various Roman traditions concerning the sites of the earliest churches are founded upon valid memories. The antiquity of the Priscilla tradition, however, which goes back to at least the middle of the second century A.D., strongly favors its truth.

2. The Prisca-Aquila Couple. If we assume that Priscilla was an aristocratic Roman woman, the fact of her marriage to Aquila, a Jewish businessman with international connections, should not in any way be astonishing. Judaism had for several decades met with outstanding success in making proselytes from all classes of society. The Jewish community of Rome was indeed so numerous and so prosperous in the first century A.D. that it maintained more than thirteen synagogues in the city. When, by imperial edict, Claudius expelled the Jews from Rome, Priscilla followed her husband eastward. It may be presumed that she had become a Jewish convert before both of them accepted the Christian faith.

As residents of Corinth, Prisca and Aquila welcomed Paul in their new home as he worked for their commercial enterprise, and it is likely that they had by then become catechists or teachers. They went with him to Ephesus, and after his departure from that city to Jerusalem, they remained in Ephesus for some months. It was then that they taught a dynamic figure from Alexandria, a man named Apollos, who held some strange views on baptism and possibly other aspects of the gospel (Acts 18:25–26). Significantly, it was Prisca, together with her husband Aquila, who was the teacher of Apollos. Here again, she is named first, before her husband. After Paul's return to Ephesus, he wrote to the Christians of Corinth and included in his letter greetings from Aquila and Prisca (1 Cor. 16:19). Years later, in a note now incorporated in the Deutero-Pauline anthology known as the Second Letter to Timothy, he once more mentioned Prisca and Aquila (4:19). Evidence points to an association and even an affectionate friendship between this amazing couple and Paul, a friendship that lasted for their lifetime.

3. The Writer of Hebrews. Many scholars believe that the authorship of "To the Hebrews," a book that differs in form and thought from any other in the entire New Testament, is unknown. Some even maintain that attempts to break its anonymity belong to the realm of romantic imagination. A few critics of solid reputation have, however, suggested Priscilla, with the collaboration of her husband, Aquila.[40] This hypothesis rests on three lines of inquiry. First, the names of all other candidates are, for one reason or another, to be eliminated. This is, to be sure, a negative observation, but it prepares the validity of the other points, which are strikingly positive. Second, the author not only knew the Greek language extremely well but was also highly educated and especially well trained in the sophisticated rhetorics of the Hellenistic culture. Third, the author was exceptionally cognizant of the Hebrew Scriptures, well acquainted with the Jewish sect of the Essenes, and thoroughly immersed in the trends of Hellenistic philosophy.

The first line of inquiry is based upon the fact that even in patristic times the church simply did not know who had written the document entitled "To the Hebrews." Perhaps the church fathers did not want the writer's name to be known. When the book was finally accepted within the literature of the New Testament, the principle of canonicity was apostolicity, yet they did not believe that the apostle Paul might have been the author. Clement of Alexandria was one of the few exceptions. He suggested that Paul had written the book in the Hebrew language and that Luke had translated it into Greek. On linguistic, stylistic, and thematic grounds, all scholars agree today that Paul could not have been the author.

It has been thought that Clement of Rome had written "To the Hebrews" because his own epistle to the Corinthians (ca. A.D. 96–97) shows many affinities with this book. A minute analysis of the two documents conclusively shows that Clement liberally quoted from "To the Hebrews" but that his language, style, purpose, and ideas were substantially different, as was his method of exposition.

Tertullian proposed Barnabas, the companion of Paul (Acts 13:2). As a former Levite, Barnabas was certainly well acquainted with the Hebrew Bible, but it is difficult to maintain that he was an unsurpassed master of the Greek language. Moreover, as a former Levite, Barnabas would not have erroneously placed the gold censer in the Holy of Holies (Heb. 9:3–4; cf. Exod. 40:5), nor would he have stated that the high priest offered "daily sacrifices" (Heb. 7:27).

Ancient and modern writers have proposed Apollos, "a native of Alexandria," who had the reputation of being "an eloquent man, well versed in the Scriptures" (Acts 18:24) and who, in Ephesus, "powerfully confuted the Jews in public, showing by the Scriptures that Jesus was the Christ" (v. 28). This description fits quite well the portrait of the author of Hebrews. Like Barnabas, Apollos was an outstanding teacher, and Paul looked upon both of them as apostles (1 Cor. 4:9), a term he probably used in the sense of preachers and interpreters of the gospel. If, however, Apollos was considered an apostle and had written "To the Hebrews," why is it that no manuscript attributes the book to him and that the early church fathers thought of other candidates?

The affinities of the book with Apollos are cast in a new light when it is conjectured that Priscilla, a Roman woman, with the collaboration of her Jewish-Christian husband, Aquila, wrote the mysterious treatise. According to the Book of Acts, Apollos was already a Christian convert when he arrived in Ephesus from Alexandria. "He began to speak boldly in the synagogue, but when Priscilla and Aquila heard him, they took him [aside] and expounded to him the way of God *more accurately*" (Acts 18:26–27; italics added). In other words, Priscilla and Aquila were teachers' teachers. They took it upon themselves to direct this brilliant but still misguided expositor of the gospel. It was they who completed his theological education in the formal sense. And since the name of Priscilla, here again, is placed before that of Aquila, it is reasonable to conjecture that she assumed the major responsibility in the task of enlightening Apollos.

The second line of inquiry deals with the linguistic, stylistic, and rhetorical features of "To the Hebrews." Its author was highly conversant with the best Greek of the Hellenistic age, although there are in the book a few Semitisms. Its morphology is correct, its syntax supple, and its vocabulary extraordinarily broad. More than 150 of its words are found nowhere else in the New Testament. Many of these, as well as others, and also a number of complex expressions, are commonly used in the philosophical fragments of the period, but the context of "To the Hebrews" at times confers upon them a distinct nuance. For example, "to be moderate in one's passions," *metriopathein,* is a term familiar to Aristotle and the Stoics as well as to Philo of Alexandria, but the author of Hebrews uses it (5:2) in the sense of "to be capable of comprehension," "to be tolerant."

The writer is a consummate stylist and rhetorician. Even in modern translations, the exordium of the book is a model of sophistication, equilibrium, movement, and other traits that match the originality of the thought:

> God, who at sundry times and in diverse manners spake in times past unto the fathers by the prophets, hath in these last days spoken unto us by [his] son, whom he hath appointed heir of all things, by whom also he made the worlds; who being the brightness of [his] glory, and the express image of his power, when he had by himself purged our sins, sat down on the right hand of the Majesty on high; being made so much better than the angels, as he hath by inheritance obtained a more excellent name than they. (1:1–4)

Again and again, the main themes are introduced by specially constructed sentences, comparable to architectural variations in a monumental edifice.

These variations announce themselves by several devices. One of them is that of alliteration, such as in the opening phrase of the exordium, where similar sounds pile up consonantally and vocally: Polumerōs kai polutropōs palai ho theos lalēsas tois patrasin en tois prophētais . . .: "Many-place-wise and many-form-wise [adverbs] in antiquity has God spoken to the ancestors through the prophets . . ." (Heb. 1:1). The contrast between "the fathers" and "the Son," which is the subject of the entire book, is thus introduced by a phonetic interlocking that immediately compels the reader's attention and conduces to memorization.

The choice of many words or expressions was clearly dictated by an awareness of the effect that the sounds or images might evoke in the reader. For example, with the clause *mēpote pararuōmen,* "lest we drift away" (Heb. 2:1), the author warns against deviation from the faith through forgetfulness or corrupting influences. This verb appeared once in the Septuagint (Prov. 3:21) and it has not been used in secular Greek or Hellenistic literature. Probably a variant form of *pararreo,* it suggested the sailor's fear of straying off course. Aristotle used it for speaking of food swallowed into the trachea, and Plutarch for false money and false rumors. The writer's purpose in "To the Hebrews" was certainly to startle and thus to provoke immediate attention.

A similar purpose was achieved by the placing in proximity of words that do not normally follow closely together, for instance, *di' hupomonēs trechōmen,* "let us run with patience" (Heb. 12:1). The phrase stands at the core of one of the most eloquent and theologically significant phrases in the treatise, perhaps of the entire Bible, and ranks in form with the artistry of a Demosthenes:

> Wherefore seeing we are encompassed about with so great a cloud of witnesses, let us lay aside every weight, and the sin which doth so easily beset [us], and let us run with patience the race that is set before us, looking unto Jesus the beginner and the finisher of our faith; who for the joy that was set before him endured the cross, despising the shame, and is set down at the right hand of the throne of God. (12:1-2)

Many other rhetorical features have been identified by commentators, such as a variety of prose rhythms, the use of chiasmus, by which parallel words or clauses appear in reverse order, and a predilection for the *inclusio poetica,* in which the beginning of a development calls for symmetry of a similar ending.

An apprentice littérateur or even an experienced teacher who was not trained in the intellectual circles of the Greco-Roman world was not likely to have mastered these techniques and to have maintained their application throughout such a long composition.

The book "To the Hebrews" ends with a personal note as if it were a letter (13:22-25), but the material that forms its body is planned according to a tightly composed structure, in which moral exhortations follow most of the theological discussions.

The subject of the book is the exaltation of Jesus over the angels, the supreme pontiffs, and the saints of the old dispensation. It falls into seven distinct parts:

1. Jesus as the New Angel (1:1—2:18)
2. Jesus as the New Moses (3:1—4:13)
3. Jesus as the New High Priest (4:14—7:28)
4. Jesus as the New Temple (8:1—9:10)
5. Jesus as the New Sacrifice (9:11—10:39)
6. Jesus as the New Head of the Faith (11:1—12:29)
7. "Jesus Christ, the Same Yesterday and Today and For Ever" (13:1–25)

No other writing of the early church amalgamates or knits together, according to a reasoned plan, catechesis and homily, theology and ethics, *theoria* and *praxis,* faith and work, life and order, Old Covenant and New Covenant.

Such a synthesis brings together the Hebraic mind and the Hellenistic culture. It displays, also, the Roman sense of architecture, and the constitutive elements of the whole are filtered, seasoned, and articulated by a burning devotion to the person of Jesus. The question is not at this point whether "To the Hebrews" offers a theology less "authentic" than the Pauline or the Johannine interpretations of the faith. What is at stake in this inquiry is the authorship of the book.

The writer belonged to "the household of faith," most probably in Rome and its vicinity. The last word, before the benediction, is "Those from Italy salute you" (13:24). Whether this refers to Italians in residence (if the letter was written from Rome) or to Italians exiled in one of the imperial provinces (if the letter was written to Romans), their mention shows the close affinities existing between the author and the capital city of the Empire.

Analysis of the vocabulary, morphology, style, rhetorical devices, and ideas demonstrates that the treatise was composed by a single hand. Yet, the first personal pronoun in the singular, "I," sometimes alternates with the plural "we." However, each pronoun, singular or plural, is found in phrases that imply the same authoritative assurance and the same affectionate feeling toward the addressees. It may be significant that the "I" belongs to the theological passages, whereas the "we" is found in the homiletical admonitions, although the last part of the book uses both "I" and "we," as if written by a couple of close collaborators. Priscilla and Aquila meet in every respect the particular features of this profile.

With her husband Aquila, Priscilla lived in Rome, left the capital for several years, and then returned to the city, where she apparently sheltered the church in her home. Then she went away from Rome again, and it is from Ephesus that she may have written "To the Hebrews." The collaboration of a Jewish-Christian husband explains the facility and versatility with which quotations from the Hebraic Scriptures are welded into the Greek rhetorical development.

That Priscilla was a Roman is indicated by archeological excavations. Prisca, or Priscilla, is a Latin, not a Greek name. Plutarch was the first to mention a man named Priscus. Discoveries in the foundations of the churches of Santa Pudenziana and Santa Prisca, as well as in the Catacomb of Priscilla, associate this extraordinary woman with a leading Roman family.

There is no need to seek for a difference between a so-called "masculine" or "feminine" approach in "To the Hebrews." Nevertheless, the parade of the heroes of faith would be astonishing indeed, had it been conceived by a man. The concern for women shows itself there in a startling way. Who would ever think that Sarah, the skeptic woman, who laughed when she heard the promise of a son while she was already of an advanced age, would be listed among the models of faith? Would it not, also, be more natural for a woman than for a man to mention pointedly that Moses "had refused to be called the son of Pharaoh's *daughter*" (11:24, italics mine)? Would it not at least be unexpected for a man to praise "Rahab, the prostitute," who "by faith did not perish with rebels, for she peacefully welcomed the spies" (11:31)? The concern for womanhood is equally obvious in the enigmatic note, "Women recovered their dead by resurrection" (11:35).

It has been objected that the author of the book "To the Hebrews" must have been a man, since the phrase, "time would fail me to tell . . ." (11:32), uses the Greek participle *diēgoumenon,* "telling," in the masculine gender. This argument reveals a faulty or biased knowledge of Greek syntax, which commonly employs such a participle not in the masculine but in the neuter (here indistinguishable from the masculine).

One commentator, unwittingly humorous, has suggested as unlikely that "a learned monk [who] would have been able to compose a document such as this homily in the first century would have been a woman."[41] There is, however, no valid evidence that "To the Hebrews" comes from the hand of a learned monk, Essene or otherwise. Affinities with the Dead Sea Scrolls are, in effect, numerous, but there are similar affinities between the Dead Sea Scrolls and other writings of the early church.

In view of the ambivalence of Christendom toward women in the second-century church, it is understandable that the name of Priscilla would have been eradicated from the manuscript of "To the Hebrews." By comparing the reading of the Greek majuscule manuscripts with the Syro-Latin recension and Codex D, Harnack has shown conclusively that the latter had reversed the order of the names "Priscilla and Aquila" in the story of the Book of Acts when it introduced the famous couple as the teachers of Apollos (Acts 18:26). Even more disturbing, the Syro-Latin recension and Codex D had emended the sentence which follows (18:27) with the result that the "brothers" who wrote a letter of introduction for the same Apollos about to depart on a missionary journey are no longer identified with

Priscilla and Aquila. There seems to have been a reluctance to recognize that the well-known pair, especially Priscilla, would have been prominent in the administration of the church at Ephesus in the first century.

One cannot demonstrate beyond doubt that a woman was the author of this book, certainly the best written in that first century church. Like natural science in general and astrophysics or molecular biology in particular, literary and historical criticism remains scientific, but its results are still open to revision. That the name of Priscilla would have been censured is, however, consistent with the mores of the time, both within and without the church. For example, Pliny the Elder, in his *Natural History,* lamented the fact that the names of women physicians had been obliterated from medical treatises of an earlier age.

Furthermore, there may have been a specific reason of theological importance for concealing the feminine authorship of "To the Hebrews." The book boldly attempted to present the relationship between "the Son" and God in a language borrowed in large part from the Wisdom of Solomon, the writings of Philo of Alexandria, and other Hellenistic mystical philosophers.

The opening words (Heb. 1:1–3) spoke of Jesus as the "splendor" or "effulgence," *apaugasma,* of God's glory, and even as the "stamp" or "engraved effigy," *charactēr,* of his "being," *hupostasis.* People who were so inclined could read into these words some specific ideas that later became the vogue in certain Gnostic circles (cf. Heb. 1:3 with Wis. 7:25–26; Philo *On Noah's Work as a Planter* 50). In view of the fact that a number of Gnostics presented Jesus as *Sophia* in the sense of a mystical and esoteric "knowledge," *gnōsis,* and the fact that many women were apparently captivated by these sectarian trends, it may well be that "To the Hebrews" needed to be divested of its feminine authorship. Yet, the book itself was too valuable to be discarded. The theology of mediation through Jesus that it proposed was sufficiently original for readers and copyists to preserve it from generation to generation.

While "To the Hebrews" used a daring and powerful terminology, its purpose may have been precisely to warn against heretical distortions of the faith, which had already appeared in the middle of the first century A.D. The phrase, "lest we drift away" (5:2) is a clear signal that the author was aware of dangers on both sides. The book therefore recommended strict adherence to a sound Christology. Against Jewish-Christian legalism it stresses divine grace and ecumenical outreach. Against antinomianism within sectarian, pseudo-mystical, pseudo-philosophical Gnosticism in its nascent stage the book emphasizes an openness to a worldwide *ecclesia* rather than a restrictive *ecclesiola.*

The Followers of Paul

The apostle Paul perished in Rome, under Nero, between A.D. 62 and 65. Modern scholars assign to his disciples some of the letters that have been traditionally ascribed to him—Ephesians, Colossians, Timothy, and Titus. As shown by statistics compiled already a hundred and fifty years ago and recently confirmed by computer calculation, these writings present peculiarities of morphology and syntax that differ markedly from those of the other Pauline epistles. Moreover, they contain non-Pauline ideas and reflect theological concerns of the second and third Christian generations. The authors of these letters were eager to preserve a few short notes dictated by the apostle during his final two years, while he was under house arrest in Rome, and also to write in his name their own recommendations on theology and ethics for the church in the face of a new situation. The practice of composing books under a great name was common among both Jews and Gentiles. These books were called pseudepigrapha.

Differences between the Pauline and the Deutero-Pauline ideas are particularly noticeable in the realm of sexual morality.

While the apostle had proclaimed the equality of male and female in Christ, his successors advocated the subservience of woman in marriage. To be sure, the bluntness of the admonition in the Epistle to the Colossians, "Wives, submit yourselves [*hupotassesthe*] to your husbands, as it is proper in the Lord" (3:18), was somewhat mitigated by the tone of a second exhortation, "Husbands, love your wives, and do not show hardness toward them" (3:19), but the reason for justifying the wives' submission as "proper in the Lord" was not given. In addition, the two sets of marital obligations are not parallel. Feminine submission is an act of obedience to be performed through a conscious act of the will. Masculine love is an emotion of inner attitude. Women are called upon to adopt and maintain subservience, whereas men are invited to feel love for them and thus to exercise generosity toward them in the name of that love.

Similar advice appears in Ephesians (5:21–32), but its motivation transcends the realm of ethics. Woman is compared to the church. In the early days of Christianity the word "church" was applied to communities that might be described today as historical phenomena. The author of the Letter to the Ephesians implied that the church was suprahistorical, hence a mythical entity, "the bride of Christ." These two themes, the ethical and the ecclesial, are treated concurrently within the same rhetorical development and they are not kept distinct. They are treated back and forth in overlapping fashion. The result of this defect in composition is a rather tortuous style as well as a notably deficient use of analogy as a rhetorical device.

First, both men and women are invited to submit themselves to each other "in the fear of Christ" (Eph. 5:21). This exhortation faithfully echoes Paul's teaching. There is no distinction of status or of responsibility between male and female. Although the expression "the fear of Christ" is not used by Paul (he favored appeals to "the motherly compassions of God," Rom. 12:1), the Pauline disciple probably meant not "dread" or "terror" but rather the Christian eagerness not to disappoint the expectations of the divine Lover.

The long-standing connotation of religious fear was not that of punishment but, to the contrary, a positive, demanding, and thrilling desire to please. Hence, the word "reverence" (RSV) is not adequate. Inherited from Israel's prophets, psalmists, and sages, religious fear implied passionate love. The first admonition introduced a divine dimension into human love. Man and woman should eagerly submit to each other in the fearful love of Christ. This initial appeal admirably fitted the sequence that preceded: "Imitate God, since you are children whom he loves.... In all things, at all times, render thanks [*eucharistountes*]" (Eph. 5:1–20). A "eucharistic" motivation was central to Hebraic and Christian worship.

Unfortunately, the author retreated after this lofty beginning, for he immediately added, "Wives, [submit yourselves] to your husbands as to the Lord, for man is the head of the woman, as also the Christ is the head of the church, being himself the Savior of his own body" (5:22–23).

The notion of the church as the body of Christ was probably derived from the old Hebraic metaphor of marriage between Yahweh and Israel. Hosea and Jeremiah had depicted their indictment of the chosen people under the figure of sexual promiscuity. God was compared to a deceived husband who still loved his wayward wife. By making the first move, he sought to bring her to better ways (Hos. 3:1–3). In the new economy of existence, Israel will no longer call her God *ba'alî*, "my master" or "my owner," but *'îshî*, "my man" or "my husband" (Hos. 2:16). Such a language implied on the part of the ancient prophet an intimate, comprehensive, and astute view of the *erōs-agapē* continuum. It left no room for an Oriental or patriarchal notion of marriage in which a wife was her husband's property. The Deutero-Pauline writer of Ephesians, like Hosea, must have been to a certain extent aware of the magnificent equilibrium that the passion of love, shared, exchanged, and returned, brought to the conjugal relationship, in which the communion of husband and wife means a reciprocity of support, of responsibility, and also of need and desire. Yet, the ecclesial analogy led the author astray in the realm of conjugal ethics.

As the bride of Christ, the church is clearly under the inspiration of her Lord. His command and judgment inform and constantly reform the life of the church. In the mind of the writer, it follows that a wife will be subservient to her husband. "As the church is submitted to the Christ, let wives be submissive to their husbands" (Eph. 5:24).

Such a unilateral exhortation, which in the traditional liturgies of the wedding ceremony is the origin of the bride's promise to "obey," was to a remarkable degree counterbalanced by the next admonition, "Husbands, love your wives, as the Christ has loved the church, and has delivered himself for her" (v. 25). This astonishing phrase implies that a wife's submission is not to be separated from her husband's self-offering of love to her. The pathos of the love of Yahweh for Israel and of Christ for his church drastically modified the injunction to wives to obey. Their husbands' devotion to them must be of the same order as that of Christ for his own body, which is the church. This utmost devotion signifies on the husbands' part a readiness to love even unto death. Women's submissiveness is thus dependent upon men's willingness to offer their own lives in self-sacrifice in their wives' behalf.

This is an awesome obligation for males, without parallel in the ancient world. Wives' obedience to their husbands cannot then be called silent or one-sided servility. Such an obedience is legitimate only when husbands love them so deeply, so completely, so unselfishly that they are willing to go to death for them. Like the church, a human bride is the recipient of total love, and her obedience becomes a response not to male tyranny but to male self-abnegation and Christ-like willingness to give all. But, are husbands Christ-like?

At this point, the writer's thinking hesitated between his theological flight into the sublime and his old male prejudices. The ecclesial analogy led him to insist upon the bride's splendor, her purity, and her stainlessness, but he was not moved to declare that husbands, unlike the Christ, require salvation and the cleansing of their sins exactly as wives do.

> [The Christ] has willed to present [the church] to himself as splendid, without stain or wrinkle, or any defect. He has willed to render his church holy and without reproach. (vv. 26–27)

By associating the human bridegroom with the Lord, the comparison passes over the shortcomings, the pride, and the self-interest of the male ego. In Ephesians there is no sexual reciprocity on a footing of sexual equality in marriage.

With a perspicaciousness based undoubtedly upon his own experience, Paul had seen the give-and-take in the delights of sexual union. He had known that the bodies of spouses belong to their mates—male as well as female (1 Cor. 7:3–5). On the contrary, the writer of Ephesians, carried away by his mythical view of the church, indulged in a grand gesture. His appeal for husbands to be Christ-like resulted only in a stress on male amour-propre.

> So ought husbands to love their wives as their own bodies. He who loves his wife loves himself. Never has any man taken his own flesh in aversion. Rather, he nourishes and cherishes it, even as the Lord the church. (vv. 28–29)

A man's love for his wife is now no longer justified as an imitation of Christ's self-offering but as the enlightened appreciation of "his own flesh." In spite of present-day psychology on self-love as a necessary element of altruistic love, one must say that this exhortation proposes a form of narcissism that does not concern itself with woman's pleasure, dignity, or freedom. By nourishing and cherishing his mate, man actually nourishes and cherishes his own being. Was the analogy with the mystical bride still valid? The writer thought so, for he added, "even as the Lord the church" (v. 29).

To call the church the body of Christ might have startled the readers. Thus, the writer felt the need to be explicit, adding further, "for we are members of his body" (v. 30). Some manuscripts append, "of his flesh and bones" (v. 30b), in an apparent effort to smooth out the abrupt lack of transition by inserting a quotation from the Genesis story of the Garden.

> Therefore man will abandon his father and mother and fasten himself to his wife, and the two shall become one flesh. (v. 31; cf. Gen. 2:24, LXX)

The writer's reasoning once more descended from the level of ecclesiology to that of human conjugality.

This sudden reminiscence from Scripture did not, however, prompt him to affirm, as shown in Genesis, the amazing status of womanhood in sexual communion with man. He was close to doing so and seemingly he suspected that his readers might think that he had done so, for he at once forestalled such an inference by adding, "This mystery is great, but I, for my part, speak of the Christ and the church" (v. 32), i.e., not of the husband and wife.

In spite of this restrictive demurral, traditional denominations of Christendom have held that marriage is a sacrament. This notion arose from a misunderstanding of Jerome's rendering of the Greek *mustērion,* "mystery," by *sacramentum,* a word that originally meant "loyalty oath" for the military, "pact," "engagement."

What did the writer mean by the statement "This mystery is great"? Did he have in mind only, as some scholars believe, that the Genesis quotation had a "secret meaning," or was he ready to hint at the mystical dimensions of human love—a physio-psychological initiation into infinity—although he hastened to refrain from such a movement of thought and warned that he referred merely to an ecclesial "mystery"? Many interpreters maintain that a comparison between the vision of the church as the bride of Christ and the Hellenistic "mystery" cults, like that of Eleusis, might well have lurked at the threshold of the author's consciousness. Almost two hundred years before his time, an Alexandrian Jewish sage had written of the *mustēs,* or "initiate," in pagan rituals (Wis. 12:5). He had even proclaimed that Wisdom herself was an "initiate," *mustis,* in the "Science, *epistēmē,* of God" (Wis. 8:4).

In any case, to the very end of his development on marriage the author of Ephesians appears to have been far more interested in the church's suprahistorical significance than in woman's status, and his final reiteration makes his position abundantly clear:

> Let every one of you in particular love his wife as himself, and let a woman [behave] in such a way as to fear man. (Eph. 5:33)

Even if this womanly "fear" of man is interpreted as stemming from the ancient Hebraic ideal of love, the discrepancy between the two sexes remains. For this follower of Paul, man and woman are not equal in marriage.

Gnostic Deviations and
Male Politics

In most religious movements epigones or followers are apt to soften the boldness of their predecessors' innovations. The first-century church was no exception. Fidelity to the founders of Christianity led the next generations of Christians to blur the daring of "the first fine careless rapture." Reactionary conservatism set in among the disciples of Paul and Peter, not only in Rome but also in Greece and Asia Minor. Such a reaction was particularly manifest in sexual ethics. It affected the position of women at home and their status in public worship.

More than the writers of Colossians and Ephesians, those Pauline disciples who composed the Pastorals and the Catholic Epistles reflect a hardened attitude of male dominance with regard to the role of women in both marriage and public worship.

The First Epistle of Peter, written in excellent Greek, arose in the Pauline circle of Rome toward the end of the first century, probably after Domitian's persecution (A.D. 95–96). The views of this Roman churchman on the subservience of wives to their husbands are expressed in an unexpected way, for they are avowedly related to the missionary growth of the community.

> You, wives, be submissive [*hupotessomenai*] to your own husbands, so that even if some of them refuse to believe in the Word, they may be won without speeches by their wives' conduct, when they see your pure and respectful behavior. (1 Pet. 3:1–2)

It may be inferred from this admonition that there were in the church at that time more women converts than men. As in the earliest communities, women probably constituted the majority of membership. While there is no indication that these women were disorderly or at least too vocal for the men's comfort, feminist activists may have clamored for women's rights in marriage, as well as in public worship. The author of First Peter believed that, in the case of mixed marriages, wives should rely upon the example of their own character rather than upon the persuasiveness of their conversation.

The church moralist went so far as to counsel married women on their hairdo and dress. A daring move.

> Let not your adornment be outwardly fashionable, with braided hair, gold jewelry, elegant dress, but let it be the hidden disposition of the heart, the incorruptible attire of a gentle and peaceful spirit, which is of great price before God. (1 Pet. 3:3–4)

The writer was apparently well versed in both the Hebrew Scripture and

Jewish oral tradition. He presented Sarah and other holy women of the patriarchal age as models for their spiritual daughters.

> Thus, in former times, holy women who placed their hope in God adorned themselves, while being in submission to their husbands; as Sarah was obedient to Abraham, calling him her lord, she whose daughters you have become as long as you are acting rightly, and letting no fear trouble you. (3:5–6)

Was this last clause alluding to the threats directed against their wives by some husbands who were still pagan? In any case, a patriarchal ideal of marriage, interpreted according to the Jewish mores of a later age, had won its way into the Roman church. It must be added, however, that husbands whenever converted to Christianity were urged to treat their wives with respect.

> You, husbands, in like manner, lead your communal existence in the knowledge of your wives' delicate nature; show them honor, since you are joint heirs of the grace of life, to the end that nothing hinder your own prayers. (v. 7)

The "knowledge" that women are "of a delicate nature," literally, "weaker vessels" (KJV) or that they represent "the weaker sex" (RSV) was not based on a careful reading of the Hebrew Bible, filled as it is with examples of strong women and heroines of singular stature. The notion of "a generally inferior sex" reflected the Jewish as well as the Hellenistic views of the time. It went back, through the Greco-Roman moralists, to Plato himself (*Republic* 5.455 ff.).

Moreover, the author of First Peter, like the other followers of Paul who wrote about husbands and wives, was influenced by the tables of household duties *(Haustafeln)* that were common among Stoic philosophers (cf. Seneca *Epistles* 94.1–2). Greek and Latin lists of family obligations dealt not only with wives and husbands, parents and children, but also with masters and slaves. This threefold pattern was exactly that used by the second and third generation of Christian writers (cf. 1 Pet. 2:13—3:7 with Col. 3:18—4:1; Eph. 5:21–33; 1 Tim. 2:8–12; 6:1–2; Tit. 2:1–10).[42]

In spite of the fact that the Roman churchman who wrote First Peter was influenced by Jewish and Stoic strictures on married women, he sought to rise above his inherited prejudices when he reminded husbands that their wives, like them, would inherit "the grace of life" (3:7). He did not quite succeed in his attempt, however, for his recommendation that men respect "the weaker sex" was blatantly male-centered. The purpose of such respect was "to the end that nothing hinder [their] own prayers." This phrase implies that participation in church services, during which men were supposed to offer their prayers, was, like synagogue services, reserved for men only. Women, although present, were excluded from active sharing in religious exercises.

It appears that by the end of the first century Christian women, just as their Jewish sisters in the synagogues, were ecclesiastically debased. The presence of women in the third-generation church was tolerated but it was not comparable to the prominence they had enjoyed in the entourage of Jesus himself or in the earliest communities of Jerusalem, Thessalonica, and Corinth.

The First Letter to Timothy, written perhaps at the same time, contains a directive on public worship that indicates an even more reactionary attitude than that of First Peter. Having noted that the faith of some had been "shipwrecked" (1 Tim. 1:19), the writer continued with an injunction on church services. While he maintained that prayers should be offered for the sake of "all human beings," *anthrōpoi* (2:1), only "men," *androi,* were permitted to offer these prayers:

> I therefore urge that in every place [of worship] men should pray, lifting [to heaven] holy hands, without anger or dispute. In the same manner also women should be dressed decently; they should adorn themselves with modesty and reserve, without braided hair, gold jewelry, pearls, or sumptuous dresses; on the contrary, they should be attired with good works, as it is fitting for women who make profession of their piety. (1 Tim. 2:8–9)

A few commentators understand the opening adverb, "in the same manner also," *hōsautōs,* as meaning that women may join with the men in vocal prayer. However, the sentence thus introduced goes on to deal with women's sobriety in appearance and with their good deeds as their sole ornaments. It then leads directly into a drastic and uncompromising command:

> During the instruction, woman must keep silent, with all submissiveness. I do not permit women to teach or to dominate [*authentein*] men. Let her keep silent! (v. 12)

This prohibition, which has played havoc with the ecclesial polity of most denominations of Christendom until modern times and continues to plague some of them, was due to an interpretation of the Garden myth common in early rabbinic Judaism.

> For it is Adam who was first formed, Eve afterwards, and it was not Adam who was seduced, but it is the woman who, seduced, fell into transgression. (vv. 13–14)

Initially expressed by Jesus ben Sirach toward the end of the third century B.C. (Sir. 25:24), this reading of Genesis implied a belief in hereditary transgression, which became known as the doctrine of original sin. Instead of speculating on the corporateness of evil in the human race and thereby abandoning the notion that the curse of Adam was transmitted to every child by the father's seed, the moralist of the Roman church ascribed to the female sex entire and sole responsibility for the corruption of the human will. The claim that "Adam was not seduced" represents a gross attempt at male exculpation. It is on account of Eve that women were to be denied a role in the preaching, teaching, and liturgical ministry of the church. The writer did not sense the deep irony of the ancient story in which man accused God as well as woman: "The man said, 'The woman, whom thou gavest me . . .'" (Gen. 3:12). Yet, his scapegoating reflex may have slightly disturbed his conscience, for he admitted a certain restriction to his verdict of woman's guilt, as if he had suddenly remembered the benefits of "motherhood and apple pie." He wrote,

> However, [woman] will be saved by her bringing up children, provided she persists in the faith, in love and in holiness with humility. (1 Tim. 2:15)

The theological implication of this remark irreducibly conflicts with Paul's proclamation of grace, since woman's salvation, in this Deutero-Pauline letter, was wholly dependent upon her persistence in virtuous conduct, in addition to the fulfillment of her maternal obligation. This moralist believed in salvation by works.

In expressing their remonstrances against womanhood, the ecclesiastics of the second and third generations of Christianity offered in spite of themselves significant information on the importance of women in the church at that time.

Prohibitions are never promulgated in a social or ethical vacuum. They betray on the part of the legislators an apprehension or even a fear provoked by a specific situation. From the severity of the tone and the abruptness of the interdiction one may infer that many women (women of means, who could afford jewels of gold, pearls, and fashionable haute couture) took an active part in the life of the Roman church. Male leaders, possibly envious of their intellectual brilliance, at least of their spiritual superiority, took umbrage of their prominence. In First Peter and in First Timothy there is no evidence whatever that these women, unlike the men, indulged in eccentricities of opinion, attitude, or behavior. In fact, the Pastorals and the Catholic Epistles are filled with appeals to preserve "the sound doctrine" (1 Tim. 1:10; 2 Tim. 4:3; Tit. 1:9) and with warnings to shun theological views that threaten the purity of the gospel. Women were not exclusively or pointedly singled out in these injunctions. These were addressed to all people.

It is nevertheless probable that more than men, women were already at that time fascinated by esoteric forms of mystical "knowledge," *gnōsis*, alien to the radical openness of Christian faith. The word "Gnosticism" is a convenient term for designating many different sects that flourished chiefly in the second and third centuries A.D. These sects differed widely among themselves in thought as well as in morals, from extreme asceticism to sexual lawlessness.

The origins of these movements are obscure, but they probably went back to centers of culture such as Antioch and especially Alexandria, where Jewish and Hellenistic religionists commingled in multifarious forms of syncretism. A veritable ferment of pseudo-philosophical mysticism seized the Greco-Roman intelligentsia as well as the masses in Eastern Mediterranean lands and soon reached Rome, the capital of the Empire.

While documentary information on the Christian Gnostics is not older than the second century A.D., since it is found indirectly in the patristic literature or directly in the more extensive papyri texts of Nag Hammadi, it is clear that such ecclesial sectarianism did not erupt overnight. There is ground for maintaining that the *Gospel of Thomas,* compiled about A.D. 140 to 170, has preserved oral traditions contemporary with those of the three Synoptic Gospels (A.D. 64–85).[43] Moreover, as early as A.D. 52, Paul had written to the divided Corinthians, "We speak in secret [*en mustēriō*] the wisdom of God which is hidden [*theou sophian . . . tēn apokekrumenēn*]" (1 Cor. 2:4). He had looked upon his fellow missionaries Cephas (Peter) and Apollos as well as upon himself as "adjutants of Christ [*hupēretas Christou*] and stewards of the mysteries of God [*oikonomous mustēriōn theou*]" (1 Cor. 4:1). The word "adjutants," a metaphor derived from the nautical and military world, was used for attendants in the cult of Apollo at Delphi and also of Mithra in Rome. The "stewards" were generally estate managers for absentee landlords. In spite of the uninformed claims of some modern ecclesiastics, these expressions do not refer to an apostolic succession or to a priestly administration of the Eucharist. Paul listed not only Peter, admittedly one of the Twelve, but also Apollos and himself, who did not belong to the original group of apostles or to any priesthood.

In alluding to a Divine Wisdom that was hidden and taught in secret, as well as to the mysteries of God, Paul employed a language bound to appeal to Gnostics,[44] especially to those who favored masculine and feminine images for describing the Deity. Not only did these sectarians claim to possess an esoteric knowledge *(gnōsis),* but some of them also identified the Holy Spirit with the Divine Mother,[45] while others spoke of Wisdom *(Sophia)* as the Mother of the Angels.[46]

Toward the middle of the first century A.D., women of the upper classes in Rome and in the large cities of the Empire had become emancipated despite the antifeminist strictures of Stoic moralists.[47] Roman women participated with men in the mystery cults, for they were attracted by the worship of Isis and other mythical manifestations of the Mother Goddess. It is quite understandable that many of them, particularly those who were of a mystical bent and had also enjoyed philosophical speculations, would frequent gnostic circles.

In the latter half of the second century A.D., Irenaeus (ca. 130–200), bishop of Lyons, vehemently regretted that "many foolish women" of his congregations were seduced and defiled in their devotion to Sophia, whom they believed to be "She who is before all things."[48]

While some of the Hermetic groups and gnostic sects indulged in sexual lawlessness and others, at the opposite extreme, attempted to live as pure spirits, maintaining a rigorous asceticism, for still others there was a middle ground. This was shown by the *Apocalypse of Asclepius* (or "The Perfect Discourse") which reveals a remarkably healthy view of sexual love, with equal concern for both partners. The "mystery" of the union consummated by man and woman is called "a marvelous image." The text continues, "At that moment, if the woman receives the power of man, then man, he also, receives upon him the power of the woman. . . . Hence, the mystery of this union is accomplished in secret."[49] Similar considerations appear in the *Gospel of Philip.*[50]

Since the various Gnostic movements had their roots in the earliest times of Christianity, even in a pre-Christian Jewish background,[51] it is easy to see why the authors of the Pastorals and of the Catholic Epistles—especially First Peter and First Timothy—sought to impose a ban on women's vocal participation in public worship and insisted upon women's subjection to men, at home as well as abroad.

With their predilection for an esoteric knowledge, gnostic women, possibly more than men, threatened the centralizing efforts of the bishops of Rome and of other imperial cities. Contemporary with the writers of First Peter and First Timothy, Clement of Rome commanded the Corinthians (ca. A.D. 96) in dry and harsh tones to restrain women.[52] Heavily influenced as he was by the thought and even by the style of the treatise "To the Hebrews," which eventually found its place in the canonical books of the New Testament, the bishop of Rome unwittingly offered an example of singular irony, if indeed Hebrews has been composed by a woman, Priscilla, with the help of her husband, Aquila. One may also readily understand why this book remained anonymous.

Opposition to women in the emerging "catholic" church appears clearly not only in the patristic literature but indirectly also in the gnostic writings themselves. According to the *Gospel of Philip*, Mary Magdalene was the object of resentment and envy on the part of the male disciples of Jesus.[53] In *Pistis Sophia*, Peter strenuously protests against the women who intervened while Jesus conversed with the Twelve.[54] Maria (the mother of Jesus?) said, "I am afraid of Peter, he hates our [race]."[55] In another passage, Peter doubts that the risen Lord spoke secretly to Mary Magdalene, a woman.[56]

Such polemic was most likely related to the emergence of a male hierarchy within the Christian communities of the Empire.[57] Bishops and priests, who in early times had been indistinguishable in rank, attempted to legitimate their authority by linking themselves to an anachronistic apostolic college, sole witness of the resurrection.[58]

In his First Letter to the Corinthians, Clement of Rome asserted with some vehemence that the leaders of the Christian communities, bishops, priests and deacons, "each in his own order," received their powers from God and therefore should be obeyed.[59] Ignatius, bishop of Antioch, claimed at about the same time (ca. 100–107) that the leaders of the churches derived their authority from God himself.[60] Toward the end of the second century, two generations later, Irenaeus, bishop of Lyons, appealed to a continuous tradition handed down from the apostles to a succession of bishops, especially those of "the universally known church of Rome," because it was founded, so he maintained, by Peter and Paul. Irenaeus concluded that every church should agree with the church of Rome on account of its preeminence.[61] Those in rebellion against this authority were declared "heretics"—i.e., "those who choose for themselves."

The politics of male dominance and eventual supremacy were intricately tied to the rejection of all who differed from the bishops.

Most of the Gnostics accepted a form of theological dualism, with the belief in a demiurge responsible for evil in this world, and they tended to confuse self-knowledge with secret speculations on divine knowledge. These views certainly did not represent the faith of Jesus or the beliefs of the early Christians. With its drive for power over the catholicity of Christendom, however, the attitude of the rising hierarchy toward womanhood was an added and major reason for the condemnation of all Gnostics as heretics. Male politics played an important part in the branding of *gnōsis* as a deviation from the gospel.

The Unresolved Tensions

No well-informed ecclesiastic or church body has today the right to proclaim that "Scripture irrevocably condemns" birth control, abortion, homosexuality, or women's equality to men. Such subjects may raise complex problems of Christian ethics, but those who quote isolated passages from Leviticus, Romans, or 1 Timothy and 1 Peter in order to support pronouncements of rigid prohibition ignore the unresolved tensions in the biblical books themselves.

Traditional denominations of Christendom still deny ordination to women and wish them to be subservient to men "on account of Eve" (1 Tim 2:13–14). By doing so, they violate the gospel of Jesus Christ. A few modern commentaries on Genesis continue to endorse the old misconceptions of "Eve, the temptress."[62] Their authors are unconsciously the victims of rabbinical and patristic prejudices. Twentieth-century monuments of Old Testament theology and New Testament theology continue to ignore woman or else to dismiss her in a few paragraphs.[63] Studies of "biblical anthropology" are, in effect, essays in "biblical andrology," since they deal with men only.[64]

A biblical theology of manhood and womanhood will not attempt to harmonize the contradictions or to resolve the tensions, for Scripture is not a single code of religion and morals. Such an undertaking will seek to view each of the contradictions in the light of its historical environment.

Emphasis has recently been laid on what has been called "canonical criticism."[65] This is not a new method of interpretation, to be used as a substitute for other techniques of modern criticism. It partakes of all these in various degrees, depending upon a given book or passage. The relevant texts will, however, be analyzed within the dynamics of biblical growth.

The word "Bible" in English designates a single entity, but it represents a Greek plural noun, *ta biblia*, "the books." Judeo-Christian Scripture is not a single literary monument but a library of sixty-six books (not counting the deutero-canonical books or Apocrypha). It must never be forgotten that Scripture was more than twelve centuries in the making.

The word canon applies not merely to a closed list of sacred writings but also to the processes of composition and of preservation through which these writings came into being.

What were the forces that presided over the selecting of oral traditions, poems, discourses, and legal codes now collected in the Pentateuch? Why were these heterogeneous yarns and bits of national memories brought together in a more or less unified tome, so lengthy that it required five scrolls and, for its safekeeping, five clay jars (in Greek, *penta-teukē,* hence the title "Pentateuch")?

It was the community at worship that, from generation to generation, unwittingly produced a "canon" of Holy Scripture.[66] When Israel gathered to celebrate her feasts, worshipers prayed and "rejoiced before the face of the Lord." They sang and they danced and they recited the rhythmic prose of their stories and commandments, which eventually became the "Scripture lesson" of their cultic ceremonies.

In postexilic times, the synagogue added to the Pentateuch the story of Israel's invasion of Canaan and the tortuous picture of the lost kingdoms together with the oracles of the prophets. Thus appeared the second canon. Still later, Hellenistic and Maccabean Jewry chanted also during the Sabbath services the poems of the wise and crowned the whole collection with "the five scrolls" sung on holy days (Song of Songs, Ruth, Lamentations, Ecclesiastes, and Esther). This third canon was still open-ended in the late first century of the Christian era.

True to its Jewish origin, nascent Christendom continued to sing the Scripture lessons of the synagogue. The churches also took the habit of reading communally the letters of Paul and of his successors as well as stories from the Gospels and the narrative which recounted the spread of the gospel from Jerusalem to Rome. Unawares, they were adding a fourth and Christian canon, which became known as the New Testament.

The three Hebrew canons were not officially closed before the end of the first century A.D. The books of the New Testament were selected through general usage. They were simply added to the three canons of the Hebrew Bible. No synodal or conciliar decision made official the final list until the sixteenth century.

Each new canon widened and lengthened the perspective from which sacred history was remembered, but did not supersede its predecessors.

Christians appropriated from Judaism their literary roots, and they consequently brought the Hebrew Bible to its culmination with the books that celebrated the life of Jesus and the diffusion of the gospel. In this slowly developed literature, we should expect to find a broad diversity of beliefs and customs concerning sexual morality. To consider the canonical dynamics of Scripture, in this area as well as in others, is a liberating enterprise. Such a task shows that the Bible is not a legal textbook of religion and morals, but a mirror of revision and of adaptation in the pursuit of a unique goal, which is the fulfilment of God's will upon earth.

Canonical dynamics is the ferment of theological thinking in a world of cultural conditions that change from century to century. Placed in their respective contexts of historical concreteness, the diversity of viewpoints, with their unresolved tensions, does not conceal a movement of continuous response, uneven as it may be, to the human understanding of the divine purpose. A biblical theology of manhood and womanhood resolutely faces the contradictions, but it attempts to appraise each one of them in the light of the crises that gave rise to canonical growth.

The early traditions of the Hebraic national epic reveal a high regard for the marvel and mystery of sexuality. They therefore assume, against the ancient Near East in general, and classical antiquity, the complementariness of men and women on an equal basis. Even those early traditions, however, harbor no illusion on the errancy of human beings—men as well as women—in all aspects of historical existence. At the conclusion of the myth of the Garden, "the man" names "the woman" and thereby objectifies and alienates his mate. The myth of the Garden becomes the myth of Adam (man) and Eve (life-giver). But the "mother of all the living" first gives birth to a murderer.

The ancestresses of Israel are depicted with a warm appreciation for their intelligence and sensitivity. As in the Song of Songs, sexual union is viewed as an act of mutual delight, in which woman shares pleasure equally with man. When Sarah, the sterile wife, overhears the announcement of her forthcoming maternity, she laughs, saying, "After I have grown old, and my husband is old, will there be sexual pleasure for me?" The word for sexual pleasure used here is a cognate of the name for the mythical garden, ʿedenah (Gen. 18:12). Precisely because the remark is incidental, it unexpectedly reveals an ancient Hebraic insight into the mystery of mutual connubiality. The woman's initial reaction is not related to the hope of motherhood but stems from her awareness of marital mutuality.

The story of Hagar and Ishmael (Gen. 16:1–16; 21:9–21) provides, however, a different picture of Sarah. Devoured by jealousy, she obtains from Abraham the expulsion of her rival and of the child she was herself not able to conceive. While the folktale may well have arisen from ethnic suspicion, since Ishmael was regarded as the ancestor of the Arabs, its preservation within the Hebraic national epic could not fail to call attention to the cruelty of bigamy and indirectly be a warning on the passion of jealousy.

Other tales of women remained in the national consciousness because they illustrated various aspects of the link between religious assimilation to the pagan environment and the barbarity of rituals concerning women. Jephtah's daughter enters the scene as the ideal of virginal femininity, but the inhumanity of the sacrifice shows how far the ideals of Moses had disintegrated when Israel accommodated her spiritual heritage of divine transcendence to the sexual worship of deified nature (Judges 11:29–40). At the same time, the style and composition of the tale convey the deep sense of pathos that the storyteller and his audience felt, as the elements of the plot slowly unfolded and a suspense in dread was maintained until the eventual denouement. Similar examples of ethical revulsion against sexual violence appeared in the tales of the Benjamite concubine's rape (Judges 19:22–30) and of Amon's incest with his half sister Tamar (2 Sam. 13:1–22). Surely, such pictures do not suggest that Israel worshiped a God of terror or that the Hebrew Bible justifies a theology of misogyny.[67] To the contrary, they reinforce indirectly the significance of the prophets' vision. These men trusted in a God whose will is to rehabilitate women as well as men without limitations of race or rite. The prophets' critique of a dehumanized cult did not prevent the exilic priests from sowing, out of fear, the seeds of legal self-justification. It was the prophets' revolutionary boldness and sapiential personification of Wisdom as the feminine side of the divine reality, open to the whole of creation, that led Jesus to violate the law for the sake of women's, as also of men's, liberation.

If some writers of the post-apostolic age retreated from the humaneness of Jesus and of Paul, was it not that they lived at a time of suspicion and perhaps hostility from the imperial administration? Respect for canonical dynamics may enable the modern theologian to see that the third-generation male leaders of the church, like the exilic priests of the Ezekielian school before them, nourished their fear of women with their fear of an alien environment. Their antifeminist legalism eventually produced the exclusively male hierarchies of the Eastern as well as of the Western churches that endure to this day, and it has also vitiated the attitudes of Protestant reformers and later sectarians. Such a male sexism does not stand up under the impact of a comprehension of canonical dynamics.

The unresolved tensions yield in the face of a dimension of grace that informs moral responsibility and always makes ethical norms relative to the full blossoming of solidarity in humaneness.

Men and women know their complementariness when their vitality is channeled in the direction of their purpose. With due consideration granted to particular vocations of virginity and to the special orientation in sexual preferences, man and woman discover their complementariness as they move on the way toward the goal of creation. This awareness anticipates the jubilation of praise.

"Till the heart sings"[68] is the end of the human pilgrimage. In God-centered humanism men and women have the opportunity to be reborn and to mature as sons and daughters of the God of Israel and of Jesus Christ. They *live* the interaction of theology and morality. Theology and morality lead to one another, and the two are integrated in the worship of the faithful Creator.

Chapter 12

Man and
Woman in Christianity

A God-centered Humanism

From Abraham to Jesus, the sweep of biblical faith opens up vistas on humanity and therefore also on divinity. Ancient Israel and early Judaism thought of God as an utterly transcendent reality; yet, they believed that this God curbed his infinity and entered finitude through his presence in Zion. The primitive church saw this entrance through the historical person of Jesus. Canonical dynamics permit the modern reader of the Bible to seize dramatically the movement through which divinity clothes itself, so to speak, in humanity. Biblical faith assumes a God-centered humanism, with a high respect for the existential destiny of women as well as men.

It was only during the Renaissance that the word "humanism" came to designate an intellectual stress on the significance of human life "here and now." With few exceptions, the Western church had considered terrestrial existence chiefly as the anteroom of heaven or hell. By and large, church fathers and medieval schoolmen had taught that human values and even human potentialities were to be appreciated as elements of preparation for death. The expectation of the cosmic end in a near future had been carried over from New Testament eschatology. Christian teaching was not concerned, on the whole, with social justice and the welfare of the individual.

For the past four centuries, at least in Western civilization, philosophers have sought to redress the balance with such ardor that humanism has become synonymous with secularism. It has led to the assumption that man, with his artistic, scientific, and even moral abilities, is the master of the universe. Today this pretense is showing itself to be an illusion, with the result that humanism, having fallen into secularism, tends now to dissolve into nihilism.

A God-centered humanism does not declare that human beings are self-sufficient in a meaningless universe. It affirms that the cosmos, with all its phenomena of frightening proportions, is an ordered and harmonious organism, and that a creative intelligence holds this cosmos moving toward its end, which is the humanizing of mankind. A God-centered humanism proposes a view of humanity that is neither arrogant nor debasing. In this respect as in many others, a biblical theology of manhood and womanhood reflects the canonical dynamics of the entire Scripture. A God-centered humanism hails woman together with man, on this earth, as the hope of creation.

The realism of Hebraic faith and the humaneness of the Hebrew prophets, psalmists, and sages provide a counterweight to the one-sidedness of Christian hope whenever this hope neglects the evils of present history. In spite of their thoroughgoing eschatology, Jesus and the first-generation thinkers— Paul at their head—dedicated their energies to the welfare and the improvement of their fellow beings already now in this world economy, while they were waiting also for the advent of a new world.

The sources of humanism have often been ascribed to Greek philosophy. Many have found its motto in the aphorism of Protagoras, "Man is the measure of all things." Protagoras himself, so it appears from the context of his teaching, knew that human beings were limited in their knowledge and fallible in their judgment.[69] In any case, "measure" does not mean "measurer." The phrase implies that on the scale of biological existence man is the canon or norm with which all things should be compared.

Be that as it may, the Hebrew prophets and poets, on the one hand, and most of the Greek and Roman philosophers, on the other, agreed in situating the human realm halfway between the animal and the divine. Both biblical and classical thinkers regretted that human beings, in spite of their potentiality for greatness, were bound by limitations of mind, corruptibility of will, and fear of mortality.

Biblical faith, however, moved beyond such generalities concerning the human condition because its initiators and reformers expressed their most decisive affirmations in the presence of a God who, they knew, cared for them. The Hebraic as well as the Christian creed was not basically a series of didactic propositions but an outpouring of the human mind *in prayer.* It never divorced intellectuality from spirituality.

One example of canonic dynamics will suffice to convey the development of this God-centered humanism. The poet of Psalm 8 praised his Creator for the near-divinity of humankind, but the writer of "To the Hebrews" adapted (Heb. 2:5–8) and thus transfigured the same psalm into a parable of the myth-and-ritual pilgrimage toward human fulfilment.

The Hebrew psalmist was surprised by a sudden awareness of the near-divine position that mankind occupies in the scale of biological existence.

> What is man, that thou art mindful of him
>   And the son of man, that thou visitest him?
> Yet, thou hast made him lack almost nothing divine,
>   And thou hast crowned him with glory and honor;
> Thou hast given him rule over thy handiwork,
>   Thou has put all things under his feet.
>
> (Ps. 8:4–6)

The poet did not dwell upon insignificance or criminality, but he was conscious of their effect upon human behavior and perhaps even of their interaction. He expressed his amazement that the Sovereign of nature would condescend to care for human creatures. The expression "son of Adam," who was made of the dust of the "soil," 'adamah, echoed the word "mortal man," 'enôsh, in the two parallel *stichoi* of the poetic line (v. 4).

In the light of his acquaintance with the rest of Scripture, especially Job and Second Isaiah, Blaise Pascal developed the thought of the psalm in his paraphrase:

> What a chimera then is man? What a novelty, what a monster, what a chaos, what a subject of contradiction, what a prodigy? Judge of all things, stupid worm of the earth; depository of truth, cloaca of uncertainty and error: glory and refuse of the universe. (*Pensées* 434)

The psalmist intimated that man is always tempted by his godlikeness. Self-sufficient humanism unwittingly enacts in history the Garden myth (Gen. 2:4b—3:24), for it presumes that man is created lord of the universe. The Garden myth shows that man is so much like God that he is prone to believe in his own divinity. Ancient Hebraism expressed in the figurative language of the tree of all-knowledge the psychological and sociological processes of idolatry. Human creatures, when they forget their creatureliness, court their self-destruction by their boast of autonomous achievement.

Christian faith transfigured the Hebraic and Hellenic visions of the human predicament because it clung to the historical figure of Jesus in the light of both *Sophia* and *Logos*.

Quoting Psalm 8 through the Greek version of the Septuagint, the author of "To the Hebrews" related the theme of the New Being to the Hebraic perception of man's tragic failure. Man has not fulfilled his Creator's expectations, although he is crowned with glory and honor and under his feet all things are to be subjected. Yet, one man has revealed and fully disclosed in his own words and deeds the image of God. The theologian of "To the Hebrews" wrote:

> As it is, we do not yet see everything in subjection to [man], but we see Jesus, who was made for a little while lower than the angels, crowned with glory and honor, because of the suffering of death, so that, by the grace of God, he might taste death for everyone. (Heb. 2:8c–9)

Instead of "by the grace of God," some manuscripts read the still more gripping phrase "without God," which may be an allusion to the cry of Jesus on the cross, quoting from Psalm 22:1 [Heb. 2], "My God, my God, why hast thou forsaken me?"

The mention of angels has puzzled many readers. The original of Psalm 8 used the name Elohim, "God," in the half-line "Yet, thou hast made [man] lack almost nothing of God" (v. 5a [Heb. 6a]). In the third century B.C., the

Greek readers of Alexandrine Jewry, shocked perhaps by the idea of a near-divine status, rendered the Hebrew text rather freely. They understood the word *Elohim* not as a plural of majesty meaning "God," but as an actual plural, "gods," and their strict monotheism led them to interpret the word as "angels" (although the Hebrew word should then have been *mal'akim*). Doctrinal orthodoxy was safeguarded, and the Christian author of "To the Hebrews," ironically, used this mistranslation for the most daring heterodoxy of all, which was to formulate the divine destiny of human beings through the divine origin of Jesus, the man par excellence.

By applying the psalm to Jesus, the author of "To the Hebrews" was able to develop a revolutionary theme, the purpose of which was to show that Jesus, in his celestial beingness, was above the angels. He was the celestial Being made man. Through his humanity, which inevitably included his mortality, he fulfilled his function as "God's compassionate and faithful high priest [who would] make expiation for the sins of the people" (Heb. 2:17). This language may sound strange to modern ears. It was admirably adapted to the readers of the treatise "To the Hebrews." It used the myth-and-ritual approach by alluding to the sacramental participation in divine forgiveness through the mediation of the high priest on Yom Kippur. Such language illumines the early stages of the intellectual process by which the church sought to put into words the unique quality of the historical figure of Jesus. At the same time, it suggested the incredible renovation, also called regeneration or new birth, through which the lives of men and women are radically reconciled to the highest purpose and meaning.

The language of "To the Hebrews," full of allusions to Jewish beliefs and rites, conferred a feminine as well as a masculine quality upon the word "sons." The author meant "children" of both sexes when the text states that Jesus will bring "many sons to glory." Whether the writer used the Hebrew original or the Greek septuagintal version of Psalm 8, the word for "man"—'*adam*, '*enôsh*, *anthrōpos*—was gender-inclusive. It designated humankind without distinction of sex. Jesus himself was made man *(anthrōpos)* in the same communal sense of male and female.

We find here the still fluid attempts to put into some form of intellectual discourse the sense of utmost wonder at the incomparableness of Jesus. His candor, his courage, the height of his perception and the breadth of his commitment to all manner of men and women, as well as his utter weakness, his tears, and his reluctance to die—these traits were remembered and commemorated as a real presence after his death. His person was more than ever the source of the healing of wounds, the erasing of guilt, the reconciliation with enemies, above all, the reinstatement in the family of God.

Looking for adequate formulas from their cultural environment, the early theologians of the church stumbled on several and tried many. Men and women saw in Jesus the true *anthrōpos* and they were easily led to experiment with the myth of the *Imago Dei*. Paul spoke of him as the Icon of God

(2 Cor. 4:4). The author of "To the Hebrews" read Psalm 8 in the light of the myth of the Son of man, which Daniel, Enoch, and other writings had rendered familiar at that time. Manifestly at home in both worlds—Hellenistic and Judaic—the author of Hebrews could use the Greek version of Psalm 8 and see in Jesus the Son of man, who was also "the splendor or reflection of God's glory," *apaugasma tēs doxēs,* and even "the print of his substance," *charactēr tēs hupostaseōs autou* (Heb. 1:3). Jesus could be hailed as "the character of God's innermost reality," for the comparison likened him to the trace of God's footprint, the sign or the mark of his authenticity, the seal of his delegated authority.

The writer stood within the theological circle of the apostle Paul, who had already bound the transformation of human beings to the person of the New Being. The New Man engendered new men and new women. This theme appears with particular power in the hymn that Paul either composed or quoted when he exhorted the Philippians to overcome their natural self-ishness by "cultivating intelligently [*phronein*] among themselves that which was also in Christ Jesus" (Phil. 2:5),

> Who, being in the form of God,
> Did not cling to his divine equality
> As if it were a prey to seize by violence;
> But he emptied himself, took the form of a slave,
> And he assumed the likeness of a man....
> (2:6–7)

The humanity of Jesus was not a model for other human beings to copy literally. Paul was aware not only of the contrast that separated the conditions of existence in the Galilean villages from those of the commercial cities of the Empire, but also of the qualitative difference that set Jesus apart from the rest of humankind. Yet, Paul laid the foundations of a new humanism by recommending the intelligent cultivation, within the church community, of the character of Jesus.

Here again, the use of the word *anthrōpos* for describing the humaniza-tion of the New Being implied the inclusiveness of genders. It did not concern men only. It represented a goal of living for both males and females.[70]

While Psalm 8 may be called the Hebraic Song of Man *(Carmen Homi-nis),* the Pauline poem is, par excellence, the Christian Hymn of the New Man *(Carmen Novi Hominis),* who combines in his person the masculine and feminine elements of *Sophia* and *Logos.*

Wisdom in the Word

In John as well as in Paul, Wisdom is linked with the Word to the creation of the world and to the destiny of man through the person of Jesus. Paul wrote that he "[spoke] the Wisdom of God in a mystery, the hidden [Wisdom], which God ordained before the world unto our glory" (1 Cor.

2:7). He had previously identified "the Wisdom of God and the Power of God" with the Christ Jesus crucified (1 Cor. 1:23–24).

In a similar fashion, the Johannine prologue sang that "the Word was made flesh and sojourned among us in a tent" (John 1:14a), and he added, "We beheld his glory" (v. 14b). Exegetes have shown that the model for this poem was a Wisdom hymn of an earlier age. In the poetic thinking of Hellenistic Judaism, *Sophia* and *Logos* had long been associated. A para-mystical philosopher had prayed thus: "God of the Fathers, Lord of Mercy, thou hast made the universe by thy word [*en logō sou*], thou hast formed man by thy wisdom [*kai tē sophia sou*]" (Wis. 9:1–2a). In the cosmic creation story (Gen. 1:1—2:4a), which was used by the exilic priests as a preface to the old Garden myth (Gen. 2:4b—3:24), the *Logos* is present in the repetition of the key phrase, "And God said." The *Logos* received a prominent place when the Sabbath became a sacrament of participation with the Lord of the cosmos. The *Logos* of Yahweh, which the great prophets had tirelessly proclaimed when they announced the condemnation of the elect people, was now vindicated by the exile in Babylon. The Sovereign of history was then clothed with the meaning of God the Creator. The people, bereaved of king, temple, and land, could regain their hope in communion with the Lord of the world. The *Logos* of creation was also the *Logos* of the new creation.

Likewise, during the centuries that followed the shabby restoration in Zion for a few and the prosperous establishment of a Diaspora for the many, the divine figure of *Sophia* was endowed with the function of a mediatrix between the Creator and all human beings (Prov. 8:30–33). Not only the Johannine prologue but also the rest of the Fourth Gospel presents Jesus as divine Wisdom coming down from above and inviting her children. A correspondence between Wisdom's plea and the invitation by the Johannine Christ is obvious throughout the Fourth Gospel.[71] Wisdom said in Proverbs,

> Come, eat my bread,
> And drink the wine I have mingled
> (Prov. 9:5)

Jesus echoed in John,

> Whosoever drinketh the water that I shall give him shall never thirst; but the water that I shall give him shall be in him a well of water, springing up into everlasting life. (John 4:14)

It was Sophia who had first proclaimed,

> Those who eat me will hunger no more.
> And those who drink me will thirst for more.
> (Sir. 24:21)

Satiety and desire are joined in a single experience of the psyche. The

Johannine saying is not contradictory to the sapiential invitation. Early Christian understanding of the person of Jesus was not independent from a sacramental relationship that united the faithful to him. What Jesus brought was the sign of who he was. The "disciples" of the Johannine Christ soon became his "children," *technia* (John 13:33). He addressed them in the same way that *Sophia* had invited her own children to listen to her, "Now, therefore, hearken unto me, O ye children!" (Prov. 8:32a). The theological movement progresses from Wisdom playing in the presence of the Creator to Wisdom giving delights to him and, finally, to Wisdom finding delights in the children of men (8:22–32).

Wisdom playing in the presence of the Creator becomes the mediatrix of human happiness through ecumenical and all-embracing ethics. The motif of Wisdom renders not only legitimate but also imperative the human quest for philosophy, the arts, and all the sciences. Since the poem is crowned with a beatitude, it sends life out on a march through the multi-lanes of Wisdom's ways. "Happy are those who keep the course on my ways!" (8:32b).

The whole of human existence is comparable to a road, and happiness is the exhilaration of those who move toward a goal and take others with them in the same direction. The macarism (from the Greek *makarios,* "happy") designates an exclamation of "sending-off-on-the-way" (from the Hebrew *ashrê,* "O the ongoingness of . . ."). Through the teaching of Jesus, steeped as they were in sapiential dynamism, the early Christians spoke of living as a marching (*peripatein,* "to go on"; 1 Cor. 7:17; 2 Cor. 10:3) or even as a beautiful race (*trachein kalōs;* Gal. 5:7; cf. Rom. 9:16; Phil. 3:14).

Responsible behavior does not primarily result from applying a code of morality. It is a walking which connotes pleasure and agreeableness in the presence of the living Lord, literally, "before him" (Luke 1:17, 75; 2 Cor. 8:21; cf. Acts 4:19). To keep the ways of Wisdom is to stay on course, although there are several modes of approach. Wisdom plays in the *oikumēnē* of the earth (Prov. 8:31). She reconciles the whole world with God.

While the writers of the infant church did not explicitly develop the motif of Wisdom at play, canonical dynamics indicate that this motif was not far from the sacramental, nurturing, feminine, and especially, maternal imagery that described the function of the living Christ. Both John and Paul comprehended his ministry, his crucifixion, and his glorification as a sacred play. In him the knot of human evil is broken, and human tragedy becomes a divine comedy. Wisdom playing before the Lord at creation (Prov. 8:30) and the Lord playing with Leviathan (Ps. 104:26) point to the drama of both nature and history. The pathos of God does not cancel out the play of God, which is never to be confused with the mocking play of the gods with men.[72] Wisdom playing at creation is the Word made flesh and put to death for the sake of man's re-creation. For the theological sages of the Hebraeo-Christian faith, "Wisdom in the Word" is the play of death and rebirth. *Sophia* and *Logos,* symbols of the feminine and of the masculine in the divine Reality, are inseparable from the liberation of men and women. The play of *Sophia,* symbol of freedom in the cosmos, becomes the play of *Logos,* sacrament of reconciliation between male and female.

Androgyny and the Eschatological Woman

The subject of androgyny has attracted much attention in recent years among psychologists, feminists, and historians of comparative religion.[73] However, the word has received a number of different meanings. In its primary sense, androgyny is almost synonymous with hermaphrodism and refers to a biological abnormality. The Greek myths of androgyny and, later, the Hellenistic paintings and statues of hermaphrodites are not relevant to this inquiry, except insofar as they have influenced the cultural environment of early Christianity.

A number of Hellenistic religions as well as gnostic and other sects cultivated some form of psychological androgyny and in effect denied sexuality. The ideal of human perfection led to the search for the *coincidentia oppositorum* in many areas, including the oneness (in the sense of identification) of male and female. The *Gospel of Thomas,* for example, several times employed the expression "to become one" in the sense of androgyny, although the last saying in the book ascribed to Jesus and Peter an attitude of sheer misogyny. When Simon Peter complained and said, "Let Mary [Magdalene] leave us, for women are not worthy of life," Jesus replied that he would make her male. The gospel of Thomas may well have been related to Jewish speculations on *Sophia,*[74] but it does not deserve to be called the fourth Synoptic Gospel.[75]

Some scholars have detected in the New Testament writings the presence of androgyny merely because Paul declares, "We, though many, are one body in Christ" (Rom. 12:5; cf. 1 Cor. 12:27), or the Johannine Christ prays that his disciples "may be one" (John 17:11). Not only does this view ignore the meaning of the word "one" *(heis)* in classical and Hellenistic Greek usage (as it has been shown above in the chapter on Paul), but it also misreads the contextual evidence, for it confuses the communality of the church with asexuality. Such a comparison betrays a distortion of the comparative method. It may be called comparativism.[76]

A few exegetes have maintained that the Pauline phrase, "There is neither male *and* female" (Gal. 3:28; italics added) does not merely indicate woman's equality with man but in fact eradicates all sexual distinction and thus amounts to an attitude of antisexuality.

Such a view disregards the entire corpus of the genuine letters of Paul, in which the mutuality of the sexes is highly extolled (1 Cor. 7:3–4). It also betrays a faulty method of interpretation. The now famous phrase of Galatians may well have been inspired in part by an early baptismal formula, in which the distinctions between Jews and Greeks, on the one hand, between slaves and masters, on the other, were not abrogated but entailed no antagonism, no division, no sense of superiority or of inferiority, and therefore promoted complete equality within the church.

The last part of the triad, "neither male *and* female" uses the word "and" instead of the "neither . . . nor . . ." of the first two pairings. As it has often been observed, this is due to the fact that Paul, whether consciously or not, was recalling the story of creation, "And God made man according to the image of God, male and female made he them" (Gen. 1:27). The Hebraic myth had nothing to do with the myth of androgyny. The phrase that immediately followed included God's blessing over the fruitfulness and multiplication of the human race (Gen. 1:28). There is no reason whatever to find in Paul's declaration the influence of a Jewish myth, preserved in a later midrash, which presented Adam as androgynous. When Paul concludes, "You are all one in Christ Jesus" (Gal. 3:29), he praises unity in spite of diversity.

The Hellenistic myth of androgyny with its antisexual or at least asexual consequences nevertheless played a part in promoting the mystique of virginity or, in any case, the practice of celibate chastity among religious orders, including its enforcement upon the parish priesthood, but not before the tenth century A.D.

Paul himself admitted that the eschatological pressure and the need to preach the gospel in time for the return of the Lord made celibacy more expedient than marriage and family obligations (1 Cor. 7:29). His concern was not the result of an ontology of a nonsexual preference. It was entirely based upon practical considerations.

Like other ethnic groups of the ancient Near East who associated sexual initiation with magical techniques, early Israel and Judaism ascribed a numinous significance to virginity. By contrast, this concern played only a marginal part in the early church. It was recorded that Philip the evangelist "had four unmarried daughters, who prophesied" (Acts 21:9). It is probable that these young women had refused marriage in order to dedicate themselves to a special vocation in total gift, comparable to the practice of sacred virginity in many Greek and Roman sanctuaries.[77]

Toward the end of the century, "widows" formed a particular class of women within the church. They had to be at least sixty years of age and to have been married only once (1 Tim. 5:9; cf. Acts 6:1; 9:39). In the second century, these widows were sometimes called virgins, a fact that may have played a part in the rise of religious orders. Chastity in men and virginity in women became the symbols of a total offering of the self to Jesus Christ in vain efforts to attain "perfection" (Matt. 19:21). Such a development contributed to the illusion of a dichotomy between a supposedly pure soul and a sinful flesh, thus shifting moral attention from humane equilibrium in social relations to the fear of sexuality and the rise of a fallacious distinction between two levels of Christian service—lay and clerical. The net result of this deviation from the teaching of Jesus and Paul led not to the sublimation of sexual desire but to an obsessiveness with its repression, which plagues to this day large segments of Christendom.

To be sure, there was in ancient Israel a special class of men called Nazirites ("consecrated ones," Judges 13:5) who were dedicated to the Deity. The legislation on the Nazirites, recorded only in exilic times (Num. 6:2 ff.), does not state whether their various vows of abstinence included sexual continence. The Nazirites still existed in Maccabean times (second century B.C.), and their ideals may have influenced the sectarians of Qumran. In the early church, men did not consider sexual continence or celibate chastity to be signs of total consecration to the divine. The Jewish practice of making vows may have been handed down to some Jewish Christians. Mention is made of young men who had vowed not to shave their heads (Acts 21:23 ff.).

It will be readily admitted that virginity for women and celibate chastity for men were not matters of theological concern either for Jews or for the first-century Christians. However, the symbol of virginity, in the sense of moral stainlessness, belonged to their religious imagination. Paul figuratively hailed the church of Corinth as "a pure bride," literally, "an undefiled virgin," *parthenos hagnē,* "betrothed to Christ" (2 Cor. 11:2).

It was surely not on account of an accidental association of feelings or ideas that the apostle immediately afterwards added, "but I am afraid that as the serpent seduced Eve in his ability to perpetrate malevolence everywhere [*panourgia*], your thoughts will lead you astray from your rectitude and from the purity of your dedication [*hagnostē*] to Christ" (2 Cor. 11:3). The theme of a seduced Eve rose at once to Paul's consciousness when he wrote of the church as "an undefiled virgin" (v. 11:2).

The expression "eschatological woman," which has been felicitously applied to any female individual liberated from her servitude by the living Christ[78] should not be restricted to this usage alone. The eschatological woman designates also the whole community of those who are bound to the new economy of eternal life—Jews and Greeks, slaves and masters, males and females. The eschatological woman is the metaphorical description of the church at the end of time. The femininity of the designation derives only in part from the myth of Eve. Christ is "the last Adam" (1 Cor. 15:45), just as the church is the new Eve, the eschatological woman.

Why should the new society of men and women who have left behind them the inequalities of class, the hatreds of race, and the resentments of sex be compared to a feminine figure who will triumph over evil at the end of time? Several answers are possible and are not mutually exclusive, the most probable of which is that the early Christian imagination, fed as it was by the hopes of the prophets and the visions of the apocalyptists, thought of the church as the ideal Israel, the youthful bride for whom Yahweh will always have maternal compassion (Isa. 54:6). In view of the recurrent reverses and persecutions endured by Jewry and now piercing the heart of nascent Christendom, the feminine imagery of bride and mother fluctuates as it passes from Israel to the church. Like Israel, the church is the mother writhing in the pangs of travail. She is not only Rachel weeping for her children (Matt. 2:18) but also the eschatological woman of the Johannine apocalypse (Rev. 12:1–17).

In a clear allusion to the descendants of Eve (Gen. 3:15), similar to that of Paul in his Second Letter to the Corinthians (11:1–3), the seer of Patmos described, toward the last decade of the first century A.D., the new Eve, whose infant son will crush the antique serpent, "the seducer of the entire world" (Rev. 12:9).

Eve, the seduced mother of all the living, is now transfigured into the second Eve, symbol of all those who will bear witness in their lives to the Lord Jesus (Rev. 12:17). While the eschatological woman of the Johannine apocalypse is not intended to be the Virgin Mary—and modern commentators, including Roman Catholic exegetes, agree on this point—it is understandable that the fluidity of the imagery permitted the identification of the Mother of Jesus with

> [the] woman clothed with the sun, the moon under her feet, and on her head a crown of twelve stars; she was with child, and she cried out in her pangs of his birth, in anguish for delivery.... (Rev. 12:1–2)

As long as the figure of the Mater Dolorosa remains associated with the ideology of the church in travail rather than with a trinitarian theology that introduces the eschatological woman within the realm of divinity, Mariological symbolism is true to biblical faith. The Second Council of the Vatican has satisfied in modern times the requirements of Scripture when it removed Mariology from theology proper (doctrine of God) and inserted it in ecclesiology (doctrine of the church).

The Lukan story of the annunciation alludes to divine presence in terms of the "thick darkness" that overshadowed the Sinai epiphany (Luke 1:35; cf. Exod. 20:21), or the "deep gloom" of the innermost room in the Jerusalem temple (1 Kgs. 8:12). The gospel of the nativity presented the mother of Jesus as the first daughter of the church.

A few artists have understood this aspect of ecclesial Mariology when they pictured the second Eve as the church in travail, from Piero della Francesca's fresco of the *Madonna del Parto* ("My Lady of the Birth") in the Monterchi cemetery chapel (Tuscany) to Jean Lurçat's modern tapestry of *The Virgin and the Dragon* in the apse of the church at Assy facing Mont Blanc (Savoy).

The theme of the eschatological woman, paradigm of a church that is in no way triumphant but suffers the agonies of all human beings in history, is concordant with the Pauline evocation of the "undefiled virgin" now at risk of being led astray (2 Cor. 11:2–3).

From Eve seduced in Genesis to Eve transfigured in Revelation, the religious symbol of femininity would not have survived throughout the twelve centuries of the scriptural span if an unswerving respect had not persisted, at least among a few in each generation, for the nobility of womanhood. The persuasive power of Hebrew-Christian faith, which overcomes the chasms of race, class, and sex, derives its language from the human experience of the *erōs-agapē* continuum.

Investigation of the relationship between man and woman in the long growth of the biblical literature has shown that progress was by no means uniform. It presents a tidal movement of action and reaction, of progress and regress, both in Judaism after Hebraism and in Christendom after Jesus and the first formative hours. Yet, a steady direction, an entelechy, a teleology, binds together the mutuality of manhood and womanhood with the human image of divinity. Theology may never be divorced from male and female anthropology. Manhood and womanhood, in the Hebraeo-Christian Scriptures, are coordinated with the vision of a divine equilibrium between masculine and feminine experiences of being human.

Recent writers on the feminine dimension of the divine have so far failed to delineate the distinction, admittedly subtle, that in the ancient religions separates the worship of the Mother Goddess—principle of fertility and the stimulus of the magical character of cultic sexuality—from the worship of the transcendent Being, whose descriptions are molded by human awareness of the masculine-feminine complementariness. When transcendence is taken seriously, masculine language in itself is not offensive. As soon as one reflects upon the processes of language, one discovers that gender is not to be confused with sex. This fact cannot be stressed strongly enough. This is the reason for which such expressions as "Beyond the Sex of God" are irrelevant. It must be emphasized again and again that language about God is always metaphorical. The change to the metaphor of mother will not solve the problem which, for some women today, arises from the metaphor of father.

The Wonders and the Pitfalls
of Human Love

A biblical theology of manhood and womanhood includes many topics, for which insights on God and the experience of living interact in language and in substance. None of these topics is more fraught with fascination and peril than that of human love.

In the course of her comments on Abélard's contribution to philosophy and to lyric poetry, the medievalist Helen Waddell quoted lines from the *Carmina Burana* ending with "Till the heart sings." Praising Abélard for "setting [Héloise's] lovely name to melodies lovelier still," she observed that "the current always flows from pure humanism to speculative theology."[79]

Perhaps she meant that theologians who speculate—that is, who look reflectively on the mystery of God—inevitably borrow from the language of true lovers. At the same time, one might add that the passion that brings together and keeps together two human beings transcends pure humanism. It goes beyond a biological urge and stems from the center of being in relation to the self and to others in an enhanced awareness of time and space. Here lies the source of the wonders and the pitfalls of human love.

When the bond that unites a man and a woman is so deep, so shattering, and so impervious to ephemerality or distance that it is ready to defy the norms of society and institutional church, it belongs to a realm akin to the religious and it requires theological analysis. The pure humanism of love does not present a secular aspect of self-sufficiency. It implies a God-inspired and a God-aiming humanism. When creatureliness discovers its authentic humanity through a liberation from existential solitude, it ushers in adoration. Not the adoration of another being, not the adoration of universal forces, but the worship of the Spirit of the universe. Humanity transfigured by love mirrors divinity.

At this moment, however, the individual lover of either sex runs the risk of confusing infinity with finitude, and human love may easily become a form of idolatry. On account of trance-like moments when the self seems to escape from reality through communion with another self, or when that other self is fused with the experience of that escape, the passage may slide from self-gift to immersion within the universe, which, in the final analysis, is self-worship.

One should discard the popular opinion that dates the rise of love lyricism in literature to the troubadours of the twelfth century A.D. In ancient Egypt, love poetry sometimes displayed a reciprocity of desire and obligation, as well as the exquisite sadness of refinement through the unfulfilled. In classical antiquity, the iconography of marriage, beyond the misogynous mores debasing womanhood to mere instrumentality, could also reveal a sentiment at once wistful and serene that defied the presence of death. This is illustrated, for example, by the alabaster sarcophagus of Vulpi (fourth century B.C.) at the Boston Museum of Fine Arts. The images of a man and a woman facing one another are seen in profile on the lid. Their embrace is at once intense and sober. Their eyes meet in eternity.

It was in the Song of Songs, however, that the *erōs-agapē* continuum appeared probably for the first time in the literature of the Western world. Its poetic and perhaps even choreographic depiction of human love exhibited a sense of passionate reciprocity, an awareness of human frailty, the agonies of absence, the extreme edge of precipitous delight, the dread of loss, the certainty of promise and hope for the future.

Although the Song of Songs did not explicitly show the lovers' attachment to the religion of Yahweh, it could not have been preserved as a musical and dancing masque of love if its inspiration had not been predicated upon the vision of the Hebrew theologians of transcendence. The Song of Songs is a riposte to the curse of Eve in the myth of the Garden.

Like the Genesis narrative, it abounds in allusions to the flora, the fauna, and the mores of a pastoral culture in transition. Nomads have just recently entered into an agrarian mode of existence. They cultivate fields, orchards, vineyards, and at times inhabit walled-in villages. Tension between the two modes of social economies may be detected in both documents. The strangeness of the imagery that adorns the Song of Songs should not be repellent to the modern temper nor conceal the profundity of the poet's purpose.

While in the myth of the Garden man is condemned to eat his bread in the sweat of his brow until he returns to the dust whence he has come (Gen. 3:17–19), the woman's burden is even heavier in the pain of childbearing (v. 16a, b). In addition, woman's submission to her husband is explained by her lust toward him (v. 16c).

The Song of Songs pointedly reverses this expression of male arrogance by employing the same Hebrew word for desire but this time applying it to the man's irresistible longing for the woman (7:10 [Heb. 11]). The poet seems to have been aware of the unfortunate effect upon the ego of male dominance produced by the story of Eden whenever it was chanted liturgically during cultic celebrations in the sanctuaries of ancient Israel. Lyricist of love, admirer of womanhood, this humane artist eulogizes the couple, and his appreciation of sexual fairness makes of him a theological polemist.

The body of each lover is candidly admired by the other. The woman's charms are extolled three times (1:1—2:2; 4:4–5; 7:2–4; cf. tables 1 and 2 in chapter 3 above), and the man's euphemistic "whole self" only once (5:13–16), but at the very center of the mirrorlike unfolding of the choreography. Ritual impurities of sexual secretions, ritual prohibitions, and the ritual gestures of cleansing, which eventually became in the official codes of the Torah a matter for exact observance, are completely ignored.

The consummation of love, with its foreplay and afterplay, is described without any sense of sin. Nudity provokes no embarrassment, either in the dream sequence or in the actuality of intimacies (2:3). The entire poem exudes the joy of the flesh. Ecstasy is equally shared by both lovers, who thus reach together the esthetic and psychological instant of total union. At the end, the poet points out that it is the woman who rightly claims the privilege of bringing to her partner *shalôm,* in the ancient, complex, and inclusive meaning of "peace inseparable from health, growth, and the blossom of being" (8:10).

The impression that here *erōs* is interwoven with *agapē* arises from the structured sequence of the Song of Songs, up to the "last word" (8:14). True love requires faithfulness and durability as well as tenderness at all times.

Both lovers know that such a love is as strong as death, or according to the intensifying parallelism of the second *stichos* in the poetic line, that such a passion is as cruel as the grave (v. 6).

This double saying is elliptical, and its meaning open to various interpretations. Does the poet wish to suggest that the two lovers are united until death? Does he imply that the act of consummation, with its physio-psychological finality of gift and gain and its traumatic sensation of rebirth after death, may symbolize an existential demand for repudiating the dread, or even for overcoming the cruelty, of death? Is there at that point in this masque of music and dance an ultimate protest against the finitude of human destiny on earth? If so, the Song of Songs includes a second and final attempt to silence the reverberations of the knell audible at the end of the myth of the Garden.

Although the poem says nothing of procreation or of the responsibilities of lovers for a family, one may see in it a prelude to monogamous marriage. Polygamy was no doubt inherited from the pre-Abrahamic culture, from which Hebraism emerged. It persisted in Israel for a long while in spite of the awareness of its baneful consequences for woman's happiness in the home, as shown by the stories of Sarah and Hagar, and of Rachel and Leah.

In his repeated efforts to reaffirm the nobility of oppressed womanhood, Jesus endorsed the Jewish ideal of monogamy. Further, he clearly implied that marriage stood on a far higher ground than economics, eugenics, or the continuity of the race. Not only did he perceive and uphold the rights of women but he also argued against the easy male-sided practice of divorce, and he pronounced a word that has captured the imagination of all Christians ever since:

> Those whom God hath joined together,
> Let no man put asunder.
> (Mark 10:9; Matt. 19:6)

The freedom that he boldly exercised in his selective application of the Torah for the sake of humaneness, whenever one of its legal provisions was unfair to women and stressed only the hardness of male minds (Deut. 24:1–4), is the very reverse of the legalism that later crept into clerical Christendom and that has prohibited the dissolution of the marriage bond under all circumstances, except through venal casuistry.

Viewed from the perspective of canonical dynamics, the myth of the Garden and its theological counterpart, the Song of Songs, raise for a biblical theology of manhood and womanhood not only the social problem that results from the biological differentiation of sexes but also the spiritual problem inherent in the ambiguity of *erōs* as soon as *erōs* is transformed by the qualities of *agapē*.

The Hebraic theology of divine transcendence over nature went counter to the cultural grain of the neolithic age. It represented a revolutionary turning around of the mores that had fashioned the human species for millenniums during its infancy. When prehistoric man and woman domesticated milk-producing animals and began to learn the arts of agriculture, the sexual drive allied itself to the whole environment of existence, cosmic as well as social. In consort with the cycles of the seasons, *erōs* was endowed with the power of achieving mystical communion with the deified forces of nature, upon which depended food, shelter, and the basic economy of survival. Periods of sexual abstinence alternated with orgiastic feasts in which the myth of Mother Earth and other powers of nature was enacted through rituals of homosexual and heterosexual promiscuity. Religion and sexuality were one. Eroticism led human beings to immerse themselves within the numinous of nature, and it coincided with the rhythm of work and leisure. Modern ecologists do not understand the temptations to which the ancient Hebrews were exposed. Actually, the European and American abuse of nature is inherited from the Assyro-Babylonians, the Persians and the Romans. The Hebraic exhortation to subdue the earth was directed against the ancient Semitic arts of agriculture with their rites of erotic espousal of Mother Earth.

The emergence of the Hebraic faith in its complete reliance upon a Creator utterly distinct from nature but always its Sovereign entailed a profound change in *erōs*. The bounty of the Lord of rain and harvest was no longer dependent upon the orgiastic celebrations of the ancient Semitic cults. To be sure, ethics of the covenant did not divorce Israel from nature, but it altered *erōs* profoundly because it transferred its numinous character from the violence and excesses of the religious orgy to the strictly human vocation of protecting the family from generation to generation.

The myth of the Garden aimed at protecting Israel from the "lure of infinity," to which for millenniums the agriculturists of Mesopotamia and the Fertile Crescent had been exposed in their seasonal worship of the gods of vegetation and animal husbandry. It opposed to the Canaanite absorption of *erōs* in the cosmos the more refined thrill of monogamy. In this ethos of love between two human beings, "the-man," *Ha-Adam*, offers a lyrical response to his discovery of the human exchange of joy. Aware of the complementariness offered by "the-woman," *Ha-Ishshah*, "the-man" exclaimed in postcoital rapture,

> This time, this-one [fem.]! She is
> Bone of my bones
> And flesh of my flesh!
> (Gen. 2:23)

In Yahwistic theology womanhood is raised from the level of erotic instrument to that of love-sharer, equal in sensual enjoyment. In the context of creatureliness, the man knows that the gift from his Maker is the crown of creation. Within a religious framework that extols the bounty of the Lord of nature—who is not to be confused with any of the natural forces—the myth of the Garden proposed a new *erōs,* not deviated but reoriented into a physio-psychological realm that prizes above all the arts the ethical mystery of the human couple.

The eating of the fruit of the tree of knowledge is not an initiation into the experience of sexuality. Rather, it designates the pantheistic lust that wishes to explode finitude and that thereby poisons the sexual relationship at the very core of the human personality. Symbolized by the ludicrous fig leaves, sexual modesty between man and woman becomes the symptom of the alienation that now separates them. The so-called enmity of the sexes—a theme overwrought in the literature of most cultures—is the consequence of a loss of trust in the transcendent Giver of all bounty.

The wonders of human love are constantly threatened by the resurgence of an *erōs* that leads women as well as men to the egocentric illusion of secular humanism. This resurgence produces sexual egotism, the love of self and the thirst for instant self-gratification. *L'amour sans lendemain* has become at once the cause and the sign of the bane which breaks down the *erōs-agapē* continuum. The trivialization of sexuality seems at first to be the opposite of its divinization, but both indicate that the cosmic eroticism of ancient times remains unregenerate.

When man or woman is used by the other sex for purely erotic purposes, *erōs* eventually fades into insignificance and banality. The myth of the Garden anticipates the observations of depth psychologists who are today baffled by the widespread incidence of frigidity and impotence.

Moreover, the myth of the Garden adds to the man's exultation the correlative judgment that situates woman, the marriage partner, at the top of the social scale:

> Therefore shall a man leave his father and mother,
> And shall cleave unto his wife,
> And they shall be one flesh;
> And they were both naked, the man and his wife,
> And were not ashamed.
>
> (Gen. 2:24–25)

The marriage bond takes precedence over ancestral lineage and even reverence for parents. The *agapē* subsumed by the "attachment," "gluing," or "cleaving" of this unicarnality also commands the quality of endurance in time.

The Song of Songs implies the same expectation of constancy. It argues against the common distortion that views the myth of the Garden as a chronological event in the history of mankind. The Genesis story is then demythicized. To historicize it is to deny its truth. When traditional churches still speak of "before" and "after" the Fall, they miss the disturbing contemporaneity of the myth, for they relegate the Genesis narrative to some original sin remote in the past, and thereby attempt to preserve themselves from the existential risk of every generation.

The canonical dynamics of human love, from the ancient Yahwists to the apostle Paul, celebrate the wonders of love whenever *agapē* motivates and invigorates *erōs*. The urge to go beyond the self in love enables one to care for the other, to give to the other, and at the highest and heroic level, to die for the sake of the other. In the altruism of its direction human love meets divine love.

That in the eighth century B.C. the prophet Hosea could liken the compassion of God to the love *(agapē)* of a man for a woman (Hos. 3:1–3) indicates, in the midst of ample evidence scattered elsewhere in the literature of ancient Israel, that *agapē* was not just the discovery of the early Christians. It derived from Hebraism at its best, which in turn inherited it from a few Yahwists and those prophetic visionaries who put into words their interpretation of life, death, and sexuality.

A biblical theology of manhood and womanhood stretches human love "till the heart sings." It views marriage not so much as an institution as a union within the third dimension. Rainer Maria Rilke expressed a similar thought poetically when he wrote,

> Once the realization is accepted that even between the *closest* human beings infinite distances continue to exist, a wonderful living side by side can grow up, if they succeed in loving the distance between them which makes it possible for each to see the other whole against a wide sky![80]

For Paul and the early church, a God-centered humanism is marching according to Christ Jesus. The theology of the Way renders the importance of "do and don't" not superfluous but derivative. *Agapē* is the energy and the destination of the march. *Agapē* is that which does not seek its own advantage (1 Cor. 13:5). It endures as well as comforts the mate in love and the neighbor in friendship (Gal. 6:2). The constancy of the movement toward the goal is not easy, unless it be that "the *agapē* of the Christ *constrains* us" (2 Cor. 5:14; italics mine). The Greek verb *sunechein* suggests not the constraint of a law, nor the restraint of a conforming to society, but the power of an *agapē* that transmutes *erōs* into self-offering. The apostle knew that love is the ultimate reality by which we are grasped, embraced, hugged, surrounded, and therefore also maintained. The French translators use *étreinte* rather than *contrainte*. *(Traduction œcuménique de la Bible)*.

The movement of this kind of love is not from pure humanism to speculative theology. It is the reverse. The *erōs-agapē* continuum flows from infinity to finitude. Then pleasure *(hēdonē)* refuses to be demonized into hedonism. Happiness is not even the static eudaemonism of an abstract philosophy of living. The art of love cannot be built upon the cult of pleasure. It stems from the pursuit of happiness, which in its turn has to be assessed not in the light of eighteenth-century deism but according to the beatitudes of divine wisdom and Jesus himself.

Human love is neither a substitute for a cosmic sacredness, which is lost, nor at the opposite end of the spectrum, a sinful accommodation to biological expediency, nor again—between these two extremes—a mere exercise in "fun and games." In the highest sense, human love is the act and the art of play, but a play within a faith that praises the glory of creation.

The love of man and woman affects their private lives rather than their public status, function, and responsibility within the church. Nevertheless, a biblical theology of humanhood "on the way," whose *erōs* is animated by *agapē* toward a common goal of living, bears also upon the question of the Christian ministry for women as well as for men.

Are women so truly the equal of men that they should be officially ordained and actually "received" by all members of the church as priestly ministers of the mysteries of Christ?

Toward a New Theology of Priesthood

The topic of ministry in the church, even more than that of love between man and woman, is far too complex for adequate treatment in this study. A biblical theology of manhood and womanhood points, however, to developments of a later age and proposes overtures, with safeguards, to contemporary ecclesiologists, whose responsibility is to prepare today for the universal church of tomorrow.

Should women be ordained to priesthood in the traditionalist denominations that still deny them their vocation as sacramental administrators? Should progressive denominations that now admit the validity of female ordination educate their membership in such a way that ordained women be fully received, accepted by all, on a par with ordained men? In its diverse forms the same question is perhaps as urgent for Protestants as it is for Greek Orthodox, Roman Catholic, and Anglo-Catholic communities of Christendom on their way to becoming the true church of Christ.

If a woman could be called an apostle *(apostolos)* or could hold the office of minister *(diakonos)* in the early church, the question of the ordination of women to the ministry becomes an entirely legitimate and even imperative and inescapable aspect of biblical theology.[81]

The canonical dynamics of Scripture call for a new theology of priesthood as well as for a new theology of the ministry.

A linguistic confusion needs to be dispelled. The English word "priest" stands for the Greek word *presbyteros* (Hebrew, *zaqen*), which means "elder," and also for the Greek word *hiereus* (Hebrew, *kohen*), which means "keeper of the sanctuary, temple official" and, eventually, "sacrificer, offerer of sacrifice." In the strict sense of the word, there was no Christian priest, male or female, in the first-century church. There were elders, evangelists, prophets (who spoke in tongues), teachers, apostles (who were originally envoys and missionaries), and special members, *diakonoi* (later institutionalized as "deacons") who were in charge of welfare for the poor. Bishops, literally "overseers," *episkopoi,* were probably officials responsible for the supervision of the treasury as well as for the maintenance of buildings and grounds.[82] No hierarchical chain of command or sacramental rank existed among the various ministers. The only priests mentioned in the canonical literature of the early church were Jewish sacrificers in the Jerusalem temple or the cultic officials of the Hellenistic sanctuaries.

The opinion has been held that Paul once referred to his apostolate in sacerdotal terms. According to the Revised Standard Version, he wrote "of the grace given me by God to be a minister of Christ Jesus to the Gentiles in the priestly service of the gospel of God" (Rom. 15:15b–16a). The Jerusalem Bible went so far as to venture an even more blatant mistranslation when it paraphrased, "[God] appointed me a priest of Jesus Christ, and I am to carry out my priestly duty by bringing the Good News from God to the pagans." The original Greek does not support these interpretations. Paul called himself not "a priest," *hiereus,* but "a minister," *leitourgos,* and here the Revised Standard Version is correct. However, did Paul consider his work to be "the priestly service," *hierourgounta,* of the gospel of God? The fact that the plural neuter *hierourgounta,* "holy works," and the word *hiereus,* "priest," which is absent in this passage, are related to the same notion of *hieros,* "holy, sacred" does not justify the translation "priestly service" for the plural neuter *hierourgounta,* used of Jewish and pagan sacrifices and other cultic acts (Philo, Lucian, Plutarch). Paul's religious vocabulary reflected that of his time. Even as late as the fifth century A.D., Jerome discerned here not an allusion to the priesthood but a reference to the holiness of the mystery of conversion. He translated the Greek phrase into the Latin as *sanctificans Evangelium Dei,* "making holy the gospel of God." Paul used sacerdotal language, but he did not think of himself as a Christian priest offering the body of Christ in the Eucharist. He referred to converted pagans offering themselves acceptably to God (Rom. 15:16b).

When the confederation of Israel's tribes settled in the land of Canaan over two centuries of infiltration, the children of the nomads were slowly initiated into the art of husbandry by the Canaanite natives. Religious syncretism was inevitable. Plowing, harvesting, and threshing were cultic acts. The Yahwist theologians attempted to "hebraicize" the agricultural feasts. Thus they taught the farmers how to offer the first fruit of the fields to the Sovereign of nature, not as a ceremonial of erotic communion with the gods of the soil and rain, but as a ritual of thanksgiving for the Lord of nature *and* of history. This solemn act took place in a sanctuary attended by a priest, whose responsibility was to remember the correct formula of the thanksgiving liturgy and to prompt the worshipers during the offering dedication (Deut. 26:1–10). The priest did not offer the sacrifice of first fruit on behalf of a laity. He was the keeper of the shrine and of the Yahwist tradition. Similarly, the priest in charge at the temple of Shiloh at the time of Samuel was not the officiant of any sacrifice. His duty was to keep a close supervision over the behavior of the worshipers (1 Sam. 1:9 ff.).[83]

Israelite priesthood was hereditary, reserved to the descendants of the tribe of Levi. The numinous character of genealogy took precedence over the moral character of the incumbents. With the rise of the monarchy, temple officials became royal functionaries, and their importance increased with time. The high priest of the Solomonic temple was not the sacramental head of the clergy. He administered ceremonies and supervised the priests who were attached to the temple. There is no evidence whatever that before the exile priests were intermediaries between God and man. In the post-exilic birth of Judaism only priests offered sacrifices. When, in the second temple, the myth of Aaron coincided with the myth of Zion, the high priest exercised many sacred duties and enjoyed special prerogatives. On the Yom Kippur, he entered the Holy of Holies and stood—so it was believed—in the immediate presence of God. Coming out of "the house of the veil" (Sir. 50:5), he would with his ritual benediction carry out, in effect, to the assembled congregation the power of the Most High (Sir. 50:12–21). The political and moral corruption that vitiated the high priesthood in the course of the centuries explains in part the brutal intervention of Antiochus IV Epiphanes (168 B.C.). The Maccabean Wars were initially caused by a feud between two rival high priests. The final revolt against the Romans (A.D. 66), which in turn precipitated the destruction of the second temple (A.D. 70), could not be ascribed solely to the corruption of the Jewish clergy, but there is little doubt that the early Christians—like their distant models, Jeremiah and other prophets of the eighth and seventh centuries B.C.—saw in the Jerusalem priesthood the very symbol of a religious system from which they had been liberated.

The notion of priesthood as an agency of divine-human mediation had been borrowed originally from the religions of the ancient Near East. For the Yahwist theologians of early Israel, priesthood was not a sacerdotal institution. The notion was used as a linguistic structure to express the mission of Israel in history.

The Sinai covenant formula conferred upon the whole people an awesome commission, "to become a kingdom of priests" (Exod. 19:6) for the sake of all nations. It was this theology of universal vocation which Second Isaiah developed centuries later when he proclaimed Israel, the servant of Yahweh, to be "a light unto the nations" (Isa. 42:6; cf. 61:6).

The early Christians returned to this same high level of discourse when they thought of Jesus as the pure High Priest (Heb. 5:5). In spite of the agonies of dissension within and hostility without, they saw in the nascent church "a chosen race, a royal priesthood, a holy nation, God's own people" (1 Pet. 2:5).

For canonical Christianity, priesthood remained a theological metaphor

destined to explain the *klesis* of the *ekklesia:* the church is the society of
those who are "called" to bring the gospel to the world. The Jewish and
pagan notion of the individual priest as the officiant of a sacrifice *(hiereus)*
was utterly alien to the spirit as well as the letter of the canonical literature
in the early church.

The sacerdotal institution remained in the mentality of those sons of the
covenant only as a semantic sign; Jesus was the High Priest, the sole head of
the society of God.[84]

Toward the end of the first century A.D., momentous changes took place
within the organization of the churches. Was it a coincidence that those
changes were simultaneous with a new emphasis on the dominance of
males, both at home and in the cult?

Clement of Rome (A.D. 95–96) alluded to a hierarchy of Christian ministers, whom he compared to the sacerdotal body within Judaism—high
priest, priest, and Levite. At the beginning of the second century A.D., the
author of the *Didache* (pseudepigraphic "Teaching of the Twelve Apostles")
enjoined the communities to support with material goods the prophets who
ministered unto them, for, he wrote, "they are your high priests" (*Didache*
13.3). The use of the expression was still metaphorical, but the subsequent
literature of the church fathers amply documents the rise of a male clergy,
distinct from the laity, set apart from all other Christian men and women.
The clergy comprised deacons, priests, and bishops, with the bishop of
Rome attempting by various methods to assert his supreme authority over
all of them.

Two factors have prominently contributed to the evolution of the
priesthood in the West. First, the growth of an antisexual bias is amply
documented by the patristic literature. Jerome, for example, wrote, *"Omnis
coitus impurus."*[85] It was the fear of sexuality that may have provoked or
followed the linking of perfection to virginity or at least to chastity. It
eventually led to an institutional enforcement of priestly celibacy and, in
effect, to a sacerdotal form of androgyny.[86] Second, the Eucharist came to
be understood no longer exclusively as an act of thanksgiving and of participation in the body of Christ (1 Cor. 10:16; 11:23–26; 14:16) but
primarily as a sacrificial offering upon the altar. These two developments,
among others, explain in part why women have been excluded from ordination to the priesthood in the traditional churches of Christendom. As long as
a male priest claims that he reenacts in a sacramental form the sacrifice of
Jesus on the cross and is thereby identified mystically with the living
Christ—the Bridegroom of the church—any discussion on the ordination of
women will remain sterile.

The canonical dynamics of Scripture show unambiguously that the
church is not a hierarchy based on "grades of existence" (Thomas Aquinas)
that are determined by God. The church is the whole people of God.

Canonical dynamics of Scripture call urgently for a new theology of priesthood.

Protestants, in practice if not in official doctrine, likewise need to reconsider their theology of the ministry. An ordained pastor, man or woman, is above all a specially trained officiant who is set apart for the celebration of the eucharistic mystery. The common usage of public worship, in several denominations that have arisen from the Protestant Reformation, reduces the ministry of the Word chiefly to the sermon, and the sermon itself to a "religious" discourse, with the pulpit at the center of the chancel. The celebration of the Eucharist belongs to the dominical service as its liturgical apex, and the altar, not the pulpit, deserves the central place. Many Protestants need to learn anew, from the synagogue and from Orthodox and Roman churches, the sacramental character of the Scripture lesson, especially of the Gospel, and the preaching of the Word as the indispensable preface, within proper liturgical movement, to the ceremonial act of eucharistic communion.

The mentality of many Protestant congregations, still hostile to the presence of a woman in the pulpit, may be, through a study of the canonical dynamics of Scripture, first nurtured into the rediscovery of the dominical service. On the Lord's day the church holds the feast of the Word made flesh.

Our Father Who Art in Heaven

The canonical dynamics of Scripture, from Genesis to Revelation, exhibit interaction between the language of human love and the description of God. On account of the cultural trends of the present day and the social disintegration of the family, the idea of divine fatherhood has become offensive to some.

Opposition, in some quarters, to the notion of divine fatherhood is due not only to the human experience of domineering and despotic fathers but also, and paradoxically, to the human experience of effeminate fathers, of absent fathers, of irresponsible fathers, and of fathers who have failed. Let it be reaffirmed that the biblical metaphor of divine father is never divorced from the memory of dual parenthood (Hosea). It never means genital procreation. Neither is the father image to be separated from the motif of love as motherly compassion in nurture; it implies both divine self-immolation in the *theologia crucis* and a human willingness to become, for women as well as for men, humble, open, and recipient like little children. Divine fatherhood has nothing to do with the American idea of manliness or virility. It points to strength in weakness, to the power of love that lives in death and beyond death.

A biblical theology of manhood and womanhood is neither a modern, systematic theology expressed in terms of the cultural environment of the twentieth century A.D., nor is it a manual of sexual ethics for our time. Rather, a biblical theology of manhood and womanhood attempts to expound, with scrupulous respect for the historical growth in all its ups and downs over twelve centuries of Near Eastern and classical antiquity, the double movement in the interaction of theology with anthropology and, conversely, of anthropology with theology. The offensiveness of naming God, Father vanishes when the speech of prayer precedes and informs theological discourse.

To say, "Our Father who art in heaven, Hallowed be thy name," is not an attribution. It is an invocation.

The Lord's Prayer lifts the metaphor of divine fatherhood far above the notion of maleness and femaleness or even of masculinity and femininity. It transcends the imagery of generation and nurture. It does not use the word "Father" alone, out of context. It does not offer an intellectual proposition. It does not detach the invocation from the hallowing of the name.[87]

When Jesus bade his disciples to pray, "Our Father," he invited them to join the whole history of salvation within the purpose of the universe. One does not talk *about* God and call him merely Father. One talks *with* God and says, "Our Father who art in heaven, Hallowed be thy name!"

A human being at the moment of death may cry out, "My God!" But the church at prayer says, "Our Father." The church follows the synagogue and invokes with the remnant of Israel in all ages, *Abinu,* "Our Father." Such an attitude operates a radical shift of emphasis, from God the genitor and dominator to Immanuel, "God with us."

First, it implies the plurality in time and space of the society of God. The mode of address in the Lord's Prayer transfers the figure of speech from the realm of individual piety, which always risks deteriorating into self-justification, self-pity, self-comfort, self-gratulation, to a higher plane. "Our Father" bespeaks a response to the teleological view of creation, the vision of a *telos,* a goal, which the prophets Hosea, Jeremiah, and Second Isaiah bequeathed to Jesus. As "Our Father," God is not the Ancestor, a metaphor of the past, but the Initiator of the new covenant, the Re-creator whose passion to save transcends the language of both paternity and maternity.

Second, the Lord's Prayer places the divine above time and space. "Our Father" is "in heaven." This figure of speech also comes to annihilation. "The heavens and even the heavens of heavens cannot contain thee." The myths of the ancient gods are "human, all too human." The myths of the modern gods are cosmic but limited abstractions or merely psychological projections. They too are brought to naught. The metaphorical language is exploded.

Third, the Lord's Prayer compels the shaking of belief into faith, and in turn the mutation of faith into commitment. Transcendence is not remote in the realm of dream, of idealization. "Name" means summons. When the church prays, "Hallowed be thy name," it answers yes to the urgency of the call. The God who is in heaven is disturbingly near, very near, for he comes with a love that liberates only as it demands. From "He Who Causes To Be" of the burning bush to "Our Father," the name seals an appointment, spells out a delegation, discloses an ambassadorship, and requires a response of acceptance.

A God-centered humanism confers upon woman as well as man the full stature of humanity. In the Pauline theology, divine fatherhood means filiality with an invitation to act. In the Johannine Gospel, divine fatherhood means the apostolate of both sons and daughters. To pray the Lord's Prayer is to face availability and commitment.

Principal Abbreviations

AJSLL	American Journal of Semitic Languages and Literatures
ALBO	Analecta lovaniensia biblica et orientalia
ANQ	Andover Newton Quarterly
ATR	Anglican Theological Review
Bib	Biblica
BJRL	Bulletin of the John Rylands University Library of Manchester
BSac	Bibliotheca Sacra
BTB	Biblical Theology Bulletin
BZ	Biblische Zeitschrift
CBQ	Catholic Biblical Quarterly
CC	Christianity and Crisis
HSCP	Harvard Studies in Classical Philology
HTR	Harvard Theological Review
HUCA	Hebrew Union College Annual
Int	Interpretation
JAAR	Journal of the American Academy of Religion
JBL	Journal of Biblical Literature
JEA	Journal of Egyptian Archaeology
JNWSL	Journal of Northwest Semitic Languages
JSOT	Journal for the Study of the Old Testament
LTQ	Lexington Theological Quarterly
NRT	La nouvelle revue théologique
Nov T	Novum Testamentum
Nov T Sup	Novum Testamentum, Supplements
NTS	New Testament Studies
RB	Revue biblique
RHPR	Revue d'histoire et de philosophie religieuses
RL	Religion in Life
TGl	Theologie und Glaube
TQ	Theologische Quartalschrift
TS	Theological Studies
TToday	Theology Today
USQR	Union Seminary Quarterly Review

VT	*Vetus Testamentum*
VTSup	Vetus Testamentum, Supplements
WTJ	*Westminster Theological Journal*
ZAW	*Zeitschrift für die alttestamentliche Wissenschaft*
ZKT	*Zeitschrift für katholische Theologie*
ZNW	*Zeitschrift für die neutestamentliche Wissenschaft*

Notes

1. Tennyson, *The Princess*, viii.243.
2. Robert Graves, "What Is Love?" *Poems 1968–1970* (Garden City, N.Y.: Doubleday & Co., 1971), 26.
3. Whether the Hebrew flowers *shoshannim* should be identified with lilies *(Lilium candidum)*, waterlilies *(Nymphaea lotus)* or red anemones *(Anemone coronaria)* is open to question. In any case, all these flowers, perhaps on account of their triangular or hexagonal shape, received from the earliest art of Egypt and the classical Orient a feminine connotation, which persisted in the Middle Ages when the lily became associated with the virgin Mary, as in the symbol of the city of Florence or in the stylized fleur-de-lis.
4. Song of Songs 6:13d literally reads, "as on the dance of Manahaim," which probably alludes to two armies facing each other in battle, or to swords or daggers that bridegrooms and brides juggle as they dance during their nuptial rites.
5. It will be observed that the woman's triple affirmation of confidence (left column) is given in the presence of the chorus, which is absent from the two scenes of tryst (right column).
6. In postbiblical Hebrew this is precisely the sense that the word *teshuqah* has acquired: loyalty. This meaning reflects perhaps indirectly the ethical reputation that Jewish women at their best in subsequent history have acquired.
7. Emily Dickinson, *The Complete Poems of Emily Dickinson,* ed. Thomas H. Johnson (Boston and Toronto: Little Brown & Co., 1960), 216.
8. In many cultures, mothers used to teach infants how to walk with special belts and straps to keep the little ones from falling.
9. The traditional rendering "I am that I am" comes from the Greek translators, who sought to proclaim during the Hellenistic period that their beliefs were not contradictory to ontological speculations on being. They in turn influenced the singers of the synagogue, who pronounced the consonantal text of Exod. 3:14 with the vocalic sounds of the indicative voice, "I am," rather than the causative voice, "I cause to be," which the name Yahweh requires.
10. The same Hebrew word *Yehudim* designates the Judahites, subjects of the kingdom of Judah, which ended in 587 B.C., and the Jews, members of a religious community that survived the deportation.
11. Rainer Maria Rilke, *Sämtliche Werke* (Wiesbaden: Insel-Verlag, 1956), II: 541.
12. There is no biblical evidence for ablation of the clitoris foreskin in females, let alone of the barbaric practice of clitoridectomy.
13. The folkloric tradition remembered that "Ishmael [was] thirteen years old when he was circumcised in the flesh of his foreskin" (Gen. 17:25).
14. See, for example, Wilfred Thesiger, *Arabian Sands* (New York: E. P. Dutton & Co., 1959), 98 ff.

15. See S. Terrien, *The Elusive Presence: The Heart of Biblical Theology* (New York: Harper & Row, 1983), 350 ff.; J. G. Gammie et al., eds., *Israelite Wisdom: Theological and Literary Essays in Honor of Samuel Terrien* (Missoula, Mont.: Scholars Press, 1978).

16. Rather than "poured out." The allusion may be to a royal or sacerdotal ritual of unction.

17. The masculine word *amon* probably means "contractor" and stands in apposition to the pronoun "him." Some prefer to follow the version of Aquila, which reads *amun*, "nursling, darling child," and renders the line: "Then I was at his side, a darling child."

18. Some versions render, "I was [in] delights," for the Hebrew merely reads, "I was delights," but this elliptical clause implies an objective effect rather than a subjective attitude or reaction. Cf. similar constructions in "Be thou a blessing," i.e., "to all the families of the earth" (Gen. 12:2), or "I am [for] peace" (Ps. 120:7).

19. See the stimulating analysis of the Egyptian iconographic material gathered by one of the scholars who have commented on this poem, Othmar Keel, "Die Weisheit 'spielt' vor Gott. Ein ikonographischer Beitrag zur Deutung des mesaḥäqät in Spr 8,30f," *Freiburger Zeitschrift für Philosophie und Theologie* 21 (1974): 1–66.

20. Contra Gerhard von Rad, *Wisdom in Israel*, trans. James D. Martin (Nashville: Abingdon Press, 1973), 144 ff.

21. From the Semitic and Hebraic root *salal I*, in the intensive voice, *pilpel*, "to titillate, to hug, to clasp to and fro."

22. Almost every one of the lines begins with a letter of the Hebrew alphabet in its traditional order.

23. Meaning uncertain.

24. From Cave XI, the so-called Psalms Scroll, column XXI, lines 11–17.

25. This gloss is found in a few Greek manuscripts.

26. *Gospel of Philip*, trans. W. W. Isenberg, in *The Nag Hammadi Library*, ed. J. M. Robinson (San Francisco: Harper & Row, 1977), 138.

27. Gertrud Kolmar, "Du," in *Poems of Gertrud Kolmar*, trans. Henry A. Smith (New York: Seabury Press, 1975), 72–73.

28. Nineteen Greek and Latin inscriptions, dating from the first century B.C. to the fourth century A.D., suggest that some Jewish women were known as heads of synagogues. It cannot be ascertained whether their titles were functional or honorary.

29. The fact that the women had been "sent" to the disciples led Hippolytus, one of the church fathers, to remark, at the beginning of the third century, that these women were in truth "apostles to the apostles" (*Commentary on the Song of Songs*, Georgian version, XXV. 6). In this bold statement there may well be one further clue to the reasons for the persistent opposition that Hippolytus manifested against four bishops of Rome in succession—Zephyrinus, Callistus, Urban, and Pontianus.

30. The tradition notwithstanding, Stephen and six other men chosen to serve at the tables were not called deacons (cf. Acts 6:1–6).

31. On a Jewish inscription found in Aphrodisias, a certain woman called Jael is listed as *prostatēs* (of a synagogue), while her son, Joshua, appears as *archōn*, "chief." See B. J. Brooten, *Women as Leaders in the Ancient Synagogue* (Chico, Calif.: Scholars Press, 1982), 151.

32. See B. Malina, "Does Porneia Mean 'Fornication'?" *NovT* 14 (1972): 10–17. Cf. *A Greek-English Lexicon of the New Testament and Other Early Christian Literature*, ed. Walter Bauer, William Arndt, and F. W. Gingrich (Chicago and London: Univ. of Chicago Press, 1979), 693.

33. The apostle hesitated to praise unreservedly the advantages of married life

and warned against its disadvantages partly on account of his eschatological expectations; time was too short for family ties. He may also have been influenced by Stoic
philosophers. When he advised servants of the gospel to be "free from anxieties,"
amerimnoi (1 Cor. 7:32) and to live "without distraction," *aperispastōs* (v. 35),
he used the same language as that of Antipater of Tarsus (second century B.C.),
Musonius Rufus, Epictetus, and Hierocles Stoicus, moral philosophers of the first
century A.D., who wrote on similar themes.

34. There is no injunction against female homosexuality. Modern anthropologists
have speculated that such injunctions were entirely superfluous. It was against the
magical use of sperm that the legislation on homosexuality was directed. The spilling
of a man's seed in masturbation (erroneously called onanism on account of Gen.
38:9, which actually describes coitus interruptus) is therefore condemned, for the
early Jewish priests reacted vehemently against any deed that was suspect as a
fertility rite.

35. See A. Néher, "Ezéchiel, rédempteur de Sodome," *RHPR* 59 (1979):
483–90.

36. This view is the more remarkable since the phraseology of the Sodom story
was apparently used in a carnal sense by the narrator of an entirely different story, in
which a woman was raped by the men of Gibeah-Benjamin (Judges 19:22–30). The
woman was offered as a substitute for the male guest, whom the men of the town
wanted "to know" (in this case, carnally).

The homosexual connotation of the crime of Sodom entered Christian circles in
the third or fourth generation of the church (Jude 7; 2 Pet. 2:6–10).

37. Here Paul disrupts the sequence of "neither . . . nor," for he apparently quotes
the LXX version of Gen. 1:27.

38. Cf. "He discarded the part of a soldier and put on that of the sophist"
(Sophista Libanius [fourth century B.C.] *Epistula* 968). Dionysius of Halicarnassus
(first century B.C.). wrote of someone who "put on [played the part of] Tarquinius"
(*Antiquates romanae* ii.5:2). The metaphor suggests that one could enter, through
the parasacramental metamorphosis that is experienced on stage by consummate
artists of the theater, into the being of another.

39. Some copyists at a later date, who probably could not believe that a woman's
name should be placed before her husband's, altered the manuscripts. See
B. Witherington, "The Anti-Feminist Tendencies of the 'Western' Text in Acts," *JBL*
103 (1984): 82–85, and the extensive bibliography listed therein.

40. Among them may be listed A. von Harnack, J. Rendel Harris, A. S. Peake, and
J. H. Moulton. First made by Harnack, the case has been strengthened by J. Rendel
Harris in "Side-Lights on the Authorship of the Epistle to the Hebrews," in *Side-
Lights on New Testament Research* (London: Kingsgate Press, 1908, 148–76), esp.
159 ff.

41. G. W. Buchanan, ed., *To the Hebrews*, Anchor Bible (Garden City, N. Y.:
Doubleday & Co., 1972), 266.

42. The second-generation retreat toward reactionary ethics in matters of
women's equality may well reflect an apologetic response to suspicion and hostility
from the Roman government. See D. L. Balch, *Let Wives Be Submissive: The
Domestic Code in I Peter* (Chico, Calif.: Scholars Press, 1981).

43. See H. Koester, "Introduction to the Gospel of Thomas," in *The Nag Ham-
madi Library*, ed. J. M. Robinson (San Francisco: Harper & Row, 1977), 117; E.
Pagels, *The Gnostic Paul: Gnostic Exegesis of the Pauline Letters* (Philadelphia:
Fortress Press, 1975), 55 and passim.

44. See R. Scroggs, "Paul, *sophos* and *pneumatikos*," *NTS* 14 (1967–68):
33–55.

45. *Gospel of Thomas*, saying 101, trans. Thomas O. Lambdin, in *The Nag Hammadi Library*, 128–29 (cf. J.–E. Ménard, *L'évangile selon Thomas* [Leiden: E. J. Brill, 1975], 172–73); *Apocryphon of John* II.1, trans. F. Wisse, in *Nag Hammadi*, 101.

46. *Gospel of Philip* II. 3.63, trans. W. W. Isenberg, in *Nag Hammadi*, 138.

47. See J. Leipoldt, *Die Frau in der antiken Welt und im Urchristentum* (Leipzig: Kohler und Amelung, 1955); C. Vatin, *Recherches sur le mariage el la condition de la femme mariée à l'époque hellénistique* (Paris, 1970).

48. Irenaeus *Adversus Omnes Haereses* I.13.5–6.

49. *Asclepius*, V. 65. 15–19, 21–24, 26–27, trans. J. Brashler, et al, in *Nag Hammadi*, 300–301.

50. See R. M. Grant, "The Mystery of Marriage in the Gospel of Philip," *Vie chrétienne* 15 (1961): 129–40; J.–P. Mahé, "Le sens des symboles sexuels dans quelques textes hermétiques et gnostiques," in *Les textes de Nag Hammadi*, ed. J.–E. Ménard (Leiden: E. J. Brill, 1975), 126 ff.; J. J. Buckley, "A Cult Mystery in *The Gospel of Philip*," *JBL* 99 (1980): 569–81.

51. See G. W. MacRae, "The Jewish Background of the Jewish Gnostic Sophia Myth," *NovT* 12 (1970): 86–101.

52. *1 Clem.* 1.3.

53. *Gospel of Philip* II. 3.63, *Nag Hammadi*, 138.

54. *Pistis Sophia* IV.146, in *Pistis Sophia*, ed. C. Schmidt and V. MacDermot (Leiden, 1978), 377.

55. *Pistis Sophia* II.72, in *ibid.*, 162.

56. *Gospel of Mary*, 7.17.18—7.18.15, trans. George W. MacRae and R. McL. Wilson in *Nag Hammadi*, 473.

57. See E. Pagels, *The Gnostic Gospels* (New York: Random House, 1979), 28 ff.

58. See H. von Campenhausen, *Ecclesiastical Authority and Spiritual Power in the Church in the First Three Centuries* (Stanford, Calif.: Stanford Univ. Press, 1969), 149 ff., 297 ff.; E. Pagels, "Visions, Appearances, and Apostolic Authority: Gnostic and Orthodox Traditions," in *Gnosis: Festschrift für Hans Jonas*, ed. B. Aland (Göttingen: Vandenhoeck & Ruprecht, 1978), 415–30, esp. 424–25.

59. *1 Clem.* 40.1–5; 41.1–3.

60. Ignatius *Epistle to the Magnesians* VI.1–6; *Epistle to the Trallians* II.1 ff., III.1–8; *Epistle to the Smyrneans* VIII.1 ff.

61. Irenaeus *Adversus Omnes Haereses* I.10.1–3.

62. Gerhard von Rad, *Genesis: A Commentary*, trans. John H. Marks (Philadelphia: Westminster Press, 1961), 87 ff.; cf. J. M. Higgins, "The Myth of Eve: The Temptress," *JAAR* 44 (1976): 639–47.

63. R. Bultmann, *Theology of the New Testament* (New York: Charles Scribner's Sons, 1951), 1:190 ff., 227 ff.; L. Köhler, *Old Testament Theology* (Philadelphia: Westminster Press, 1957), pp. 129 ff.; Gerhard von Rad, *Old Testament Theology* (New York: Harper & Row, 1960–62), 1:152 ff., 458 ff.; 2:275 ff.; W. G. Kümmel, *Theology of the New Testament*, trans. John E. Steely (Nashville: Abingdon Press, 1973); C. Westermann, *Theologie des Alten Testaments in Grundzügen* (Göttingen: Vandenhoeck & Ruprecht, 1978), 81 ff. [ET: *Elements of Old Testament Theology*, trans. D. W. Scott (Atlanta: John Knox Press, 1982), 94–102].

64. C. Spicq, *Dieu et l'homme selon le Nouveau Testament* (Paris, 1961), 185 ff.; idem, *Théologie morale du Nouveau Testament* (Paris, 1965), 2:187, 530 ff.; W. G. Kümmel, *Man in the New Testament* (Philadelphia: Westminster Press, 1963); H. W. Wolff, *Anthropology of the Old Testament*, trans. Margaret Kohl (Philadelphia: Fortress Press, 1974); H. D. Wendland, *Ethik des Neuen Testaments* (Göttingen: Vandenhoeck & Ruprecht, 1978), 80 ff.

65. See Samuel Terrien, "The Play of Wisdom: Turning Point in Biblical Theology," *Horizons in Biblical Theology: An International Dialogue* 3 (1981): 125 ff.; J. A. Sanders, *Canon and Community: A Guide to Canonical Criticism* (Philadelphia: Fortress Press, 1984).

66. While G. Östborn, in *Cult and Canon: A Study of the Canonization of the Old Testament* (Uppsala and Leipzig, 1950), may have insisted too heavily on the role of the autumn feast (myth and ritual) in the inception of sacred books, he paved the way for further studies. Cf. A. Weiser, *The Psalms: A Commentary* (Philadelphia: Westminster Press, 1962), 25–26; A. S. Kapelrud, "Tradition and Worship: The Role of the Cult in Tradition Formation and Transmission," in *Tradition and Theology in the Old Testament*, ed. D. A. Knight (Philadelphia: Fortress Press, 1977), 101–2; R. B. Laurin, "Tradition and Canon," ibid., 261 ff.

67. Cf. P. Trible, *Texts of Terror: Literary-Feminist Readings of Biblical Narratives* (Philadelphia: Fortress Press, 1984).

68. "Surge cantilena de pectore," *Carmina Burana, MSS. of Benedictbeuern*, cxl. 6 in *The Wandering Scholars: The Life and Art of the Lyric Poets of the Latin Middle Ages*, ed. and trans. Helen Waddell (Garden City, N.Y.: Doubleday & Co., 1955), 116; cf. *Mediaeval Latin Lyrics*, trans. Helen Waddell (New York: W. W. Norton & Co., 1977), 226–27.

69. Diogenes Laertius *Protagoras* IX.51.

70. For further comments on the relation between this hymn and the Garden myth, see S. Terrien, *The Elusive Presence*, 459–64.

71. F.–M. Braun, "Saint Jean, la Sagesse et l'histoire," in Neotestamentica et Patristica (Festschrift O. Cullmann), Nov T Sup 6 (Leiden: E. J. Brill, 1962), 123–33.

72. See E. Fink, *Le jeu comme symbole du monde*, trans. H. Hildenbrand and A. Lindenberg (Paris: Editions de Minuit, 1966), 125 ff., 177–78, passim; D. L. Miller, "From Leviathan to Lear: Shades of Play in Language and Literature," in *The Plays of God and Men*, ed. R. Ritsema, *Eranos* (1982), 69.

73. See H. Baumann, *Das doppelte Geschlecht* (Berlin, 1955); M. Delcourt, *Hermaphrodite: Mythes et rites de la bisexualité dans l'antiquité classique* (Paris, 1958); Mircea Eliade, *Mephistopheles and the Androgyne* (New York: Sheed & Ward, 1966), 78–124; W. A. Meeks, "The Image of the Androgyne: Some Uses of a Symbol in Earliest Christianity," *History of Religions*, 13 (1973–74): 165–208.

74. S. Davies, *The Gospel of Thomas and Christian Wisdom* (New York: Seabury Press, 1983), passim.

75. S. Davies, "Thomas—The Fourth Synoptic Gospel," *Biblical Archeologist* 46 (1983): 6–9, 12–14.

76. "Saint Paul and the Gospel of John already counted androgyny as one of the characteristics of spiritual perfection" (Eliade, *Mephistopheles and the Androgyne*, 107).

77. Biblical theology knows nothing of the status of virginity as an ecclesiastical office. It also ignores the later concept of the virgin as the bride of Christ, which the church fathers found in the Song of Songs.

78. R. Scroggs, "Paul and the Eschatological Woman," *JAAR* 40 (1972): 283–303; idem, "Paul and the Eschatological Woman Revisited," *JAAR* 42 (1974): 532–37.

79. Helen Waddell, ed. and trans., *The Wandering Scholars: The Life and Art of the Lyric Poets of the Latin Middle Ages*, 116.

80. *Letters of Rainer Maria Rilke, 1892–1910*, trans. J. B. Greene and M. D. H. Norton (New York: W. W. Norton & Co., 1945), 57–58.

81. "One cannot adduce any New Testament text in support of the ordination of women. One cannot adduce any New Testament text in support of the ordination of

men" (J. L. McKenzie, in *Women Priests: A Catholic Commentary on the Vatican Declaration,* ed. A. Swidler and L. Swidler [New York: Paulist Press, 1977], 213).

82. The word was commonly used in Hellenistic Greek to designate administrators, guardians, or watchmen. Cf. Phil. 1:1; 1 Tim. 3:1–7; Acts 20:28; Titus 1:7. Whether or not the early *episkopoi* were similar to the *mebaqqerim (episkopoi)* of the Qumran texts cannot be demonstrated. Cf. B. E. Theiring, "*Mebaqqer* and *Episkopos* in the Light of the Temple Scroll," *JBL* 100 (1981): 59–75. It was only after the end of the first century A.D. that the episcopate became an office endowed with monarchic authority.

In the Roman church of St. Praxedis—one of the two martyred daughters of Senator Cornelius Pudens—a fifth-century mosaic represents the head of a certain Theodo[ra] (the final syllable is obliterated) with the title of *episcopa.* Even at this relatively late date, a woman may have been a bishop in Rome. See Joan Morris, *The Lady Was a Bishop* (New York: Macmillan Co., 1973), 4 ff. Other epitaphs have been found, especially one with the inscription *"femina episcopa."*

83. In the course of time, priests came to offer incense and burnt offerings at the altars. In the early days, they also acted as diviners who used Urim and Thummim. Nevertheless, even as late as the reform of Josiah (seventh century B.C.), it was a woman and a prophetess (Huldah), not a priest, who was asked to authenticate "the book of the law."

84. The figure of Melchizedek, king of Salem, priest of the Most High, remained in Jewish lore the paradigm of the divine mediator at the end of time (Gen. 14:18; Ps. 110:4). It was easily applied to the sacerdotal function of Christ (Heb. 7:1–3).

85. Jerome *Against Jovinian* I.20.

86. G. Koepgen, *Die Gnosis des Christentums* (Salzburg, 1939), 130 ff.; N. Berdyaev, *The Meaning of the Creative Act* (New York: Collier Books, 1962), 173 ff.

87. See C. Geffré, "'Father' as the Proper Name of God," in *God and Father,* ed. E. Schillebeeckx and J. B. Metz, Concilium vol. 143 (New York: Seabury Press, 1981), 45–46; Samuel Terrien, *The Elusive Presence,* 121 ff., 138 ff.

Selected Bibliography

Not included in this partial bibliography are biblical commentaries and articles in biblical dictionaries.

1. General

Adams, Q. *Neither Male nor Female: A Study of the Scriptures.* Ilfracombe: Stockwell, 1973.

Amsler, S., et al. *Le canon de l'Ancien Testament.* Geneva: Labor et Fides, 1983.

Barr, J. *The Scope and Authority of the Bible.* Philadelphia: Westminster Press, 1980.

———. *Holy Scripture: Canon, Authority, Criticism.* Philadelphia: Westminster Press, 1983.

Beer, G. *Die soziale und religiöse Stellung der Frau im israelitischen Altertums.* Tübingen: J. C. Mohr, 1919.

Bird, P. "Images of Women in the Old Testament." In *Religion and Sexism,* ed. R. R. Ruether, 41–88. New York: Simon & Schuster, 1974.

Blackman, A. "On the Position of Women in the Ancient Egyptian Hierarchy." *JEA* 7 (1921): 8–30.

Boer, P. A. H. de. *Fatherhood and Motherhood in Israelite and Judean Piety.* Leiden: E. J. Brill, 1974.

Breyfolge, C. "The Religious Status of Woman in the Old Testament." *Biblical World* 35 (1910): 405–19.

———. "The Social Status of Woman in the Old Testament." *Biblical World* 35 (1910): 107–16.

Bruns, J. "Old Testament History in the Development of a Sexual Ethics." In *The New Morality,* ed. W. Dunphy, 55–81. New York: Herder & Herder, 1967.

Collins, A. Y., ed. *Feminist Perspectives on Biblical Scholarship.* Chico, Calif.: Scholars Press, 1985.

Deen, E. *The Bible's Legacy for Womanhood.* Garden City, N.Y.: Doubleday & Co., 1969.

Döller, J. *Das Weib im Alten Testament.* Biblische Zeitfragen 9, Heft 7/9. Münster: Aschendorff, 1920.

Dubarle, A. *Amour et fécondité dans la Bible.* Paris: Dépôt Diffénet, 1967.

Eichrodt, W. *Theology of the Old Testament,* 2 vols. Philadelphia: Westminster Press, 1967.

Emswiler, S. *The Ongoing Journey: Women and the Bible.* New York: United Methodist Church Board, 1977.

Engelsman, J. *The Feminine Dimension of the Divine.* Philadelphia: Westminster Press, 1979.

Fraine, J. de. *Women of the Old Testament.* De Pere, Wisc.: St. Norbert Abbey Press, 1968.

Gadala, M.-T. *Le féminisme dans la Bible,* 2 vols. Paris: Geuthner, 1930–51.

Grimal, P. *Histoire mondiale de la femme,* 3 vols. Paris, 1966.

Hurley, J. B. *Man and Woman in Biblical Perspective.* Grand Rapids: Wm. B. Eerdmans, 1981.

Jacob, E. "Man Is Created Male and Female." In *Theology of the Old Testament,* 172–73. New York: Harper & Row, 1958.

Jewett, P. *Man as Male and Female: A Study in Sexual Relationships from a Theological Point of View.* Grand Rapids: Wm. B. Eerdmans, 1975.

Knierim, R. "The Role of the Sexes in the Old Testament." *LTQ* 1 (1975): 1–10.

Köhler, L. *Hebrew Man.* Nashville: Abingdon Press, 1953.

Leonard, H. *Women in the Bible: A Bibliography.* Durham, N.C.: Privately printed, 1977.

Loewe, R. *The Position of Women in Judaism.* London: SPCK, 1966.

MacDonald, E. *The Position of Women As Reflected in Semitic Codes of Law.* Toronto: Univ. of Toronto Press, 1931.

Maxey, M. "Beyond Eve and Mary." *NovT* 14 (1972): 207–29.

McMillan, C. *Women, Reason, and Nature: Some Philosophical Problems with Feminism.* Princeton, N.J.: Princeton Univ. Press, 1982.

Molan, G. "Toward a Biblical Understanding of Womanhood." *Ministry* 8 (1967): 3–9.

Mollenkott, V. *Women, Men, and the Bible.* Nashville: Abingdon Press, 1977.

Ochs, C. *Behind the Sex of God: Toward a New Consciousness—Transcending Matriarchy and Patriarchy.* Boston: Beacon Press, 1977.

Otwell, J. *And Sarah Laughed: The Status of Woman in the Old Testament.* Philadelphia: Westminster Press, 1977.

Patai, R. *Sex and the Family in the Bible and the Middle East.* Garden City, N.Y.: Doubleday & Co., 1959.

Patterson, R. "The Widow, the Orphan, and the Poor in the Old Testament and the Extra-Biblical Literature." *BSac* 130 (1973): 226ff.

Phillips, A. "Some Aspects of Family Law in Pre-Exilic Israel." *VT* 23 (1973): 349ff.

Phillips, J. A. *Eve: The History of an Idea.* San Francisco: Harper & Row, 1984.

Phipps, W. "Adam's Rib: Bones of Contention." *TToday* 33 (1976): 263–73.

Price, E. *The Unique World of Women in Bible Times and Now.* Grand Rapids: Wm. B. Eerdmans, 1969.

Rad, G. von. *Old Testament Theology,* 2 vols. New York: Harper & Row, 1962–65.

Raitt, J. "The *Vagina Dentata* and the *Immaculatus Uterus Divini Fontis.*" *JAAR* 48 (1980): 415–32.

Reed, E. *Woman's Evolution, from Matriarchal Clan to Patriarchal Family.* New York: Pathfinder Press, 1975.

Russell, L. *The Liberating Word: A Guide to Nonsexist Interpretation of the Bible.* Philadelphia: Westminster Press, 1976.

Sakenfeld, K. "The Bible and Women: Bane or Blessing?" *TToday* 32 (1975): 222–33.

Scanzoni, L. *All We're Meant to Be: A Biblical Approach to Women's Liberation.* Waco, Tex.: Word Books, 1974.

Schaef, A. W. *Women's Reality.* Minneapolis: Winston Press, 1981.

Schelkle, K. *Der Geist und die Braut: Frauen in der Bibel.* Düsseldorf: Patmos, 1977.

Schüssler Fiorenza, E. *In Memory of Her: A Feminist Theological Reconstruction of Christian Origins.* New York: Crossroad, 1983.

———. *Bread Not Stone: The Challenge of Feminist Interpretation.* Boston: Beacon Press, 1985.

Seltman, C. *Women in Antiquity.* London: Thames & Hudson, 1956.

Siddons, P. *Speaking Out for Women: A Biblical View.* Valley Forge, Pa.: Judson Press, 1980.

Smith, C. Ryder. *The Biblical Doctrine of Womanhood in Its Historical Evolution.* London: Epworth Press, 1923.

Smylie, J. "The Woman's Bible and the Spiritual Crisis." *Soundings* 59 (1976): 305–28.

Stanton, E. C. *The Original Feminist Attack on the Bible.* New York: Arno Press, 1975.

Starr, L. A. *The Bible Status of Woman.* New York: Revell, 1926.

Stendahl, K. *The Bible and the Role of Women: A Case Study in Hermeneutics.* Philadelphia: Fortress Press, 1966.

Stone, M. *When God Was a Woman.* New York: Dial Press, 1976.

Swidler, L. *Biblical Affirmations of Woman.* Philadelphia: Westminster Press, 1979.

Terrien, S. "Toward a Biblical Theology of Womanhood." In *Male and Female: Christian Approaches to Sexuality,* ed. R. T. Barnhouse and U. T. Holmes, 17–27. New York: Seabury Press, 1976.

Tolbert, M. A., ed. *The Bible and Feminist Hermeneutics.* Semeia 28. Philadelphia: Fortress Press; Chico, Calif.: Scholars Press, 1983.

Trible, P. "The Depatriarchalizing of Biblical Interpretation." *JAAR* 41 (1973): 30–48.

_____. "Biblical Theology as Women's Work." *RL* 44 (1975): 7ff.

_____. *God and the Rhetoric of Sexuality.* Philadelphia: Fortress Press, 1978.

_____. *Texts of Terror: Literary Feminist Readings of Biblical Narratives.* Philadelphia: Fortress Press, 1984.

Vaux, R. de. *Ancient Israel,* 2 vols., 1:24–40. New York: McGraw Hill, 1961.

Vos, C. *Woman in Old Testament Worship.* Delft: Judels & Brinkman, 1968.

Vriezen, T. "Man and Woman." In his *An Outline of Old Testament Theology,* 208–12. Oxford: Basil Blackwell, 1958.

Wagner, W. H. "The Demonization of Women." *RL* 42 (1973): 56–74.

Walsh, J. "Genesis 2:46—3:24: A Synchronic Approach." *JBL* 96 (1977): 161–77.

Williams, J. "Yahweh, Women, and the Trinity." *TToday* 32 (1975): 234–42.

Wolff, H. W. *Anthropology of the Old Testament.* Philadelphia: Fortress Press, 1974.

Zschokke, H. *Die biblischen Frauen des Alten Testamentes.* Freiburg-im-Br.: Herder, 1882.

_____. *Das Weib im Alten Testamente.* Vienna: H. Kirsch, 1883.

2. The Myth of the Garden

Alonso-Schökel, L. "Sapiential and Covenant Themes in Genesis 2—3." *Theology Digest* 13 (1965): 3–10.

Bailey, J. "Initiation and the Primal Woman in Gilgamesh and Genesis 2—3." *JBL* 89 (1970): 137–50.

Barthélemy, D. "'Pour un homme,' 'Pour l'homme,' 'Pour Adam'? [on Gen. 2:20]." In *De la Torâh au Messie* (Mélanges Henri Cazelles), ed. M. Carrez et al., 47–53. Paris: Desclée et Cie., 1981.

Bravmann, M. "The Original Meaning of ' . . . a Man Leaves His Father and Mother.' " In his *Studies in Semitic Philology,* 593–95. Leiden: E. J. Brill, 1977.

Brueggeman, W. "Of the Same Flesh and Bone (Gn 2, 23a)." *CBQ* 32 (1970): 532ff.

_____. *Genesis.* Atlanta: John Knox Press, 1982.

Bruns, J. "Depth-Psychology and the Fall." *CBQ* 21 (1959): 78ff.

Carmichael, C. M. *Women, Law, and the Genesis Traditions.* Edinburgh: Edinburgh Univ. Press, 1979.

Coppens, J. *La connaissance du bien et du mal et le péché du Paradis: Contribution à l'interprétation de Gen. II–III.* Analecta lovaniensia biblica et orientalia 2.3. Gembloux: Duculot, 1948.

Fraine, J. de. *La Bible et l'origine de l'homme.* Brugge: Desclée de Brouwer, 1961.

Fuss, W. *Die sogenannte Paradies Erzählung; Aufbau, Herkunft und theologische Bedeutung.* Gütersloh: Gerd Mohn, 1968.

Gilbert, M. " 'Une seule chair' (Gn 2, 24)." *NRT* 100 (1978): 66ff.

Gordis, R. "The Significance of the Paradise Myth." *AJSLL* 52–54 (1935–36): 86–94.

———. "The Knowledge of Good and Evil in the Old Testament and the Qumran Scrolls." *JBL* 76 (1957): 123–38.

Higgins, J. M. "The Myth of Eve: The Temptress." *JAAR* 44 (1976): 639–47.

Humbert, P. *Etudes sur le récit du paradis et de la chute dans la Genèse.* Neuchâtel: Secrétariat de l'Université, 1940.

Joines, K. "The Serpent in Gen. 3." *ZAW* 87 (1975): 1–11.

Lagrange, M.-J. "La paternité de Dieu dans l'Ancien Testament." *RB* 17 (1908): 481ff.

Leach, E. "Lévi-Strauss in the Garden of Eden: An Examination of Some Recent Developments in the Analysis of Myth." In *Claude Lévi-Strauss: The Anthropologist as Hero,* ed. E. N. Hayes and T. Hayes, 51ff. Cambridge: M.I.T. Press, 1970.

Massart, A. "L'emploi, en égyptien, de deux termes opposés pour exprimer la solitude." In *Mélanges bibliques* (Festschrift André Robert), 38–46. Paris: Blond et Gay, 1957.

Mendenhall, G. "The Shady Side of Wisdom: The Date and Purpose of Genesis 3." In *A Light unto My Path* (Festschrift Jacob M. Myers), ed. H. Bream and R. Heim, 326ff. Philadelphia: Temple Univ. Press, 1974.

Meyers, C. "Procreation, Production, and Protection: Male-Female Balance in Early Israel." *JAAR* 51 (1983): 569–93.

Ricoeur, P. *The Symbolism of Evil,* 235ff. Boston: Beacon Press, 1969.

Rigaux, B. "La femme et son lignage dans Genèse III, 14–15." *RB* 61 (1954): 321–48.

Ruppert, L. "Die Sündefallerzählung (Gen 3) in vorjahwistischer Tradition und Interpretation." *BZ* 15 (1971): 185–203.

Soggin, J. "The Fall of Man in the Third Chapter of Genesis." In his *Old Testament and Oriental Studies,* 88ff. Biblica et Orientalia 23. Rome: Pontifical Biblical Institute Press, 1975.

Steck, O. *Die Paradiserzählung. Eine Auslegung von Genesis 2, 4b—3, 24.* Neukirchen-Vluyn: Neukirchener Verlag, 1970.

Stern, H. "The Knowledge of Good and Evil." *VT* 8 (1958): 405–18.

Thompson, P. "The Yahwist Creation Story." *VT* 21 (1971): 197–208.

Wambacq, B. " 'Or tous deux étaient nus, l'homme et sa femme, mais ils n'avaient pas honte' (Gn 2, 25)," in *Mélanges bibliques en hommage au R. P. Béda Rigaux,* ed. A. Descamps and A. de Halleux, 547ff. Gembloux: Duculot, 1970.

Westermann, C. *Genesis,* 245–380. Neukirchen-Vluyn: Neukirchener Verlag, 1974. ET: *Genesis 1—11.* Minneapolis: Augsburg Pub. House, 1984.

Zacklad, J. "Création, péché originel et formalisme (Gen. I—III)." *RHPR* 51 (1971): 1–30.

3. The Song of Songs

Angénieux, J. "Note sur les trois portraits du Cantique." ALBO IV.35 (1966).

Audet, J.-P. "Le sens du Cantique des Cantiques." *RB* 62 (1955): 197ff.

Cook, A. *The Root of the Thing: A Study of Job and the Song of Songs.* Bloomington: Indiana Univ. Press, 1968.

Dubarle, A.-M. "L'amour humain dans le Cantique des Cantiques." *RB* 61 (1954): 67–86.

Exum, J. C. "A Literary and Structural Analysis of the Song of Songs." *ZAW* 85 (1973): 47–70.

Fox, M. "Love, Passion, and Perception in Israelite and Egyptian Poetry." *JBL* 102 (1983): 219–28.

Gerleman, G. *Ruth. Das Hohelied.* Neukirchen-Vluyn: Neukirchener Verlag, 1963.

Gordis, R. *The Song of Songs: A Study, Modern Translation, and Commentary.* New York: Seabury Press, 1954.

Graves, R. *The Song of Songs.* London: William Collins Sons, 1973.

Kramer, S. "The Sacred Marriage and Solomon's Song of Songs." In his *The Sacred Marriage Rite,* 85–106. Bloomington: Indiana Univ. Press, 1969.

Krinetzki, L. "Die erotische Psychologie des Hohen Liedes." *TQ* 110 (1970): 404–16.

Lambert, W. "The Problem of Love Lyrics." In *Unity and Diversity: Essays in the History, Literature, and Religions of the Ancient Near East,* ed. H. Goedicke and J. J. M. Roberts, 98ff. Baltimore: Penguin Books, 1975.

Landy, F. "The Song of Songs and the Garden of Eden." *JBL* 98 (1979): 513–28.

Littlewood, A. "The Symbolism of the Apple in Greek and Roman Literature." *HSCP* 72 (1967): 147–81.

Lys, D. *Le plus beau chant de la création: Commentaire du Cantique des Cantiques.* Lectio Divina 51. Paris: Editions du Cerf, 1968.

Murphy, R. "Form-Critical Studies in the Song of Songs." *Int* 27 (1973): 413–22.

_____. "The Unity of the Song of Songs." *VT* 29 (1979): 436–43.

Phipps, W. "The Plight of the Song of Songs." *JAAR* 42 (1974): 82–100.

Pope, M. *The Song of Songs.* Anchor Bible. Garden City, N.Y.: Doubleday & Co., 1977.

Robert, A., R. Tournay, and A. Feuillet. *Le Cantique des Cantiques.* Paris: Editions du Cerf, 1963.

Rylaarsdam, J. "The Song of Songs and Biblical Faith." *Biblical Research* 10 (1965): 11ff.

Sadgrove, M. "The Song as Wisdom Literature." *Studia Biblica* 1 (1978): 245–48.

Schott, S. *Les chants d'amour de l'Egypte ancienne.* Paris: Adrien Maisonneuve, 1956.

Snaith, N. H. "The Song of Songs: The Dances of the Virgins." *AJSLL* 50 (1933–34): 129–42.

Soulen, R. "The *Waṣfs* of the Song of Songs and Hermeneutics." *JBL* 86 (1967): 183–90.

Tournay, R. *Quand Dieu parle aux hommes: Le langage de l'amour; études sur le Cantique des Cantiques.* Paris: J. Gabalda, 1983.

_____ and M. Nicoläy. *Le Cantique des Cantiques: Commentaire abrégé.* Lire la Bible 9. Paris: Editions du Cerf, 1967.

White, J. B. *A Study of the Language of Love in the Song of Songs and Ancient Egyptian Poetry.* Missoula, Mont.: Scholars Press, 1978.

Winandy, J. *Le Cantique des Cantiques: Poèmes d'amour mués en écrit de Sagesse.* Paris: Casterman, 1960.

4. The Gender of God

Ahlström, G. *Aspects of Syncretism in Israelite Religion.* Lund: C. W. K. Gleerup, 1963.

Andreasen, N.-E. A. "The Role of the Queen Mother in Israelite Society." *CBQ* 45 (1983): 179–94.

Bleeker, C. "The Divine Lady." In his *The Sacred Bridge,* 83–111. Leiden: E. J. Brill, 1963.

_____. "Isis and Nephtys as Wailing Women." In *The Sacred Bridge,* 190–205.

Brooks, B. "Fertility Cult Functionaries in the Old Testament." *JBL* 60 (1941): 227–54.

Bruns, J. *God as Woman, Woman as God.* New York: Paulist Press, 1973.

Crenshaw, J. "Journey into Oblivion: A Structural Analysis of Gen. 22:1–19." *Soundings* 58 (1975): 243–56.

Davies, P. R., and B. D. Chilton. "The Aqedah: A Revised Tradition History." *CBQ* 40 (1978): 514–46.

Diner, H. *Mothers and Amazons: The First Feminine History of Culture.* Garden City, N.Y.: Doubleday & Co., 1969.

Donner, H. "Art und Herkunft des Amtes der Königinmutter, im Alten Testament." In *Festschrift Johannes Friedrich zum 65. Geburtstag . . . gewidmet,* ed. R. von Kienle, 105–45. Heidelberg, 1959.

Doyle, E. "God and the Feminine." *Clergy Review* 49 (1971): 866–77.

Eliade, M. "La Terre-Mère et les hiérogamies cosmiques." *Eranos Jahrbuch* 22 (1953): 57–95.

Gynz-Rekowski, G. von. *Symbole des Weiblischen in Gottesbild und Kult des Alten Testaments.* Zurich: Rascher, 1963.

Harrelson, W. *From Fertility Cults to Worship.* Garden City, N.Y.: Doubleday & Co., 1969.

Hirschberg, H. "Some Additional Arabic Etymologies in Old Testament Lexicography." *VT* 11 (1961): 373ff.

Hoffner, H. A., Jr. "Symbols for Masculinity and Femininity: Their Use in Ancient Near Eastern Sympathetic Magic Rituals." *JBL* 85 (1966): 326–34.

Holladay, W. "Jeremiah and Women's Liberation." *ANQ* 12 (1971–72): 4.213–23.

James, E. *The Cult of the Mother Goddess: An Archaeological and Documentary Study.* London: Thames & Hudson, 1955.

Junker, H. "Die Frau im alttestamentlichen ekstatischen Kult." *TGl* 21 (1929): 68–74.

Kruijf, T. *The Bible on Sexuality.* De Pere, Wisc.: St. Norbert Abbey Press, 1966.

Legrand, L. *The Biblical Doctrine of Virginity.* London: Geoffrey Chapman, 1963.

Lipiński, E. "Les 'voyantes des rois' en Prov. XXXI 3." *VT* 22 (1973): 246.

Löhr, M. *Die Stellung des Weibes zu Jahwe-Religion und Kult Untersucht.* Leipzig: J. C. Hinrichs, 1908.

Néher, A. "Le symbole conjugal—expression de l'histoire dans l'Ancien Testament." *RHPR* 34 (1954): 30–49.

―――. *L'essence du prophétisme,* 247ff. Paris: Presses Universitaires de France, 1972.

Ochshorn, J. *The Female Experience and the Nature of the Divine.* Bloomington: Indiana Univ. Press, 1981.

Patai, R. *Sex and Family in the Bible and in the Middle East.* Garden City, N.Y.: Doubleday & Co., 1959.

―――. *The Hebrew Goddess.* New York: Ktav Pub. House, 1967.

―――. *Man and Temple in Ancient Jewish Myth and Ritual.* New York: Ktav Pub. House, 1967.

Phipps, W. E. "The Sensuousness of Agape." *TToday* 29 (1978): 370–79.

Reventlow, H. Graf. *Opfere deinen Sohn: Eine Auslegung von Genesis 22.* Neukirchen-Vluyn: Neukirchener Verlag, 1968.

Roellenbeck, E. *Magna Mater im Alten Testament.* Darmstadt: Claassen & Roether, 1949.

Schemp, P. "L'homme et la femme d'après l'Ecriture Sainte." *Foi et Vie* 44 (1948): 228–39.

Schuttermayr, G. "RHM—Eine lexikalische Studie." *Bib* 51 (1970): 499ff.

Speiser, E. "The Wife-Sister Motif in the Patriarchal Narratives." In *Biblical and Other Studies,* ed. A. Altmann, 15–28. Cambridge: Harvard Univ. Press, 1963.

Terrien, S. "The Omphalos Myth and Hebrew Religion." *VT* 20 (1970): 315–38.

Vos, C. J. *Woman in Old Testament Worship*. Delft: Judels & Brinkman, 1968.

Ward, W. "La déesse nourricière d'Ugarit." *Syria* 46 (1969): 225–39.

Westman, H. "The Akedah." In his *Springs of Creativity*, 512–28. New York: Atheneum, 1961.

Yeivin, S. "Social, Religious, and Cultural Trends in Jerusalem under the Davidic Dynasty." *VT* 3 (1953): 162ff.

5. Divine Wisdom

Bailey, K. "Women in Ben Sirach and in the New Testament." In *For Me to Live* (Festschrift J. L. Kelso), ed. R. A. Coughenoor, 56–73. Cleveland: Dillon/Liederbach, 1972.

Blenkinsopp, J. *Wisdom and Law in the Old Testament*. New York and London: Oxford Univ. Press, 1983.

Bonnard, P. E. "De la Sagesse personnifiée dans l'Ancien Testament à la Sagesse en personne dans le Nouveau." In *La Sagesse de l'Ancien Testament,* ed. M. Gilbert, 117–49. Gembloux: Duculot, 1979.

Braun, F.-M. "Saint Jean, la Sagesse et l'histoire." In *Neotestamentica et Patristica* (Festschrift O. Cullmann), 123–33. Nov T Sup 6. Leiden: E. J. Brill, 1962.

Cahill, P. "The Johannine Logos as Center." *CBQ* 38 (1976): 54–72.

Cazelles, H. "L'enfantement de la Sagesse en Prov. VIII." *Sacra Pagina* 1 (1959): 511–15.

Childs, B. "Proverbs, Chapter 7, and a Biblical Approach to Sex." In his *Biblical Theology in Crisis,* 184–200. Philadelphia: Westminster Press, 1970.

Christ, F. *Jesus Sophia: Die Sophia-Christologie bei den Synoptikern.* Abhandlungen zur Theologie des Alten und Neuen Testaments 57. Zurich: Zwingli-Verlag, 1970.

Conzelmann, H. "The Mother of Wisdom." In *The Future of Our Religious Past* (Festschrift R. Bultmann 2), ed. J. M. Robinson, 230–43. New York: Harper & Row, 1971.

Crenshaw, J. *Old Testament Wisdom: An Introduction*. Atlanta, Ga.: John Knox Press, 1981.

_____. "Wisdom and Authority: Sapiential Rhetoric and Its Warrants." *VT* Sup 31 (1981): 10–29.

Dahood, M. "Proverbs 8, 22–31. Translation and Commentary." *CBQ* 30 (1968): 512–21.

Davidson, A. B. "Sirach's Judgment of Women." *Expository Times* 6 (1894–95): 402–4.

Feuillet, A. *Le Christ, Sagesse de Dieu d'après les épîtres pauliniennes*. Paris: J. Gabalda, 1967.

Fourniez-Bidoz, A. "L'arbre et la demeure Siracide XXIV 10–17." *VT* 34 (1984): 1–10.

Freed, E. "Some Old Testament Influences on the Prologue of John." In *A Light unto My Path* (Festschrift J. M. Myers), ed. H. N. Bream et al., 145–61. Philadelphia: Temple Univ. Press, 1974.

Gese, H. "The Prologue to John's Gospel." In *Essays on Biblical Theology,* trans. K. Crim, 167–222. Minneapolis: Augsburg Pub. House, 1981.

_____. "Wisdom, Son of Man, and the Origins of Christology: The Consistent Development of Biblical Theology." *Horizons in Biblical Theology* 3 (1981): 22–57.

Gilbert, M. "L'éloge de la Sagesse (Siracide 24)." *Revue théologique de Louvain* 5 (1974): 326–48.

_____. "Le discours de la Sagesse en Proverbes 8: Structure et cohérence." In *La Sagesse de l'Ancien Testament,* ed. M. Gilbert, 202–18. Gembloux: Duculot, 1979.

Habel, N. "The Symbolism of Wisdom in Proverbs 1—9." *Int* 26 (1972): 131–57.

Harris, S. L. "Wisdom or Creation: A New Interpretation of Job XXVIII 27." *VT* 33 (1983): 419–27.

Heinisch, P. *Personifikationen und Hypostasen im Alten Testamente und im Alten Orient.* Münster: Aschendorff, 1921.

Hermisson, H.-J. "Observations on the Creation Theology in Wisdom." In *Israelite Wisdom: Theological and Literary Essays in Honor of Samuel Terrien,* ed. J. G. Gammie et al., 43–57. Missoula, Mont.: Scholars Press, 1978.

Hulsbosch, A. *Sagesse créatrice et éducatrice (Job XXVIII et Proverbes I-IX).* Rome: Collegium Internationale Augustianum, 1963.

Imschoot, P. van. "La Sagesse de l'Ancien Testament est-elle une hypostase?" *Collationes Gandavenses* 21 (1934): 10ff.

Jacob, E. "Wisdom and Religion in Sirach." In *Israelite Wisdom: Theological and Literary Essays in Honor of Samuel Terrien,* ed. J. G. Gammie et al., 247–60. Missoula, Mont.: Scholars Press, 1978.

Kayatz, C. *Studien zu Proverbien 1—9.* Neukirchen-Vluyn: Neukirchener Verlag, 1966.

Keel, O. "Die Weisheit 'spielt' vor Gott . . ." *Freiburger Zeitschrift für Philosophie und Theologie* 21 (1974): 1–66.

Knox, W. "The Divine Wisdom." *JTS* 38 (1939): 230–37.

Landes, G. "Creation Tradition in Proverbs 8:22–31 and Genesis 1." In *A Light unto My Path* (Festschrift J. M. Myers), ed. H. N. Bream et al., 279–93. Philadelphia: Temple Univ. Press, 1974.

Lang, B. *Frau Weisheit: Deutung einer biblischen Gestalt.* Düsseldorf, 1975.

Larcher, C. *Etudes sur le livre de la Sagesse,* 398–410. Paris: Librairie Lecoffre, 1969.

Levêque, J. "Le contrepoint théologique apporté par la réflexion sapientielle." In *Questions disputées d'Ancien Testament: Méthode et théologie,* ed. C. Brekelmans, 183–202. Gembloux: Duculot, 1974.

Mack, B. L. "Wisdom Myth and Mytho-logy: An Essay in Understanding a Theological Tradition." *Int* 24 (1970): 46ff.

———. *Logos und Sophia: Untersuchungen zur Weisheitstheologie im hellenistischen Judentum.* Göttingen: Vandenhoek & Ruprecht, 1973.

Marböck, J. *Weisheit im Wandel: Untersuchungen zur Weisheitstheologie bei Ben Sirach.* Bonn: Peter Hanstein, 1971.

Marcus, R. "On Biblical Hypostases of Wisdom." *HUCA* 23.1 (1950–51): 157–72.

Miller, E. L. "The Logic of the Logos Hymn: A New View." *NTS* 29 (1974–75): 552–61.

Pfeiffer, G. *Ursprung und Wesen der Hypostasen Vorstellungen im Judentum.* Stuttgart: Calwer Verlag, 1967.

Rad, G. von. *Wisdom in Israel.* Nashville: Abingdon Press, 1972.

Rendel Harris, J. "Athena, Sophia, and the Logos." *BJRL* 7 (1922–23):56–71.

Richter, G. "Die Fleischwerdung des Logos im Johannesevangelium." *NovT* 13 (1971): 81–126; 14 (1972): 257–69.

Rickenbacher, O. *Weisheitsperikopen bei Ben-Sira,* 14–15, 123ff. Göttingen: Vandenhoek & Ruprecht, 1973.

Ridderbos, J. "The Structure and Scope of the Prologue to the Gospel of John." In *Studies in John* (Festschrift J. N. Sevenster), 180–201. NovT Sup 24. Leiden: E. J. Brill, 1966.

Ringgren, H. *Word and Wisdom: Studies in the Hypostatization of Divine Qualities and Functions in the Ancient Near East.* Lund: H. Ohlssons Boktr., 1947.

Robinson, J. M. "Jesus as Sophos and Sophia: Wisdom Tradition and the Gospels." In *Aspects of Wisdom in Judaism and Early Christianity,* ed. R. L. Wilken, 1–16. Notre Dame, Ind.: Univ. of Notre Dame Press, 1975.

Sanders, J. A. "Sirach 51:13ff." In his *Psalms Scroll of Qumran Cave XI*, 79ff. Vol. 4 of *Discoveries in the Judean Desert of Jordan*. New York: Oxford Univ. Press, 1965.

———. "Sirach 51:13ff." In his *The Dead Sea Psalms Scroll*, 112ff. Ithaca, N.Y.: Cornell Univ. Press, 1967.

———. "The Sirach 51 Acrostic." In *Hommages à André Dupont-Sommer*, 429–38. Paris: Adrien Maisonneuve, 1971.

Schmithals, W. "Der Prolog des Johannesevangeliums." *ZNW* 70 (1979): 16–43.

Schüssler Fiorenza, E. "Wisdom Mythology and the Christological Hymns of the New Testament." In *Aspects of Wisdom in Judaism and Early Christianity*, ed. R. Wilken, 17ff. Notre Dame, Ind.: Univ. of Notre Dame Press, 1975.

Scott, R. B. Y. "Wisdom in Creation: The 'AMON of Proverbs viii 30." *VT* 10 (1960):213–23.

Sheppard, G. T. *Wisdom as a Hermeneutical Construct: A Study in the Sapientializing of the Old Testament*. Berlin: Walter de Gruyter, 1980.

Skehan, P. "The Acrostic Poem in Sirach 51; 13–30." *HTR* 64 (1971): 387–400.

———. "Structures in Poems on Wisdom: Proverbs 8 and Sirach 24." *CBQ* 41 (1979): 365–79.

Spicq, C. "Le Siracide et la structure littéraire du Prologue de Saint Jean." In *Mémorial M.-J. Lagrange*, 183–95. Paris: J. Gabalda, 1940.

Stecher, R. "Die persönliche Weisheit in den Proverben Kap. 8." *ZKT* 75 (1953–54): 411–51.

Suggs, M. J. *Wisdom, Christology, and Law in Matthew's Gospel*. Cambridge: Harvard Univ. Press, 1970.

Terrien, S. *The Elusive Presence: Toward a New Biblical Theology*, 350ff. San Francisco and New York: Harper & Row, 1978.

———. "The Play of Wisdom: Turning Point in Biblical Theology." *Horizons in Biblical Theology* 3 (1981): 125–53.

Tournay, R. "Proverbs 1—9: A First Theological Synthesis of the Tradition of the Sages." In *The Dynamism of the Biblical Tradition*, ed. P. Benoit et al., 51–61. Concilium vol. 20. New York: Paulist Press, 1966.

Trible, P. "Wisdom Builds a Poem: The Architecture of Proverbs 1:20–33." *JBL* 94 (1975): 509–18.

Vawter, D. "Proverbs 8:22: Wisdom and Creation." *JBL* 99 (1980): 205–16.

Whybray, R. *Wisdom in Proverbs: The Concept of Wisdom in Proverbs 1—9*, 82–103. London: SCM Press, 1965.

6. Man and Woman in Early Judaism

Baron, S. *A Social and Religious History of the Jews*, 1:111–14. New York: Columbia Univ. Press, 1952.

Bigger, S. F. "The Family Laws of Leviticus 18 in Their Setting." *JBL* 98 (1979): 187–203.

Daube, D. *The New Testament and Rabbinic Judaism*, 72ff, 373ff. London, 1956.

Douglas, M. *Purity and Danger: An Analysis of Concepts of Pollution*. Harmondsworth, England: Penguin Books, 1970.

Eliade, M. *Rites and Symbols of Initiation: The Mysteries of Birth and Rebirth*. New York: Harper & Row, 1965.

Epstein, L. M. *Sex Laws and Customs in Judaism*. New York: Bloch Pub. Co., 1948.

Eslinger, L. "The Case of an Immodest Lady Wrestler in Deuteronomy XXV 11–12." *VT* 31 (1981): 271–81.

Fox, M. V. "The Sign of the Covenant: Circumcision in the Light of the Priestly 'ôt Etiologies." *RB* 81 (1974): 557–96.

Guillaumont, A. "A propos du célibat des Esséniens." In *Hommages à André Dupont-Sommer*, 395–404. Paris: Adrien Maisonneuve, 1971.

Harding, M.E. *Woman's Mysteries, Ancient and Modern: A Psychological Interpretation of the Feminine Principle as Portrayed in Myth, Story, and Dreams.* New York: Bantam Books, 1973.

Hyman, P. "The Other Half: Women in the Jewish Tradition." *Conservative Judaism* 26 (1971–72): 14–21.

Isaac, E. "Circumcision as a Covenant Rite. *Anthropos* 59 (1964): 444–56.

Jeremias, J. "The Social Position of Women." In his *Jerusalem in the Time of Jesus,* 358–76. Philadelphia: Fortress Press, 1969.

Kosmala, H. "The 'Bloody Husband.' " *VT* 12 (1962): 14–28.

Loewe, R. *The Position of Women in Judaism.* London: SPCK, 1966.

McKeating, H. "Sanctions Against Adultery in Ancient Israelite Society . . ." *JSOT* 11 (1968): 57–72.

Meyers, C. "Procreation, Production, and Protection: Male-Female Balance in Early Israel." JAAR 51 (1983): 569–94.

Mitchell, T. "The Meaning of the Noun ḤTN in the Old Testament." *VT* 19 (1969): 93ff.

Morgenstern, J. *Rites of Birth, Marriage, Death, and Kindred Occasions Among the Semites,* 48–66. Cincinnati and Chicago: Quadrangle Books, 1966.

Murphy, R. E. "GBR and GBWRH in the Qumran Writings." In *Lex tua veritas* (Festschrift H. Junker), ed. H. Gross, 137–44. Trier, 1961.

Neusner, J. *A History of the Mishnaic Law of Purities.* Leiden: E. J. Brill, 1974.

———. *A History of the Mishnaic Law of Women,* 5 vols. Leiden: E. J. Brill, 1980.

Nunberg, H. *Problems of Bisexuality As Reflected in Circumcision.* London: Imago, 1949.

Schlossman, H. "Circumcision as Defense: A Study in Psychoanalysis and Religion." *Psychoanalytic Quarterly* 35 (1966): 340–56.

Sierksma, F. "Quelques remarques sur la circoncision en Israël." *Oudtestamentische Studien* 9 (1951): 136ff.

Stagg, E. and F. *Woman in the World of Jesus.* Philadelphia: Westminster Press, 1978.

Thiessen, G. *Sociology of Early Palestinian Christianity.* Philadelphia: Fortress Press, 1978.

Weiss, C. "Motives for Male Circumcision among Preliterate and Literate Peoples." *Journal of Sex Research* 2 (1966): 69–88.

Wit, C. de. "La circoncision chez les anciens Egyptiens." *Zeitschrift für ägyptische Sprache und Altertumskunde* 99.1a (1972): 41–8.

7. Jesus, Woman, and Divine Fatherhood

Becker, U. *Jesus und die Ehebrecherin.* Berlin: A. Töppelmann, 1963.

Bernaulle, C. A. "Le Dieu-Père de Jésus d'après les Synoptiques." *Actes du Congrès International d'Histoire des Religions* 2.211ff. Paris, 1925.

Bode, E. *The First Easter Morning: The Gospel Accounts of the Women's Visit to the Tomb of Jesus.* Analecta Biblica 45. Rome: Pontifical Biblical Institute Press, 1970.

Bonnard, P. *Notre Père qui es aux cieux. La prière oecuménique.* Paris: Editions du Cerf, Les Bergers et les Mages, 1968.

Bruckberger, R. *Marie-Madeleine: soror mea sponsa.* Paris: La Jeune Parque, 1952.

Burkitt, F. "Mary Magdalene and the Sister of Martha." *Expository Times* 42 (1930–31): 157–59.

Brown, R. E. "Women in the Fourth Gospel." *TS* 36 (1975): 688–99.

Daly, M. *Beyond God the Father: Toward a Philosophy of Women's Liberation.* Boston: Beacon Press, 1973.

Daube, D. "The Anointing at Bethany and Jesus' Burial." *ATR* 32 (1950): 186–99.

Delobel, J. "L'onction de la pécheresse: La composition littéraire de Lc. vii, 33, 36–50." ALBO 4.4 (1966); *Ephemerides theologicae lovanienses* 42 (1966): 415–75.

Derrett, J. D. M. "Law in the New Testament: The Story on the Woman Taken in Adultery." *NTS* 90 (1963–64): 1–26.

Faxon A. *Women and Jesus.* Philadelphia: United Church Press, 1973.

Fitzmyer, J. A. *The Gospel According to Luke I-IX.* Garden City, N.Y.: Doubleday & Co., 1981.

Garrison, W. *Women in the Life of Jesus.* Indianapolis: Bobbs-Merrill, 1962.

Grassi, J. "Abba, Father (Mark 14:36): Another Approach." *JAAR* 50 (1982): 449–58.

Grelot, P. "Le père et ses deux fils; Luc, xv, 11–32; De l'analyse structurale à l'herméneutique." *RB* 84 (1977): 538–65.

Gyllenberg, R. "Gott der Vater im Alten Testament und in der Predigt Jesus." *Studia Orientalia* 1 (1925): 51–60.

Hamerton-Kelly, R. *God the Father: Theology and Patriarchy in the Teachings of Jesus.* Philadelphia: Fortress Press, 1979.

Hengel, M. "Maria Magdalena und die Frauen als Zeugen." In *Abraham unser Vater* (Festschrift O. Michel), ed. O. Betz et al., 243–56. Arbeiten zur Geschichte des Spätjudentums und Urchristentums 5. Leiden: E. J. Brill, 1963.

Holst, R. "The One Anointing of Jesus: Another Application of the Form-Critical Method." *JBL* 95 (1976): 435ff.

Hosie, L. *Jesus and Woman: A Study of Christ's Attitude to Women As Recorded in the Gospels.* London: Hodder & Stoughton, 1956.

Jeremias, J. *The Lord's Prayer.* Philadelphia: Fortress Press, 1964.

_____. "Abba." In his *The Central Message of the New Testament,* 9–30. Philadelphia: Fortress Press, [1965] 1981.

_____. *New Testament Theology,* 1:61–67; 178–203; 223–27. New York: Charles Scribner's Sons, 1971.

Julian, F. "The Maleness of God." *Hibbert Journal* 52 (1954): 343ff.

Ketter, P. *Christ and Womankind.* Westminster, Md.: Newman Press, 1952.

Köberle, D. "Vatergott, Vaterlichkeit und Vaterkomplex im christlichen Glauben." In *Vorträge über das Vaterproblem in Psychotherapie, Religion und Gesellschaft,* ed. W. Bitter, 17ff. Stuttgart: Calwer Verlag, 1954.

Légasse, S. *Jésus et l'enfant.* Paris: J. Gabalda, 1969.

Malvern, M. *Venus in Sackcloth: The Magdalen's Origins and Metamorphoses.* Carbondale: Southern Ill. Univ. Press, 1975.

Manson, T. W. "The Pericope *de Adultera* (Joh 7,53—8,11)." *ZNW* 44 (1952–53): 255–56.

Marchel, W. *Abba! La prière du Christ et des chrétiens. Etude exégétique sur les origines et la signification de l'invocation à la divinité comme père, avant et dans le Nouveau Testament.* Analecta Biblica 19. Rome: Pontifical Biblical Institute Press, 1963.

McCutchen, L. "The Father Figure in Psychology and Religion." *JAAR* 40 (1972): 176–92.

McFague, S. "God the Father: Model or Idol?" In her *Metaphorical Theology: Models of God in Religious Language,* 145ff. Philadelphia: Fortress Press, 1982.

Moll, W. *Father and Fatherhood.* Notre Dame, Ind.: Univ. of Notre Dame Press, 1966.

Muilenburg, J. "A Meditation on Divine Fatherhood." *USQR* 5 (1950): 21–27.

_____. "Father and Son." *Theology and Life* 3 (1960): 177–87.

Nel, P. "The Concept 'Father' in the Wisdom Literature of the Ancient Near East." *JNWSL* 5 (1977): 53–66.

Phipps, W. *Was Jesus Married?* New York: Harper & Row, 1970.

Pohier, J. "Au nom du Père." *Esprit* (1966): 480–500, 947–70.

———. "La paternité de Dieu." *L'Inconscient,* no. 5 (Jan. 1968): 3–59.

Ricoeur, P. "Fatherhood: From Fantasm to Symbol." In his *The Conflict of Interpretations,* 468–97. Evanston, Ill.: Northwestern Univ. Press, 1974.

Sanders, J. N. "Those Whom Jesus Loved." *NTS* 1 (1954–55): 29–41.

Schilling, F. A. "The Story of Jesus and the Adulteress." *ATR* 37 (1955): 91–106.

Sergio, L. *Jesus and Woman.* McLean, Va.: EPM Pub., 1975.

Stagg, E. and F. *Woman in the World of Jesus.* Philadelphia: Westminster Press, 1978.

Swidler, L. "Jesus Was a Feminist." *Catholic World* 212 (1970–71): 177–83.

———. "Jesus Was No Chauvinist." *Inside* 3 (Jan. 1972): 15–16.

Tellenbach, H. *Das Vaterbild im Mythos und Geschichte: Ägypten. Griechenland. Altes Testament. Neues Testament.* Stuttgart: Kohlhammer, 1976.

Vetterling-Braggin, M., ed. *"Femininity," "Masculinity," and "Androgyny": A Modern Philosophical Discussion.* Totowa, N.J.: Rowman & Littlefield, 1982.

Visser 't Hooft, W. *The Fatherhood of God in an Age of Emancipation.* Philadelphia: Westminster Press, 1982.

Wahlberg, R. "Jesus and the Uterus Image." *TToday* 31 (1974–75): 228ff.

———. *Jesus According to a Woman.* New York: Paulist/Newman Press, 1975.

———. *Jesus and the Freed Woman.* New York: Paulist Press, 1978.

Witherington, B. "On the Road with Mary Magdalene, Joanna, Susanna, and Other Disciples—Luke 8:1–3." *ZNW* 70 (1979): 243–48.

———. *Women in the Ministry of Jesus: A Study of Jesus' Attitudes to Women and Their Roles As Reflected in His Earthly Life.* New York and Cambridge: Cambridge Univ. Press, 1984.

Zeller, D. "God as Father in the Proclamation and in the Prayer of Jesus." In *Standing Before God* (Festschrift J. M. Oesterreicher), ed. A. Finkel and L. Frizzell, 117–30. New York: Ktav Pub. House, 1981.

8. Early Christianity

Baltensweiler, H. *Die Ehe im Neuen Testament.* Abhandlungen zum Theologie des Alten und Neuen Testaments 52. Zurich: Zwingli-Verlag, 1967.

Benko, S. "A New Principle of Mariology: The Kenotic Motif." In *OIKONOMIA: Heilsgeschichte als Thema der Theologie* (Festschrift O. Cullmann), ed. F. Christ, 259–72. Hamburg-Bergstedt: Reich, 1967.

Blum, G. "Das Amt der Frau im Neuen Testament." *NovT* 7 (1964): 142ff.

Braun, W. *Die Frau in der alten Kirche.* Berlin-Lichtenfelde: Edwin Runge, 1919.

Brown, R. E. *The Birth of the Messiah,* 356–65. Garden City, N.Y.: Doubleday & Co., 1977.

——— et al., eds. *Mary in the New Testament.* Philadelphia: Fortress Press; New York: Paulist Press, 1978.

Cazelles, H. "Fille de Sion et théologie mariale dans la Bible." *Mariologie et œcuménisme* 3 (1964): 54ff.

Coppens, J. *Les affinités qumrâniennes de l'Epître aux Hébreux.* ALBO 4.1 (1962).

Daniélou, J. *The Ministry of Women in the Early Church.* London: Faith Press, 1961.

Donaldson, J. *Woman, Her Position and Influence in Ancient Greece and Rome and Among Early Christians.* London: Longmans, Green & Co., 1907.

Dupont, J. *Etudes sur les Actes des Apôtres.* Paris: Editions du Cerf, 1967.

Gelin, A. "Marie et son chant de pauvreté." In his *Les pauvres de Yahvé,* 121–32. Paris: Editions du Cerf, 1953.

Greeley, A. *The Mary Myth: On the Femininity of God.* New York: Seabury Press, 1977.

Gryson, R. *Le ministère des femmes dans l'Eglise ancienne.* Gembloux: Duculot, 1972.

Guldan, E. *Eva und Maria, Eine Antithese als Bildmotiv.* Graz and Cologne: Böhlau, 1966.

Heiler, F. "The Madonna as a Religious Symbol." In *The Mystic Vision: Papers from the Eranos Yearbooks,* 348–74. Bollingen Series 30.6. Princeton, N.J.: Princeton Univ. Press, 1968.

Hoppin, R. *Priscilla: Author of the Epistle to the Hebrews, and Other Essays.* New York: Exposition Press, 1969.

Lagrand, J. "How Was the Virgin Mary 'Like a Man' [. . .]?" *NovT* 22 (1980): 97–107.

Langdon-Davies, J. "Women and the Early Christian Church." In his *A Short History of Women.* London: Watts, 1938.

Laurentin, R. *Structure et théologie de Luc I—II,* 82ff. Paris: J. Gabalda, 1957.

McHugh, J. *The Mother of Jesus in the New Testament.* London: Darton, Longman & Todd, 1975.

Meeks, W. "The Image of the Androgyne: Some Uses of a Symbol in Earliest Christianity." *History of Religions* 13 (1974): 165–208.

Morris, J. *The Lady Was a Bishop.* New York: Macmillan Co.; London: Collier, 1973.

_____. *Against Nature and God: The History of Women with Clerical Ordination and the Jurisdiction of Bishops.* London and Oxford: A. R. Mowbray & Co., 1974.

Pagels, E. *The Gnostic Gospels.* New York: Random House, 1979.

Pape, D. *In Search of God's Ideal Woman: A Personal Examination.* Downers Grove, Ill.: Inter-Varsity Press, 1976.

Pomeroy, S. *Goddesses, Whores, Wives, and Slaves: Women in Classical Antiquity.* London: Robert Hale, 1976.

Räisänen, H. *Die Mutter Jesu im Neuen Testament.* Helsinki: Akateeminen Kirjakauppa, 1969.

Rollet, H. *La condition de la femme dans l'Eglise,* 1–17. Paris: Fayard, 1975.

Ruether, R. *Mary—the Feminine Face of the Church.* Philadelphia: Westminster Press, 1977.

Schneider, F., and W. Stenger. "Die Frauen im Stammbaum Jesu nach Mattäus." *BZ* 23 (1979): 187–97.

Schreiber, J. *Primitive Christian Traditions: Toward the Historical Structure of Primitive Christianity.* Evanston, Ill.: Garrett Theological Seminary Library, 1968.

Tannehill, R. "The Magnificat as a Poem." *JBL* 93 (1974): 263–75.

Thomas, W. D. "The Place of Women in the Church at Philippi." *Expository Times* 83 (1971–72): 117–20.

Wilson, S. G. *The Gentiles and the Gentile Mission in Luke-Acts.* New York and Cambridge: Cambridge Univ. Press, 1973.

9. Paul on Human Liberation

Allmen, D. von. *La famille de Dieu: La symbolique familiale dans le Paulinisme.* Fribourg: Editions Universitaires, 1981.

Balch, D. L. "I Cor 7:32–35 and Stoic Debates about Marriage, Anxiety, and Distraction." *JBL* 102 (1983): 429–39.

Barré, M. "To Marry or to Burn: *Pyrousthai* in I Cor 7:9" *CBQ* 36 (1974): 193–202.

Barth, M. *Ephesians 4—6.* Anchor Bible. Garden City, N.Y.: Doubleday & Co., 1974.

Bligh, J. *Galatians: A Discussion of St. Paul's Epistle.* Householder Commentaries 1. Langley, Bucks.: Society of St. Paul, 1969.

Boldrey, R. and J. *Chauvinist or Feminist? Paul's View of Women.* Grand Rapids: Wm. B. Eerdmans, 1976.

Boswell, J. *Christianity, Social Tolerance, and Homosexuality,* 91–117, 333–35. Chicago: Univ. of Chicago Press, 1980.

Boucher, M. "Some Unexplored Parallels to I Cor. 11, 11–12 and Gal. 3, 28: The New Testament on the Role of Women." *CBQ* 31 (1969): 50–58.

Byrne, B. "Sinning Against One's Body: Paul's Understanding of the Sexual Relationship in 1 Corinthians 6:18." *CBQ* 45 (1983): 608–16.

Caird, G. "Paul and Woman's Liberty." *BJRL* 54 (1971–72): 268–81.

Campbell, R. C. "Women's Liberation and the Apostle Paul." *Baptist Leader* (March 15, 1972): 307–9.

Chanson, P. *Le mariage chrétien selon St. Paul.* Paris: Editions du Levain, 1953.

Conzelmann, H. *1 Corinthians: A Commentary.* Hermeneia. Philadelphia: Fortress Press, 1969.

Feuillet, A. "L'homme 'gloire de Dieu' et la femme 'gloire de l'homme' (I Cor., xi, 7b). *RB* 81 (1974): 161–82.

————. "La dignité et le rôle de la femme d'après quelques textes pauliniens." *NTS* 21 (1974–75): 157ff.

Fuchs, E. "Gloire de Dieu, gloire de l'homme: Essai sur les termes *kauchasthai, kauchêma, kauchêsis* dans la Septante." *Revue de theologie et de philosophie* (1977): 321–32.

Hall, B. "Paul and Women." *TToday* 31 (1974–75): 50–55.

Hommes, N. "Let Women Be Silent in the Church: A Message Concerning the Worship Service and the Decorum to Be Observed by Women." *Calvin Theological Journal* 4 (1969): 5–22.

Hooker, M. "Authority on Her Head: An Examination of I Cor. XI.10." *NTS* 10 (1963–64): 410–16.

Hurley, J. "Did Paul Require Veils or the Silence of Women? A Consideration of 1 Cor. 11:2–16 and 1 Cor. 14:33b–36." *WTJ* 35 (1972–73): 190–220.

Jaubert, A. "Le voile des femmes (I Cor. xi.2–16)." *NTS* 18 (1971–72): 419ff.

Kümmel, W. *Man in the New Testament.* Philadelphia: Westminster Press, 1963.

Kürzinger, J. "Frau und Mann nach I Kor 11, 11f." *BZ* 22 (1978): 270–75.

Leslie, W. H. *The Concept of Woman in the Pauline Corpus in Light of the Social and Religious Environment of the First Century.* Evanston, Ill.: Northwestern Univ. Press, 1976. Microfilm.

Meier, J. P. "On the Veiling of the Hermeneutics (I Cor 11:2–16)." *CBQ* 40 (1978): 212–26.

Menoud, P. "Saint Paul et la femme." *Revue de theologie et de philosophie* (1969): 318ff.

Mercadante, L. "From Hierarchy to Equality: A Comparison of Past and Present Interpretations of 1 Cor. 11:2–16 in Relation to the Changing Status of Women in Society." Ph.D. diss., Regent College, 1978. Vancouver: Privately printed, 1978.

Murphy-O'Connor, J. "Sex and Logic in 1 Corinthians 11:2–16." *CBQ* 42 (1980): 482ff.

————. "The Divorced Woman in 1 Cor 7:10–11." *JBL* 100 (1981): 601–6.

Odell-Scott, D. W. "Let the Women Speak in Church: An Equalitarian Interpretation of 1 Cor 14:33b–36." *BTB* 13 (1983): 90–93.

Orr, W. F., and J. A. Walther. *1 Corinthians,* 205ff. Anchor Bible. Garden City, N.Y.: Doubleday & Co., 1976.

Pagels, E. "Paul and Women: A Response to Recent Discussion." *JAAR* 42 (1974): 538–49.

Scroggs, R. "Paul: Chauvinist or Liberationist?" *The Christian Century* 89 (1972): 307–9.

_____. "Paul and the Eschatological Woman." *JAAR* 40 (1972): 283–303.

_____. "Paul and the Eschatological Woman: Revisited." *JAAR* 42 (1974): 532–37.

_____. *The New Testament and Homosexuality.* Philadelphia: Fortress Press, 1983.

Seyer, H. "The Stewardship of Spiritual Gifts: A Study of First Corinthians, Chapters Twelve, Thirteen, and Fourteen, and the Charismatic Movement." Ph.D. diss., Univ. of Wisconsin, 1974.

Spicq, C. "La morale néotestamentaire: Morale chrétienne et morale de la charité." In *Neotestamentica et Patristica* (Festschrift O. Cullmann), 228–39. NovT Sup 6. Leiden: E. J. Brill, 1962.

Stacey, W. *The Pauline View of Man in Relation to Its Judaic and Hellenistic Background.* New York: Macmillan Co., 1956.

Tannehill, R. *Dying and Rising with Christ: A Study in Pauline Theology.* Berlin: Walter de Gruyter, 1967.

Tenney, M. *Galatians: The Charter of Christian Liberty.* Grand Rapids: Wm. B. Eerdmans, 1950.

Vaux, R. de. "Sur le voile des femmes dans l'Ancien Orient." In his *Bible et Orient,* 407–24. Paris: Editions du Cerf, 1967.

Walker, W. O., Jr. "1 Corinthians 11:2–16 and Paul's Views Regarding Women." *JBL* 94 (1975): 94–110.

Warren, M. *The Gospel of Victory: A Study in the Relevance of the Epistle to the Galatians for the Christian Mission Today.* London: SCM Press, 1955.

Weeks, N. "Of Silence and Head Covering." *WTJ* 35 (1972–73): 21–27.

Williams, D. *The Apostle Paul and Women in the Church.* Glendale, Calif.: Regal Books, 1979.

10. Man and Woman
in the Church

Bailey, D. S. *Sexual Relation in Christian Thought.* New York: Harper & Brothers, 1959.

_____. *The Theology of Sex and Marriage.* London: The Church of England, 1953.

Beckwith, R. T. *Priesthood and Sacrament.* Appleford, Berks.: Marchem Manor Press, 1964.

Bell, D. H. *Being a Man: The Paradox of Masculinity.* New York: Lewis Pub. Co., 1984.

Biéler, A. *L'homme et la femme dans la morale calviniste.* Geneva: Labor et Fides, 1963.

Blenkinsopp, J. *Sexuality and the Christian Tradition.* Dayton: Pflaum Press, 1969.

Bliss, K. *The Service and Status of Women in the Churches.* London: SCM Press, 1952.

Bockle, F., and J.-M. Pohier, eds. *Sexuality in Contemporary Catholicism.* Concilium vol. 100. New York: Seabury Press, 1976.

Boucher, M., et al. "Women and Priestly Ministry: The New Testament Evidence." *CBQ* 41 (1979): 608–13.

Bourke, M. "Reflections on Church Order in the New Testament." *CBQ* 30 (1968): 493–511.

Brown, R. E. *Priest and Bishop: Biblical Reflections.* New York: Paulist Press, 1970.

_____. *Biblical Reflections on Crises Facing the Church.* New York: Paulist Press, 1975.

Buckley, M. *Morality and the Homosexual: A Catholic Approach to a Moral Problem.* Westminster, Md.: Newman Press, 1960.

Callahan, S. *Beyond Birth Control: The Christian Experience of Sex.* Retitled: *Exiled to Eden: The Christian Experience of Sex.* New York: Sheed & Ward, 1968.

Carmody, D. L. *Feminism and Christianity: A Two-Way Reflection.* Nashville: Abingdon Press, 1982.

Clark, E., and H. Richardson, eds. *Women and Religion: A Feminist Sourcebook of Christian Thought.* New York: Harper & Row, 1977.

Cody, A. *A History of Old Testament Priesthood.* Analecta Biblica 35. Rome: Pontifical Biblical Institute Press, 1969.

Colson, J. *Ministre de Jésus-Christ ou le sacerdoce de l'Evangile. Etude sur la condition sacerdotale des ministres chrétiens dans l'Eglise primitive.* Paris: Beauchesne et ses fils, 1966.

Davis, G. "Woman and the Church." *RL* 44 (1975): 338ff.

Decter, M. *The New Chastity and Other Arguments Against Women's Liberation.* New York: Coward, McCann & Geoghegan, 1972.

Dixon, J. W. "What the Priesthood Is All About." *The Christian Century* 92 (1975): 244–45.

Dodd, W. H. "Toward a Theology of Priesthood." *TS* 28 (1967): 683–705.

Dumas, A. "Biblical Anthropology and Participation of Women in the Ministry of the Church." In *Concerning the Ordination of Women.* Geneva: World Council of Churches, Commission on Faith and Order, 1964.

Elliott, J. H. *The Elect and the Holy: An Exegetical Examination of 1 Peter and the Phrase βαδίλειστν ἱεράτευμα.* Leiden: E. J. Brill, 1966.

Ermarth, M. *Adam's Fractured Rib: Observations on Women in the Church.* Philadelphia: Fortress Press, 1970.

Frost, J., and L. Morrison. "On the Ordination of Women." *Christianity and Crisis* (March 6, 1972).

Fuchs, E. *Sexual Desire and Love: Origins and History of the Christian Ethic of Sexuality and Marriage.* New York: Seabury Press, 1983.

Gardiner, A. M., ed. *Women and Catholic Priesthood: An Expanded Vision.* New York: Paulist Press, 1976.

Gössmann, E. "Women as Priests?" in *Apostolic Succession,* ed. H. Küng, 115–25. Concilium vol. 34. New York: Seabury Press, 1968.

Goman, J. *The Ordination of Women: The Bible and the Fathers.* Claremont, Calif.: Claremont School of Theology, 1976. Microfilm.

Grelot, P. *Le ministère de la Nouvelle Alliance.* Paris: Editions du Cerf, 1967.

Grévy-Pons, N. *Célibat et nature: Une controverse médiévale.* Paris: Centre national de la recherche scientifique, 1975.

Gross, R. M., ed. *Beyond Androcentrism: New Essays on Women and Religion.* Missoula, Mont.: Scholars Press, 1977.

Gryson, R. *Les origines du célibat ecclésiastique du premier au septième siècles.* Gembloux: Duculot, 1970.

Harkness, G. *Women in Church and Society.* Nashville: Abingdon Press, 1972.

Hauret, C. "Eve transfigurée . . . : De la Genèse à l'Apocalypse." *RHPR* 59 (1979): 327–39.

Heilbrun, C. G. *Toward a Recognition of Androgyny.* New York: Alfred A. Knopf, 1973.

Horner, T. *Sex in the Bible.* Rutland, Vt.: C. E. Tuttle Co., 1974.

————. *Jonathan Loved David: Homosexuality in Biblical Times.* Philadelphia: Westminster Press, 1978.

Howard, R. *Should Women Be Priests? Three Sermons Preached Before the University of Oxford.* Oxford, 1949.

Jones, H. K. *Toward a Christian Understanding of the Homosexual.* New York: Association Press, 1966.

Kendall, P. *Women and the Priesthood: A Selected and Annotated Bibliography.* Philadelphia: Episcopal Diocese of Pa., 1976.

Kerényi, C. *Eleusis: Archetypal Image of Mother and Daughter.* Bollingen Series 65.4. Princeton, N.J.: Princeton Univ. Press, 1967.

Komonchak, J. "Theological Questions on the Ordination of Women." *The Catholic Mind* 75 (1977): 13–28.

Kress, R. *Whither Womankind? The Humanity of Women.* St. Meinrad, Ind.: Abbey Press, 1975.

Küng, H., ed. *Apostolic Succession: Rethinking a Barrier to Unity.* Concilium vol. 34. New York: Seabury Press, 1968.

Lea, H. C. *History of Sacerdotal Celibacy in the Christian Church,* 2 vols. New York: Macmillan Co., 1907.

Legrand, L. *The Biblical Doctrine of Virginity.* New York: Sheed & Ward, 1963.

McGrath, A. *What a Modern Catholic Believes about Women.* Chicago: Thomas More Press, 1972.

McNeill, J. J. *The Church and the Homosexual.* Mission, Kans.: Sheed Andrews & McMeel, 1976.

Mascall, E. *Women and the Priesthood of the Church.* London: Church Union, Church Literature Assn., 1960.

Meer, H. van der *Woman Priests in the Catholic Church? A Theological-Historical Investigation.* Philadelphia: Temple Univ. Press, 1973.

Moltmann-Wendel, E. *Liberty, Equality, Sisterhood: On the Emancipation of Women in Church and Society.* Philadelphia: Fortress Press, 1978.

Moore, P., ed. *Man, Woman, and Priesthood.* London: SPCK, 1978.

Nelson, J. B. "Homosexuality and the Church: Towards a Sexual Ethics of Love." In *Christianity and Crisis* 37, no. 5 (April 4, 1977): 63–69.

Peters, J. "Is There Room for Women in the Functions of the Church?" in *Apostolic Succession,* ed. H. Küng, 126–38. Concilium vol. 34. New York: Seabury Press, 1968.

Piper, O. A. *The Biblical View of Sex and Marriage.* New York: Charles Scribner's Sons, 1960.

Pittenger, N. *The Christian View of Sexual Behavior.* Greenwich, Conn.: Seabury Press, 1954.

_____. *Time for Consent: A Christian's Approach to Homosexuality.* London: SCM Press, 1967.

Ramin, Ida. *The Exclusion of Women from the Priesthood: Divine Law or Sex Discrimination?* Metuchen, N.J.: Scarecrow Press, 1976.

Ricoeur, P. "La sexualité: La merveille, l'errance, l'énigme." *Esprit* (Nov. 1960): 1665ff.

Robinson, D. W. B. "The Priesthood of Paul in the Gospel of Hope." In *Reconciliation and Hope* (Festschrift L. L. Morris), ed. R. Banks, 231–45. Grand Rapids: Wm. B. Eerdmans, 1974.

Ruether, R. R. *Religion and Sexism: Images of Woman in Jewish and Christian Traditions.* New York: Simon & Schuster, 1974.

_____. *New Woman—New Earth: Sexist Ideologies and Human Liberation.* New York: Seabury Press, 1974.

Ruether, R. R., and E. McLaughlin, eds. *Women of Spirit: Female Leadership in the Jewish and Christian Traditions.* New York: Simon & Schuster, 1979.

Ryrie, C. C. *The Place of Women in the Church.* Waco, Tex.: Word Books, 1974.

Schillebeeckx, E. *Autour du célibat des prêtres.* Paris: Editions du Cerf, 1967.

Schneiders, S. M. "Women in the Fourth Gospel and the Role of Women in the Contemporary Church." *BTB* 12 (1982): 35–45.

Shideler, M. "Male and Female Created He Them." *RL* 43 (1974): 60–67.

Slusser, M. "Fathers and Priestesses: Footnotes to the Roman Declaration." *Worship* 51 (1977): 434–45.

Smith, B. *Breakthrough: Women in Religion.* New York: Walker & Co., 1978.

Stuhlmueller, C., ed. *Women and Priesthood: Future Directions, A Call to Dialogue.* Collegeville, Minn.: Liturgical Press, 1978.

Swidler, A., and L. Swidler, eds. *Women Priests: A Catholic Commentary on the Vatican Declaration.* New York: Paulist Press, 1977.

Swidler, L. *Women in Judaism: The Status of Women in Formative Judaism.* Metuchen, N.J.: Scarecrow Press, 1976.

Tavard, G. *Woman in Christian Tradition.* Notre Dame, Ind.: Univ. of Notre Dame Press, 1973.

Terrien, S. "The Numinous, the Sacred, and the Holy in Scripture." *BTB* 12 (1982): 99–108.

Thielicke, H. *The Ethics of Sex.* New York: Harper & Row, 1964.

Thompson, J. A. "The Significance of the Verb *Love* in the David-Jonathan Narratives in 1 Samuel." *VT* 24 (1974): 334–38.

Thrall, M. *The Ordination of Women to the Priesthood: A Study of the Biblical Evidence.* London: SCM Press, 1958.

Valente, M. *Sex: The Radical View of a Catholic Theologian.* Saint Paul, Minn.: Bruce Pub. Co., 1970.

Wahl, J. A. *The Exclusion of Woman from Holy Orders.* Washington: Catholic Univ. of America, 1959.

Way, P. "An Authority of Possibility for Women in the Church." In *Women's Liberation and the Church,* ed. S. B. Doely, 77–84. New York: Association Press, 1970.

Wilhelmsen, F. D. *The Metaphysics of Love.* New York: Sheed & Ward, 1962.

Indexes

Passages

Subjects

Authors